EAST ASIA

East Asia

FROM CHINESE PREDOMINANCE TO THE RISE OF THE PACIFIC RIM

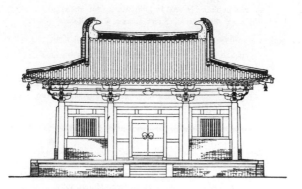

Arthur Cotterell

OXFORD UNIVERSITY PRESS
New York   Oxford

Oxford University Press

Oxford   New York   Toronto
Delhi   Bombay   Calcutta   Madras   Karachi
Kuala Lumpur   Singapore   Hong Kong   Tokyo
Nairobi   Dar Es Salaam   Cape Town
Melbourne   Auckland   Madrid

and associated companies in
Berlin   Ibadan

Copyright © 1993 by Arthur Cotterell

First published in 1993 by John Murray (Publishers) Ltd.
50 Albemarle Street, London W1X 4BD

First issued in cloth by Oxford University Press, 1994

Oxford is a registered trademark of Oxford University Press

Library of Congress Cataloging-in-Publication Data
Cotterell, Arthur.
East Asia : from Chinese predominance to the rise of the Pacific
rim / Arthur Cotterell.
p. cm.
Originally published: London : John Murray, 1993.
Includes bibliographical references and index.
ISBN 0-19-508840-9
ISBN 0-19-508841-7 (paper)
1. East Asia — History.   I. Title.
DS511.C82   1994
950 — dc20   93-26263

Title page decoration: part of the Nanchan monastery in Shanxi province

2 4 6 8 10 9 7 5 3 1

Printed in the United States of America

CONTENTS

Contents

ILLUSTRATIONS

between pages 148 and 149

1. The terracotta army at Mount Li, northern China
2. Kiyomizu temple in Kyoto, Japan
3. Ananda temple at Pagan, Burma
4. Borobodur, central Java
5. The Bayon, near Angkor Wat, Cambodia
6. The mosque at Songei Poear, Sumatra
7. Pu Yi, the last Chinese emperor, flanked by ministers, New Year's Day, 1933
8. Dr Sun Yatsen and Jiang Jieshi, 1923
9. Guomindang troops during the Sino-Japanese War, 1937
10. The arrival of HMS *Prince of Wales* at Singapore on 2 December 1941
11. Japanese soldiers in Singapore, February 1942
12. Aung San, the wartime Burmese leader
13. Mao Zedong in Yan'an, northern China
14. Kamikaze attack on USS *Bunker Hill*, March 1945
15. British troops during Korean War, April 1951
16. The Japanese surrender aboard USS *Missouri*, 2 September 1945
17. Premier Yoshida Shigeru in Paris, 1954
18. US aerial destruction of Vietnam during the 1960s
19. President Marcos with US Presidential envoy Philip Habib (left) and US Ambassador to the Philippines Steven Bosworth, Manila, 1986

vii

The author and publisher would like to thank the following for permission to reproduce illustrations: Plate 1, the Chinese authorities; Plates 2, 17, 23, Keyphotos, Tokyo; Plate 3, Christine Osborne; Plate 4, John A. Stevens/ Popperfoto; Plates 6, 18, Popperfoto; Plates 7, 9, 12, Hulton–Deutsch Collection; Plate 8, Camera Press Ltd/Robert Hunt Library; Plates 10, 15, Imperial War Museum; Plates 11, 13, Robert Hunt Library; Plate 14, US National Archives/ Robert Hunt Library; Plate 16, the Press Association; Plates 19, 20, Popperfoto/ Reuter; Plate 21, Associated Press; Plate 22, Simpson Fitzherbert Berman.

FOREWORD

From Chinese Predominance to the Rise of the Pacific Rim

The events of the past fifty years have more than converted the Far East into East Asia. Besides toppling the antiquated notion in the West that Europe is the centre of the world, the changes set in motion by the Japanese endeavour to conquer the whole area can be seen as the trigger for the resurgence of a third of mankind. Even without the recent realisation that by the next century East Asia will be the workshop of the world, it is obvious that the long struggle against Western colonialism has been decisively won. An irony of this alteration in the balance of power is the role played by Japan, first as a Western-style empire, then as an economic superpower.

The purchase of Hollywood film studios is only one sign of Tokyo's new strength. Future historians are likely to see this transfer of capital as just a single transaction along the Pacific Rim, the global economic pace-setter of the twenty-first century. The fact that shortly Japan will not however have such a favourable balance of payments requires no crystal ball. Its historical advantage will be eroded through the hectic pace of development amongst its neighbours, the greatest of which, the People's Republic of China, has only just started to compete as an exporter.

For the social and economic direction that the Chinese people eventually decide to take must prove as decisive for the future of East Asia as it has for its past. The almost terminal decline of China at the end of the nineteenth century under the last imperial house, and the chaotic conditions prevalent during the ill-fated republic which followed earlier this century, blinded many Westerners to the resilience of its people. Forgotten were the previous crises through which the world's oldest continuous civilisation had passed since the days when its hegemony was taken for granted in East Asia. It is that persistent lack of a perspective on what is the most dramatic transformation taking place in the contemporary world which this book attempts to remedy. The area covered includes South-East Asia for the good reason that periodically it was very much part of the East Asian sphere of influence, something the advent of Islam and early European colonisation has until recently tended to obscure.

The three parts into which this short history is divided therefore represent distinct periods of East Asian civilisation. The first considers the era of Chinese supremacy; the second the new balance of power inaugurated by the rise of northern peoples such as the Mongols and the Manchus; while the third deals with the impact of modern times. That Japan, the catalyst for so much change, has been the front-runner of the Pacific Rim is hardly surprising. Because Japan was the first East Asian nation to develop an industrialised economy, its ability to shape the area's affairs outside the People's Republic of China can be expected to last for some years before it is overtaken. But ultimately relations between the Chinese and the Japanese are the factor which will determine the future of East Asia.

The author wishes to acknowledge the assistance of Ray Dunning in preparing the line drawings for publication. He is also indebted to his wife, Yong Yap Cotterell, for her help with translation.

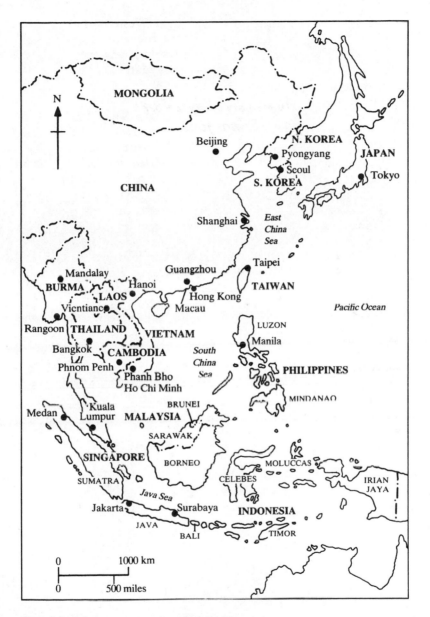

East Asia today

In memory of my teacher
Esmor Jones

PART I

Chinese Predominance

The determining influence on China, the cradle of East Asian civilisation, was its isolation from the other great civilisations, notably India, West Asia, Egypt and Europe. Arising first in the second millennium BC, early China was, during its formative stage, a world apart, cut off by mountains and deserts from India, Mesopotamia and Egypt. Over a millennium had passed before, in 126 BC, the Chinese learned from an envoy of the existence of other civilisations. Even then the difficult journey via the oasis towns of Central Asia kept contact to a minimum, though foreign merchants carried along the Silk Road, as this caravan route became known, the greatest Chinese import before modern times – Buddhism. The fact that this Indian belief arrived so late in China, penetrating all parts of the country only towards the end of the fourth century AD, helps explain why it failed to dislodge Confucianism – with its stress on filial piety, reverence for ancestors and on moderation and harmony in all things – as the state ideology.

A struggle between the classical legacy of China, as expressed in Confucian support for a centralised state under the rule of an enlightened emperor, and the spiritual individualism of the Buddhist faith, after the ninth century AD marked the closing phase of early East Asian history. Nowhere was this clearer than in the Japanese attempt to adopt a Chinese-style bureaucracy, which foundered through the rivalry of Buddhist sects as well as the combativeness of feudal lords. In both Korea and Japan, nevertheless, Buddhism did much during the seventh and eighth centuries to contribute to the process of building a national state. Similarly, in ninth-century South-East Asia, Hindu and Buddhist beliefs, imported from India, assisted the rise of kingdoms in Burma,

1

Cambodia and Indonesia. Only in Vietnam was the Confucian-Buddhist conflict evident, as this country was then incorporated into the southern defences of the Chinese empire.

Even within China there was a phenomenal growth of Buddhism; the government's response was laicisation. In 845 the Tang emperor Wu Zong sent monks and nuns home 'with their heads wrapped up' as a sign of returning to ordinary life. The Japanese monk Ennin, an eyewitness of the event, was surprised at the official thoroughness, noting that 'every action is reported to the throne'. By contrast, in Japan Oda Nobunaga slaughtered, on a single day in 1571, 4000 residents at the Enrakuji monastery at Mt Hiei, north of Kyoto. Afterwards he ordered his troops to fire the buildings.

That China could successfully employ less violent tactics to suppress a rich and powerful Buddhist church demonstrates the strength of the rational, sceptical mould of the Confucian outlook. A Chinese political tradition which took for granted strong central authority, embodied in the emperor as the Son of Heaven, was too firmly rooted for Buddhism to alter permanently either the social or the spiritual landscape. But though the Buddhist church was brought within the scope of the state in China, there, as throughout East Asia, its metaphysical speculation was to have a lasting influence by integration with Neo-Confucianism, the dominant philosophy in the region until modern times. Neo-Confucianism's great exponent was Zhu Xi (1130–1200), who advocated above all else the pursuit of moral perfection through harmonious social relations.

The Chinese cultural and political hegemony in East Asia was interrupted temporarily in the early fourth century by the Tartar occupation of north China. Japanese principalities, for instance, sent envoys to China in 57, 107, 239, 249, 245, 247, 265 and 266, but tribute failed to arrive regularly again until 413. Three years later the Chinese dynasty to which the Japanese envoys again travelled in Nanjing dispatched an expedition northwards, but nearly two more centuries had to pass before the country was reunited, a process abetted by the sinisation of the Tartars. The absorptive power of Chinese culture undoubtedly sustained the country during such periods of crisis, making it an exception to the general rule that large states did not long endure in the pre-modern age.

As a result China was both the Greece and Rome of early East Asia: the imperial boundaries enclosed the civilised world; the Chinese writing system passed to neighbouring peoples no matter how unsuited to their own languages. Superior Chinese technology was

Chinese Predominance

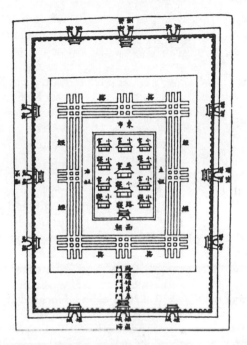

Fig. 1. Idealised plan of Luoyang, the Zhou kings' residence from the late eighth century BC. It reveals the deep-rooted Chinese veneration of encircling walls

also a welcome import, especially as an essentially defensive posture belied the fact that Chinese arms were in advance of all others until around 1500. The nation that built the Great Wall also invented the crossbow before 450 BC and the gun in the thirteenth century, two weapons put to lethal use elsewhere. The Lateran council of 1139 felt obliged to anathematize all those who used the diabolical crossbow against Christians. China's own decline as a great power in East Asia was relative to the extent to which its northern enemies borrowed the military equipment developed for its own imperial armies. Not until the Mongols enrolled in their force subject allies with up-to-date weaponry were they in 1279 able to conquer China and, afterwards, the greater part of East Asia.

1

CLASSICAL CHINA

From the Shang to the Qin Dynasty
(1650–206 BC)

THE SHANG AND EARLY ZHOU DYNASTIES (*c*. 1650–771 BC)

More than a prelude to the classical age of China (which spanned the six centuries until the foundation of the Han empire in 206 BC) were the first two dynasties from which written records survive. These dynasties of Shang and Early Zhou witnessed the earliest civilisation in East Asia, and with it the emergence of values that the Chinese later were to refine before passing them on to the Koreans, Vietnamese and Japanese. In Shang oracle inscriptions are found an emphasis on reverence, filial piety, kingly virtue, and propriety in the performance of ritual. In the recorded actions of the Early Zhou there is a courtesy and uprightness that, later, seemed to the philosopher Confucius (551–479 BC) almost a lost ideal; he claimed that his own teachings sought to 'follow Zhou' in establishing a moral code for 'all under Heaven', and insisted: 'I am a transmitter, not a creator. I believe in things old and love them.' Society's rootedness in the past was always taken for granted by the early Chinese.

Tradition credits Tang, the founder of Shang rule, with ending the cruel tyranny of Jie, the king of the previous dynasty, the Xia. The *Book of History (Shujing)*, a collection of documents edited in the fourth century BC, calls the Xia the first Chinese dynasty of all. Before that, rulers were chosen by merit. The first Xia king was Yu, and it was because of his achievement in containing the Flood through an extensive scheme of water-control works that he was permitted to found a dynasty. That the early Chinese associated this privilege with hydraulic conservancy (though the major schemes

5

actually only appear from the fifth century BC onwards) must mean that the throne was always held responsible for natural calamities and their amelioration. King Yu had spent thirteen years 'mastering the waters' without once returning home to see wife and children.

The *Book of History* pointedly contrasts the wisdom of Yu in his respect for the five elements with the indifference of the king before him. Yu received the Mandate of Heaven (*tianming*) to rule over the north China plain in accordance with 'the nine divisions and unvarying principles', which illustrate many facets of early Chinese thought. The first of the nine divisions comprised the five elements: water, fire, wood, metal and earth. The second division concerned personal behaviour, and included respectful demeanour, careful speech, clear vision, attentive listening as well as balanced ideas. The third listed the objects of government as food, wealth and articles of convenience, sacrifices, public works, instruction, punishment of crime, courtesy to guests, and finally, the army. In the fourth were the dividers of time, the calendar being a prerequisite of established rule.

The fifth division treated the ethics of sovereignty; the sage-king concentrated happiness in his own person, then diffused it for the benefit of the people, who responded positively to royal benevolence. This doctrine later formed the core of Confucius' own ethical system: hereditary privilege did not entitle the gentleman or nobleman to a position of social superiority, but only qualities of personal virtue that commanded respect.

Royal righteousness was also the subject of the sixth division, on the need for flexibility in dealing with subjects. Guidance could be sought from Heaven by means of divination, reminded the seventh division: 'When the king uses the tortoise shell, or the divining stalks, to consult the ancestral spirits, the ministers and the officials, as well as the common people, all agree about a course of action. This is called the Great Accord.'

The eighth of the nine divisions dealt with correspondences. Just as rain, sunshine, heat, cold, wind and seasonableness in their proper order caused vegetation to grow abundantly, so ceremony, orderliness, wisdom and knowledge contributed to the salvation of the kingdom. The last division, the ninth, sets the five sources of happiness: longevity, wealth, soundness of body and serenity of mind, love of virtue, and a good death, against the seven extreme evils: misfortune, a short life, illness, distress of mind, poverty, wickedness and weakness.

As the ruler was styled the Son of Heaven, it is hardly surprising that he interceded with the chief deities in person. Should his entreaties and sacrifices fail, then responsibility for whatever was amiss rested squarely on his shoulders. Tang himself narrowly averted such a crisis. The problem was a drought, which, according to traditional chronology,

began a year after his accession, and lasted for seven years, bringing great hardship to the people. During this time rain almost ceased to fall, and sorrow and distress stalked the country. Many of Tang's poorest subjects were reduced to such straits that they were compelled to sell their children as slaves in order to fend off starvation. Relief measures failed to alleviate the suffering, with the result that a general conviction arose that a human sacrifice would have to be offered to Heaven. Without a second thought Tang expressed his willingness to die for the sake of the kingdom. Having fasted and prepared himself spiritually for the sacrifice, the king cut his hair, clipped his nails, and donned a robe of white rushes, before riding to a mulberry grove in a simple carriage drawn by a team of white horses. There, as Tang offered himself as a divine victim, the drought ended in a heavy downpour.

The rain-making dragons sent by Shang Di, the high god of heaven, refreshed the land and saved Tang, and indeed the newly founded Shang dynasty. Now demonstrably blessed by Heaven, Tang had confidence to demote the untrustworthy lesser deity responsible for the drought. The divine and natural worlds were held to mirror feudalism (mountains and rivers were styled duke or count). That Tang, with the agreement of Heaven, should remove a laggard deity from his fief seemed perfectly reasonable.

On the terrestrial level Tang was just as energetic. To support campaigns needed to defend his kingdom, he promoted efficient government and encouraged agriculture, the cornerstone of the Chinese state. Although in the People's Republic today Shang society is held to have depended upon slaves, solicitude for the welfare of the peasantry is evident in the oldest surviving texts. The *zhong*, the 'multitudes', were strictly supervised but they remained distinct from war captives and debt-slaves. Oracle inscriptions reveal that peasant-farmers cultivated fields belonging to the king and the nobility, participated in royal hunts, formed a sizeable part of the army, and undertook garrison duties.

Shang slaves were largely non-Chinese war captives from beyond the northern and western frontiers of the kingdom. They worked alongside the *zhong* in the fields and as servants and grooms within noble households. Doubtless from their ranks were drawn those destined for sacrifice. During the laying of foundations both human beings and animals were ritually killed and interred. In the second Shang capital of Ao, sited at modern Zhengzhou, a ditch below one palatial floor contains about 100 sawn-off human skulls. Human sacrifice lingered on after the fall of the Shang dynasty in 1027 BC, but declined before the humanist teaching of Confucius and his followers.

The Shang used human sacrifice most in the grave pits of the eleven royal tombs at Anyang. But the last Shang king, Di Xin, had no place in this cemetery since he was burned to death when the city fell to Zhou attackers. In the decisive battle which preceded the fall, 'those in the front ranks of the royal army turned their spears and fought those behind until they fled'. The stratagem would have been the work of dissident nobles secretly in contact with Wu, the Zhou leader, and their defection would have been seen as a public declaration that the heavenly mandate no longer resided with the Shang house.

The reader should guard against a tendency among Chinese chroniclers to explain changes of dynasty in terms of virtue sweeping aside cruelty and corruption. Ancient historians perceived events as moving in cycles: a new cycle began when a hero-sage toppled the worthless tyrant of the old house and set up a new rule.

Though the usurpation of Wu is always credited with the over-throw of a tyrant and the restoration of feudal order, the Zhou house was not effectively founded until after his death. The man responsible was Wu's younger brother Tan, who acted as regent during the minority of the second Zhou king. Well acquainted with Shang ways from his many years as a young man at the Shang court, this elder statesman was able to unite the nobility, draw up new laws, establish a central bureaucracy, organise schools throughout the realm, and show proper respect for the fallen house by arranging for the continuation of ancestral sacrifices. His most conciliatory gesture was finding employment for Shang officials, a precedent that during subsequent changes of dynasty freed scholar-bureaucrats from slavish devotion to any particular royal lineage.

The Zhou claimed descent from the deity Houji, 'he who rules the millet', while another leading clan traced its first ancestor to Houji's mother, Jiang Yuan. Both these clans, which intermarried, derived their names from tributaries of the Wei river, on the banks of which the new capital of Hao was founded. Hao's natural defences should have aided the Zhou dynasty, but in 771 BC it was sacked by an alliance of barbarian tribesmen and relations of the queen, who had been set aside because of the king's preference for a concubine. The great vassals rallied to the throne, and the dynasty survived the catastrophe of the king's death, though a new capital had to be established at Luoyang some distance down the Yellow river. Royal prestige was shattered and real power allowed to shift to the nobles who held the largest fiefs, and were independent in all but name.

With the advantage of hindsight, a chronicler noted that

Another unwise act was the ennoblement of the chief of the Qin people. Out of gratitude for sending soldiers to guard him on his way to the new capital, Ping not only raised the chief to noble rank but also gave him sufficient land to sustain his new position, the chief city of which was the old capital which he had just abandoned . . . The very duties ennobled Qin would be called upon to perform would inevitably develop his ambition, for the military skills of his people could not but be improved by their constant struggles with raiding tribesmen along the western frontier.

From this Qin chief would eventually descend Zheng, the unifier of China and its First Emperor.

THE SPRING AND AUTUMN PERIOD (790–481 BC)

Though the Son of Heaven became a ceremonial figure within a small domain surrounding Luoyang, feudalism enjoyed a brief flourish during the so-called Spring and Autumn period, called after annals of the same name. In their own domains, feudal lords conducted sacrifices to their ancestors and local deities that over time assumed almost as much significance as those at Luoyang. A few of these quasi-states were almost the size of a modern province, even though many consisted of little more than a few walled towns along with the villages in countryside around them. At the start of the Spring and Autumn period there were some 120 feudal states; by its end less than twenty survived. The tendency for powerful states to swallow up their smaller neighbours was even more marked later, during the Warring States period (481–221 BC), when only seven states were able to marshal adequate forces for war. Powerless, successive Sons of Heaven watched as two great semi-barbarian powers, Qin and Chu, gained territory until the last Zhou king was rudely pushed from his throne by Qin troops in 256 BC. By 221 BC the strength of Qin was sufficient to destroy all its rivals and unify China as an empire.

The chief reason for the unending conflict was undoubtedly the succession disputes that erupted on the deaths of feudal lords. Intrigues arose through the custom whereby a ruler chose which of his sons, by his wife or his concubines, should be his heir. The other sons were frequently assigned to posts in outlying lands, where there were opportunities to build up individual power bases. Violence for instance marred the funeral of Huan in 642 BC. The struggle between his sons delayed burial until the condition of the corpse became scandalous. Worms were seen crawling out of the room in which it lay, and so putrid was the flesh that final preparations could not be undertaken in daylight.

Huan had been the first *ba* ('hegemon' or 'overlord'). To fill the vacuum created by the decline of Zhou power, the custom had arisen by which leading feudal lords became hegemon in turn to exercise authority in the Son of Heaven's name. Huan was duke of Qi, a prosperous north-eastern state in Shandong province. Though Qi's economic strength was securely based on salt, iron and irrigation, Huan's elevation resulted from the energetic measures he took in dealing with barbarian incursions and inter-state rivalry. Confucius told his disciples a century or so later that his campaigns against the northern barbarians had saved Chinese civilization: otherwise 'we should now button our clothes down the side and wear our hair down the back'.

Huan was ably assisted by his chief minister Guan Zhong (died 645 BC), one of the earliest statesman to be associated with a body of political theory. The rival schools of Confucianism and Legalism were both influenced by Guan Zhong's ideas, even though Confucius reacted unfavourably to his concentration on the ruler's position. Mencius (372–288 BC), the greatest follower of Confucius, singled out for criticism the authoritarian outlook of Guan Zhong when he argued for consistency in the treatment of the people. Whereas Mencius considered the will of the people to be a decisive political factor which might express itself in justified rebellion against tyrannical government, Guan Zhong looked upon a docile people as the natural instrument of a ruler's will. 'For one who is skilled in using the people,' Guan Zhong said, 'can kill them, imperil them, work them, exhaust them, cause them to suffer hunger and thirst; indeed, the ruler who knows how to use the people may achieve these extremes, yet among the people will be no one plotting harm to him.' Yet he did not advocate any reliance on terrible punishments – branding on the forehead, cutting off the nose, cutting off the legs, castration, and death by cutting in half – unlike his fellow chief minister Shang Yang, who died in 338

BC. This fervent believer in Law said bluntly: 'In an orderly state, punishments are numerous and rewards are rare. Therefore the good ruler punishes the bad people, but does not reward the virtuous ones.' For it had to be made worse for someone to fall into the hands of the police than to go to war.

Huan always claimed to act on behalf of the Son of Heaven, but in fact pursued ambitions for his own benefit. While he preferred to settle problems through diplomacy rather than on the battlefield, he was obliged to go to war twenty-eight times as hegemon. The family feud for the succession on Huan's death ruined Qi and allowed the hegemony to pass first to neighbouring Song, and then in 636 BC to Jin, the biggest state of all until internal troubles in 403

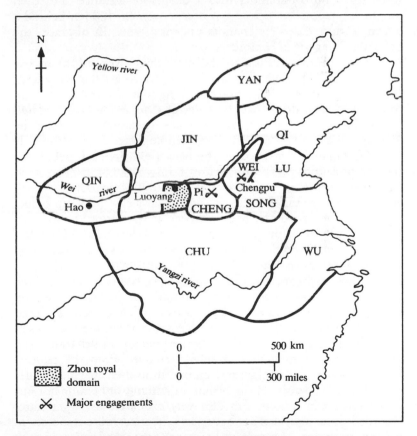

The Middle Kingdom during the Spring and Autumn period (790–481 BC), showing the principal states

BC split it into three separate units: Han, Wei and Zhao. Jin's duke felt grand enough to summon and dismiss the Zhou king without ceremony.

In the warfare of the Spring and Autumn period is encountered the Chinese equivalent of the epic battles of Greek and Indian warriors. Two battles stand out: Chengpu and Pi. The first was a defeat inflicted on Chu by hegemon Wen, duke of Jin. In 632 BC the Jin army marched to the relief of its ally Song, the capital of which had been besieged for several months. The bulk of the Chu forces withdrew on the approach of Wen, but one general refused, in defiance of his orders. He could not accept the taunt: 'A man of virtue cannot be opposed'. At the border town of Chengpu, Wen lured this Chu commander into a dangerous advance, and then caught his exposed troops in a pincer movement hidden behind a screen of dust raised by chariots dragging trees. In disgrace, the defeated Chu general committed suicide.

The engagement at Pi in 595 BC more than revenged the reverse at Chengpu. 'Through this defeat,' a Jin counsellor remarked, 'Heaven is perhaps giving a grave warning to our state.' There were so many Jin casualties that the ruler of Chu seriously considered 'piling up the bodies to make an imposing monument'. That he was persuaded to erect an ancestral temple instead accords exactly with the gallantry displayed on the battlefield. In a lull before the start of hostilities three Chu heroes riding in a chariot had challenged the Jin lines. Pursued by a squadron of charioteers, these adventurers were making their escape when a stag leapt up before them. They downed the beast with their last arrow, halted and presented it to their pursuers, who accepted the gift and broke off the chase. The Jin nobles let the Chu chariot get away in recognition of the prowess and courtesy of their foe.

But these mannered skirmishes were not to last. The eclipse of the chariot in the face of the deadly crossbow during the fourth century BC destroyed the link between aristocracy and war. Battles turned into large-scale infantry actions, with massed armoured columns of foot soldiers supported by crossbowmen, cavalry and chariots. The new riveted iron mail-coats were far removed from the padded jackets or treated sharkskin and animal hide used in Huan's lifetime. With the demise of the hegemon system war became not just professional and serious, but also very expensive as larger states absorbed their smaller neighbours and diverted more resources to military purposes. The powerful states of Qin and Chu could each put into the field over a million soldiers.

THE WARRING STATES PERIOD (481–221 BC)

Because the core of the contending armies consisted of regulars, highly trained and well-equipped, rulers were anxious not to waste in unprofitable engagements what was a considerable investment. Sun Zi's *Art of War (Bingfa)*, the oldest known military treatise in the world, cautions the eager commander against taking unnecessary risks with his forces: 'Under fragrant bait there is certain to be a hooked fish.' Nor should advantage be pressed too hard: 'Never press an enemy at bay. Always leave a way of escape, or your foe will be forced to fight to the death.' The realism of this fifth century BC strategist stemmed from his appreciation of logistics, and their burdensome cost:

Operations inevitably require 1000 fast chariots, 1000 wagons, and 100,000 mail-clad foot soldiers. When provisions are transported for 1000 km the expenditure at home and at the front, including entertainment of allies, the cost of materials such as glue and lacquer, and sums spent on chariots and armour, will amount to 1000 pieces of silver a day. Such is the outlay required to put into the field an army of 100,000 men. When the actual fighting commences, and a victory is slow in coming, the weapons of troops grow dull and their morale weakens. When a city is besieged, you quickly exhaust your army's strength. Again, if a campaign is protracted, the resources of the state will prove unequal to the strain. When your weapons are dulled and morale is weakened, your strength exhausted and your treasure spent, other rulers will take advantage of your distress. Then no adviser, however clever, will be able to save your state.

Perhaps the Japanese should have heeded this advice in 1937 when they began in China a campaign that led, within a decade, to their own defeat. The furious determination of Sun Zi himself in military affairs is not to be underestimated, however. When hostilities broke out between the states of Lu and Qi, he offered his services to the duke of Lu, who hesitated to accept Sun Zi's expert advice because of his marriage to a native of Qi. The issue of loyalty was settled by her killing. Sun Zi said that he could find another wife more readily than an opportunity to direct a campaign.

This cold-blooded murder can stand as a symbol of the Warring States period. The ruthlessness of the battlefield could be disguised no longer: 'blood for the drums' ceased to be the occasional execution of a handful of prisoners after the fight when, in 260 BC at Chang Ping, the Qin generals ordered the wholesale slaughter of Zhao prisoners.

The policies ultimately responsible for the new aggression were those of Shang Yang. A new spirit of government, a quest for efficiency without regard to traditional morality, already permeated several states, but none of them adopted as enthusiastically as Qin the harsh tenets of Legalism. Arriving in 356 BC from Wei, where he was descended from a concubine of the ruling house, Shang Yang found the Qin ruler ready for far-reaching change. At once Shang Yang was given permission to introduce a new legal code, which strengthened the state's military power by weakening the influence of the aristocracy, breaking up powerful clans, and freeing the peasantry from bondage. In place of customary ties he substituted collective responsibility as the method of securing order. So Shang Yang

ordered the people to be organised into groups of five and ten households, mutually to control one another's behaviour. Those who did not denounce the guilty would be cut in half; those who denounced the guilty would receive the same reward as if they had decapitated an enemy . . . Everyone had to assist in the fundamental occupations of tillage and weaving, and only those who produced a large quantity of grain or silk were exempted from labour on public works. Those who occupied themselves with trade were enslaved, along with the destitute and the lazy. Those of noble lineage who had no military value lost their noble status. The social hierarchy was clearly defined and each rank allotted its appropriate fields, houses, servants, concubines, and clothes. Those who had value were distinguished by honours, while those without any value, even if they were wealthy, could have no renown whatever.

Shang Yang's singlemindedness made him unpopular and, like Sun Zi, he did not long survive his master's death. Confucian opponents saw the totalitarian dangers in subjugating the state to a ruler's needs. For, on the contrary, they held the good of the people to be the objective of politics, and regarded ethics as the standard of life. Rulers possessed no absolute authority, because every level of society had mutual responsibilities. When asked about government, Confucius replied: 'Let the prince be a prince, the minister a minister, the father a father, and the son a son.' Officials were obliged to obey a ruler's commands only as long as they were ethical. 'If it becomes necessary to oppose a ruler,' remarked Confucius, 'withstand him to his face, and don't try roundabout methods.' This firmness of principle was destined to be the cardinal virtue of the later imperial civil service; high officials would perish at the hands of impatient emperors, but would be admired for generations afterwards.

Mencius extended the concept of righteous opposition to unjust

Fig. 2. Confucius, the most influential thinker in East Asian history. He died in 479 BC

Fig. 3. Qin Shi Huangdi, First Sovereign Qin Emperor, who died in 210 BC

government into the right of the people to take up arms against wicked rulers. Whenever a ruler lost the goodwill of his subjects and resorted to oppression, the Mandate of Heaven was said to have been withdrawn and the ruler's replacement on the throne by a more suitable candidate justified. It was perfectly practicable for Mencius to argue the case for rebellion: offensive weapons from the Warring States period onwards were always superior, first the crossbow, then later the gun, ruling out an armoured domination akin to that of the medieval knight in the West.

Mao Zedong was the Communist leader who fully appreciated the revolutionary dynamic inherent in the agrarian revolts which punctuated Chinese history. Even in the worst years of World War Two he remained convinced that Japanese brutality would rouse the peasantry to action and cause the emergence of 'a more progressive China'. Mao Zedong was just as aware of how Confucian political theory had turned popular discontent into a safety-valve for the traditional order, a viewpoint shared by the third major school of classical philosophy, Daoism. For the Daoists social evolution had started to go wrong with feudalism; their ideal was the primitive collectivist society that was supposed to have existed prior to the Xia dynasty.

An older contemporary of Confucius, Lao Zi (born 604 BC) the founder of Daoism, was keeper of the archives at the Zhou court. Access in Luoyang to more ancient records than anything available to Confucius in the eastern states of Lu, Song and Qi may have persuaded him of the falseness of traditions glorifying the feudal past. Unlike Confucius he was convinced that the causes of disorder in the world lay not in the shortcomings of Zhou institutions but rather the fact that institutions themselves were an unsatisfactory method of achieving order. Benevolence and righteousness, Lao Zi argued, usually acted as a mask for princely ambition. The book associated with Lao Zi's name, *The Way of Virtue (Daodejing)*, set the rivalry of princes in a cosmic perspective:

> Who would prefer the jingle of jade pendants,
> Once he has heard stone growing in a cliff?

Man's rootedness in nature, an inner strength that made all men wiser than they knew, was looked upon as the means to personal salvation. The artificial demands of feudal society had so disturbed the innate abilities of the people that instead of following the natural way of living, they were circumscribed through man-made codes of honour, love and duty. Daoist quietism was practised by a number of Lao Zi's followers, one of whom, Zhuang Zi (350–275 BC), rejected the premiership of the great southern state of Chu. As he succinctly commented: 'A thief steals a purse and is hanged, while another steals a state and becomes a prince.' In the turmoil of the Warring States period, the only sensible policy for the sage was to live the life of a recluse.

Such an attitude was anathema to Confucian thinkers, who regarded service to the state as a moral obligation. The problem for the Daoists was that in classical times China had no popular institutions similar to those which appeared in Greece: there was nothing for them to use in the furtherance of a practical democratic philosophy. Withdrawal from service in government, or becoming a hermit, could never be more than a political protest. Though the idea was to prove attractive during periods of disturbance or foreign conquest, scholarly retreat could not advance political development beyond the imperial system, which lasted with interruptions from 221 BC till 1912. The only revolutionary glimmer to survive at all was in Daoist religion, a transformation of Daoist philosophy brought about largely by the need for solace amongst the peasantry when crisis overtook the early empire in the third century AD. Chang Daoling, the first heavenly teacher of the Daoist church, even established for a time a small, semi-independent state on the borders of Sichuan and Shaanxi provinces. His organisation of the peasants living there in a quasi-religious, quasi-military movement was the first of many such ventures. It is reputed that Chang Daoling dramatically acquired immortality when in 156 he disappeared except for his clothes.

That the tomb of Lao Zi is unknown indicates more than an indifference to the Confucian value placed on ancestor worship. It shows how Daoism was always connected with the pursuit of the elixir of life. The First Emperor, Zheng, was to devote a fortune to this end, dispatching embassies to the tops of mountains in order to establish relations with the spirits as well as sending them overseas to find 'the three isles where the immortals dwell'. Absurd though this seems now, it has been plausibly argued that in Daoist observation of Nature and experiments in alchemy are the dim beginnings of scientific method.

The 'Hundred Schools' of philosophy, said to have existed during the Warring States period, represents an intellectual ferment unmatched in the later monolithic unity of the empire. With one exception, the philosophers appear to have been *shi*, members of the scholar-gentry and administrative class. Their social position entitled them to a freedom of thought and movement denied as much to noblemen as to peasants and artisans. They wrote books because rulers would rarely listen to advice. Only the glibbest advisers could expect to avoid miserable ends. Even the politically astute Li Si, the guiding spirit behind the rise of Qin, found palace intrigue beyond his powers in 208 BC, when he was executed at the instigation of the chief eunuch Zhao Gao. From 237 BC onwards Li Si had the ear of Zheng, the ruler of Qin. Strengthened economically through large-scale irrigation schemes, and especially the Chengkuo canal which had opened a decade earlier, the state of Qin became ready for a final open clash with its rivals. Troops were deployed in campaign after campaign, in the words of the Han historian Sima Qian 'as a silkworm devours a mulberry leaf'. Between 230 and 221 BC the 'Tiger of Qin', as Zheng was called, overcame all the other feudal states to make himself sole ruler of China.

QIN UNIFICATION (221–206 BC)

Zheng chose to be called Qin Shi Huangdi, First Sovereign Qin Emperor, to show his supremacy ever the rulers he had deposed. The character for emperor (*di*) in the title may have contained the notion of divinity, or at least divine favour. As early as 219 BC Zheng tried to associate himself with the immortals by obtaining the elixir of life, the same year that work started on his own mausoleum at Mt Li. Assassination attempts not only served to increase his dread of dying; they also encouraged his aloofness from all but a small circle of advisers and, indirectly, abetted those intrigues so disastrous to the Qin dynasty on his sudden death in 210 BC.

Although the Qin dynasty was brief it represents a turning-point in East Asian history, not least because the bureaucratic form of government developed under the Qin emperors became the model for future Chinese organisation. The significance of the change the First Emperor began, and Liu Bang, the founder of the following Han dynasty, completed, cannot be overstated; the unified empire gave China over two millenniums of internal stability and external influence.

In his drive for uniformity the First Emperor relied on military force. Feudal holdings were abolished and noble families compelled to take up residence in Xianyang, now the capital of all China; the peasants were given greater rights over their land but became liable for taxes; weapons were also brought to the capital, where they were melted and cast into twelve colossal statues; the empire was divided into administrative districts, garrisons planted strategically, and a body of inspectors established to audit accounts as well as check on the administration of justice; there was standardisation of weights and measures, currency, written script and axle wheels; a national road network was built and canals improved for the supply of the army; and, as a counter to the Xiongnu (probably the Huns who later invaded the Roman empire), the Ordos desert region was annexed and defended by the Great Wall, which ran for over 1000 km from Gansu province in the west to the Liaodong peninsula in the east.

General Meng Tian was sent with a force of 100,000 men to expel the nomads, plant numerous walled cities and, using 'the natural mountain barriers', erect 'ramparts and installations where they were needed'. When, in 210 BC, the general and the heir apparent to the imperial throne, Fu Su, were ordered to commit suicide in an edict forged by Li Si and Zhao Gao, Meng Tian admitted:

I have indeed a crime for which to die. Beginning at Lintao and extending to Liaodong, I have made walls and ditches over more than 10,000 *li*, and in this distance it is impossible not to have cut through the veins of the earth. This is my crime.

The historian Sima Qian, however, comments that the general's death had less to do with upsetting natural forces than his 'disregard for the distress of the people'. As a compliant servant of the First Emperor, Meng Tian had shut his eyes and ears to the sufferings of the conscripted labourers who toiled and died in their thousands building the Great Wall.

The First Emperor was anxious to halt any drift of the Chinese people to the north in case the farmers of the northern outposts might abandon agriculture and take up stock-rearing, so strengthening the nomad economy. The Great Wall was intended to keep his subjects in as well as shut his enemies out. To encourage a southward population movement imperial armies appropriated more land to the south. By 210 BC operations had extended the First Emperor's authority into the West river basin, reaching the coast in the vicinity of modern Hong Kong. While the peoples of Nanhai, 'South Sea', were by no means assimilated or firmly controlled, they were irrevocably tied to the empire. The cutting of a canal which joined the Yangzi and West river systems facilitated the southward flow of settlers, many of whom were convicts or 'unproductive' persons such as traders. Both the First Emperor and his chief minister Li Si endorsed the Legalist policy of encouraging agriculture and repressing commerce.

When, in 213 BC, the First Emperor discovered that his edicts drew criticism from scholar-gentry of the Confucian persuasion, he followed the advice of Li Si and burned all books except those on medicine, forestry, agriculture and divination. Then the disloyal would be 'unable to use the past to discredit the present,' Li Si said. 'As for persons who still wish to study, let them take the officials as their teachers.' Radical though this attempt was to make knowledge an imperial monopoly, the proscription of books under Qin rulers was not new; Shang Yang had burned the *Book of History* among other classics. But the result of Li Si's advice was more profound. When, in 206 BC, a rebel army burned Xiangyang, the conflagration engulfed the imperial library and destroyed the sole surviving copies of many books. The loss caused a definite break in consciousness, for when, under the patronage of the Han emperors, ancient texts were painfully reconstructed from memory and badly tattered copies hidden in 213 BC at great risk were unearthed, the feudal age was remote. The book-burning gave later scholars a lasting revulsion against the Qin dynasty, although this did not entirely prevent censorship in later years.

Renewed criticism in 212 BC drove the First Emperor to conduct a purge of scholars, some 460 being condemned to death. Zheng's heir, Prince Fu Su, was sent to oversee Meng Tian's operations on the northern frontier for daring to criticise this act. His banishment and subsequent death removed the most vigorous and able member of the imperial family at a critical moment, since popular rebellions soon broke out in protest at the severity of Qin rule and the heavy burden of labour on public works. Li Si's motive in plotting against Fu Su appears to have been personal anxiety, a weakness skilfully played upon by the chief eunuch Zhao Gao. Because he was unwilling to risk demotion, Li Si not only acquiesced in the installation of Hu Hai, the worthless second son, but he pandered to his lust for power. In 209 BC Li Si wrote to Hu Hai: 'The intelligent ruler makes decisions solely himself and does not let his authority lie in the hands of his ministers.' Only then could he 'devote himself to using the empire for his own pleasures'.

The circumstances of the First Emperor's death in 210 BC had given Li Si and Zhao Gao their chance. Having on a tour of inspection a dream of a sea-god interpreted as an evil spirit keeping him from contact with the immortals, the First Emperor roamed the shore of Shandong province until he dispatched what was most likely a whale with a repeater crossbow. Shortly afterwards he sickened and died, but Li Si and Zhao Gao suppressed the news and brought the imperial litter back to Xianyang, behind a cartload of mouldering fish in order to disguise the stench of the corpse. As a result of the terror inspired by the imperial title, there was neither an onlooker to question the arrangements for the homeward journey, nor on arrival in the capital an official to oppose the forged will they used to place Hu Hai on the throne.

Neither of the conspirators gained permanently from their actions. Zhao Gao engineered Li Si's execution in 208 BC, and in the ensuing year forced the Second Emperor, now called Ershi Huangdi, to take his own life, but the usurpation then attempted by the scheming eunuch was effectively opposed. 'Realising that Heaven had refused to grant him the imperial mandate,' the historian Sima Qian relates, 'and that the officials as a whole would not aid his ambition, Zhao Gao summoned the nephew of the First Emperor and reluctantly handed over the imperial seal.' Within two months,

Fig. 4. Three early official seals. Left, Warring States period (481–221 BC); middle, Qin dynasty (221–206 BC); right, Former Han (206 BC–AD 9)

Fig. 5. Seal belonging to the brother of the Later Han emperor Gwangwu Di, who allowed his close relatives to rule small kingdoms within the imperial boundaries

early in 206 BC, this hapless nephew was a prisoner of Liu Bang, the first of the rebel leaders to reach Xianyang. The arrival of the main force under Xiang Yu, a Chu nobleman, shortly after the Qin surrender, brought death to the entire imperial clan in a general massacre. 'Palaces and houses were looted and fired. The burning lasted several months. So it was', Sima Qian states, with some satisfaction, 'that the Qin empire was lost.'

2

THE EARLY CHINESE EMPIRE

From the Han Dynasty to the Mongol Conquest
(206 BC–AD 1368)

THE HAN DYNASTY (206 BC–AD 220)

Four issues dominated the empire under the Han: its administration, the economy, the intrigues of powerful families, and the northern frontier. The dynasty struggled with these, and the deposition of the usurping Xin emperor, the reformer Wang Mang, was caused in AD 23 by a combination of them all. His short reign did more than divide the Han dynasty into the Former (206 BC–AD 9) and the Later (25–220); by eclipsing for a while the imperial house, Wang Mang made the Later Han emperors reliant on the landowners responsible for restoring their dynasty. As one of these landowners thoughtfully remarked: 'In present times, it is not only the sovereign who selects his subjects. The subjects also select their sovereign.'

That Han society would be divided by literacy could hardly have been foreseen in 202 BC, the year the first Han emperor Liu Bang took the title Gaozu, or High Ancestor. He was almost certainly illiterate and not a little intolerant of scholars. Yet as a result of his policies the fundamental distinction in imperial times was always between the rulers and the ruled, between the educated gentry from which the officials were drawn and the peasants who could not read or write. The ruling class, however, was neither closed nor unchanging. Old feudal families lost ground during the Former Han, while Later Han society was even more open to the rise of new ones. Imperial consorts' families, in particular, tended to reach the highest levels, though when their downfall came it was usually swift and catastrophic. Below the élite were the mass of the peasants, living in villages, working owned or share-crop land, paying rents and taxes, providing manpower for public works and the army, surviving at subsistence level. The opening up of new lands, together with improvements in agricultural techniques, took the population to almost 53 million, a total in excess of the entire Roman empire.

Gaozu had a peasant dislike of the excessive ceremony attached to learning. When some scholars came to him in costume, he snatched one of their elaborate hats and urinated in it. But he was moderate in comparison with the nobleman Xiang Yu, who thought nothing of boiling an outspoken follower alive. Gaozu's mildness seems to have been genuine, a signal virtue in that very violent age, and it made his accession popular: people felt that he would govern in their interests, unlike the absolute rulers of Qin. Gaozu neither aped aristocratic manners nor slackened his compassion for the peasantry, and his habit of squatting down, coupled with an earthy vocabulary, unsettled polite courtiers. He knew the value of learned and cultivated advisers and assistants, however. To bring order to the daily life of his new palace at Chang'an ('Forever Safe'), across the Wei river from the old Qin capital, he commissioned a new court ceremonial for his boisterous followers. His only instruction was 'Make it easy'.

Despite the brief unification imposed by the First Emperor, China had remained a confederation of recently independent states with still vigorous regional cultures. But Confucian standards and rituals together with inherited Qin practice brought some cultural unity. By turning to scholars untarnished by the harsh policies of Legalism, Gaozu paved the way for the ultimate Confucianisation of a bureaucratic empire. The transformation was a slow one because the first Han emperor settled for a political compromise after the oppression of the First Emperor. He allowed the restoration of certain feudal houses and granted fiefs to his own close relatives, but these diminished holdings were intertwined with districts controlled by imperial officials.

In 154 BC emperor Han Jing Di (156–141 BC) used a rebellion among his vassals to alter the laws of inheritance. Inherited land now had to be divided between all sons in a family which hastened the breakdown of large units. Emperor Han Wu Di (140–87 BC) completed the dispossession of the old over-powerful aristocracy.

His most zealous agent was Chang Tang, a justice official who, if he knew the emperor wanted a person condemned, would turn the case over to the harshest judges. The Han historian Sima Qian

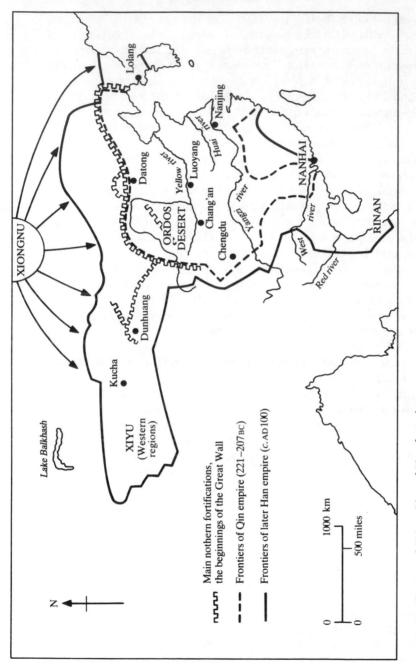

Lake Balkhash

XIYU
(Western regions)

Kucha

XIONGNU

Dunhuang

Datong

Lolang

Yellow river

ORDOS DESERT

Luoyang

Chang'an

Huai river

Nanjing

Chengdu

Yangzi river

NANHAI

West river

Red river

RINAN

N

Main northern fortifications,
the beginnings of the Great Wall

Frontiers of Qin empire (221–207 BC)

Frontiers of later Han empire (c. AD 100)

1000 km

500 miles

0

0

Imperial Unification of China: Qin and Han dynasties

records an attack on Chang Tang in front of Wu Di himself. A senior official declared

People say that petty clerks with their brushes and scrappers have no business becoming high government officials. How right they are! It is men like this Chang Tang who have turned the empire into a state where men are afraid to look each other in the eye or to put one foot down beside the other for fear of breaking the law!

Unimpressed though Wu Di was with this viewpoint, he allowed open discussion in court. This official had to retire, but in the end it was Chang Tang who committed suicide on a charge of corruption. On hearing how Chang Tang's mother was so put out by his sudden fall that she forbade a decent funeral, Wu Di commented, 'If she weren't that kind of mother, she could never have borne that kind of son!'

Through his persistence and severity, Wu Di ended the power-sharing with the nobility, and then bent to his own will the officials who replaced it. Gaozu had summoned scholars to assist with administration, but Wu Di was the first emperor who set examinations for would-be officials. He would even revise the pass list personally when he spotted a candidate whose ideas he liked. The total bureaucracy, from ministers to minor officials, in 5 BC numbered about 135,000, a figure thought to be slightly higher than in Wu Di's reign.

An ideal official, a graduate from the imperial university in Chang'an, was said to be distinguished by abundant talents, respect for the family, loyalty to the throne, moral rectitude, and deep learning. Education had begun its enduring role as arbiter of power and prestige outside the imperial house itself. The blocking of all avenues of social advancement to merchants, a Confucian attitude reinforced by Legalism, always meant that a poor scholar without an official position would prefer farming to trade as a means of livelihood, lest he spoil any future opportunity of a civil service career.

Action in the economic sphere, however, was forced on Wu Di's officials by mounting difficulties in the production and distribution of basic commodities, the worsening condition of the peasantry, the growing wealth of merchants, and inflation caused by the private minting of coin. To meet immediate financial commitments Wu Di was advised to sell titles and call in privately minted coins by issuing treasury notes made from the skin of a rare white stag. In 119 BC merchants were forbidden to own land and state monopolies were declared over iron and salt. Control was given to officials until their incompetence compelled the recruitment of merchants in these essential industries. To counter speculation in foodstuffs Wu Di established public granaries and ordered provincial officials to buy when prices were low and to sell in times of shortage.

Wu Di was equally vigorous in dealing with the Hunnish Xiongnu, whose raids south of the Great Wall were a perpetual threat. Manned by soldiers with crossbows, this fortication had proved effective only when combined with substantial annual gifts to the Xiongnu equivalent of the Son of Heaven, who in return, policed the steppes along the northern border. Now Wu Di adopted a different tactic. In 138 BC an envoy named Zhang Qian was dispatched westwards to stir up the enemies of the Xiongnu in Central Asia: he reported finding, in what is now Afghanistan, 'cities, mansions and houses as in China'. This was in the recently conquered Graeco-Buddhist kingdom of Bactria, a remnant of Alexander's dominions. The Chinese court was amazed; it had never suspected the existence of other civilisations. What particularly interested Wu Di in Zhang Qian's account, though, were the large horses he had noticed, since these could be used to carry heavily armed men against the Xiongnu on their smaller Mongolian ponies. Military expeditions by 101 BC established Chinese suzerainty in the Ferghana basin and secured enough horses for stud purposes.

The arrival of Chinese arms in Central Asia disturbed the balance of nomad power, and for nearly half a century the Xiongnu were contained. In order to deny them supplies new colonies were also planted in the north-east as a protection for the overland route to Korea. Although these victories made Wu Di famous, he recognised by 91 BC that the strain of continuous campaigning was becoming intolerable. No Chinese ruler could wage a prolonged war and avoid rebellion or being overthrown. Imperial armies depended on a nationwide militia that supplemented small forces of professional soldiers. Conscription lasted for only two years, though time-expired militiamen were liable for recall in an emergency.

Wu Di himself ensured in 87 BC the smooth succession of his youngest son Zhao Di, but court intrigue later undermined his successors and ultimately brought to power Wang Mang's brief dynasty, the Xin (AD 9–23). Recurring economic problems and renewed activities of the Xiongnu were also factors in Wang Mang's rise to power; the radical measures he took to deal with them brought about his own death and his dynasty's fall.

Wang Mang sought to limit the wealth of powerful families, whose holdings of land had once more increased, and to alleviate the distress of the peasants, obliged to sell their farms and pledge their service to the rich during famine years. The buying and selling of land as well as slaves was banned, and small families with large estates were forced to surrender land for distribution to those who had none. Low-interest government loans, funded by state monopolies, enabled poor peasants to buy tools and seed.

Resistance to Wang Mang's radical measures was aided by the lukewarm attitude of officials, often themselves relatives of important landowners. It became irresistible when famine and misman-aged aid drove the northern provinces into a rebellion that coincided with large-scale operations against the Xiongnu. In AD 24 the head of the usurper, exhibited in the market-place at Chang'an, was stoned by the crowd. This final indignity did not lead to an immediate restoration of the Han house, however. Gwangwu Di, the first Later Han emperor was one of twelve to claim the right to don the yellow robe.

The transfer of the seat of imperial government downstream from Chang'an to Luoyang was tacit acknowledgement of a shift of the centre of the nation's economy eastwards and southwards. The lower Yangzi and Huai river valleys had overtaken Shaanxi as the most developed region in the empire. The later break-up of China during the Three Kingdoms period (221–265) can be seen as a continuation of this same process in that the southern kingdoms of Shu and Wu were sufficiently strong to challenge for many years the northern state of Wei, which was the rump of the Han empire.

In contrast to the Former Han capital, Luoyang appeared almost frugal. The splendours of Wu Di's reign were gone. With 500,000 inhabitants, Luoyang was nonetheless still the most populous city in the world. But it was destroyed soon after the massacre of the eunuchs in 189. Enraged at the assassination of a renowned general at court, troops stormed the imperial palace and later razed the city. The Later Han emperors had taken to using their eunuch followers against powerful families, but these conflicts tended only to make the eunuchs powerful in turn, until at last their plots drew the army into politics. The beneficiary of this particular coup was another general, the soldier-poet Cao Cao (155–220), who assumed authority in all but name: the Later Han dynasty was tolerated as long as Cao Cao considered it politically useful.

Despite the decline of the Chinese empire during the Later Han, there were significant technical advances connected with imperial patronage. In 31 the state-owned iron industry took advantage of the invention of a water-powered metallurgical machine, which

may have led directly to the production of steel. Another step forward in the imperial workshops was the perfection of paper-making
around 105. The earliest known printed book, a Buddhist text,
dates from much later, in 868, but by that date Chinese prisoners of
war had already introduced paper-making to the Arabs, who eventually passed the technique to Europe about the eleventh century.
Paper-making assisted the spread of hygienic habits throughout
society too: in lavatories toilet paper became available. Health also
improved as a consequence of imperial interest in longevity, since
from Daoist magic a systematic approach to diet and medicine
developed. The first official dissection was actually carried out in 16
by special order of Wang Mang.

Communications were enhanced through extensive canal-
building. Steering was aided by the invention of the stern-post
rudder, whose prototype has been discovered in a pottery model of a
vessel excavated from a Former Han tomb. This rudder and the
watertight compartment allowed junks to become large deep-ocean
craft several centuries before European ships could venture on the
high seas. The wheelbarrow, an improved equine harness, and the
stirrup put land transport equally ahead.

THE CRISIS OF THE EARLY EMPIRE (220–589)

Once in charge, Cao Cao obliged the shaken throne to let him eliminate other military leaders. In 208 he felt strong enough to tackle
the Sun family, a serious rival established on the Yangzi river at
Nanjing, but the superior nautical skills of the southerners discom-
forted Cao Cao at the battle of Chibi and he had to accept a division
of China into three. Following the accession of his son Cao Pi as the
first Wei emperor, the Sun declared itself in 229 the imperial Wu,
and not long afterwards at Chengdu in Sichuan province Liu Bei,
who claimed to be connected with the deposed Han house, added
his own claim as the imperial Shu.

The rivalry of Wei, Wu and Shu is celebrated in the famous novel
The Romance of the Three Kingdoms (Sanguo Yanyi), written by
Luo Guanzhong in the fourteenth century. To the Chinese the
period has always appeared legendary, so much so that from one of
its generals they have derived Guan Di, the Confucian god of war.
However, this deity sought to prevent hostilities.

The struggle between the Three Kingdoms was finally ended in
280 by the Western Jin dynasty, which had toppled the Wei house
fifteen years earlier. The first Western Jin emperor, Sima Yan,

was another northern general in the mould of Cao Cao, though he outdid him by briefly achieving the reunification of the whole country. His strength came partly from the manpower of barbarians allowed to settle within the Great Wall, a policy with dire consequences. For the Western Jin dynasty lasted only till 316, when most of the northern provinces passed into the hands of peoples from the steppe – generally Tartars – and the remnant of Sima Yan's line fled southwards to Nanjing. There they founded the diminished Eastern Jin dynasty (317–420). Nomad encroachment had been a worry since the time of Gaozu, but it was the more conciliatory Later Han who weakened the northern defences and let barbarians carve out territories within the empire. In 383 the Eastern Jin army managed to halt at Feishui the southern movement from the steppe, thus confirming the independence of the Chinese settled south of the Huai river valley. The line of partition was the northern boundary of the wet-rice growing area, country unsuited to nomad cavalry. But the victory at Feishui could not avert the division of China for almost three centuries.

The Tartar partition (317–589) brought very different historical experiences to each half of China. The south had to adjust to the loss of the ancient heartland of the country; as a result, Confucian ideas rapidly lost ground to both Daoism and Buddhism. Buddhist monks even dared to assert their independence of secular authority as they had in India. In the barbarian north, by contrast, Tartar rulers expected obedience. There the Tuoba Tartars gradually defeated rival tribesmen, setting up in 386 a dynasty known as the Tuoba Wei. The Chinese at court, however, managed to reassert their influence and by the reign of Xiao Wen Di (471–99) formed the leading element, even persuading the emperor to move his capital from Datong to Luoyang as a token of his claim to rule 'all under Heaven'. In the 490s Xiao Wen Di introduced further measures: in the interests of administering the vast Chinese state, he prohibited Tartar speech, dress and costume.

This astonishing instance of the absorptive power of Chinese culture in part explains the survival of the empire, even its continuation down to modern times. The impact of barbarian settlement on the western provinces of the Roman empire was entirely different, since a definite cultural break occurred with the retreat of Latin learning behind monastery walls. In north China there existed an alternative social structure to central authority in the groupings of powerful families, whose estates could offer security to peasants and employment to scholars. Although these local magnates could be troublesome, they were accepted by the Tartar invaders as permanent, and ultimately produced a Sino-barbarian synthesis.

The transfer of the capital to Luoyang did not revive Confucianism at once. While Xiao Wen Di favoured this philosophy, he found that popular opinion would not countenance any limit on Buddhist temples and monasteries within the city walls. He had to sanction gigantic sculptures at nearby Longmen to replace those left at the former capital. The phenomenal rise of Buddhism was indeed the chief event of this period. Introduced by way of Central Asia during the Later Han, it developed initially as a sect of Daoism. Daoists spread Buddhist symbols and cults, just as Jewish communities helped to spread Christianity in the eastern Roman empire. That Buddhism became such an eclectic faith was due as much to the circumstances of its arrival as to the ability of the Chinese mind to hold different propositions simultaneously without apparent distress. The earliest Buddhist converts had few texts, depended on the testimony of foreigners, and had scant knowledge of India, where Buddha had preached.

Mahayana (Great Vehicle) was the form of Buddhism carried to China, and thence transmitted to Korea and Japan. This more evolved version of the faith contrasts with *Hinayana* (Lesser Vehicle), the dominant form in South-East Asia, in its worship of an extended pantheon of saints and deities. Of particular importance was the *bodhisattva*, or 'being who is possessed of the essence of Buddhahood', a divine person whose selfless desire to bring enlightenment to others more than matched the wisdom thought to be possessed by the monk, the *Hinayana* ideal. Translation of the manuscripts brought back by pilgrims, or introduced by Central Asian monks, quickly drew criticism from Confucian scholars, who accused the new teachings of being unfilial. To counter such a charge, scriptures were translated that showed concern for the family, although not until the open clash between Confucianism and Buddhism under the late Tang emperors would Buddha finally become the epitome of the filial son.

Of all the southern rulers during the Tartar partition, the greatest patron of Buddhism was Liang Wudi (502–50). Converted in about 511, the Chinese emperor invited 3000 monks from India and established at Nanjing a translation school for Buddhist texts. Only with difficulty was he dissuaded from becoming a monk himself.

Each day the emperor and the empress became more and more absorbed in their devotion to Buddhism. The empress built a magnificent temple close to the palace, where she could worship at all hours of the day, and as a work of merit she erected a pagoda thirty metres in height, which could be seen for a long distance in every direction, and which reminded the people of the hold that Buddhism was taking upon those in high positions in the land. In order to adhere strictly to its tenets, the emperor forbade the taking of life and even issued an edict that no figures of animals should in future be embroidered on any cloth, because tailors in making up garments were obliged to cut through them, and so might accustom themselves to cruelty.

Nothing was said to have daunted Liang Wudi's religious enthusiasm, not even an apocryphal interview with Bodhidharma, the founder of the Chan sect, which in Japan eventually became Zen. When asked by the emperor what merit he had acquired by good works, Bodhidharma replied, 'No merit at all!' Amazed, he then asked his uncompromising visitor about the first principle of Buddhism. 'There isn't one,' was the reply, 'since where all is emptiness, nothing can be called Holy.'

THE SUI AND TANG DYNASTIES (589–906)

The sinicisation of the Tartars living in north China left the way open for reunification. Like the Qin dynasty which first united the country, the Sui began its reconquest in the northern provinces,

Fig. 6. Bodhidharma, founder of the Chan sect in China. In Korea this radical Buddhist teaching was known as Son, in Japan as Zen

only to fall itself within a few decades. And, once again, a subsequent imperial house built on the foundations it laid. Under the Tang emperors China experienced a notable cultural renaissance.

Notwithstanding his forbidding manner, the first Sui emperor Wen Di (589–604) knew that military conquest of the southern provinces would not alone restore unity; traditional beliefs must be revived and imperial patronage granted to both Daoism and Confucianism. By 595 examinations for civil service candidates were open once again to all, except merchants and artisans; but examination questions were based exclusively on a Confucian curriculum, despite Wen Di's personal sympathy for Buddhism, because Confucianism provided the only available body of political theory and ritual precedents for running the state. Confucian learning was thus re-established as the passport to official office and wealth, though the focus of intellectual interest remained Buddhism, whose rapid development even attracted monks from Korea and Japan.

Early in his campaign of reunification, Wen Di proclaimed his purpose in religious terms when he said: 'With a hundred victories in a hundred battles, we promote the practice of the Buddhist virtues.' Possibly the emperor's birth in 541 in a Buddhist temple, and his upbringing until the age of twelve by a nun, had a more profound effect than was at first realised. A soldier from his fourteenth year, Wen Di expected unqualified obedience and enforced stern discipline, in early days even taking a horse-whip himself to those who slacked in their duties. Towards the end of his reign, however, Buddhist observances grew more frequent and more elaborate at court. In 601, in imitation of the great Indian ruler Aśoka, Wen Di had reliquaries built throughout the empire. But this fervent espousal of a gentle faith failed to save his own life. Plotting among the imperial concubines brought about the downfall of the heir apparent and the elevation of his second son Yang Di, who in 604 assassinated his father.

As soon as Yang Di came to power as the second Sui emperor, he abandoned his father's austerity and commissioned a new capital at Luoyang. His next project was the Grand Canal linking the northern and the southern provinces permanently together. Construction involved reopening existing but derelict waterways as well as cutting extensive new sections. At the same time, repairs initiated by Wen Di on the Great Wall continued. Millions toiled on these gigantic projects: shirkers could expect execution, flogging, neck weights or the confiscation of property.

Yet for all this, it was Yang Di's foreign policy that ruined the

Sui, in particular the failure of successive campaigns against Koguryo, a Korean kingdom with its capital at Pyongyang. Militarily Koguryo was a threat only in alliance with its nomad neighbours, but border incidents were magnified by Yang Di as personal affronts so that he persisted in squandering his armies in the face of disaster. Unseasonable weather, supply difficulties, and stubborn Korean resistance effectively decimated three enormous Chinese expeditions. Fortunately for China, in 614 exhaustion caused the king of Koguryo to end hostilities and become an imperial vassal. Meanwhile, peasant rebellions had begun in 611 with a rising in Shandong province, and their number and intensity increased in the north-east as the pressure of each failure bore down on the population.

A shaken Yang Di ordered the empire back to peacetime pursuits, but his edict rang hollow in provinces in rebel hands. In 617 Li Yuan (566–635), one of the most powerful Sui generals, marched his forces on the capital and captured it. He did this at the prompting of his second son, Li Shimin, the future Tang emperor Tai Zong. 'Follow the desire of the people,' he had been urged, 'raise a righteous army, and convert calamity into glory.' The assassination of Yang Di a year later offered the rebellious general scope to consolidate his position. However, the exceptional service rendered by Li Shimin in the struggle to secure the Tang dynasty (618–906) provoked an immediate crisis. Rivalry with the heir apparent became a feud, which in 626 left Tai Zong's elder and younger brothers dead, and his father dethroned.

The support of his own troops in the coup of 626 made the second Tang emperor, Tai Zong, very sensitive to dangers from the army, and led him to shift power from military to civil officials. He increased the number and frequency of civil service examinations and instituted a scholarship system to encourage learning, so that during his long reign (624–49) the imperial administration was gradually taken over by professional bureaucrats recruited on the basis of personal talent and education. The rise of men committed to a central government changed the position of the emperor: he was no longer just the chief aristocrat, whose pedigree might even be suspect; with no aristocracy to challenge his authority, and with a loyal bureaucracy, the imperial clan became set apart from the people in quite a new way, and the emperor started to accrue powers that would culminate in virtual despotism under the Ming dynasty (1368–1644).

Tai Zong was a self-conscious ruler, deeply concerned over the record of his reign. In China it was customary from the Former Han onwards for specially appointed scholars to write an account of their times, and only they were allowed to read what they had written. As each document was composed, it was deposited in an iron-bound chest, which remained locked until the dynasty ceased to rule. Then the chest would be opened and the documents edited into a 'veritable record'. In 641 Tai Zong asked one of these officials about the possibility of examining documents before they were deposited, but was respectfully fobbed off. Pressed by Tai Zong, the official said: 'My duty in office is to uphold the brush, so how could I not record bad points?' The emperor often professed ignorance of state affairs. Once he said:

We appreciate that as yet We are not good at making judgements. We conquered the empire with bows and arrows, but Our knowledge even of these is poor. How much less We understand then about ruling the empire!

This show of modesty aside, Tai Zong was an energetic and successful administrator, who possessed the happy knack of attracting first-rate subordinates. One of them was Wei Zheng (580–643), a Confucian moralist of uncompromising directness. Although rarely involved in the details of administration, Wei Zheng was renowned as a salutary restraint on imperial power. More than once Tai Zong exploded in rage at his opposition, shouting aloud, 'I'm going to have to kill that old country bumpkin!'

Wei Zheng's outspokenness rested on the conviction that the fall of the Sui dynasty was attributable to Yang Di's reluctance to heed the advice of his ministers, and that its inability to deal with internal unrest resulted from an obsession with foreign conquest. In 640 he opposed an expansionist policy in Central Asia, much to Tai Zong's annoyance. Vigorous action in the 660s did eventually destroy Koguryo, but an offensive by the Korean state of Silla soon drove the Tang garrisons out of the peninsula. By then China had a formidable power to worry about on its western frontier. Tibet had become, under Sron btsan sgampo (605–49) a unified kingdom for the first time; it put pressure on Gansu province and threatened communications with Central Asia.

Along this route the great Buddhist pilgrim Xuang Zhang, or Tripitaka, had left China in 629 and returned in 645, after fifteen years in India, with hundreds of scriptures. Tai Zong granted him a personal interview. Some seventy texts were translated under Xuang Zhang's supervision, supported by imperial funds, while at Tai

Zong's request a translation of the *Daodejing*, the Daoist classic, was made into Sanskrit for transmission westwards. This commission was meant to reaffirm religious policy, since in 637 an edict had ordered that Daoist monks and nuns should have precedence over Buddhists in all imperially sponsored ceremonies. It was becoming obvious that the activities of the powerful Buddhist church had to be controlled. Eventually, illegally ordained monks might be condemned to death, and interference by them in secular matters became a punishable offence. But Tai Zong was unsuccessful in his attempt to forbid monks and nuns receiving homage from their parents, a practice incompatible with ancestor worship.

Imperial notice of Buddhism was unavoidable, given the endless proliferation of sects and movements. In part the diversity of Chinese Buddhism arose from the absence of a sacred language, like Latin or Greek in the West. Few monks could emulate Xuan Zhang and consult the original texts, so that the founders of new schools usually started from Chinese translations. Another factor was the coalescence of the imported faith with existing modes of Chinese thought, and especially Daoism. Chan Buddhism (Son in Korean, Zen in Japanese) represents an admixture of Buddhist and Daoist ideas, the most obvious a profound distrust of words.

Intrigue at court resulted in the ninth son of Tai Zong succeeding him in 649 as emperor Gao Zong. Weak and prone to physical illness, Gao Zong was overshadowed by his clever empress, Wu Ze Tian, who virtually ran the empire even before his death in 683. Afterwards Wu Ze Tian continued to control the court and ruthlessly pushed aside two of her sons before, in 690, becoming the only

Fig. 7. The only woman to have occupied the imperial throne, Wu Ze Tian, who styled herself emperor Sheng Shen (690–705)

woman in Chinese history to don the yellow robe.

Allowing for Confucian commentators' hatred of her usurpation, it is clear that Wu Ze Tian was exceptionally gifted and constructive. A streak of cruelty created terror, but she was always careful to balance those who served her violent ends with talented administrators. These able men had risen to the highest posts by way of the examination system, by means of which Wu Ze Tian weakened her opponents within the imperial administration. The extension of opportunity this entailed was not the empress's only claim to fame, for it was through her influence that poetry became a requisite in examinations for higher qualifications. The subsequent poetical outpouring was block-printed in an anthology comprising 48,000 poems by no less than 2200 authors.

During the long reign of Xuan Zong (712–56) the Tang dynasty reached its peak, and suffered a disaster in the revolt of Turkish general An Lushan from which its authority never recovered. The preoccupation of its ruler, towards the close of his reign, with the concubine Yang Yuhuan is the conventional explanation for the destruction visited upon Chang'an and the northern provinces of the empire. In the 740s Yang Yuhuan became a close friend of An Lushan, and in 751 adopted the grotesquely fat commander of the north-eastern armies as her son.

Threats from mobile enemies had made permanent formations of long-serving troops necessary along the northern frontier, replacing the conscripts whose ranks had been thinned by an expansionist foreign policy. That Chinese arms were seriously overstretched was clear from two serious defeats in 751. One occurred in Yunnan at the battle of Dali, when an army of 60,000 men was annihilated by the forces of Nanzhao, an independent kingdom; the second reverse took place on the banks of the Talas river in distant Turkestan. At the town of Atlakh the desertion of the Qarluqs, a Turkish tribe, in the middle of the engagement handed victory to the Arabs, who subsequently incorporated large parts of Central Asia into the Muslim world.

In 755 the ambitious An Lushan rebelled, with over 100,000 men, comprising regular troops as well as contingents of nomadic tribesmen. Nothing could halt his advance on the capital, and Xuan Zong reluctantly quit the city. The flight involved great hardship, and mutinous troops compelled the emperor to execute Yang Yuhuan, whom the chief eunuch strangled. By the time the rebels had been beaten in 763, the empire had abandoned outlying territories and was struggling to fend off enemy thrusts. The

Tibetans not only managed to sack Chang'an in a surprise attack, but in 787 also captured Dunhuang at the western end of the Great Wall. Further losses ceased only when the Tibetan kingdom collapsed following the assassination in 842 of its king by a Buddhist hermit.

The Tang dynasty survived, but central government was weakened by semi-autonomous administrations in the provinces, the result of demands for greater freedom of action from the military commanders who had restored the imperial house. When the last Tang emperor was deposed in 906, the country fragmented into nearly a dozen states. New methods of warfare may have had an effect: gunpowder is first mentioned in the ninth century.

One event stands out in the late Tang era: the assault on Buddhism. As is made clear in the diary kept by the Japanese monk Ennin, who was travelling in China between 838 and 847, pressure against the Buddhist church, because of its wealth, had been gradually building up, and this broadened into full-scale suppression in 845. Emperor Tang Wu Zong (840–6) shut down the 44,600 retreats, shrines, temples and monasteries housing the 260,500 registered Buddhist monks and nuns. Few exceptions were granted, according to Ennin, who saw

numerous monks and nuns being sent back to their places of origin with their heads wrapped up. The monasteries are destroyed, and their money, estates, and bells are confiscated by the government. An imperial command says that the bronze and iron Buddhas of the land are to be smashed, weighed, and handed over to the Salt and Iron Bureau. Every action is reported in detail to the throne.

Although the persecution ended after Wu Zong's death, the Buddhist church never again rivalled the state. A personal motive of Wu Zong was almost certainly inspired by the Daoist idea of an elixir of life, a will-o'-the-wisp peculiarly attractive to Chinese rulers. Ennin noted a series of edicts intended to help in its acquisition: wheelbarrows were forbidden on pain of death, and black animals ordered to be destroyed.

This persecution was mild compared to the later actions of military dictators in Korea and Japan; but the Chinese laicisation still caused considerable distress, for as Ennin observes, 'those who are sent home lack clothes to wear and food to eat . . . they are forced to steal the property of others, and in many places all monks returned to lay life are under arrest'. Some escaped to take up arms in the widespread rebellions that preceded the fall of the dynasty.

THE SONG DYNASTY (960–1279)

The half-century of disunity that separates the Tang and Song empires was ended by a northern general, who was elevated to the throne of the northernmost state by his mutinous troops. But the first Song emperor, Tai Zu, was determined that his own would be the last military coup, and he persuaded his senior officers to retire early. Then the administration was overhauled so that the army no longer controlled territory, the entire conduct of affairs being placed under civil officials. Not surprisingly, the other petty states into which China had fragmented viewed these changes with interest and sympathy. Two of them submitted to the new Song dynasty by diplomatic arrangement; the majority surrendered after brief campaigns, while the last independent principality held out against Tai Zu's successor only till 979. But in the same year the Song army met a disastrous defeat at Gaolinghe, near modern Beijing, when it tried to dislodge the Qidans, a nomadic people from Manchuria, from the territory they had occupied south of the Great Wall. The Qidans had recently set up a few agricultural settlements and established a Chinese-style dynasty in what they called the Liao kingdom. After further reverses, the Northern Song dynasty (960–1126) was always on the defensive; it is known as the Northern Song because in 1126 the nomadic Jin, having disposed of the Qidans, fell upon the capital at Kaifeng and drove the dynasty south to Hangzhou,

Fig. 8. A Buddist pagoda, over 30 m high, built by a Northern Song emperor near Kaifeng, the imperial capital

Fig. 9. An example of the renowned calligraphy of the Song emperor Hui Zong (1101–25). His misjudged alliance with the Jin led to the collapse of the Northern Song dynasty, and the transfer of the capital southwards to Hangzhou where, as the Southern Song, the imperial house lasted till 1279. Apart from the Liao kingdom, the northern frontier was also threatened by the partially sinicised Tibetan state of Xia. In 1044 an annual gift of silver and silk was agreed as the price of peace. In striking contrast to the Han and Tang empires, Song foreign policy was never expansionist but aimed at containment of the northern peoples. Foreign invasion remained a threat and was the cause of the final overthrow of the Song dynasty, but the subjection of military officials to civilian control reflects the pacific tenor of the times.

The administration was modelled on the Tang, but there was a significant widening of the curriculum on which candidates for the bureaucracy were examined. During the ascendancy of the reformer Wang Anshi (1021–86), technical and scientific subjects could be offered as special subjects. Although engineering and medicine did not long survive Wang Anshi's fall in 1076, the extension indicated a rise in scientific consciousness among educated Chinese. Wang Anshi's own humble background may account for his interest in labour-saving devices, but no country could then compare with China as an industrial power. The world's first mechanised industry was born at the same time that the printing of books facilitated the exchange of scientific knowledge derived from observation and experiment. At the throne's behest in 1111, the twelve most eminent doctors compiled an encyclopedia of current practice.

Although the Song empire reached the edge of modern science and underwent a minor industrial revolution, there was no social and economic transformation as happened later in Europe and, to a much lesser extent, in Japan. However, Song officials were not uninterested in the benefits of inventions, and the imperial workshops themselves acted as a spur to progress.

Try as the early Song emperors might to reassert control, circumstances were far different from those prior to the rebellion of An Lushan. Lack of central direction had allowed the growth of commercial centres, unwalled cities largely beyond state regulation, while inflation exacerbated by the use of paper currency, sharpened competition for land. Thus Song society presented problems of order that were not easily suspectible to direct action. Political disenchantment drove thinkers such as Zhu Xi (1130–1200) to redefine human nature and the values needed to appeal to its best side. As a young man, Zhu Xi was powerfully attracted by Chan Buddhism and he never lost that school's appreciation of the natural strength hidden within each person. Where his thought parted company with Buddhism as well as Daoism was in formulating

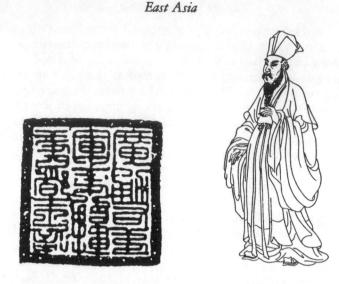

Fig. 10. An army seal dated to the year 1079, and found in Hebei province. Northern Song troops stationed here faced the forces of the sinicised Liao kingdom

Fig. 11. The Song reformer Wang Anshi (1021–86), a minister who was conscious of the technical and scientific advances of his time

principles for the regulation of human conduct. The purpose of intellectual and moral self-cultivation, he argued, was to live in harmony with a pre-ordained pattern in Nature. This alone justified the exercise of authority over other people. But Zhu Xi denied the immortality of the soul and the existence of a deity. What anchored his pronouncements in daily life was the Confucian notion that society could be governed only through individual and collective self-discipline: in his memorable phrase, 'cultivation of the self and ordering the state'. It was a reassertion of moral perfection exactly suited to the inward-looking societies typical of medieval China, Korea and Japan.

With his voluminous commentaries on the Confucian classics Zhu Xi remoulded the Chinese mind, since the Neo-Confucianism he developed as a philosophy was adopted under the Southern Song as the official orthodoxy and the curriculum for civil service examinations. Even in Tokugawa Japan (1603–1868), where no state education existed, Zhu Xi exercised a pervasive influence. As late as the 1850s, when the threat of war with the United States loomed, would-be reformers struggled to relate Neo-Confucian concepts with the Western knowledge that they desperately required for

Japan's continued survival as an independent country. The visual arts first became respectable when the Song emperor Hui Zong (1101-25), a keen painter of birds and flowers himself, added painting to the subjects candidates could offer for the highest examinations. Interest in gardening as an art ran parallel to that of landscape painting. Both were looked on as aids to meditation, and probably grew out of Buddhism. The Tang poet and painter Wang Wei (699-761) had first shown a practical way of finding contentment by designing a garden. More spontaneous than either the geometrical arrangements favoured in Europe or the stereotyped landscapes in Japan, the Chinese garden always sought irregular and unexpected features which appealed more to imagination than reason. The basic elements were the same as in landscape painting, mountains and water, which could be interpreted simply as rocks and a pond.

The gardens outside the walls of Hangzhou still preserve today something of the Southern Song. The pinnacle of urban luxury were its floating restaurants, which catered for a sophisticated official class as well as wealthy merchants. With reluctance the Southern Song emperors had agreed that the irregular and unplanned features of Hangzhou would be graced by the construction of an imperial palace. In Marco Polo's *Travels*, Hangzhou is called *Kinsai*, a corruption of 'temporary residence'. It was a prophetic name because in 1210 the Mongol horde under Genghis Khan (1162-1227) invaded China. That nearly half a century of war was necessary before in 1279 the last member of the Song imperial house fell in battle is testimony to Chinese skilful defence, exploiting terrain unfavourable to cavalry tactics. Another factor was military technology: explosive grenades and bombs were launched from catapults; rocket-aided arrows with poisonous smokes, shrapnel and flame-throwers were deployed alongside a primitive armoured vehicle and armoured gunboats; and in close combat a prototype gun, the 'flying-fire spear', discharged flame and projectiles. The Mongols, like the Tartars, became irresistible only when they adopted Chinese equipment. Yet they outdid these previous invaders in becoming the first nomadic people to conquer the whole of China. In 1263 the grandson of Genghis Khan and the first Yuan, or Mongol emperor, Kublai Khan (1214-94), moved his capital from Karakorum to Beijing.

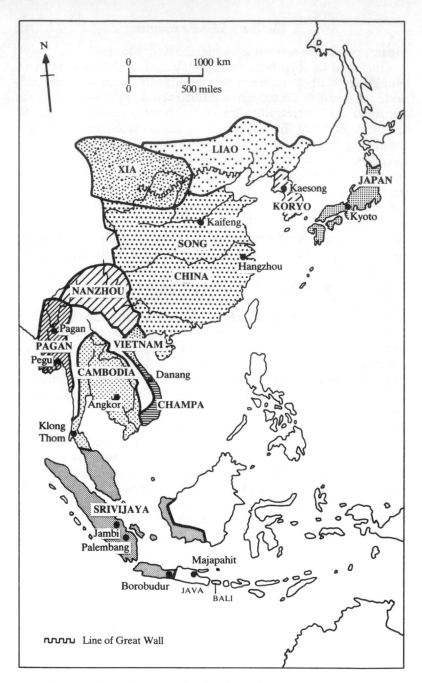

East Asia in the eleventh century, showing the main powers

THE MONGOL CONQUEST (1279–1368)

The Mongol conquest reflected a fundamental change in the balance of power in East Asia. China's military weakness had been apparent well before the Song, but the territory reunited by the Northern Song was smaller than even the late Tang empire, and its northern frontier relied for protection on payments to powerful neighbours as well as on force of arms. Once the Chinese court fled from the northern provinces in 1126, Korea and Tibet among others no longer offered tribute. Only through the arrival of a Mongol dynasty could the rulers of China restore hegemony on mainland East Asia. Unlike the Chinese, these conquerors chose direct control. Kublai Khan would not tolerate other sovereign states to exist at all.

The Mongol onslaught was unleashed on the world by Genghis Khan, who ruled that any resistance shown by cities should be punished with total extermination. When in 1222 his favourite grandson, Mutugen, fell at the siege of Kakrak, a fortress in present-day Afghanistan, he vowed to kill every living thing in the surrounding valley. As every Mongol tribesman was a soldier, the continuous military activity started by Genghis Khan forced the horde to rely on servile labour. When necessary, women and children entered the fray and acted as auxiliaries. At most there were 300,000 Mongol males of fighting age, but they had several advantages. The Mongol warriors were unswervingly loyal and obedient; and their horses, noted Marco Polo, 'are so well broken-in to quick-change movements, that upon a signal given, they instantly turn in every direction, and by these rapid manoeuvres many victories have been won'. The Mongols invariably conscripted defeated armies into their own ranks; these new recruits formed the infantry and artillery. At the battle of Wahlstadt in 1241 they deployed a Chinese smoke-producing device to cause disarray among the combined forces of the Poles and the Teutonic knights, prior to a victorious Mongol cavalry charge.

The sedentary auxiliaries, called up to supplement the nomadic tribesmen, were a late development. At the outset, the conflict was a struggle between the nomadic culture of the steppe and the civilisation of intensive agriculture. There is a revealing incident reported in the so-called *Secret History of the Mongols*, commissioned by Genghis's successor Ogodei Khan (1229–41). During the Afghan campaign Genghis Khan questioned two learned men from nearby Turkistan about the puzzling phenomenon of the city. To the

Fig. 12. The great Mongol leader Genghis Khan, who laid down the rule that any resistance should be punished by death

Mongol leader, the city with its cultivated fields was something unnatural, a threat.

A critical change in Mongol attitudes to conquered areas of settlement occurred shortly after 1218, when Yelu Chucai (1190–1244) was summoned to the Mongol capital, Karakorum. Genghis Khan expected that this Qidan nobleman would welcome service in the Mongol court because of the enmity between the Qidans and the Jin, whom the Mongols had just overthrown. But sinicised Yelu Chucai spoke respectfully of the Jin, to whom his father and grandfather had rendered loyal service. Rewarded for his honesty with the post of secretary-astrologer, Yelu Chucai was able to play on the avarice of Genghis when Mongol advisers recommended genocide as a means of turning fields back to pasture. He convinced the Khan that it was better to gather taxes and military supplies than corpses.

Although Yelu Chucai's influence increased after the election of Ogodei Khan, when he rose to become head of the secretariat, the proposals he put forward drew the animosity of the anti-Chinese faction at court. His temporary restarting of civil service examinations in 1237 at least freed a thousand scholars from Mongol slavery, but it could not arrest the drift of the dynasty towards becoming an entirely alien domination. The decision to rely on non-Chinese officials in 1239, the year tax-farming was made a preserve of Muslim businessmen, marked the end of any chance of compromise in China. Trouble was already brewing during the reign of Kublai Khan. Nominally Kublai was the last *khaghan*, 'khan of khans', but the lesser princes of Central Asia, Persia, and Russia were so restive that before his death the limits of his actual authority were confined to East Asia. Even here, his wishes did not go unchallenged, a situation his own pride found unsustainable.

Chinese emperors had usually preferred to bring foreign rulers into their orbit by peaceful means – gifts, grants of titles, and favourable trade relations. Beyond acknowledging Chinese suzerainty through the presentation of tribute, a subordinate ruler was subject to few demands and remained autonomous within his own territory. The Mongols, by contrast, required much more of their dependent states, and they imposed garrisons to ensure demands for goods and services were swiftly met. Thus the Korean navy was requisitioned for the two invasions of Japan, in 1247 and 1281.

In the early fourteenth century the strain was clearly evident in the differences between the Mongol clans, which in twenty-five years raised nine candidates to the throne. This conflict at court opened the way to a partial recovery of influence by Chinese officials in the administration, but the restarting of the examination system in 1315 came too late to rally lasting support to the Mongol dynasty, against whom popular rebellions increased in number and extent. Imperial authority was already restricted to the environs of the capital at Beijing, and isolated provinces such as Yunnan, when in 1368 its last emperor fled to Mongolia.

3

EARLY KOREA

From Choson to the Fall of Koryo
(194 BC–AD 1392)

Appropriately, perhaps, the earliest documented event in Korean history involves China. After an unsuccessful rising in 194 BC against the first Han emperor Gaozu, the defeated rebels sought refuge beyond the north-eastern imperial frontiers. One, named Wiman (Wei Man in Chinese), took over the state of Choson; he started by defending the border with China but quickly engineered a coup. Wiman, who wore his hair in a non-Chinese style, astutely showed favour to existing Korean officials in his administration. He seems to have been concerned to accommodate well-established native traditions, and not simply to pull Choson into the Chinese orbit.

Above all there was the question of language. The settlers of the Korean peninsula appear to have come originally from present-day Manchuria and Siberia. They spoke a polysyllabic and highly inflected language, in striking contrast to the monosyllabic and uninflected Chinese tongue. The Korean language, like Japanese, is now regarded as part of Altaic speech, a linguistic family named after the Altai mountains in Mongolia. Other modern languages belonging to this group include Turkish and Mongolian. Despite the obvious differences between Chinese and Korean, the Chinese script was adopted because it represented much more than the sole means of writing available in East Asia at the time. Its mastery allowed access to the Chinese classics, the contemporary standard for civilised living. The significance of sinicised Choson, and later set-

46

tlements in Korea sponsored by the Han emperors, lay in their long-term cultural influence on Japan. In time the Korean peninsula became the main conduit through which Chinese culture flowed to the Japanese islands.

During the first decades of the Han dynasty the Chinese emperors were content to let Choson become the dominant power in Korea. Wiman's introduction of an iron industry gave his state a military and economic edge which allowed it to monopolise trade in the peninsula and enrich itself greatly. The Chinese authorities may not have entirely approved of the situation, but, given the likelihood of ties between Choson and the Xiongnu, officials were disinclined to intervene as long as the nomads remained quiet. By the reign of Wu Di (140–87 BC), though, incursions were so serious a threat that Han China was forced to take the offensive. In 128 BC the Chinese unsuccessfully attempted to occupy the Yalu river valley and put pressure on Choson, but it was not until 109–108 BC that northern Korea was taken into imperial control, and four commanderies set up to administer the area. On the pretext that Choson was harbouring Chinese deserters, Wu Di dispatched forces. Defence was undermined by the murder of Ugo, Wiman's grandson, and conflict in the capital, Pyongyang. Following its surrender, the core of Choson was established as the chief commandery of Lolang, a census taken shortly afterwards recording a population of over 400,000. Lolang remained a centre of Chinese civilization for centuries after it ceased to be an actual colony in the fourth century AD. It was absorbed by the Korean state of Koguryo, which asserted its independence from China in AD 12.

The first purely native state to develop, Koguryo arose in the mountains along the middle course of the Yalu river valley. Its mounted warriors were a thorn in the imperial side until 668, when an expedition sent by the Tang emperor Gao Zong captured Pyongyang. The destruction of Koguryo was the result of an alliance between China and another state, Silla, Koguryo's rival in southern Korea. Yet this kingdom ultimately had the satisfaction of giving its name to modern Korea: Koguryo was revived as Koryo after the demise of Silla, and that name was used for the united kingdom until the Japanese annexation in 1910.

THE THREE KINGDOMS (c. 350–688)

The conquest of Koguryo ended the period known as the Three Kingdoms, although a number of smaller states also existed. The three main ones were Koguryo in the north, Paekche in the south-west, and Silla in the south-east.

Koguryo's conflict with China had become particularly intense during the reign of T'aejo (53–146), the first Korean ruler effectively to resist Chinese expansion. By subjugating Okcho, a small Korean state opposite the Han commanderies, T'aejo was able to challenge Chinese arms in the peninsula itself. The Lolang commandery survived his attack, which coincided in 75 with a general Chinese troop withdrawal, but the other three surrendered, including the one strategically placed in the lower Yalu river valley. Lolang was entirely surrounded by hostile territory, but continued in existence almost until the Tartars completed their conquest of the northern provinces of China in 317.

Koguryo had grown from its initial struggle for survival in a barren landscape. The adoption of a Chinese title did not alter the role of the ruler: he was a war-leader and expected to win for his mounted followers a regular supply of spoils – new land, slaves and domestic animals. Everything Koguryo did confirmed Chinese prejudices about the warlike nature of the northern peoples.

However, Koguryo kings seem to have been willing to share power with the chieftains of the Korean groups they steadily overcame. Taxes were levied in kind, for example in cloth, salt and fish. As in China, the officials responsible for the collection of taxes resided in the walled towns which formed centres of royal authority. During the third century kingship came to be seen as the preserve of a single house, succession passing automatically from father to son. King Sosurim (371–84) probably set the pattern for subsequent Korean rulers when, after setbacks at the hands of the Tartars, he reshaped Koguryo institutions. In 372 he introduced Buddhism as the state religion, founded a national academy to train officials according to Confucian concepts, and promulgated a legal code. The revival of Koguryo fortunes led the warlike Kwanggaet'o (391–413) to proclaim his reign as *Yongnak*, 'eternal rejoicing'. The inscription on the great stele presently standing by his tomb at Kungnae-song proudly asserts equality with the Chinese empire, then reduced by the Tartar partition to the southern provinces.

Kwanggaet'o was succeeded by Changsu (413–91), who adroitly used the political division of China to his own ends. By siding at one time with the Tartar houses of the north, then at another with the weakened Chinese rulers in the south, Changsu held his non-Korean enemies in check throughout a long reign. The respite allowed Koguryo to give its full attention to the southern part of the peninsula. As a result, Paekche was forced to abandon large tracts of land and twice transfer its own capital southwards. While that state clung to a diminished independence, neighbouring Silla bestirred itself to more effective long-term defence.

Centred near modern Kyongju, in the extreme south-east of the peninsula, Silla was converted under the strong rule of Nulchi (417–58) into a robust state, gradually extending its boundaries while still beneath the shadow of Koguryo. For more than a century opposition to Koguryo united Paekche and Silla, till in 554 Silla's occupation of the Han river valley, territory jointly won from the common enemy, caused a fatal rift.

Of the Three Kingdoms most is known about Silla. It appears as a typically aristocratic state, with a weak monarchy. Strife in the Korean peninsula must in part be blamed for a surviving aristocratic tendency, since grants of land and prisoners of war after successful campaigns strengthened the position of the nobles, who set up special villages for captives or criminals. An independent peasantry, subject, as in China, to taxation, labour duties and military service, comprised the largest section of society, but constant warfare did much to reduce its numbers and lower its status. In Koguryo the plight of the landless labourers was acknowledged and liability for taxes reduced. To aid the poorest peasants who possessed their own land there was also an equivalent of the Chinese system of grain control, introduced by the Han emperor Wu Di; peasants could borrow from state granaries during a spring shortage and make repayment after the autumn harvest.

Villages formed the basis of each kingdom, each under the authority of an appointed headman. Higher officials lived in towns or cities, and especially in the capital where the court was situated. Despite the adoption of Confucianism, no Korean ruler ever exercised the power of the Chinese emperor, and imported bureaucratic titles defined hereditary privileges rather than described official functions. The so-called 'bone-rank' hierarchy of Silla clearly reveals the structure of an aristocratic society. The top rank, 'true-bone', was reserved for the royal house of Kim and close relations; the aristocracy held several lower ranks called *tungnan*, literally 'hard to get'; below these ranks, at least in theory, there existed three further gradations among the ordinary people. Without membership of an appropriate upper rank, it was impossible to occupy any of the seventeen levels of official appointment. Moreover, dwellings and clothing were dictated by rank as well; as only a true-bone ranker could live in a large house or drive an elaborate chariot.

The strong aristocratic tradition of Silla may have hindered the southern advance of Buddhism. Whereas the new faith was readily accepted at court in Koguryo and Paekche during the fourth century, Buddhist monks met with concerted resistance in Silla until Pophung came to the throne in 514. He overruled the nobles and in 534 ordered the construction of Silla's first Buddhist monastery. The self-sacrifice of a devout courtier, Pak Yomch'ok, otherwise known as Ich'adon, finally gave Pophung the upper hand by accepting execution as the price to be paid for advocating the introduction of the faith. According to the *Lives of Eminent Korean Monks (Haedong Kosung Chon)*, Ich'adon predicted two miracles which would prove the 'virtue of Buddha' – that after decapitation, his head would fly to a mountain top, and his blood would shoot up like milk a hundred metres in the air. Legend says that these events were accompanied by an earthquake and a darkened sky, which so overawed the nobles that they embraced the new religion along with their king.

But the arrival of the gentle faith of Buddhism in Silla, as elsewhere in East Asia, did nothing to discourage war. The climax of the Three Kingdoms period was marked by a protracted struggle between China and Koguryo, which unexpectedly left most of the peninsula united under Silla. Hostilities began with a bold Koguryo thrust beyond the Liao river in 598. The reunifier of China, the Sui emperor Wen Di, launched a counter-attack but it was his successor, and assassin, Yang Di, who took up the fight once he had rebuilt the Great Wall and repaired the Grand Canal. These immense projects, coupled with three massive expeditions against Koguryo, ended with Yang Di's murder in 618. But credit for the collapse of that emperor's dynasty, pulled down as it was by widespread rebellion in China, really belongs to the generalship of Ulchi Mundok, the Koguryo commander. Ulchi Mundock seems to have caught the Chinese off guard after staging a number of mock defeats and withdrawals. In 612 Yang Di personally accompanied an expedition of over a million men to northern Korea. Impatient with the investment of frontier towns along the Yalu river, the Chinese emperor divided his army in order to rush Pyongyang. The advancing force was lured by Ulchi Mundock into a trap at Anju. Two more disastrous expeditions served to ruin Yang Di.

The Tang dynasty, which succeeded the Sui in 618, was no more successful against Koguryo until Silla became an ally. The overconfidence of Yon Kaesomun, a military dictator, allowed this dangerous encirclement. Having killed the Koguryo king and cowed the aristocracy, he chose to antagonise Silla by refusing an alliance against resurgent Paekche. As a consequence Silla came to an agreement with the Tang emperor Gao Zong and the Chinese invaded Paekche in 660. In the following year the new allies turned on Koguryo. Although Yon Kaesomun defeated the Chinese and pushed back a Silla attack, his personal position was much weakened. Once he had been forcibly removed from power, the time was right for another joint offensive. In 668 Koguryo ceased to exist as a separate kingdom. This suited the Tang court, which ordered the setting up of commanderies in Paekche and Koguryo. Silla took a different view of victory and drove the occupying Chinese troops out of the peninsula.

SILLA (688–918)

By 676 a series of reverses convinced Gao Zong that further campaigning against Silla was unwise. Fully engaged against the Tibetans, the Chinese empire was unable to spare troops. Tibetan pressure threatened China's western trade routes until 842, when civil war engulfed the Tibetan kingdom. This respite was critical for Korea, not least because Silla laid the foundation for the independent historical development of its people. Though Silla did not succeed in unifying the whole peninsula, the territory it controlled was destined to form the heartland of Korea, as the northern border ran to the south of Pyongyang.

The old core area of Koguryo, as far north as the Sungari river valley, became Parhae, the Korean pronunciation of Bo Hai, which was the name by which the Chinese finally recognised there a new state. The founders of Parhae were Koguryo nobles who rejected the overlordship of both Silla and China. But the Tang court at least hoped that Parhae might prove a useful ally in case of future Chinese hostilities with the Qidan nomads, whose raids across the Great Wall had begun in 605. The greatest of all the Parhae kings, Tae Hummu (737–94), chose to model his state on Tang China, much as Silla and Japan had also done. The Chinese court always accorded sinicised states far greater respect.

At this period the Chinese finally absorbed Buddhism and developed traditions of their own. One such school, the Hua Yan, which had no Indian counterpart at all, found devotees in Silla. Hua Yan (Hwaon in Korea) was preached during the 640s in Yongju, the Silla capital, at the Pusok-sa temple by a Korean follower of the second Chinese master of the school. Its subtle doctrine taught that every-

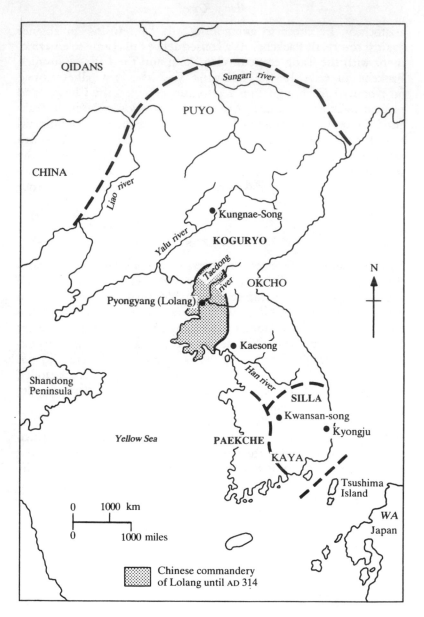

Korea during the Three Kingdoms period (second to seventh centuries)

thing in the universe, animate and inanimate, was a representation of the same supreme mind. Everything was in harmony – a favourite image referred to the apparently separate waves belonging to a single stretch of water – because all led to one point, Buddha, in the centre. This absolute idea was well suited to a centralised state under a strong ruler: hence its attraction to empress Wu Ze Tian, who, after the death of her husband Gao Zong in 683, dominated the Chinese court, and usurped the throne itself. Equally impressed was the Silla king Sinmun (681–92), who firmly established authority over the nobles. Less abstruse, and so more popular with unlettered Koreans, was Pure Land Buddhism (in Korean Chongt'o; in Chinese Jing Tu; in Japanese Jodo), which stressed the simple act of calling on Buddha's name: if one performed this devotion, one could be reborn in the Pure Land, the western paradise where Amitabha Buddha dwelt. As it had in China, the simplicity of Pure Land worship appealed to a population ravaged by war.

A profound scholar, Wonhyo (617–86) was admired for the austerity of his life as a wandering Buddhist monk. What may have driven him beyond the monastery walls was a curious experience he had had on his way to study in China. One night he took shelter in a cave. Thirsty during the night he drank water from a cup he found in the cave. In the morning, he was horrified to discover that his bed was a grave and his cup a skull. First nausea, then enlightenment overwhelmed him: he realised that reality was dependent on our perceptions, and that in China there was nothing for him to learn.

Wonhyo's son, on the other hand, rejected Buddhism in favour of the other great Chinese import – Confucianism. The appearance of its teachings to rival Buddhism indicates how thoroughly Silla came to adopt Chinese culture. In 788 selection to official posts was even made subject to examination. Candidates were graded according to their proficiency in reading Chinese classics. As admission to higher study was restricted to the aristocracy though, this innovation failed to undermine the Korean hereditary privilege.

Yet a growth in royal power was an important consequence of the rise of Silla. King Sinmun used an attempted coup in 681 to eliminate several aristocratic families altogether, but even that left the bone-rank hierarchy largely undisturbed. Unfortunately the custom of having leading provincial families send representatives as low-level officials in Kyongju only served to reinforce bone-rank aspirations, especially as the king dared not favour these provincials, whose presence was essentially intended to guarantee the good conduct of their kinsmen. The bone-rankers could still make a concerted effort to usurp royal authority. After deposing one king in 780, various factions struggled for supremacy and unrest spread throughout society. A series of peasant rebellions swept the peninsula. For over a century no central government exercised general control, until in 936 a soldier named Wang Kon reunited the whole kingdom as Koryo.

Notwithstanding the later difficulties of Silla, the period was a golden age for both secular and religious achievements. Stone and brick pagodas arose, along with fine wooden buildings modelled in the Chinese style; bas-reliefs were carved in man-made caves such as Sokkuram, near Kyongju; and magnificent bronze statues as well as bells were cast. The largest surviving Korean bell, dedicated in 771, is presently housed in the Kyongju museum: it measures 2.27 m in diameter and is 3.3 m high. The most famous Silla scholar was Kim Saeng (born 711). An anecdote recalls the power of Kim Saeng's calligraphy. The large characters he employed to write the name of a certain Buddhist temple made the structure lean to one side, when hung up. By hastily re-writing the name the calligrapher caused the temple to resume an upright position!

KORYO CONSOLIDATION (918-1392)

By blocking all avenues of political advancement to provincial families, the bone-rank aristocrats of Silla forced them to look beyond the peninsula for opportunities. Trade thus developed with China and Japan: in Shandong province there were permanent settlements with Korean magistrates and temples, while on the island of Tsushima the Japanese stationed extra Korean interpreters. Foreign trade had been carried on previously by official missions, but these gave place to private enterprise with the result that wealth and, ultimately, power shifted away from the capital at Kyongju toward commercial centres in outlying places. One of these was Kaesong, the home of the grandfather of Wang Kon, the founder of the Koryo dynasty.

The loosening of ties between the provinces and the capital allowed local leaders to collect forces together and fortify their homes. Known as castle lords, they controlled much of the countryside, and made it almost impossible for government officials to collect taxes from the peasants. The reduction of central revenues provoked, in 889, a determined effort by the government, but that resulted only in a series of revolts, as the peasants found themselves mercilessly squeezed between an extravagant court aristocracy and the exactions of the castle lords. The initial uprisings were not contained by Silla troops, and insurgent bands soon combined into large forces capable of holding wide territories, once leaders arose to direct their energies. One such man was Kyonhwon, a soldier of peasant stock from the mountainous interior. Seizing several towns and cities in the south-west, Kyonhwon endeavoured to restore the old state of Paekche. In 927 he was strong enough to sack Kyongju, execute the king of Silla, and carry off the royal treasury.

Kyonhwon might have survived as the most powerful Korean ruler but for his despotic nature and opposition from the northern part of the peninsula. The backers of his chief rival, Wang Kon, seem to have been the commanders of the fortresses strung along the border. They probably saw that Wang Kon's familiarity with international commerce, and his proven abilities as a general, offered the country the best chance it had of lasting unity. They would have been pleased, too, with his determination to be the champion of all Korea and the successor of the Koguryo kings. In 918 he named his dynasty Koryo, an abbreviation of Koguryo and the origin of our name Korea. Whereas Silla means 'new silk' and Choson 'morning freshness', Koryo refers to the 'hills and streams' that feature so prominently in the Korean landscape.

Having moved his headquarters to Kaesong, his own home area near the mouth of the Han river, Wang Kon prudently set about conciliating the northern castle lords and preparing for a clash with Kyonhwon. Because of Wang Kon's caution, the struggle was not to end till 936, a year after the last local ruler of Silla voluntarily submitted to Koryo. When Parhae went down before the Qidans at about the same time, those families of Korean descent fled south, where Wang Kon warmly welcomed them to his new state of Koryo and gave them lands. In 947 the Qidans called their state Liao, a sinicised name, and adopted Chinese culture. For almost two centuries Liao was the dominant state in East Asia. Then in 1125 Liao was seized by the warlike Jin, another northern people, who went on to conquer most of northern China.

Against the Qidans and the Jin, Song China and Koryo Korea may have hoped for some sort of alliance; but in 1022 all official contact between China and Korea was even forbidden by Liao, an unprecedented situation. In comparison with the losses sustained by the Song emperors on the battlefield, the Koryo kings did not fare badly and they managed to take over old Parhae territories south of the Yalu river, which now became Korea's definitive northern frontier.

Wang Kon himself swept away the bone-rank system that had so hindered the Silla monarchy. He showed his concern for tradition in his choice of a Silla princess for his queen, his appointment of Silla nobles to Koryo posts, and his coldness towards the former supporters of Kyonhwon, yet not for a moment would he agree to inherit the aristocratic difficulties of Silla.

Unification of all the Korean people in Koryo was not enough to bring lasting peace on its own. The age-old tendency to fragment into a number of separate states was finally stopped, but the influence of the castle lords remained strong, as did the power of the military commanders who had first supported Wang Kon. Within two years of Wang Kon's death rebellion broke out. Chongjong (945-9), who put it down, decided to move the capital to Pyongyang, away from troubled Kaesong, but died before he could do so. His successor Kwangjong (949-75) adopted a tougher policy. He struck at the manpower held by military commanders and local gentry by decreeing that former commoners enslaved through war or poverty should be freed. In 958 he introduced civil service examinations for the appointment to official posts of scholars unconnected with powerful families. His last reform was a scheme which regularised the grants of land made to officials as stipends: he made sure these properties reverted to the state when they died. As soon as the old guard dared to show their displeasure at these edicts, Kwangjong slew them without hesitation, even though they were descended from the original supporters of the dynasty. But Kwangjong was still compelled for administrative purpose to lean on aristocrats, since only these men could afford to prepare themselves as examination candidates. So it was that once again the deep Korean respect for lineage gradually converted Koryo into an educated aristocratic state with the king as supervisor of a centralised administration.

Under Songjong (981-97) Confucian scholars were first dispatched from the capital to take charge of local government in twelve newly established provinces. By this period Kaesong, which had become the capital, had grown into a large city. A surrounding wall was built in 1029 by 30,000 labourers, its gates crowned by buildings with tiled roofs as in China, unlike the majority of its houses which appear to have been thatched. Dwellings belonging to the aristocracy were constructed in wood and protected by tiles. The royal palace itself stood at the foot of a mountain, a site chosen largely for its propitious qualities: geomancy was taken into strict account by the Koryo court. Students were admitted to the various colleges that constituted the national university according to rank, junior members of the aristocracy and commoners being restricted to institutions offering technical studies such as law, accountancy and calligraphy. There was also in Kaesong a host of private academies catering for pre-university education. The first of these was opened by the Confucian scholar Ch'oe Ch'ung (984–1068), who gave lectures on the Chinese classics to young aristocrats. His spiritual descendant was Kim Pusik (1075–1151), who wrote the first Korean history. Like the true Confucian minister that he was, Kim Pusik did not hesitate to lead the government troops who crushed the rebellion of Myoch'ong in 1136.

The Buddhist monk Myoch'ong had gained ascendancy at court by means of his skill in divination. King Injong (1122–46) was inclined to heed the ambitious monk's recommendation that he quit Kaesong, where the royal palace had been burned to the ground in recent disturbances, and move to Pyongyang (where Myoch'ong intended to seize the reins of power for himself). A royal palace was built there in 1129, but Injong was dissuaded from moving the court by Kim Pusik, who rightly feared that the king would be drawn into unnecessary conflict on the northern frontier. When it was obvious that Injong would not move northwards, Myoch'ong and his supporters rose in arms but were defeated by the resolute action of Kim Pusik.

The plot of Myoch'ong reveals the extent of Buddhist belief in Koryo. The faith was seen as more than a personal way of salvation: as in early Japan, pious acts and occult knowledge were assumed to have influence over the fortunes of the state. Wang Kon himself had built many temples in gratitude for his successes. His successors were bluntly told that 'the great enterprise of founding Our dynasty entirely depended upon the protective powers of the many Buddhas'. It was their duty to ensure that proper ceremonies were performed for the welfare of Koryo. The most splendid temple, the Hungwang-sa, was dedicated along with its gold statue of Buddha in 1067, after nearly twelve years of construction.

Buddhist festivals were often combined with shamanistic practices. As in China, the spirit world of the northern steppe was never entirely banished from ritual. Though shamanism never enjoyed in Korea anything like the prestige it acquired when incorporated into Chinese Daoism, Korean adepts still mediated between the worlds of the spirits and of mankind, and they played a critical role in regional festivals which celebrated the seasons. By the time of the Koryo dynasty, nonetheless, the nobles had transferred their allegiance to a Buddhist calendar of festivals. Sharing the concern of the king for the prosperity of the realm and the safety of its borders, they contributed generously to the costs of Buddhist festivals as well. Nearly 100,000 monks were fed together at seasonal vegetarian feasts held in Kaesong. Another popular observance was the propagation of the Buddhist scriptures. Monks were sponsored to recite them, or simply parade the sacred texts in the streets. Although beautiful hand-made copies of key passages were specially commissioned, it was acknowledged how the greatest merit belonged to the throne for block printing between 1016 and 1087 the entire Buddhist canon. The woodblocks cut for this purpose were later destroyed by the Mongols in the thirteenth century.

All these endeavours brought Buddhism to a height in Korea never attained again. Its subsequent decline, as in China and Japan, may be attributed to a confusion of doctrine and a readiness to absorb native ideas. In the seventh century Wonhyo had already condemned the rivalry of the various Buddhist sects, along with their competing claims for supremacy in matters of doctrine. Another eminent monk who took the same view was Uich'on (1055–1101), fourth son of the Koryo ruler Munjong, who set about reconciling in Korea the chief antagonists among the flourishing Buddhist sects: the Hwaon and the Son.

The earlier predominance of the Hwaon school, especially under the Silla kings, had long passed away. Before the foundation of Koryo the introduction of Son (Zen in Japanese) was welcomed by the provincial gentry. They were pleased to exchange the complex Hwaon doctrines for the more contemplative and less erudite Son. Drawing on Daoist disdain for the written word, the Chinese followers of Bodhidharma, the Indian founder of the Chan school, had discarded sacred scriptures, images and rituals, concentrating instead on the cultivation of the mind. They maintained that the purpose of Buddhism was enlightenment – necessarily a personal experience. They also believed that they should work, as the moment of insight into one's own nature could occur anywhere. This practical outlook helped Chan Buddhism in China weather the general persecution of 845, when the Tang emperor Wu Zong temporarily shut down monasteries, temples and shrines. Moreover, Son proved to have considerable appeal for smaller Korean landowners, who valued their simple independence at a safe distance from the elaborate and uncertain ways of the capital.

To bring Hwaon and Son Buddhists together, Uich'on advanced the doctrines of Ch'ont'ae school (Tiantai in Chinese; Tendai in Japanese) because they laid emphasis on both intellectual understanding and insight. Conscious of the conflicting claims of Buddhist sects, Ch'ont'ae was comprehensive and encyclopedic in its scope, finding room for the scriptures, monastic discipline, and individual enlightenment. Its basic idea was the oneness of existence. The acceptance of Ch'ont'ae inaugurated a new phase in Korean Buddhism, but it was not enough to reinvigorate the religion, which went into steep decline under the Yi kings, the rulers of Korea from 1392 onwards. In an age that gave priority to the this-worldly teachings of Confucius, Buddhism degenerated into little more than popular superstition.

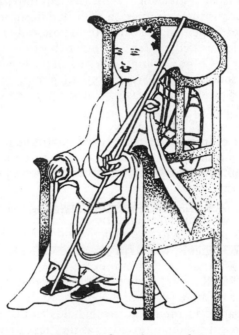

Fig. 13. The royal monk Uich'on, a firm advocate of the Ch'ont'ae school of Buddhism. In 1086 he brought back from Song China 3,000 volumes for the library of holy books already established at Kaesong

The rise of Confucianism stemmed naturally from the prestige of Chinese literature and calligraphy. An aristocratic education was based on the Chinese classics, in addition to their extensive commentaries written by Confucian scholars. Their emphasis on the virtues of the scholar-bureaucrat, the minister loyal to the throne, seems almost wishful thinking during the military unrest that bedevilled late Koryo. Trouble erupted as the pay of the army officers fell notably below that of the civil service. In 1170 and again in 1173 the palace guard staged coups, deposing the king and slaying civil officials. When the disorder spread to the peasantry, the whole structure of the state began to fall apart, a process only just halted by the military dictator Ch'oe Ch'unghon (1149–1219). Having removed in 1196 his military opponents, close kinsmen and fellow officials alike, Ch'oe Ch'unghon took direct command of the palace guard and stationed near Kaesong units personally loyal to him. That in the space of sixteen years he needed to depose two kings and set four others on the throne worried the dictator even less than his dismissal of all civilian ministers. His disregard for niceties allowed a successful confrontation with Buddhism too. When several thousand armed monks tried to oppose military rule, Ch'oe Ch'unghon let his soldiers drive them forcibly from the capital.

The power of Ch'oe Ch'unghon rested on the loyalty and courage of his own soldiers. They were a mixed group, including many impoverished peasants and slaves. Unlike for instance in Japan, the soldiery was neither raised directly from feudal holdings nor from any specific part of the country. This may be explained by the permanent requirement of the central government for a force to defend the northern frontier. Another influence was undoubtedly the low esteem for the military, an attitude imported via Confucianism direct from China.

After the death of Ch'oe Ch'unghon in 1219 an accommodation was made between the army and the civil service, since a number of civil officials returned to the government. The compromise was forced by the Mongols, who kept up an attack on Koryo from 1225 to 1259. Hostilities arose from excessive Mongol demands for tribute. In 1232 Kaesong had to be abandoned and the court took refuge on the offshore island of Kanghwa, while the peasantry was ordered to gather in mountain strongholds and conduct guerrilla warfare against the Mongol invaders as they repeatedly ravaged the land. The invasion of 1254 was dreadful: the Mongols took away 200,000 captives and left behind countless piles of severed heads. When, four years later, the last of the line of military dictators was assassinated, the Koryo court swiftly took advantage of the interregnum to sue for peace.

King Wonjong (1259–74) was able to resume occupation of Kaesong and, with Mongol aid, even reassert his authority over army leaders. The price of Koryo survival was cession of the northern part of the peninsula, elimination of the anti-Mongol party among the military leadership, and assistance with two Mongol assaults on

Japan. The Mongols, who had already overrun a vast area in Asia and Europe, were poised to conquer the outlying countries of East Asia. The removal of the Mongol capital in 1264 from Karakorum on the steppe to Beijing in north-east China was a signal that Kublai Khan, the grandson of Genghis, had decided on permanent domination. As a 'son-in-law' nation, allied by marriage between Wongjong's son and a Mongol princess, Koryo was expected to furnish supplies for the expeditionary force, and to build the fleet that would ferry it to Japan.

In reality the Koreans had little choice. Rather like Britain in 1940, Japan was fortunate to be surrounded by sea. The Mongols were wonderful horsemen, but incompetent sailors. Kublai Khan also underestimated the strength of the Japanese opposition. In 1274 he dispatched a small invasion force of 23,000 Mongol, Chinese and Korean troops in a fleet of several hundred ships. The island of Tsushima was taken without much difficulty, but on Kyushu the invaders met desperate resistance, though by means of superior weaponry and discipline they got the best of the fighting. A deterioration in the weather then led the Mongol generals to re-embark their troops and limp back through a gale to Korea. Stung by the reverse, Kublai Khan ordered another invasion in force, and this went ahead in 1281, three years after the Mongols had completed their conquest of China, but the Japanese had prepared their defences and, together with a timely typhoon, they beat off the attack once again.

The burden on Korea of these abortive efforts was intolerable. The resources of the peninsula had been recklessly consumed, and famine stalked the land. Only the presence of Mongol soldiers held the peasants in check, and all realised that the Koryo dynasty was little more than a puppet. Yet for a century the Mongols continued to prop up Koryo kings. Without this support there would have been no central government at all, for great estates were being formed by the nobles for their own benefit and not the royal treasury. The collapse of Mongol power in China in the 1360s left a vacuum in Korea, which the aristocracy naturally attempted to fill. The contest lasted till 1392, the year that Yi Songgye usurped the throne and founded the Yi dynasty. This general had marched his army not against the Chinese force then massing on the border in order to punish Koryo for remaining pro-Mongol, but against the Korean court itself. An immediate consequence of this shrewd move was the acceptance of Yi Songgye as a vassal by the powerful new Ming dynasty of China.

4

EARLY JAPAN

From the Wa Kingdoms to the End of the
Kamakura Shogunate
(Third century AD–1336)

THE FOUNDATION OF THE JAPANESE STATE

Although Japan lay beyond the perimeter of the Chinese empire,
its rulers in early times were regarded by Chinese emperors as subordinate princes. Chinese cultural influence had been imported by
way of Korea for centuries and the Chinese script used for records
from 400 onwards, but only in the seventh century did the Japanese
begin consciously to organise their country according to the Chinese
model. A passage in the history of the Tang dynasty (*Hsin Tang
Shu*) throws a fascinating light on this era:

Japan was once called Wa . . . There are no fortifications and walls in that
country, only barriers made by placing strong stakes together. The roofs of
all buildings are thatched with grass . . . The people can read and write,
and they honour the teachings of Buddha. In government there are twelve
official ranks. The name of the royal family is Ame . . . and a recent king
has moved the palace to the province of Yamato. In the year [631], the
Japanese sent an embassy to the imperial court. Recognising the distance
that the ambassador had to travel, the Chinese emperor declared that an
annual visit was not required . . . In the year [663] an envoy came to the
imperial court accompanied by some Ainus, who also dwell on the islands.
The beards of the Ainus were four feet long. They carried bows and arrows,
which they shot so well that they never missed a gourd placed on a man's
head at ten paces . . . At this time [670] the Japanese who knew the
Chinese tongue came to dislike the name Wa and changed it to Nippon.
According to the Japanese ambassador, the new name was chosen because
his country was so close to where the sun rises.

The passage goes on to speculate about the truthfulness of the ambassador but, brief and unsure though it is, the main events of early Japanese history are recorded in the passage.

The issue of Japan's name was not new. The second Sui emperor Yang Di had been annoyed to receive a communication in 607 from Japan which began: 'The Son of Heaven in the land where the sun rises addresses this letter to the Son of Heaven of the land where the sun sets.' Yang Di was so displeased by the effrontery of a barbarian king in treating him as an equal that Chinese officials were careful to keep Nippon in its proper place thereafter.

More pertinent are the references to the Ainu and the transfer of the capital to Yamato province, on the island of Honshu at the head of the Inland Sea. Mountainous Kyushu, the original centre of the Wa kingdoms, had insufficient land for cultivation, so a general eastward migration took place. Whether the lands bordering the Inland Sea were united by Yamato arms, or whether they coalesced naturally as a result of several warring factions settling their differences, a single state came into existence; it was destined to control all Japan and give the world its present oldest reigning dynasty. Fierce opposition from the Ainu, the aboriginal inhabitants who spoke a non-Altaic tongue and lived in tribal groups, may have encouraged solidarity. The Ainu were durable enough to dominate the northern island of Hokkaido until the nineteenth century.

Entirely missing from the Chinese text is Shotoku (574–622), who, although he exercised power for thirty years, never ascended the throne. He was regent for his aunt, the empress Suiko, who had been enthroned in 592 after a ferocious struggle between two rival clans. Her husband, the emperor, died in this strife, and so it was with relief that she entrusted government to Shotoku, whose name can be translated as 'royal moral authority'. Such were the gifts of the prince, according to the *Chronicles of Japan* (*Nihongi*), that 'he could speak as soon as he was born, and was wise enough when he grew up to be able to attend to the suits of ten men at once and decide them all without error. He knew beforehand what was going to happen.'

There is no doubt that Shotoku's reforms laid the foundation of the Japanese state. In 604 he issued the so-called *Seventeen Article Constitution* (*Jushichijo Kempo*), a set of principles for good and stable government. These precepts introduced Chinese institutions and thought in that they proposed the supremacy of the ruler within a centralised state, administered by salaried officials. Shotoku was an ardent Buddhist as well as a worshipper in the Japanese cult of

Shinto, but it was to the teachings of Confucius that he had turned for guidance in practical matters. Thus the first article of his constitution quotes Confucius in condemning factionalism: 'Harmony should be held a treasure, and the person who eschews selfish opposition should receive honour.' The Buddhist faith would also help to sustain order, because 'few men are utterly bad', the second article asserts.

It is not impossible that the constitution was written as a memorial to Shotoku a generation or more after his death, when Chinese ideas were better known. If so, its existence is an indication of the esteem in which his regency was held. However, the *Chronicles of Japan* offer little information on Shotoku's activities other than his introduction of ranks for court officials, a system intended to replace an hereditary one not unlike the bone-rank hierarchy found in the Korean state of Silla. That something akin to the Korean nobility should exist in early Japan is likely, considering the close relations between them. Nearly a third of the Japanese nobility had ancestors who were originally refugees from Korean states or Chinese commanderies. But the purpose of the new officials' ranks was the reduction of noble power. To strengthen the position of the ruler embassies were sent to the Chinese court, the first in 607 carrying that irritating letter to Yang Di.

The *Seventeen Article Constitution* reveals an uncertain relationship between the political precepts of Confucianism and the spiritual demands of Buddhism. The emphasis on Buddhism in the protection of Japan as a country indeed suggests the survival of an older native tradition. It accords with Chinese accounts of the Wa ruler as a female shaman. The early Japanese emperor, or empress, was expected to be the medium through which the powers ruling over the world communicated their will. For Shotoku Buddhism probably offered an up-dated version of divine protection for both the throne and the state: by sponsoring the new religion he hoped that the warring nobles might embrace a faith identified with the rule of a peaceful monarch. Patently, Buddhism was to act as a civilising agency which would help to solidify the nation.

With the peculiarly Japanese talent for absorption and imitation, Shotoku had made foreign learning his own. But his interest in the native Shinto faith seems to have been positive, too, possibly for the reason that worship was already entwined with the imperial family, which traced its divine descent from the sun goddess Amaterasu. Indeed, her gifts of a sacred bronze mirror and a sword are still part of the imperial regalia today.

Shinto, 'the way of the gods', was so called to distinguish native beliefs from the foreign 'way of Buddha'. Never more than a loose body of cultic practices descended from shamanism, Shinto failed to evolve into a unified faith and, until the nineteenth century, was subordinate to Buddhism. Its deities were amalgamated as local manifestations of Indian and Chinese Buddhist divinities, and its shrines were run as branches of the larger Buddhist temples. Amaterasu was associated eventually with Dainichi-nyorai, the 'Great Brilliant One', a radiant version of Buddha.

Buddhism was attractive to the Japanese at this period because of its sophisticated doctrines and elaborate rituals, but especially because its emphasis on peace did much to curtail the bloody quarrels of the nobility that plagued the country. The emperor was in time compared to Dainichi-nyorai, as the guarantor of peace in earthly affairs. Emperor Shomu went so far as to declare in 749 that the laws of Buddha and the imperial edicts were identical.

The high-water mark of imperial government during the Nara period (710–84) was not ushered in without further violence and reform, however. Shotoku's own son fell victim to intrigue and Yamato remained in turmoil until 645, when the future emperor Tenchi (668–71) employed assassins to rid the court of unwanted noble advisers. Their dispersal gave scope for a second series of Chinese-inspired reforms, called the *Taika* (Great Change): they were to reproduce the organisation of the Tang empire in Japan. A decree of 646 ordered that the capital was to be regulated, along with districts and provinces. In the countryside, every fifty houses were placed under a headman, whose tasks included superintendence of agriculture, administration of justice, collection of taxes, and organisation of labour duty on public works. Change would have been far-reaching had not the nobles occupied most of the senior posts in the provinces. As it was, they were able to maintain most of their privileges, although the state steadily improved its performance in taxation and social control. Rebellions continued – a particularly serious one after the death of Tenchi in 671 – but the imperial house was able to lay out in 710 a capital at Nara.

NARA PERIOD (710–84)

The first requirement of a Chinese-style state was a permanent capital, something alien to the early Japanese. As they believed that a dwelling place was polluted by death, the court had moved to a new site whenever a ruler died. Reformers finally succeeded in estab-

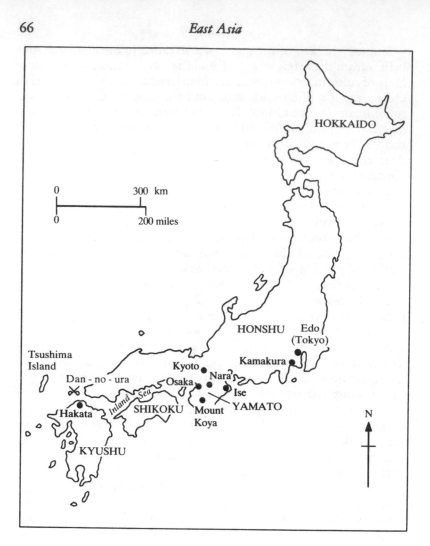

Japan

lishing at Nara a city modelled on the Chinese capital, Chang'an. Its streets ran in the same grid pattern and the imperial palace was situated at the northern end. But there were no city walls, an omission unheard-of in China, and the street plan had to make allowance for existing Buddhist and Shinto buildings. These monasteries and shrines, and forty-eight new Buddhist temples built there, were to form later the nucleus of Nara following the removal of the court to Kyoto, north of Yamato province. The reason for leaving Nara, still incomplete in 784, was that the city had become a stronghold of the Buddhist clergy, who tried to dominate its political life. The move to Kyoto was destined to last, for in name at least the capital remained there until the Meiji restoration in the nineteenth century.

The place of Buddhism in Japan was defined in law, which acknowledged the role of the religion in maintaining the welfare of the state, confirmed the property rights of its institutions, and laid down guidelines for the conduct of monks and nuns. The spread of Buddhism beyond the capital was accelerated by the emperor Shomu (abdicated 749). Not only did he commission a bronze Buddha, over 18 m high, but he ordered the construction of a temple, a monastery and a nunnery in each province, and sent out to them copies of the scriptures. Imperial patronage was very beneficial to the Buddhist clergy, some 25,000 of whom were ordained during the Nara period. Temples received both public and private donations and started to amass great wealth. While rulers continued to officiate in Shinto, Buddhism was the chief preoccupation of the court, a circumstance soon exploited by an unscrupulous monk. The crisis arose through the decision in 764 of the empress Shotoku, who had already abdicated, to resume the throne. Under the spell of a monk named Dokyo, she announced her return to power as a nun in these terms: she had a duty 'first to serve the Three Treasures (Buddha, the scriptures and the monastic orders), then to worship the gods (Shinto), and next to cherish the people (rule the state)'. Dokyo was appointed chief minister and for a time he outwitted the aristocratic opposition, led by the Fujiwara family.

The Fujiwara first won imperial favour during the reform struggle of 645, and ever since the family had held on to a prominent position by its natural talents and a practice of marrying its girls to imperial princes. But in 765 the leading Fujiwara was killed, the young emperor exiled, and Dokyo left supreme. Soon, no member of the court could be unaware of Dokyo's ambitions. With difficulty the empress was prevented from abdicating in his favour, and only her death in 770 allowed the Fujiwara family to exile him.

This episode led to efforts to limit the power of the Buddhist clergy, but the moment was not right; the building in 768 of a Buddhist temple at Shinto's holiest shrine, the seat of Amaterasu herself, was a sure indication of the growing popularity of Buddhism. Not till the sixteenth century would the economic, and by then military, power of the faith be broken by the warlord Oda

Nobunaga and his equally ruthless successors. But the fall of Dokyo had an immediate effect on the constitution in that Japan accepted the political wisdom of China and thereafter barred women from accession to the throne.

Although the government at Nara was supposed to be a replica of Tang China, the Japanese situation was in reality quite different: there was no disguising the fact of continued noble influence. Officials sent to administer the provinces were often kinsmen of local magnates. And the imperial university was not used to open up an official career to talent; as in Korea, it served as a finishing school for the sons of court aristocrats. The central bureaucracy upon which a unified state must depend failed to emerge in Japan possibly because opening office to scholars was too democratic an idea for a tradition that associated power with birth.

The rise of the Fujiwara during the Heian period is a barometer for measuring decline from the Tang imperial model. But both before and after the move from Nara, the impact of Chinese culture on Japan was profound, not least because of the adoption of the Chinese script. Unsuited though its characters were to the inflected and polysyllabic Japanese language, scholars persevered and greatly excelled in calligraphy. Inspired by Tang achievements, Japanese poets in 760 produced the first national anthology, the *Collection of Myriad Leaves (Manyoshu)*, containing over 4000 poems.

The northern frontier came under Ainu attack from 776 onwards. Early in the Heian period the throne admitted that it could no longer hold these incursions in check, and the Chinese principle of a conscripted army was dropped. Defence was left in the hands of provincial landowners, who raised their own forces to protect their property. By 812 the threat had passed, but so had the independence of the emperor, for now even the palace guard was the preserve of the aristocracy.

THE HEIAN PERIOD (794-1184)

On the site of modern Kyoto, the emperor Kammu (781-806) built in 794 a city named 'Capital of Everlasting Peace' (*Heian-kyo*), after the meaning of Chang'an. Although the emperor strictly forbade the Nara monasteries and temples from moving to Kyoto, he allowed new Buddhist schools there that would contribute to the welfare of the state. A small shrine already erected by Saicho, the descendant of a Chinese immigrant family, was regarded as a good omen for the new city. Disgusted at the worldliness of the Nara clergy, the monk

Saicho (767–822) had sought solitude as a recluse on Mt Hiei, part of a range of hills north-east of Kyoto. Impressed, Kammu sent him to China in 804. There he concentrated on the doctrines of the Tiantai school and, after one year of instruction, returned with scriptures to Japan to found the Tendai sect. Perhaps the significance of Saicho's mission turns as much on the circumstance that Tiantai was an authentic Chinese school as on the encouragement shown by the throne. Tiantai bore no Indian imprint at all. It interpreted Buddha's teachings in a variety of ways, thereby dealing with the contradictions within the scriptures; differences ceased to exist when the devotee realised the unity of all phenomena. This typically Chinese synthesis of Buddhist doctrines meant that all men could achieve enlightenment, because they all shared the nature of Buddha.

Tendai was espoused by the educated. Not only did the sect have a great influence on art, but many of the founders of later Buddhist schools were originally its members. From the middle of the Heian period onwards the sons of court nobles and provincial gentry began to swell the ranks of the Buddhist establishment, and the scene was set for a repeat of the Nara court experience. An idea of the Kyoto monasteries' wealth and power can be gained from Saicho's own foundation, Enryakuji on Mt Hiei, which developed into a complex spread over twenty square kilometres, housing 3000 monks. Its influence, moreover, reached into a number of provinces because it acted as the co-ordinator of another 370 institutions.

But power at court was gradually acquired by the Fujiwara family. Few emperors had the determination of Kammu and the practice of abdication so weakened the throne that by the end of the ninth century the emperor was little more than a cipher. Always modest in the display of power, the Fujiwara family ruled Kyoto in everything but name; yet the denial of all opportunity at court to non-Fujiwara nobles proved in the end to be a fatal policy. These unwanted aristocrats went to seek their fortunes elsewhere, and many married into provincial families, enhancing their wealth by incorporating vast tracts of uncultivated land into their holdings. Two great warrior-clans so formed were the Taira and the Minamoto. The name Taira was first adopted in 824 by Takamochi, a grandson of emperor Kammu. Seeing all prospects of advancement blocked in Kyoto, he moved east and settled on the Kanto plain, north of present-day Tokyo. Without entirely cutting themselves off, his descendants built up an effective power base beyond central control. Rivals to the Taira family were the Minamoto, also descended from imperial stock. With their residence closer to the capital, they came to enjoy an unofficial alliance with the Fujiwara.

It was to Minamoto arms that a Fujiwara regent looked in 1050 to deal with some unrestrained behaviour of the nobles in Mutsu province, at the extreme north of Honshu. Appointed as governor of the area, Minamoto Yoriyoshi (995–1082) led his forces northward. Having overwhelmed the opposition after a difficult campaign, Yoriyoshi sent his son to court with the rebel leader's head. The warriors who fought in the campaign were samurai, literally 'those who serve'. Samurai were the armed retainers of the provincial aristocracy, not the throne, and were recognisable by their box-like armour of metal and leather, extravagantly horned helmets, and razor-sharp curved swords slung from the belt. In time their conduct, with its emphasis on loyalty and honour, was codified as *bushido*, 'the way of the warrior'. Although this philosophy evolved long after the heyday of the warrior had passed, the samurai class never lost its vigour and in the nineteenth century brought about the Meiji restoration. The warrior tradition ended rather sadly in the Second World War, when disgraced officers of the Imperial Japanese Army impaled themselves on their own swords and ordinary soldiers fell before enemy fire in suicidal charges.

Curiously, between 858 and 1868, hardly an emperor can be said to have ruled. The notable continuity of the dynasty was a result of its impotence. Those who ran Japan – in turn the Fujiwara, Taira, Minamoto, Hojo, Ashikaga and Tokugawa families – had no need to ascend the throne. They wielded power under titles awarded on their own recommendation. For in Japan, unlike China, there was

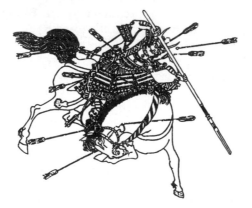

Fig. 14. Samurai fighting on horseback, the favourite method of combat in early Japan

no central bureaucracy to hold the power of a military aristocracy in check, and so surplus imperial sons naturally tended to join its ranks rather than strive for any imperial revival.

By the end of the Heian period Japan had abandoned all pretence at central government and moved back to the loosely federated feudal holdings which prevailed before Shotoku's constitution. But a new factor in the political equation was a strengthened Buddhism, whose institutions, through tax exemptions and land grants, had become centres of considerable economic power. In order to protect these assets, and the independence they conferred on the clergy, it was soon customary for them to maintain 'warrior-monks'. Many were runaway peasants, some even petty criminals or bandits, but their prowess approached that of the samurai, because the monasteries also recruited men capable of giving them thorough training.

It is a paradox that wars between monasteries devoted to the worship of gentle Buddha should mark the collapse of civil government and the advent of military domination in Japan. Since the move of the capital there had been intense rivalry between the older foundations of Nara and the new ones built on Mt Hiei. In 963 a religious conclave held at court only added further ill-will. Even within the favoured Tendai sect a split had occurred shortly after the death of Saicho's greatest successor, Ennin (793–864). This monk accompanied a Japanese embassy to China in 838, kept a fascinating diary of the nine years he spent abroad, and returned to be abbot of Enryakuji for more than two decades. The split led to competition between Enryakuji and its twin foundation of Miidera, on the southern slope of Mt Hiei.

In 989 Enryakuji sent warrior-monks to attack one of the monasteries in Nara. In 1036 it turned on Miidera and, years later, following a dispute over the election of the abbot, burned that monastery to the ground. Several thousand buildings were utterly destroyed. Enryakuji was certainly the most belligerent foundation during the Heian period, its army of 6000 warrior-monks marched time and again on the imperial palace. Often they would emphasise their presence by carrying a piece of celestial artillery, a portable shrine which contained a Buddhist or Shinto divinity. Fearful of giving the portable god any offence the inhabitants of the capital would anxiously await the decision of the court on the monks' latest demand. Typical are these chronicle entries:

May 1102   The monks of Kofukuji, bringing with them a sacred tree, entered Kyoto and demanded that priests recently

	chosen to take part in a memorial service for Fujiwara Makatari be dismissed.
Aug. 1104	The monks of Enryakuji destroyed the quarters of their abbot and drove him out.
Jan. 1105	Monks from Enryakuji, bearing a portable Shinto shrine, went to the headquarters of the palace guards and complained threateningly about the abbot of a rival monastery.
Dec. 1105	Monks from Enryakuji and Shinto priests got into a fight, and many were wounded or killed in a disturbance which filled the streets of Kyoto.

The growing reliance of the Fujiwara on Minamoto arms in handling these disturbances drew the provincial nobility into court affairs. As long as the great families quarrelled away from Kyoto, their battles had little effect on the overall political situation, but once the Minamoto and the Taira took sides in the capital the end of Fujiwara supremacy was in sight.

Their first clash occurred in 1156, when two imperial princes vied for the throne. Taira Kiyomori (1118–81) supported one, Minamoto Tameyoshi (1096–1156) the other. Without waiting for reinforcements from Enryakuji, then allied to the Minamoto, Tameyoshi began the action before dawn. This proved a mistake: the palace buildings caught fire, the Minamoto forces inside perished, and Tameyoshi was executed. Victory made Taira Kiyomori the strongman of Japan. With the Fujiwara in eclipse, it seemed that an era of Taira power was about to start. In the event, Minamoto fortunes were restored by a son of the former leader, named Yoritomo.

The conflict was renewed in 1180 by Yoritomo's uncle, an old man whom Taira Kiyomori had allowed to stay at court. Monasteries in Kyoto and Nara supported the uprising, but at the battle of Uji, midway between the two cities, Kiyomori crushed his opponents with the aid of the Ashikaga, another rising warrior-clan. Enraged by the intervention of the warrior-monks, Kiyomori fired the monasteries at Nara, badly damaged the great bronze Buddha dedicated by the emperor Shomu, and brought back the heads of 1000 monks for public display in the capital.

Still exiled in south-eastern Honshu when the battle was fought, Minamoto Yoritomo (1147–99) gathered followers and prepared to resist. On his death-bed in the ensuing year, Taira Kiyomori told his own sons to forget about Buddhist rites and bring to his grave the head of this dangerous rebel. This advice went unheeded at great cost, and Taira forces were frittered away in actions against other enemies. The destruction was compounded by epidemics and famine, which reached a peak around 1182. Taira power was finally broken in 1185 at Dan-no-ura, a sea battle in the waters separating the islands of Kyushu and Honshu. The Minamoto fleet was commanded by Yoritomo's younger brother, Yoshitsune. By directing archers' fire at the oarsmen in the Taira boats, he disabled them and caused a mass suicide of samurai. The Taira leader donned two suits of armour to weigh him down, and then joined his men over the side. American sailors were to be amazed at chilling repetitions of such voluntary drownings during the Second World War.

In 1192 the emperor made Yoritomo *shogun* – best translated as 'generalissimo' – in recognition of his absolute military authority. This was the first such appointment to be made permanent. Yoritomo used his new power in an entirely different way from Fujiwara and Taira leaders: ignoring the capital, he ruled from Kamakura, a city on the coast near modern Tokyo, from which came the name for the last period in early Japanese history.

Despite all the bloodshed, the culture of Kyoto at this period was sophisticated and rich. A close survey of the manners and sensitivities of court life, the *Tale of Genji* (*Genji monogatari*), ranks as a masterpiece of fiction. Lady Murasaki, the author, readily explores Genji's feelings about his life and times and, as she makes the prince himself comment, an imaginative writer 'sets virtue by the side of vice, and mingles wisdom with folly.' Sei Shonagon, a lady-in-waiting at the close of the tenth century, offers in her *Pillow Book* (*Makura no soshi*), a less romantic view of the court and the lovers she attracted to her bed. Aristocratic manners were the subject of

Fig. 15. The first shogun, Minamoto Yoritomo. He was the first military leader in Japan to demand obedience to himself rather than the throne

painters, too, but so were the battles that raged both inside and outside the walls of the capital. The burning of the imperial palace was too good a subject to miss.

THE KAMAKURA PERIOD (1185–1333)

The Minamoto triumph ended the court system and established a feudal state centred on a military dictatorship. Although the emperor reigned, and the court nobility lived in Kyoto, effective government was at Yoritomo's headquarters in Kamakura. It was called *bakufu*, or 'tent government', after the accommodation used by the generalissimo on campaign.

Yoritomo left no one uncertain as to his intentions. Taira estates were confiscated and awarded to loyal vassals, while those who accepted any appointment from the throne were declared his enemies. The obedience he demanded dramatically altered the political landscape of Japan, for until the battle of Dan-no-ura the government never really had control over the whole country. The imperial house failed to match the general authority of a Chinese dynasty. This was unacceptable to Yoritomo, who reduced outlying territories to obedience, removed potential rivals from their estates, and cut down members of his own family. In 1189 Yoshitsune, the victor of Dan-no-ura, was forced was forced to commit hara-kiri – by cutting open the stomach with a dagger.

In 1199 Yoritomo was thrown from his horse, and died from his injuries. Without capable sons, his loss was immediately felt by the Minamoto. After a short period of confusion, during which the court attempted a last bid for power, the Hojo family of Yoritomo's widow Masako seized control. From 1219 onwards Hojo regents dominated the Kamakura shogunate through puppet Minamoto leaders, just as the . ijiwara had kept emperors on the throne in Kyoto. This recurring indirectness may show a Japanese reluctance to abandon traditional forms that lingers on today, but above all it shows the wisdom of Yoritomo's political settlement. Despite the unrest immediately after his own death, Japan enjoyed peace at home for a century, no mean achievement in comparison with the turmoil of the Mongol wars in the rest of East Asia. But then the repulse of the Mongol invasions of 1274 and 1281 would be among the finest achievements of the samurai. Thousands of vassal families loyal to the shogunate would send forth their best sons at the moment of national crisis.

The Hojo family had Taira blood, but found its fortunes best served by the Minamoto cause. So closely associated were the Minamoto and Hojo families that Yoritomo's father-in-law, Hojo Tokimasa (regent 1203-5), seems to have harboured no ambitions for himself or his descendants. Anxious to preserve the shogunate, he decided a Hojo regency would perpetuate the feudalism upon which it rested. Had the first shogun's two sons proved less incompetent, Hojo power might have grown more slowly. As it happened, the first was obliged to abdicate as shogun in 1203 in favour of his younger brother, Minamoto Sanetomo (1192-1219). Two years later, Tokimasa's failure to warn of an attempt on the new young shogun's life shocked Kamakura, and led to Tokimasa's retirement to a Buddhist monastery. His inaction implied that there were better candidates for the shogunate. Other nobles agreed, but Sanetomo was not assassinated until the position of the second regent Hojo Yoshitoki (1183-1242) was almost impregnable. The court misread the situation and, egged on by former emperor Go-Toba (abdicated 1198), declared the Hojo regent an outlaw. The imperial forces, hurriedly collected from discontented nobles and raw levies raised from the peasantry, were no match for Yoshitoki's army. Driving the remnant into a burning Kyoto, he surrounded the palace and had the throne condemn its own supporters: in 1221 Go-Toba left for exile, his noble supporters were beheaded, and their lands fell into the hands of the regent's closest allies.

Although the downfall of the imperial rebels disposed of all opposition, the outstanding commander of the campaign, Hojo Yasutoki, was no dictator. Succeeding his father as a regent in 1224, he installed the boy who was to be the next shogun and set up a council to advise himself as regent. This body gave senior nobles a voice in government, a safety-valve for their discontent and a useful check on the regency. When the direct descendants of Minamoto Yoritomo became extinct in 1252, the Hojo regents could even allow imperial princes to fill the ceremonial post of shogun.

It was fortunate that Japan was so well governed. The panic caused at court in 1266 by a letter from Kublai Khan is a reminder of what would have happened without the shogunate. Kublai Khan addressed the Japanese ruler as a vassal king, demanding submission to his will. Brushing aside the fears of the court, the Hojo regent sent the Mongol envoys back empty-handed. There could be no question of negotiation, even less surrender: only death could stop a Japanese warrior.

Under the energetic leadership of Hojo Tokimune (regent 1268-84) preparations went ahead. Vassals on the northern coasts of

Kyushu and Honshu were put on alert, stockades planted at strategic points, and weapons made ready. Diplomatic exchanges achieved nothing and, in spite of a heroic stand, in 1274 a Mongol fleet overwhelmed the island of Tsushima, by sheer weight of enemy numbers. Once the invasion force had landed on Kyushu, near the town of Hakata, the odds were less unfavourable for the Japanese, although the enemy had surprises ready. The first was tactics. Whereas the Japanese warrior always sought to be the first into battle and the greatest collector of severed heads, the Mongol soldier willingly sank his individuality and behaved as a member of a combat unit. No matter how bravely mounted samurai charged the Mongol ranks, they could not break up the formation. A second shock was the invaders' weapons. Besides powerful crossbows and catapults, they had missiles which exploded in the air; these frightened the horses, and wounded men with iron fragments. 'When the fighting began,' a Japanese chronicler recounts, 'mighty iron balls were flung towards our men. Some were simply rolled along the ground, but they still sounded like thunder and looked like bolts of lightning. As many as 3000 balls were used at a time, so that many died of burns.'

The determination of the samurai also surprised the Mongol generals, who were aware that reinforcements would soon approach from Honshu. When the Korean sea captains advised that the invasion fleet sail so as to avoid being dashed on the rocks by an imminent storm, the generals evacuated the coast, after first firing a number of villages and temples. But heavy rain doused the flames and a strong wind soon whipped the sea into a rage. The Mongols struggled back to Korea, losing a proportion of their vessels on the way.

Between 1274 and 1281 Kublai Khan was too busy with the conquest of southern China to worry about Japan. Hojo Tokimune knew that he had time to prepare for a full-scale invasion. His main decision was to build a long wall to deny the Mongols the landing-place near Hataka, the best anchorage on the island of Kyushu. This could not defeat the invaders on its own, and arguably Tokimune might have built ships instead, but the five years spent building the wall stiffened the Japanese will to resist.

When the invasion fleet was sighted in the summer of 1281 there was confidence among the defenders, at least until it was realised that the ships were only an advance squadron of a combined armada from Korea and southern China, carrying 140,000 men. As the assault was about to start on the shore in front of the long wall, a typhoon suddenly destroyed much of the Mongol fleet. The kamikaze, or 'divine wind', was believed to have been sent by the sun goddess Amaterasu at the behest of the throne. It was all the crippled Mongol fleet could do to get away under the blast.

The myth of this miraculous salvation so entered the Japanese consciousness that it was vividly recalled in the last, desperate stages of the Second World War. Less well known than the air attacks of kamikaze pilots is the solitary sacrifice of the battleship *Yamato* on 7 April 1945. Entirely unprotected by aircraft, the great ship sailed from the Inland Sea on a one-way voyage to Okinawa, then invested by the U.S. Pacific Fleet. After the captain had explained the mission, an officer roused the fighting spirit of the crew by shouting: '*Kamikaze Yamato*, be truly a kamikaze!'

The Mongol threat was over, yet the changed circumstances on mainland East Asia were not at once appreciated in Japan, where large forces were kept together for many years. The burden of defence was heavy, especially as the invasions had left no spoils. The lack of reward rankled in the minds of the loyal vassals. This was dangerous for the Hojo family which soon suffered a notable decline in talent. Its enemies needed only a cause to unite the aristocracy against Kamakura. That was provided by a squabble over the imperial succession, which in normal circumstances the regent would have treated as irrelevant to the real business of government. Through hesitation and blunders, however, the domestic strife of the palace was allowed to come to a head in 1331, when emperor Go-Daigo resorted to arms against Kamakura. Unsuccessful at first, Go-Daigo found himself briefly on the winning side in 1333 when Ashikaga Takauji (1305–58) switched allegiance.

The defection of this great lord was a signal for a general revolt against the Hojo regency. Kamakura was sacked and the Hojo family slain. Two imperial courts were set up in rivalry, provoking a civil war that lasted half a century; and though in 1338 Takauji eventually took the title of shogun, there could be no return to the unity won by Yoritomo, for the fighting inaugurated a period of protracted strife.

5

EARLY SOUTH-EAST ASIA

From the Chinese Annexation of Vietnam
to the Mongol Invasions
(111 BC–AD 1292)

THE BIRTH OF VIETNAM

When the early Chinese empire was consolidated under the Former
Han dynasty (206 BC–AD 9) the people of what is now northern
Vietnam were incorporated into the imperial defences, remaining
under the control of the emperor or separate southern Chinese states
for a millennium. They became independent only when China itself
fragmented following the fall of the Tang in 906: even then Ngo
Quyen, the first Vietnamese ruler, looked north for the model of his
new kingdom; a sinicised aristocrat, he recognised no alternative.
Despite an anti-Chinese reaction after his death in 944, the *Historical Records of Dai Viet (Dai Viet su ky)*, compiled in the thirteenth
century by Le Van Huu, state that Ngo Quyen 'aroused the people
and established a kingdom, with the result that the northerners
dared not come back again'.

Before its conquest by Former Han armies in 111 BC southern
China was called Nan Yueh, from which the name Vietnam derives.
Notionally incorporated into the empire by the earlier Qin dynasty,
around 213 BC, Nan Yueh was treated as semi-dependent till
internal strife compelled emperor Han Wu Di to send his forces
southwards. Nine commanderies in 111 BC were set up to administer the captured territory, which included what is now northern
Vietnam. The three Vietnamese commanderies were Jiaozhi, Jiuzhen
and Rinan, whose southernmost boundary reached as far as Hué.

At first Chinese policy was to uphold the local chieftains, the Lac
lords. Legend claims that these earliest rulers descended from Lac

Long Quan, the Lac dragon-lord, who came from the sea, subdued evil spirits, taught the Vietnamese how to grow rice and wear clothes, and offered to return if they were ever in distress. This they were when a Chinese ruler, finding the land without a king, claimed it himself. Lac Long Quan came back and captured Au Co, the new ruler's wife. The Chinese invader quit and the sons Au Co bore the dragon-lord became the first Lac lords.

The closeness of the Vietnamese relationship with China is clear from this myth, although credit for civilisation and independence goes to the local culture-hero. It is likely that the Lac lords' maritime inheritance was the mythical background to the introduction of water into rice-fields and the consequent increase in production. Chinese records indicate that efforts were made to switch from hunting and fishing to the cultivation of rice, with the aid of iron implements. As sub-prefects within the Han administration, the Lac lords would have been expected to encourage agriculture. Their co-operation was also necessary for the sinicisation that accompanied this fundamental shift in economic activity. This transformation was not unopposed, however. In AD 40 two aristocratic sisters, Trung Trac and Trung Nhi, led a major rebellion.

General Ma Yuan, with an army of 20,000 Chinese troops, dealt with the rebels and strengthened the administration in the Vietnamese commanderies. An outspoken but loyal supporter of the Later Han emperor Guangwu Di, whom he had restored to the Chinese throne after the usurpation of Wang Mang, Ma Yuan believed that economic progress depended on direct rule. 'Wherever he passed,' the Chinese record says, 'Ma Yuan promptly set up prefectures and districts to govern wall-towns and their environs, and dug ditches to irrigate the fields in order to sustain the people living in those places.' Garrisons protected the imperial officials, who were directly responsible for implementing the regulations by which Ma Yuan bound the Vietnamese to the empire. Old customs had to operate within the confines of imperial edicts. The Vietnamese came more and more under Chinese influence. Many intermarried with the flood of Chinese immigrants which now poured into the commanderies, gradually making them just another province of the empire.

The legacy of Ma Yuan was full Chinese administration. The beheading of the Trung sisters in 42 showed how far the independence of Vietnam had declined since the days of the mythical Au Co. The influence of China penetrated no further south than Hué, until an independent Vietnam started expanding in that direction at the expense of the Indianised kingdom of Champa. This loosely organised state first attacked the commandery of Rinan in 399.

The presence of Sanskrit inscriptions in central Vietnam, dating from this time, reveals an important cultural divide in South-East Asian history. Except for the three commanderies incorporated into the Chinese empire, the core of modern Vietnam, all the other early states that arose in the region were dominated by India, but through trade and religious contacts rather than conquest. Champa, Cambodia, Pagan on the mainland, and the island empire of Srivijaya, always looked westwards for inspiration and guidance.

Chinese relations with the coastal kingdom of Champa were often strained by border clashes, but for several reasons China was never tempted by annexation. Lying so far to the south, Champa's climate was uninviting and believed to be dangerous – the expected casualty rate in an army of occupation as high as 50 per cent. Supply lines would also be stretched to the limit, and reinforcement in an emergency almost impossible.

That Ma Yuan's settlement was effective in northern Vietnam is seen from the brick-built tombs excavated in the Red river valley. These traditional Chinese graves, the very epitome of ancestor worship, served the needs of the great provincial families who arose towards the end of the Later Han period (25–220). Their fortified encampments controlled the countryside, offering security to indigenous peasants as well as employment to immigrant scholars, and in times of disorder they acted as the last bastions of Chinese authority. But the Vietnamese language survived, and within a generation or two the local magnates proudly spoke it alongside the official Chinese tongue. Vietnam shared in the population growth of the southern provinces, and its total by 140 probably passed one million; but prosperity attracted raids from the unassimilated Lao peoples of the highlands.

Although imperial rule in Vietnam was weakened by the disturbances that split China into the Three Kingdoms (221–65), Chinese involvement slackened neither then nor during the Tartar partition of China (317–589). On the contrary, displaced Chinese fled south, and the regime established in Nanjing – too weak to challenge the Tartars – tended to expand southwards instead.

The Vietnamese rose in general revolt only in the sixth century, with the first major outbreak in 541. It was led by Ly Bi, like many rebel leaders in the Chinese empire, a disappointed candidate for provincial office. His cause was helped by the avarice of the provincial governor, the emperor's nephew. An enraged population supported Li By and independence. In the spring of 542 the imperial counter-attack, launched foolishly at the beginning of the rainy season, met with disaster as the casualty rate from illness and guerrilla warfare rose above 70 per cent. Here is an early instance of that deadly combination always faced by the foes of the Vietnamese – an exhausting terrain ideally suited to irregular tactics. Having also beaten off a Cham invasion prompted most likely by Chinese diplomacy, Li By proclaimed himself in 544 the ruler of Vietnam. He called his kingdom Van Xuan, 'Ten Thousand Springtimes', rather optimistically because in the ensuing year an experienced sea-borne Chinese force defeated him at Chu-dien. The Chinese then pursued Li By upriver to the site of present-day Hanoi and savaged his followers again. Undaunted, Li By fled into the mountains and rallied the rebels, including a number of Lao chieftains. It looked as if his genius for survival would outlast the strength of the imperial army, but the rebellion largely collapsed with his assassination in 547 by the Lao, who exchanged his head for Chinese gold.

Two further rebellions were crushed by 602, and Chinese arms punished the Cham king Sambhuvarman for attacks on Rinan, the southernmost commandery. Tang China (618–906) was able to hold on to northern Vietnam, then known as Annam, 'the pacified south'. But its quietness had little appeal to imperial officials, and the administration was barely sustained by the victims of court intrigue, exiled princes, ministers, scholars and soldiers sent to govern it. In 855 Annam's distress attracted neighbouring Nanzhao, the original homeland of the Thai peoples, which combined with Vietnamese rebels in a bitter war. The uneasy peace that ensued hardly survived the fall of the Tang dynasty. Independence was achieved eventually by Ngo Quyen, who ruled as king from 939 to 944, but was followed by turmoil. Order was restored in 968 by Dinh Bo Linh, who overcame local centres of power and united the country. He also patronised Buddhism, endowing monasteries and building temples.

In spite of the strenuous efforts of Dinh Bo Linh's successors to strengthen the national defences, credit for the formation of the Vietnamese state really belongs to the Later Li dynasty (1010–1225). The first Vietnamese emperor Le Long Dinh (1010–29) constructed a capital at Hanoi, protected by huge earthen ramparts. From here his successors ruled a Chinese-style state for two centuries, presiding over a cultural renaissance and keeping foreign powers at bay. In 1076 a pre-emptive strike was delivered against China, where the reforming minister Wang Anshi favoured southern expansion, but the greatest military threats did not appear until the Later Li dynasty was supplanted by the Tran (1225–1400). The first assault came from Cambodia, whose warrior-king Suryavarman II led two expeditions in the early 1130s. Champa, another victim of Cambodian aggression, was inclined to an alliance with Vietnam rather than the hostilities that traditionally marked its border. The Chams then concentrated their efforts on Cambodia and even sacked the capital at Angkor, much to the relief of the Vietnamese.

Differences such as these, however, were about to be dwarfed by the Mongol threat. Mongol armies invaded Vietnam in 1257, 1285 and 1287; they ravaged Champa and raided Cambodia in 1283, and dominated Burma after Pagan fell in 1287. They had earlier overrun Nanzhao (present-day Yunnan) and pushed many of its Thai inhabitants towards their present-day home in Thailand. They seized Hanoi on three occasions, but the guerrilla tactics adopted by the Vietnamese under the determined generalship of Tran Quoc Toan eventually forced them out of the country. Emperor Tran Nhan Tong (1278–93), the general's cousin, was thus able to resume the throne in triumph.

The Mongol invasions may have strengthened Vietnamese cultural ties with the subjugated Chinese. As early as 1076 the cult of Confucius had been introduced, and subsequent reforms confirmed an imperial model of government. Emphasis was placed on obedience to the throne, administration by salaried officials, the payment of taxes, and large-scale irrigation schemes. Not surprisingly the resurgent Ming dynasty in China, the scourge of Mongols, found in the Vietnamese rulers congenial tributaries, once all ambition of annexation was forgotten after 1427.

CAMBODIA, THE KHMER EMPIRE

The foundation myth of Cambodia, like that of Vietnam, concerns the generosity of a dragon-lord. According to this tale, probably borrowed from southern India, a brahmin named Kaundinya appeared one day off the shore of Cambodia. When the local dragon-princess paddled out to greet the stranger, he fired from a magic bow an arrow into her boat, with the result that she agreed to marry him. Before the wedding Kaundinya gave the dragon-princess clothes to wear, and in exchange her father, a mighty dragon-lord, enlarged her dowry by drinking up the water that covered the land. He also built them a fine capital, and changed the name of the country to Kambuja.

In contrast with the Vietnamese story, there is no confrontation here with a conqueror; the foreign Indian priest has the blessing of the existing overlord. His gift is a recognition of the way that water-control schemes had always sustained the Cambodian kingdom. Without them, for example, the enormous temple-city of Angkor could not have existed. The unpredictable rainfall was never adequate for the agricultural economy on which this complex depended. Another feature of the tale is the expertise of Kaundinya in sacred matters, for Cambodia unreservedly accepted the Hindu concept of kingship. The king was a living god, an embodiment of Siva or Vishnu, even Harihara, the composite deity whose sculpted form is much in evidence at Angkor. His duties encompassed both the spiritual and the temporal realms because the early Cambodians regarded them as indivisible. The capital was designed around the sanctity of the ruler: its chief building was his own temple, and the mausoleum of his ancestors, the previous kings.

A consequence of this union between the dragon-princess and the brahmin was the absence of anything like the Vietnamese consciousness of prolonged struggle against invaders. Later hardships suffered by Cambodia, wedged uncomfortably between the rival powers of Thailand and Vietnam, did not change this. Before French colonial rule in the nineteenth century Cambodia was a traditional society built around a hallowed throne.

The Cambodian imperial age spanned the years from 802 to 1440. It is called the Khmer empire after the people who extended its frontiers to incorporate the lion's share of mainland South-East Asia. The Khmers were a long-established people whose language is found widely scattered throughout the region, the islands included. An inscription tells of a ceremony held in 802 to make their unifier Jayavarman II (802–50) a *devaraja* or 'god king'. The historical significance of the god-king ceremony is a matter of debate. One school of thought argues that it marks a rejection of Javanese overlordship. In 767 Chinese troops had struggled to repulse a massive Javanese raid on Vietnam. As sea-borne assaults are also known to have fallen on Champa, there is no reason to believe that Cambodia had not suffered at all. Alternatively, the royal progress of Jayavarman II through his new dominions may have been marked by other religious ceremonies intended to ensure Cambodian security from all invaders, and not just Javanese overlords. Whatever the purpose of the brahminical ritual, the king was able to build his capital at Hariharalaya, present-day Roluos, some 20 km south-east of the future Angkor.

The warring principalities that Jayavarman II drew together must have evolved from chiefdoms enriched by trade in jungle commodities. Chinese records call the area Zhenla and give the impression that originally it was a vassal of Funan in the Mekong river delta. Excavation at the modern Vietnamese village of Oc-Eo has disclosed a trading settlement, with finds ranging from Roman coins to Indian artefacts. If this port once belonged to Funan, then it was probably part of a larger trading network, for a Chinese source mentions a link between Funan and Dunsun, present-day Klong Thom on the Kra isthmus in the far south of Thailand. There 'East and West meet together so that daily in the market are innumerable people, precious goods and rare merchandise. There is nothing which is not for sale.' The city of Dunsun may have been a vassal too: the Chinese records say that 'the king of Funan ordered the construction of great ships and crossing right over the Gulf of Siam, attacked more than ten states'. All this notwithstanding, Funan hardly seems to have been a major kingdom.

By the reign of the usurper Indravarman I (877–89), Cambodia stretched into the Mekong river delta and the Khorat plateau of north-eastern Thailand. That war led to this expansion is clear, from an inscription at Hariharalaya, which claims that Indravarman I, 'the conqueror', now stands 'above the lordly heads of the rulers of China [Annam], Champa and Yavadvipa [Java]'. Besides adding territories, he initiated public works that included irrigation projects and temple construction. A massive reservoir was dug to the north of the capital, and brick funerary towers were built for his forbears. To justify his usurpation, Indravarman bypassed Jayavarman II and claimed descent from a senior line with more ancient ancestors. His greatest work, a pyramidal temple in stone called the Bakong, was completed in 881 and anticipated several features that were to become important later – mountainous piles, elaborate carving, surrounding walls and moats.

Indravarman's son, Yasovarman I (889–910), began to lay out a new capital within a three-kilometre square at Angkor. Although the city was abandoned in the 1440s, Buddhist monks worshipped there until the arrival of the French. Hence the title of its major temple, Angkor Wat, 'the city that has become a Buddhist temple'. From the start Yasovarman I set out to surpass his father's own temple-shrine, the Bakong. Yasodharapura, as the city was then called, was large and well supplied with water. Along its southern shore eclectic Yasovarman had monasteries built for sects that honoured Siva, Vishnu and Buddha. His own temple-mountain stood on a small hill at the centre of the new capital. Construction on this scale, coupled with the building of over a hundred temples in the provinces, could be accomplished only through a massive mobilisation of labour. Many of the extra hands at Yasovarman's disposal would have been enslaved, enemy prisoners, captives taken in raids, or forcibly enrolled peasants. Yet this was not an outright slave state. No satisfactory picture of Cambodian society exists for the early period, beyond the confines of the court. Slavery was undoubtedly widespread, but it did not conform to usual patterns, because 'slaves' are known to have married members of the royal family, and to have owned slaves themselves. Nor, as far as we can tell, was the Indian caste system ever imitated.

Yasovarman I was succeeded by two of his sons. Little is recorded about their reigns, except for the building of a rival capital to the north of Angkor by an uncle, Jayavarman IV (928–42). This usurper claimed to rule as a universal monarch, in whose person the divinity of Siva was manifest. The formula was copied by later rulers, at least till the worship of Vishnu rose to the fore in the twelfth century. Though a king might claim a special relationship with Siva, this god never enjoyed the exclusive patronage of the throne, as temples dedicated to Vishnu and Buddha also received royal largesse. Typical of Cambodian tolerance is the syncretic figure of Harihara, a name meaning 'grower-remover'. Hari, a popular name for Vishnu, refers to the natural cycle of renewal and growth, while Hara ('he who takes away') is a common epithet for Siva. With Vishnu shown on the left side and Siva the right, carvings of Harihara at Angkor and other early sites bear witness to the supreme harmony of those great opposites: creation/destruction, life/death.

With the accession of Rajendravarman in 944, the capital was returned to Angkor, where the new king repaired older buildings and built several new ones, including his own pyramidal temple on an island in the middle of the Eastern Baray. An inscription praises his decoration of houses 'with shining gold, and palaces glittering with precious stones'. Rajendravarman secured his position through greater control in the provinces, and successful wars; in 946 an invasion of Champa produced a notable haul of gold. Rajendravarman was succeeded in 968 by his young son, Jayavarman V, who died in 1001, whereupon Cambodia broke into two antagonistic states. The struggle was ended by Suryavarman I (1010–50), a determined ruler whose success may have depended on an alliance with the priestly families who now dominated Angkor. He reduced the influence of the provincial aristocracy, demanding absolute

loyalty to the throne; extended the area under cultivation by granting tracts of wasteland to new religious foundations; advanced the
western frontier as far as Lopburi on the central plain of Thailand;
and, not least, greatly expanded Angkor. Its largest reservoir, now
the Western Baray, was dug at his command. Since merchants from
Champa, China and Vietnam are frequently mentioned in inscriptions, as a matter of policy Suryavarman I may have encouraged
trade and urban settlement in order to increase his revenues. Economic development seems to have been a priority from his reign
onwards, with the agricultural surplus steadily growing as a result of
a second rice harvest each year.

Reverses at the hands of the Chams in 1074 and 1080 brought
division once again to Cambodia. The political situation was not
stabilised until Suryavarman II (1113–50) reasserted Khmer claims
to the outlying territories. Suryavarman was even recognised as an
important vassal by the Chinese Southern Song dynasty which ruled
from Hangzhou, near the mouth of the Yangzi river. The southern
location of the capital naturally drew Hangzhou's attention to
South-East Asia and a permanent navy of twenty squadrons was
maintained to protect Chinese interests in southern waters. Given
Suryavarman's complete control of the shores of the Gulf of Siam,
the Southern Song emperors might need his help in time of trouble.
Suryavarman II's devotion to Vishnu led him to commission the
largest Cambodian monument of all, the temple-tomb and obser-
vatory now known as Angkor Wat. At its centre once stood a statue
of the god. Today the miraculous deeds performed during his
numerous incarnations can be seen carved in relief on the walls of
the temple.

Thirty years of chaos following Suryavarman II's death, around
1150, almost destroyed Cambodia. In 1177 the Chams brought
their navy up the Mekong river, sailed straight across the great lake
Tongle Sap, and overwhelmed Angkor. Only the resolute actions of
Jayavarman VII (1181–1219), the last of the Khmer warrior-kings,
gave the empire a temporary respite. His bloody revenge against
Champa and his grand reconstruction of Angkor, though, seems to
have imposed a crushing burden on Cambodia, already under pressure in the north from Thai infiltrators.

Following a Mongol raid in 1283, the Cambodian monarch hurriedly sent tribute to Kublai Khan. By the time the first Mongol
embassy reached Angkor in 1296–7, the capital was in danger of
turning into a splendid stage set. The envoy noted with wonder a
royal procession:

Troops march at the head, in front of banners, flags and music. Several hundred palace women, wearing flowered cloth and flowers in their hair, follow holding lighted candles, even in broad daylight . . . Ministers and princes ride on elephants topped by red umbrellas. They are followed by the wives and concubines of the king in chairs and carriages, or on horseback and elephants. Their umbrellas are flecked with gold. Behind them comes the ruler himself, standing proudly on an elephant, sword in hand. The tusks of this creature are covered with burnished gold.

All this was in marked contrast to Beijing, where, following Chinese practice, the rare movements of the conquering Mongol emperor outside the palace entailed a general clearance of the streets. Yet behind the display Cambodia was showing signs of exhaustion: the last stone monument ever to be built at Angkor had already been completed. The envoys were observant enough to note that the Buddhist monasteries were the only buildings allowed to have tiled roofs besides the palace and the houses of high officials. They owed their privileged position to Jayavarman VII, whose great monument to the faith was the Bayon, an outstanding group of fifty towers festooned with faces of Siva. Merit had also accrued to the king for his charitable works, notably 102 hospitals permanently supported by the labour of over 80,000 peasants and slaves. Good intentions, however, could not save Angkor in the fourteenth century. Having gained their independence from the Khmer empire the Thai attacked and captured the city in 1352. On their withdrawal in 1394, they left Cambodia an enfeebled power. Some allegiance was still forthcoming from the Lao people, but the constant Thai threat from the state of Ayudhya to the west made Angkor so vulnerable that, after a siege in 1431, the capital was shifted downriver to Phnom Penh, where it has stayed ever since.

THE KINGDOMS OF BURMA

Situated on the western edge of South-East Asia, Burma remained isolated for many centuries. It was savagely introduced to East Asian politics in 1287, when Mongol forces destroyed the Burmese kingdom of Pagan, and left the country divided for over two centuries.

The complicated settlement of Burma has always tended to produce division. Modern Burmans descend from a tribe which arrived in the north during the ninth century. Their Sino-Tibetan language is quite different from Mon, the tongue belonging to the ancient inhabitants of the lowlands and a close relation to Khmer. The history of Burma till comparatively recent times was in fact a struggle between the kingdoms of the interior and the kingdoms of the Irrawaddy river delta. Despite the abundant rainfall which makes the delta so fertile, the dry interior enjoyed a number of distinct political advantages. First, the need for irrigation and land clearance drew the farmers together as a force. A second advantage was the availability of Thai-speaking Shan auxiliaries for extended campaigns. Of the hill peoples only the Karen were in contact with the Mon-speaking southern kings. But the closeness of highlanders was also always a double-edged weapon, as Anawrahta (1044–77), the great Burman warrior-king of Pagan found through the southern movement of the Thai. He seems to have prevented a general coalition against his kingdom only by a judicious marriage to the daughter of a leading Shan chieftain.

Details about Pyu, the earliest southern kingdom, are found in Chinese records of embassies sent from Nanzhao to the Tang court in 802 and 807. Astride the Irrawaddy river, Pyu's contact with the advanced civilisation of India was facilitated by the monsoon winds of the Bay of Bengal; vessels regularly crossed to and from, and left an Indian imprint on the kingdom. According to the Chinese records, there were many Buddhist monasteries where children received religious instruction till the age of twenty. And the gentle tenets of the faith were evident in the absence of torture, criminals never being punished with more than a bamboo cane – with the sole exception of those found guilty of murder.

The ruins of the Pyu capital, Shrikshetra, are believed to be at Hmawza, a few kilometres east of Prome, where fortified gateways and towers of the wall are still visible today. The city fell to a Nanzhao army in 832, and a large number of its inhabitants were deported. The kings of Nanzhao had already brought under their control the upper reaches of the Irrawaddy river, where they accepted the vassalage of local chiefdoms, many of them Thai. With the weakening of the Tang dynasty in China, Nanzhao armies marched out of the Yunnan plateau against Cambodia, Annam, and Burma. In 829 they even sacked Chengdu, the capital of Sichuan province, and laid waste large areas of China nearby. The speed and scale of these attacks were alarming, but their ultimate effect was to open lines of overland communications, and to encourage the movement of peoples.

Following the fall of Pyu, the delta ports were incorporated into the Mon kingdom of Hamsavati, whose capital was Pegu, a city founded about 825 much nearer the sea. Mon does not appear to have been the tongue of the Pyu kingdom, but rather a language akin to Burmese. Hamsavati also had to endure Nanzhao attacks, and later to cede large areas in the lower Irrawaddy valley to the incoming Burmans. Between 849, when Pagan, the Burman capital, is said to have been fortified by a legendary king, and the accession of Anawrahta in 1044, the historical record is scant. Like the other new arrivals such as the Thai, the Burmans may have served in the forces of Nanzhao as vassals. There is no doubt that some accommodation was necessary until the end of the tenth century, when Nanzhao ceased to be a major power. Once Anawrahta came to the throne of Pagan, the country was freed from outside interference, especially after his conquest of the Irrawaddy delta in 1057. This annexation of Hamsavati could have been assisted by Indian arms, however: a tradition of the southern Chola kings relates a devastating raid on Pegu in 1025–7.

The far-flung campaigns of Anawrahta are unlikely to have been as effective as this rare Indian intervention in South-East Asian affairs. Over-optimistically he is credited in Burman tradition with the defeat of Arakan, an Indianised kingdom to the west of Pagan; an invasion of Cambodia, for which no record exists at Angkor; and, most prestigious of all, a successful campaign against the once-mighty Nanzhao.

Anawrahta's relations with Sri Lanka are better known. The Sinhalese king, Vijayabahu I (1056–1101), sent one of Buddha's teeth as a present to Anawrahta, who enshrined it in the Shwezigon pagoda. Another powerful influence on the Burmans was Mon culture, following a compulsory transfer of population to Pagan, the captive king of Hamsavati erecting several monuments there himself. But Buddhist enthusiasm brought no peace to Burma after Anawrahta's death in 1077. Almost immediately his son was killed in a rebellion of the southern provinces, and fierce fighting was needed to restore order under Kyanzittha (1084–1112). A younger son of Anawrahta, this king greatly admired Mon culture as well as Buddhism, two preferences which wonderfully united in the construction of the Ananda temple at Pagan, the masterpiece of Burmese architecture. Brilliant white with towers of gold, the temple celebrates in a series of reliefs the entire life and ministry of Buddha, and houses four statues of him in gilded wood, each ten metres high.

Kyanzittha also paid for repairs to Buddhist monuments in India, where the religion was rapidly approaching extinction. Embassies were dispatched to China, too, as a counter-balance to Nanzhao. Kyanzittha's successors maintained close relations with Sri Lanka,

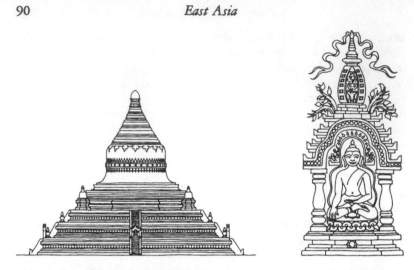

Fig. 16. One of the many stupas of Pagan, the capital of Burma until the Mongol conquest in 1278. Relics of Buddha were incorporated in such sacred structures

Fig. 17. A representation of Buddha from Pagan, a Burmese city in close contact with Sri Lanka, an island renowned for its devotion to Buddhism

drawing inspiration from its religious reforms, but in 1164 a Sinhalese ruler was obliged to attack the Burmese coast in reprisal for interference with shipping on the Sri Lanka–Cambodia trade route. The longest reign was that of Jayasura II (1174–1210). It witnessed the introduction of new Buddhist doctrines, a surge of literary composition in Pali, the language of its scriptures, the compilation of a law code, and more monuments at Pagan.

Peace was shattered by the arrival of the Mongols in Yunnan, where they were the first to subdue Nanzhao. Ignoring the warning, Narathihapate (1256–87) foolishly executed Mongol envoys and then attacked a client-state of Kublai Khan. The inevitable riposte in 1277 saw the Burman army utterly routed. In panic Narathihapate abandoned Pagan and his kingdom collapsed. The Mongols incorporated northern Burma into their dominions, and left the rest of the country to petty rulers. Shortlived though Mongol rule was in Burma, the division it reintroduced in the country lasted till the sixteenth century, not least because Thai chieftains were quick to profit from this disorder and set up states of their own, even in the south. Those Burmans who wished to avoid Thai domination gradually concentrated at Toungoo in the remote Sittang river valley. This tiny principality was later to form the nucleus of national revival, and give its name to the dynasty that reunited Burma.

Fig. 18. *Wayang kulit*, painted and perforated leather puppets from the Hindu island of Bali. Arjuna is on the left, and Krisha on the right

THE ISLAND POWERS

Relatively little is understood about the early history of Indonesia, the other centre of civilisation in South-East Asia. Archaeology has hardly compensated for the scarcity of records: the great island of Sumatra, where the Srivijaya empire arose, remains almost unexcavated. So important was this power as a centre of Buddhist learning that the Chinese pilgrim I Tsing recommended to his countrymen who wanted to go on to India to collect Buddhist texts that they should spend a year there beforehand.

According to I Tsing, the state of Srivijaya dominated nearly all Sumatra from the city of Palembang. Jambi, situated to the northwest, was probably the capital of the rival state, Malayu. An inscription from Palembang, dated to 683, refers to an expedition of 20,000 men against an unspecified enemy that brought vast booty to Srivijaya. The wealth of Suvarnadvipa, the 'golden isle', as Sumatra was then called, would have come from trade, for its size and strategic position on early communication routes conferred greater advantages than those enjoyed later by the trading states of Malacca and Brunei. Military operations were obviously profitable too: the distinction between trade and piracy was never easy to draw, especially when rulers wished to safeguard their commercial interests. Such rivalry may have been the spur to the invasion of Java, which was launched by the new Sailendra dynasty at Srivijaya around 750. The local Javanese king retreated to the eastern end of the island, where close ties evolved with the Hindu kingdom of Bali.

Fig. 19. Kublai Khan. The disfigurement of his envoys in 1289 brought about the Mongol expedition to Java

The Balinese king Udayana (989–1001) is known to have married a Javanese princess and adopted her language for his royal decrees.

Sailendra domination of western and central Java was celebrated in the construction of the vast Buddhist shrine at Borobodur, a name that could mean simply 'many Buddhas'. The enormous sanctuary, adorned with carvings illustrating the quest for enlightenment, was built shortly after 778, three and a half centuries before Angkor Wat. The virtual absence of inscriptions on Sumatra and Java leaves the empire of Srivijaya shrouded in mystery. Chinese records indicate that between 960 and 988 nine embassies from Srivijaya bore tribute to Northern Song emperors. Later envoys reported wars on Java, presumably with the resurgent house in the eastern part of the island. In 1017 the Chinese emperor also learned of an attack by the Cholas, the southern Indian kings who are said to have pillaged Burma a few years later. In 1025 another Chola expedition reached the capital of Srivijaya. The weakness of Sumatra after this attack brought about a compromise with the Javanese kings, whose own anxieties were stimulated by yet another Chola raid in 1068. But Srivijaya's decline became pronounced only in the thirteenth century, when the neighbouring state of Malayu asserted its independence at Jambi, and on Java the new powers of Singosari and Majapahit rose to the fore. In 1281 it was Malayu, and not Srivijaya, that dispatched the Sumatra tributary mission of the island to China.

Mongol intervention against Kertanagara, the king of Singosari, finally transformed the early political situation in the Indonesian archipelago, and left Majapahit the dominant power. News of the failure of Kublai Khan's invasions of Japan and Vietnam may have encouraged this Javanese ruler to show defiance in 1289. His disfigurement of the Mongol envoys' faces was an unnecessary affront and brought a fleet of 1000 ships to Java three years later. As Kertanagara was dead by then and Vijaya, his heir, deposed by a rebellion, it is odd that the Mongols should have decided to restore that prince in return for the payment of tribute and acceptance of suzerainty. They took the capital at Kediri and proclaimed Vijaya king, without realising his secret determination to continue an anti-Mongol policy. Caught in a guerrilla war of resistance, they satisfied themselves with vast quantities of loot and headed home. No sooner had their wake disappeared than Vijaya established himself at Majapahit, nearer the coast. The move reflected his desire to create a second Srivijaya, an ambition his successors more than achieved by controlling for a century almost the whole of modern Indonesia.

PART II

A New Balance of Power

For most of East Asia the thirteenth century meant the end of a world – a world that acknowledged the regional power of the Chinese emperors. Mongol arms not only conquered all China, but incorporated it into the largest continuous land empire in the history of mankind. The Great Mongol State (*yeke mongghol ulus*) controlled territory from the Pacific to the Mediterranean. The obligations of vassals are graphically explained in a message demanding that West Asian rulers join a Mongol campaign against the Assassins:

If you are negligent and slow in carrying out the command then as soon as we, with God's help, finish the Assassins, we will certainly head in your direction and deal with your homes and countries in the same manner we dealt with them.

In the face of such ferocity, the complete destruction of the Assassin's forts in 1256–7 was a foregone conclusion. Dependent rulers from Persia, Armenia and the Caucasus knew that a Mongol summons was no idle threat.

But shortly after the accession of Kublai in 1260 as *khaghan*, 'khan of khans', the Mongol empire split into a number of separate states. The portion under the direct control of Kublai Khan comprised East Asia, with its capital strategically placed at Beijing. His enthronement in 1280 as a Chinese-style emperor may have been intended to signify the permanence of his dynasty, but the Mongol habit of continuous conquest died hard, and expeditions were sent to Japan, Burma, Vietnam, Champa and Java. Their success was mixed and they were very destructive, even in Japan: the samurai threw the Mongols back but the feudal order broke down in the aftermath of the attack.

Fig. 20. Emperor Ming Yong Le, the usurping uncle. He facilitated the Chinese recovery after the Mongol conquest by strengthening the northern defences and dispatching Zheng He into the 'southern oceans' (see p. 99)

Though medieval Japan may have belonged to the well-born warrior, the most successful contender for power was a peasant, Toyatomi Hideyoshi. No other Japanese has ever matched his rise to undisputed authority. Also surprising was his indifference to homosexual love. Hideyoshi's predecessor, the military dictator Oda Nobunaga, was killed fighting alongside his favourite page. Homosexual relationships appear to have increased samurai valour, though there is no report of anything comparable with the Sacred Band of ancient Thebes: 150 warrior couples, wiped out to a man in central Greece at Chaeronea in 338 BC, and found as paired corpses. Ritual suicide, however, often ended for a samurai the agony of an impossible love affair.

Francis Xavier unhappily noted the extent of homosexuality in Japan. His arrival in 1549 on a Portuguese vessel introduced another factor in the new balance of power brought about by the Mongol invasions: the beginning of Western pressure. Mercenaries and matchlocks had an immediate effect in the wars between the Burmese and the Thai. Their impact on a partially restored China was delayed until another foreign dynasty, the Qing, chose to ignore the arrival of modern times. In general, the rulers of East Asian nations failed to prepare for the transformation that an end to isolation would inevitably bring. Only the Japanese and the Thai grasped the nettle of modernisation. As a result, neither was ever colonised by a Western power.

6

THE LATE CHINESE EMPIRE

From the Ming Dynasty to the Founding of the Republic
(1368–1912)

Widespread unrest under the Mongols culminated in the 1340s in the uprising of the White Lotus society, whose members believed in the imminent appearance of Maitreya, the future Buddha. Centred on the Huai river valley, the rebels halted grain supplies to the capital and defeated imperial troops. Though the area later was pacified, the movement encouraged insurrection and mutiny elsewhere so that the last Mongol emperor, Togan Temur, soon ruled securely over little more than the capital. But because the Chinese leaders of the rebel armies could not agree together the Mongol dynasty enjoyed a breathing space before it faced the combined wrath of the insurgents.

The struggle among the rebels was intense in the lower Yangzi river valley, then the richest part of China. The eventual winner was Zhu Yuanzhang, a famine orphan saved from beggary by a Buddhist monastery. It was therefore apt that many of this former monk's followers were members of the White Lotus, a secret society whose doctrines were a mixture of Daoist and Buddhist ideas.

Having secured his position after the battle of Boyang Lake in 1363, and over the next five years organised the superior resources of the lower Yangzi valley, Zhu Yuanzhang was ready to march northwards on Beijing. Togan Temur did not even wait for the rebel army's arrival but promptly fled to Mongolia, leaving the empire in the care of the first Ming emperor Hong Wu (1368–98), as Zhu Yuanzhang styled himself. In breaking with the time-honoured custom of taking for the dynastic title an ancient name of a locality associated with the imperial house, and choosing instead the epithet 'bright' (*ming*), Hong Wu was perhaps making the point that the empire needed to be restored to its former brightness.

As the provinces had been wracked by warfare for thirty years, reconstruction and economy were essential. 'We should not pluck the feathers of an infant bird,' Hong Wu said, 'nor should We shake a newly planted tree.' When he entered Beijing, his commanders showed him a magnificent tower, which drew the dry response: 'If the Mongols had paid as much attention to the welfare of the people as they did to building such a costly but unnecessary structure as this, they would still be the rulers of China now.' He then gave orders for its obliteration. As a consequence of Hong Wu's frugality, court expenses were reduced and surplus monies immediately applied to reclamation schemes. Aware that hydraulic conservancy projects were a unifying force in imperial history, Hong Wu forced through the completion of over 40,000 water-control works.

Although there was more than a millennium between them, Ming Hong Wu and Han Gaozu are often compared as the two commoner-emperors who overthrew tyrannical regimes and founded strong dynasties. Both were of humble origin and succeeded by a combination of outstanding leadership and peasant cunning. Both were prepared to use the administrative skills of scholars in order to consolidate their authority, but in the relationships they maintained with officials there were marked differences. Anxious to dissociate himself from the totalitarian excesses of Qin rule, Gaozu adopted the role of a Confucian prince, the benevolence of whose actions would elicit virtue from a people still steeped in feudalism.

The situation in 1368 was quite different. As the leader of a successful rising against invaders, Hong Wu's personal authority was more absolute than that of any previous Chinese ruler. When, for example, ministers and generals were charged with sedition, he ordered mass executions. To strengthen the power of the throne, Hong Wu used these purges as an excuse to abolish many senior appointments, thus bringing the heads of bureaux and the armed forces into direct contact with the emperor. This move towards despotism, which was to be the major trend of the late Chinese empire, had considerable dangers for its stability, not least when children or weak emperors were seated on the throne. It was not until many years later, in 1449, that the drawbacks of this change became apparent. Then the eunuchs foolishly persuaded emperor

Ying Zong into mounting an unnecessary military expedition, which ended at Tumubao in his capture by Mongol tribesmen.

In 1400, two years after Hong Wu's death, a fierce struggle broke out between members of the imperial clan when his grandson, the emperor Hui Di, tried to assert his authority. The civil war ended in 1402 with the sack of Nanjing by Hui Di's uncle, who appointed himself as third Ming emperor Yong Le (1402–24). Yong Le's accession proved to be a very violent start to an otherwise remarkable reign. According to the dynastic record, he

behaved with the utmost cruelty and barbarity to those who had been loyal to his unfortunate nephew, and pursued them with relentless savagery. All the great men responsible for Hong Wu's elevation to the throne were likewise driven to suicide, or they were killed in the most cruel way. He also ordered that all relatives, both on the father's and the mother's side, should be seized and executed. One minister, for instance, was put to death for delaying the edict that declared his accession to the throne.

Vindictive though his character undoubtedly was, Yong Le proved himself as a statesman and a general. Even before he usurped the throne, his swift action in 1396 had foiled a Mongol counter-attack, when he marched beyond the Great Wall and caught the enemy force ill-prepared.

Although it was not until Yong Le's reign that serious attention was given to foreign affairs, there were a number of significant developments before the first Ming emperor died in 1398. While Yunnan was annexed as a province around 1392, a large army had to be stationed on the south-west frontier because the Mongol invasions of Burma and Thailand had left those countries in a state of turmoil, especially after the collapse of Pagan and the Khmer empire. The permanent incorporation of Yunnan was really a consequence of Mongol expansion, since its largely Thai population had fought off all previous invaders.

For the Ming dynasty, Japanese raids were a serious worry, and from 1387 a network of fortifications had been built along the coastline. These defensive measures were of little avail against small, fast-sailing squadrons, as it was impossible to garrison every estuary and inlet. To enlist the aid of the Japanese authorities in the suppression of piracy, Yong Le sent to the shogun Ashikaga Yoshimitsu a delegation carrying the regalia of a subordinate ally – a crown, a seal and robes of state. The acceptance of these gifts by the thrustful shogun in 1405 meant that pirate bases were no longer safe in

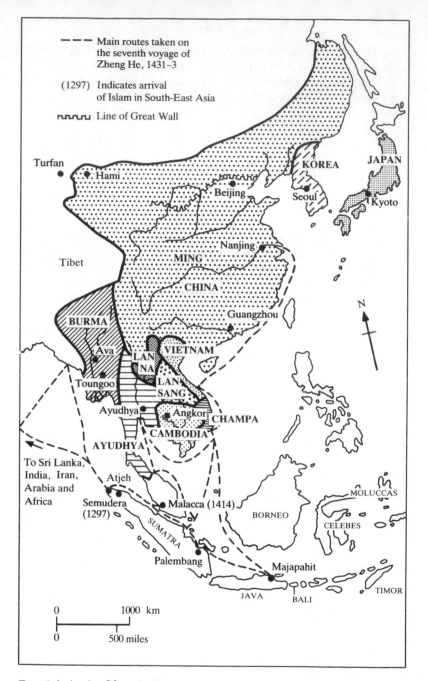

East Asia in the fifteenth century, showing the situation after the Vietnamese forced the Chinese to withdraw in 1427

Japanese waters, through attacks on them decreased somewhat after Yoshimitsu's death, three years later. Unrest in Japan itself after 1467 led to a falling away of raids, but the impression was left in the Chinese mind that all foreigners who arrived by ship were both unreliable and violent, a belief soon confirmed by the advent of European buccaneers.

Yet danger from the sea in the Ming period was never more than an irritant. Under Yong Le the might and splendour of the late empire was greater than that of any other state in East Asia, so that only Tamerlane, the fierce Central Asian conqueror, might have challenged the Ming, had he not died in 1405 on the north-western border of China. In 1407–8 imperial forces invaded northern Vietnam following a request by the son of its murdered king. The death of this prince in the fighting brought about re-annexation, and the setting up again of the old Tang commanderies. Yong Le personally dealt with the Mongols, who had regained strength after their hurried withdrawal from China: the blow of 1396 was seconded by a campaign in 1408, which reduced Mongol strength for a generation. A direct result of these victories on the northern frontier was the revival of Chinese influence in Central Asia, although direct Ming control stopped at the western end of the Great Wall.

At the same time as imperial forces campaigned in northern Vietnam, Yong Le revived the Chinese navy by dispatching a great fleet to visit countries in South-East Asia and the Indian Ocean. Between 1405 and 1433 the Ming dynasty mounted seven major seaborne expeditions. As a result the authority of the Son of Heaven was acknowledged by more foreign powers than ever before, even distant Egypt sending an ambassador. The admiral who commanded these ocean voyages was the grand eunuch Zheng He (1371–1435), a Muslim from Yunnan province, who proved a great seaman, a brave commander and an excellent envoy. The renown of the late empire was increased by his visits to friendly rulers who in return for accepting the suzerainty of Beijing, were presented with gifts and guaranteed protection. These voyages comprised the heroic years of the Ming dynasty, before reverses at the hands of the Vietnamese forced a Chinese evacuation in 1427, and the disastrous defeat at Tumubao in 1449, when the emperor Ying Zong was taken a Mongol prisoner, resulted in the contraction of the northern frontier to the line of the Great Wall.

A purpose of the seaborne expeditions was the restoration of state trading, first introduced to protect the precious metals of China. The import of luxury items such as ivory, drugs and pearls had been a severe drain on the limited supply of silver available, and a regulation issued in 1219 specified the commodities to be used to pay for foreign imports – silk, brocades and porcelain. The last became the chief item of exchange under the Ming emperors, pieces of the famous 'blue and white' turning up in places as far away as Borneo and East Africa. That Zheng He's intentions were essentially peaceful distinguishes Chinese maritime exploration from the policies of the Portuguese, the first Europeans to sail eastwards. Instead of spreading terror, slaving, and planting fortresses, Zheng He engaged in an elaborate series of diplomatic missions, exchanging gifts with distant kings from whom he was content to accept merely formal recognition of the Son of Heaven. The greed and intolerance of the *conquistador* was entirely absent. On only three occasions did Zheng He resort to force of arms.

The exact limits of Zheng He's exploration are hard to determine, but a reasonable supposition would be that the Chinese invention of the magnetic compass allowed reconnaissance squadrons to reach the southernmost extremity of Africa, touch the northern coast of Australia, and sail widely in the Pacific. The observations of Ma Huan, who went as an official translator on three of the expeditions, provide invaluable detail of life in contemporary South-East Asia. He notes in his *Overall Survey of the Ocean's Shores* (*Yingya Shenglan*) how in Malacca, for instance, 'all trading takes place on a wooden bridge, which the ruler has constructed over a river. It possesses twenty-seven pavilions, ample room for the exchange of every kind of article.' The local goods were incense, ebony, pitch and tin. The nodal position of Malacca, at a meeting point of several routes, was understood by Yong Le, who entertained its ruler in Beijing and granted him a war-junk, so that he might return to his country and protect his land. Between the first expedition of 1405–7 and Ma Huan's visit in 1413 the country had converted to Islam.

A Muslim himself, Ma Huan did not miss the fact of Atjeh's enthusiastic embrace of Islam. This state, at the northern tip of Sumatra, had converted earlier than any other country in South-East Asia. In Ayudhya Ma Huan speculated on the closeness of Chinese to the Thai language, which sounded to him rather like one of China's southern dialects. He also wondered at the use of penis balls, then a widespread example of erotic surgery:

When a man has attained his twentieth year, they open the foreskin with a fine knife and insert a dozen tin beads under the skin. They look like a cluster of grapes . . . If it is the king of the country, a great chief or a wealthy man, then they use gold to make hollow beads, inside which

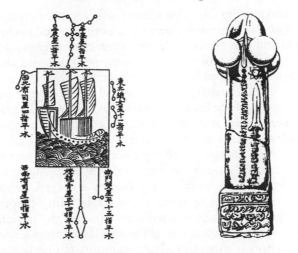

Fig. 21. Star map of the kind used for navigation by Zheng He's ships. It covers the Sumatra to Sri Lanka run

Fig. 22. Penis balls represented in a linga in a Hindu temple, central Java. This South-East Asian sex aid seems to have been popular until the sixteenth century

grain of sand is placed. When such a person walks about, the tinkling sound which occurs is considered to be beautiful. The men who have no beads inserted at all belong to the poorer classes.

The Thai were not alone in their preference for this sex aid, as European colonists were to find out. The Spaniards took a particular dislike to it in the Philippines, but the coming of Islam effectively suppressed the practice throughout most of South-East Asia. Just as odd to Ma Huan's informants would have been the contemporary Chinese delight in binding women's feet. Though Marco Polo does not mention foot-binding, it seems to have spread from court circles during the Southern Song dynasty and reached its vogue under the Ming emperors. Neither the Mongols nor the Manchus allowed their own women's feet to be bound, and the latter issued repeated edicts banning the practice, the last of them in 1902.

On the death of Yong Le in 1424 voyages were suspended and, despite the seventh expedition of 1431–3, the era of maritime exploration and diplomacy came to an end. Not all the reasons are apparent for this reversal of policy, which left a power vacuum in the Indian Ocean and China Sea – into which Vasco da Gama and Europe unwittingly sailed. A combination of circumstances seems to have been responsible. The scholar-officials, strongly against the voyages from the beginning, were even more opposed to the prestige Zheng He and the eunuchs derived from their success. They were also becoming less profitable as trading ventures and the cost of mounting them pressed hard on the imperial exchequer.

Another consideration was the removal of the capital in 1421 to Beijing, the site of the former Mongol seat of power. The laying out of a city and a palace there shifted the centre of imperial gravity northwards and concentrated attention on the Great Wall. This line of defence soon ranked as the top priority, not least because of an important change among the nomadic peoples living to its north. On the steppe, a series of strong leaders emerged, who created confederations embracing most of the tribes. Ming preoccupation with this new threat caused a swift reduction of the imperial fleet, which Manchu indifference to sea-power later compounded, leaving China entirely exposed to European imperial ambitions. After the Mongol capture of emperor Ying Zong at Tumubao in 1449 the security of the northern frontier became a subject of heated debate between the advocates of offensive and defensive strategy.

Instrumental in the policy of strengthened defences being accepted at the Ming court was Qiu Jun (1420–95), an official who argued that unless the Chinese controlled the Ordos, the expanse of semi-desert enclosed by the great northern loop of the Yellow river, the nomads were left with a perfect starting-point for attacks in a number of directions. New ramparts and strongholds were eventually built across the southern part of the Ordos, their line in the early sixteenth century being extended eastwards across mountainous country to the north of Beijing, until the coast was reached at Shanhaiguan. Its immense fortress, constructed astride the main route between China and Manchuria, was famous for the inscription carved above the outer gate: First Entrance under Heaven. Through this portal the Manchus in 1644 were to be admitted by general Wu Sangui as allies in the bitter civil war that ensued after the Ming collapse.

Impressive though the Ming rebuilding of the Great Wall was, for the first time China fell behind other countries in technology and science, experiencing a rude shock when in the 1590s imperial troops exchanged fire in Korea with Japanese expeditionary forces dispatched there by Toyotomi Hideyoshi. The invaders were armed with superior guns based on the Portuguese matchlock. The Ming soldiers were themselves well equipped with cannon and explosives, but hardwood rather than copper or iron was the material from which their hand-guns were made, suggesting an underlying weakness in metallurgy. In the last decades of the dynasty the services of Jesuits in the casting of guns were much appreciated.

The first European ships had put into Guangzhou as early as 1514 but the Portuguese crews' behaviour led to bloody clashes, which were not contained until nearby Macao was leased in 1557 as a trading base. Edicts restricting trade with foreigners were eased, at least until in 1622, when the Dutch arrived to continue their quarrel with the Spanish crown, then ruler of the entire Iberian peninsula. Repulsed from Macao with heavy loss by the defenders, the Dutch turned their attention to other parts of the Chinese coast, repeating the outrages of the Portuguese. To the dismay of the Chinese, English ships then appeared and behaved in a similar fashion.

One foreign visitor who favourably impressed senior officials was the Jesuit missionary Matteo Ricci (1552–1610), whose tolerance of practices with an obvious moral purpose such as ancestor worship was later denounced by other religious orders, until in 1705 a papal legate arrived to settle the controversy. But the Manchu emperor Qing Kangxi was not then prepared to countenance the claim of the Pope to international authority, and he announced that 'henceforth We will admit to China those Westerners alone who choose

Fig. 23. A seal of a Ming official, who during the final years of the dynasty had responsibility for the salt monopoly and coastal defences in eastern China

Fig. 24. A multiple gun used by the Ming army. Under the Qing emperors China for the first time fell behind the West in technology, much to its cost in the nineteenth century

permanent residence'. Possibly the lack of headway made by Christianity can also be explained by the contemporary reform of Buddhism, through the mission of Yungqu Zhuhong (1535-1615). Responding to the decline of the faith in a secular age, this monk placed emphasis on respect for life and social philanthropy. Those who chose the monastic path had to reject the world; the rest could find enlightenment through charity, filial piety and loyalty to the throne. It was the final Confucianisation of the Buddhist faith.

Religious revival aside, the final years of the Ming dynasty were typified by eunuch corruption, major epidemics, recurrent famines and, inevitably, frequent peasant revolts. Increased taxation drove people into rebellion under several leaders, one of whom, Li-Zicheng, felt strong enough to declare himself first emperor of the Shun dynasty and in 1644 boldly march on Beijing. As there was little resistance to the advance, his followers easily took control of the capital, and in despair the last Ming emperor hanged himself.

QING EXPANSION AND DECLINE (1644-1839)

Poised on the north-eastern frontier to strike at the faltering Ming dynasty, the Manchus tried to exploit the rebel movement. Several times they offered an alliance with Li Zicheng and, although no military co-operation took place, separately each served the other's cause by keeping imperial forces divided. The peasant leader felt no need of outside assistance, unlike his chief opponent Wu Sangui, the general responsible for defending the Great Wall immediately north of the capital. Wu Sangui had been summoned to the defence of Beijing, with the order to abandon all posts beyond the Sanhaiguan fortress. *En route* news reached him of the fall of the Ming dynasty, the capture of his own father by Li Zicheng, and the rebel abduction of his favourite concubine. Retreating to Shanhaiguan, the disappointed general reached an agreement with the Manchus and opened the 'First Entrance under Heaven'. Whatever he might have hoped to gain from the pact, the abandonment of the highway between Manchuria and China was a fatal error, for upon it the late empire's northern defences hinged.

In the short term, Wu Sangui was grateful for the timely support, because of the imminent arrival of Li Zicheng's forces. The records add that 'to strengthen his position the rebel leader brought with him the father of Wu Sangui as well as the son of the late Ming emperor'. The former implored his son to surrender and save his life. When Wu Sangui declared that he was a loyal supporter of the

Ming, his father was executed before his eyes, an event that only hardened his resolve. In the ensuing battle, the decisive moment came as '20,000 iron breast-plated Manchu horses madly galloped into the rebel host'. Unnerved by the surprise attack, the rebels fled, following the ignominious example of Li Zicheng.

While Wu Sangui hunted down Li Zicheng, the Manchus took advantage of the power vacuum in Beijing to instal their seven-year-old king as the first Qing emperor Shunzhi (1644–61). Related to the Jin tribesmen who had ruled north China from 1125 to 1212, the Manchus had grown in strength by borrowing agriculture and ironworking as well as bureaucratic administration from the late empire. The regent Dorgon in 1644 outlawed plunder and substituted as a means of livelihood for Manchu warriors the income derived from land allotments on seized imperial estates. Although the demise of this old nomad trait did much to reduce friction between Manchus and Chinese, the dividing line of conquest was still marked by Dorgon's order concerning the hair-style to be worn by Chinese men – what Europeans were to call the pigtail. To protect the organisation of the Eight Banners, which formed the basis of Manchu military power, bannermen were also forbidden to engage in commerce or agriculture, serving purely as military or civil officials. In practice though, idle garrisons of bannermen lost their military skill as a long period of peace gave them no opportunity to use it. Hunting expeditions could never replace the experience of battle.

For thirty years the authority of the newly founded Qing dynasty was limited to north China, with the southern provinces under the control of Wu Sangui and other military leaders who helped in defeating a variety of Ming pretenders. Had the ennobled Wu Sangui raised the standard of revolt earlier than 1673, the Manchus might have been driven out altogether, but the slowness of the Chinese to rally to this despised soldier meant that their eventual uprising was met by an energetic and capable young ruler, the second Qing emperor Kangxi (1662 –1722). With the aid of loyalist Chinese commanders, Kangxi imposed direct authority over south China, the last centre of resistance on Taiwan falling in 1683. Not previously under Chinese jurisdiction, the Manchus incorporated the island into the late empire, thanks to the services of hired Dutch transports.

Under the direction of Kangxi and his immediate successors, the resources of China combined with Manchu military ambitions to annex the outlying territories that now form part of the People's

Fig. 25. The Manchu emperor Kangxi, the effective founder of the Qing, the last imperial dynasty in China

Republic. Conflict with the Russians resulted in the Treaty of Nerchinsk (1689), the first treaty ever agreed by China with a European power and the first to accord diplomatic equality with the other signatory. 'Going to war is a terrible thing,' Kangxi said more than once. And his kindness was evident in the treatment of defeated opponents. Referring to the son and daughter of the Mongol rebel Galdan, the dynastic chronicle notes how 'instead of ruthlessly putting them to death, the Emperor made one a high official and married the other into a respectable family'.

Qing armies were drawn westwards again in 1715 by new disturbances. The campaigning extended over great distances as the mobile forces of various Mongol princes, who aspired to rule Central Asia, switched from one stronghold to another. As Tibet was drawn into the conflict, Lhasa was occupied and a puppet Dalai Lama installed there. Ever since the rebellion of Wu Sangui, Kangxi had harboured suspicions over the attitude of the Tibetans, for while the old Dalai Lama had protested his innocence of any support for the rebellious general, he did his country no favour in Manchu eyes by suggesting around 1675 a peace based on the division of China.

Attention was later given to strengthening the southern frontier by the fourth Qing emperor Qianlong (1736–96). Both Vietnam and Burma renewed their submission to the Son of Heaven, but in 1766 it was judged necessary to invade northern Burma. The four-year campaign ended in stalemate, with the Burmese paying the same tribute to China as before. Much to Qianlong's anger his army was compelled to conclude hostilities by melting down its cannon,

Fig. 26. Seal of the Qing emperor Qianlong. It was stamped on a painting in the imperial collection, a habit in which Qianlong over-indulged

more easily to carry the metal home. A rare victory achieved in the Himalayas soothed imperial pride, however, where in 1790-1 the Gurkhas'defeat forced Nepal to send 'elephants and horses as tribute to the Emperor every five years'. Two Nepalese attacks on Tibet had necessitated this intervention.

Emperor Qing Kangxi proved to be not only a great commander but also a model ruler and voracious reader of the Confucian classics. His dislike of unnecessary violence was founded on an appreciation of the human potentiality for goodness, for as he reflected: 'It is best to search for the good points in a person, and overlook the bad; because suspicion of others will always rebound upon oneself.'

In 1684 Kangxi visited the shrine of Confucius at Qufu in Shangdong province, a pilgrimage first undertaken by a Chinese emperor in 62, when Han Ming Di offered sacrifices to the sage as one 'who had given good laws to the people'. There the Manchu ruler heard the ritual music and listened to debates on points of Confucian interpretation: he was shown the famous collection of relics and had pointed out to him the place where a descendant of the philosopher had hidden the classics when the First Emperor burned the books. But scholars already knew that they need have no fear of Kangxi's intentions: the emperor had set the Manchus on a course that could end only with their total assimilation of Chinese culture. Reassuring though this was after the country's conquest, the identification of the Qing dynasty with Confucian orthodoxy was to promote a dangerous conservatism in government circles.

An excessively antiquarian outlook singles out the Qing encyclopedists from their Ming predecessors: perspiration had replaced all inspiration. Although in Yuan Mei (1716-79) the dynasty was blessed with a distinguished poet as well as an expert in cookery, and

in *A Dream of Red Chamber* (*Hong Lou Meng*) at least one outstanding novel, the final centuries of the late empire were devoted
to making collections of masterpieces belonging to the past rather
than the creation of new works. By the 1850s a declining imperial
house clung adamantly to traditional usage when it was obvious that
the sole hope for China as a sovereign state lay in adaptation to the
conditions of the modern world.

Scholars in the southern provinces, by contrast, looked less enthusiastically upon Kangxi's learning, their luke-warmness towards the
Manchus deriving in part from a different experience of conquest.
The easy entrance afforded by the gate at Shanhaiguan meant for
the population in north China a more or less peaceful take-over of
power, unlike the devastation of the south caused by Wu Sangui's
rebellion. The material benefits of the new regime, too, were felt
in the northern provinces because the Manchus preferred to retain
Beijing as the capital for the reason it was near their homeland. Not
a few southerners thought that the wealth of south China was being
drained northwards for the sake of a foreign house. Sometimes
overlooked is the fact that the Taiping revolutionary movement
(1851–66), which crippled the late empire, and the republican revolution of 1912, which swept it clean away, were both southern
assaults directed against the Qing.

A real cause of grievance was the operation of the official examination system. It was decreed that civil service posts should be split
equally between Manchus and Chinese. Since, at the beginning of
the Qing dynasty, the vast majority of the 250 million Chinese had
their homes in the southern provinces, the practice of holding
separate examinations for north and south China, at Beijing and
Nanjing respectively, served only to exacerbate the problem. Candidates who converged on the examination compound in Nanjing
represented three-quarters of the late empire's population, yet they
competed for a quarter of the official posts. As a consequence,
southerners who qualified tended to be the most intelligent members of the civil service, while Manchu officials, almost certain of
their posts from birth, had no need of exceptional talents to gain
office. It was near the close of Qianlong's reign that the flawed
nature of the late empire was recognised by Lord Macartney, the
first British ambassador to China. As he was astute enough to
notice:

the ancient constitution of China differed essentially from the present.
Although the Emperor was styled despotic, and decorated with all the
titles and epithets of oriental hyperbole, the power and administration of

the state resided in great councils or tribunals, whose functions were not to be violated or disturbed by court intrigue or ministerial caprice . . . The government as it now stands is properly the tyranny of a handful of Tartars over more than three hundred millions of Chinese . . . Superiority animates the one, depression is felt by the other. Most of our books confound them together, and talk of them as if they made only one nation, under the general name of China.

That the polite but indifferent reception accorded to the British trade mission of 1793–4 was determined by a wish to leave Manchu power undisturbed in China Lord Macartney was in no doubt. The sheer extent of the late empire might have allowed Qianlong to ignore economic changes outside China, but there was a danger in self-satisfaction, not least, noted Lord Macartney, because 'a nation that does not advance must retrograde and finally fall back into barbarism and misery'. Though Lord Macartney was prophetic, the reluctance of the emperor to end restrictions on international trade tallied with a tradition of control going back to Ming times. Lord Macartney was informed by Jesuits in Beijing that his embassy would have met fewer problems had it arrived in China before news of the French Revolution.

CHINA UNDER SIEGE (1839–1912)

The purpose of Lord Macartney's diplomatic mission was to persuade Beijing of the financial advantages of a freer approach to Chinese markets. That it failed, along with later attempts to open up trade by Lord Amherst in 1816 and by Lord Napier in 1834, can be explained perhaps in the darker side of trading activities. In order to acquire sufficient silver to sustain the unfavourable balance of payments involved in the China trade, caused largely by massive purchases of tea, the English East India Company deliberately stimulated the production of opium in India. Except for a single year, 1782, when its own ships sold the drug in Guangzhou because of an acute shortage of bullion, Company policy was careful to leave its distribution to private merchants. The Manchu emperors were not fooled by this ruse and, five years after Lord Macartney's return to London, the first ban was placed on all transactions involving opium at Guangzhou. With the expiration of the East India Company's charter in 1834, any restraint that may have existed on the British side was entirely removed, and the numbers of vessels arriving with cargoes of opium increased each year.

So concerned was emperor Dao Guang (1821–50) at the level of drug addiction in the southern provinces, and the mounting export of silver to pay for the harmful habit, that in 1839 he dispatched a commissioner with instructions to stamp out the whole business. First Lin Zexu broke up the network of Chinese importers and suppliers. Next he destroyed the opium stocks of European merchants without compensation, and obliged them to promise to end traffic in the drug. Since he found it impossible to believe that the opium trade was carried on with the assent of the British sovereign, Lin Zexu also addressed a letter in early 1840 to Queen Victoria. In it he appealed to her sense of decency, when he wrote:

I am told that in your country opium smoking is forbidden under severe penalties. This means that you are aware of how dangerous it is. But better than to forbid the smoking of opium would be to outlaw its sale and, better still, to outlaw the production of the drug altogether. As long as you avoid opium yourselves, but continue to make it and tempt the people of China to buy it, you will be seen to have compassion for your own lives, but none whatsoever for the lives of people who are ruined by your pursuit of gain . . . And, who can say whether one day your own subjects will not only make opium, but also smoke the drug themselves.

Had the young queen received this communication she might well have thought again about Lord Palmerston's justification for war. As it was, her first minister maintained that the only way to end the opium traffic was the suppression of the drug's use in China – not an argument given much credence today. The 1840 House of Commons debate revealed some of the worst attitudes of nineteenth-century European imperialism. Profit carried the day, and British gunboats were ordered to overturn Lin Zexu's measures.

The pretext for British intervention arose from a drunken brawl in Guangzhou. When none of the British and American sailors responsible for the disturbance were handed over for justice, Lin Zexu ordered that supplies be withheld from all foreign shipping. A clash then occurred at Kowloon, where several British vessels tried to obtain food illegally from local villagers. As a result of casualties being sustained on both sides, the British were excluded from Chinese waters. In retaliation an expeditionary force of twenty ships arrived off Macao with 4000 British and Indian troops. After attacking Guangzhou in the summer of 1840, the force received further soldiers from India, and sailed northwards inflicting heavy damage on coastal cities. With nothing to pit against the superior fire-power of the invaders, Dao Guang two years later was forced in the Treaty of Nanjing to open more ports to international commerce, including the import of opium.

The shock of capitulation to such a small expeditionary force in 1842 was enormous, for the fragility of the late empire was demonstrated to the world. It signalled that China was besieged, and an easy target for any industrial power bent on war. The siege can be said to have lasted almost to the present day, since only through the foundation of the People's Republic in 1949 has the country recovered enough strength to deter modern predators. Indeed, the 1984 accord with Britain over the return of Hong Kong can be seen as a belated admission by its old aggressor of China's proper place on the world stage.

The dynastic weakness that made China vulnerable to foreign assault also decreased the late empire's resistance to internal rebellion, which reached its climax in the 1851 Taiping rising. The growing instability was worsened by population growth, as the last census before this great rebellion returned the surprising figure of 417 million. An overburdened economy struggled to keep pace, but the demand for foodstuffs pushed agriculture more and more towards grain production at the expense of commercially valuable crops. Chinese handicrafts were unable to benefit from international trade as a consequence of the Qing policy of self-isolation. The underlying financial crisis was evident in the receipts of the imperial exchequer from the 1820s onwards. As few provinces could meet their annual taxation targets, supplementary revenue had to be found through new imposts on a hard-pressed peasantry already on the edge of banditry, if not outright rebellion.

To deal with the growing disorder the Qing emperors turned to regional militias formed by local gentry, some of which were allowed to develop into real armies. This step they were very loath to take, but the abject state of purely Manchu units, whose abilities had been sapped by generations of garrison duty, drove the embattled throne to abandon the bannermen. The new Chinese armed forces, however, remained loyal to the dynasty and put insurrection down, sometimes with foreign help. One of their later commanders was Li Hongzhang (1823–1901), who encouraged in 1865 the establishment in Shanghai of a factory for making rifles, field guns and ammunition. Impetus for adopting Western arms during the struggle against the Taipings came from the experiments of foreign adventurers, who successfully armed and trained Chinese mercenaries for the protection of the treaty ports.

But Li Hongzhang had to reconcile the adoption of foreign ways with traditional values: 'Western learning for practical purposes' and 'Chinese learning for fundamentals'. The only previous borrowing from abroad on any scale had been from India, when the Chinese accepted the Buddhist faith. As perceptive scholars saw, there were dangers to the Confucian state in the wholesale import of Western-style factories. The dilemma was put succinctly by Liu Qihong, a member of the first permanent mission sent in 1876 by China to the West. Noting how steamships, railways, mines and roads were 'mutually related', he wrote in his diary: 'One will lead to another, and we will not be able to refuse them.'

A certain amount of material progress resulted from the Taiping rebellion, but so damaged was the late empire in the upheaval that the remainder of Qing rule represents little more than an attempt to stave off foreign demands for further territory and concessions. The heavenly Taiping kingdom, which Hong Xiuquan (1814–64) declared in 1851, countenanced revolutionary ideas in land reform, the liberation of women, and attitudes to foreigners. A tragedy for the Taipings, in spite of their professed Christian belief, was the coldness of the majority of the Europeans living in China, especially those with commercial interests at stake or missionaries anxious over differences concerning doctrine. The Taipings soon learned that Europeans were neither co-religionists nor allies against the Man-chus. Drawing on Protestant tracts and visions experienced after his disappointment in the civil service examinations, Hong Xiuquan preached the overthrow of the Qing dynasty and the conversion of the Chinese people to Christianity. His Society for the Worship of God achieved astonishing victories over government forces, acted as

Fig. 27. A portrait of Hong Xiuquan, from a Taiping propaganda leaflet. His Christian rebellion against the Manchus incorporated a number of advanced ideas, such as the liberation of women

Fig. 28. A Qing seal made of silver, with Manchu and Mongolian scripts. It was presented in 1871 to a Mongolian leader for the part he had played in throwing back Russian forces from Xinjiang

a magnet for oppressed peasants, and by 1853 he made its centre Nanjing.

Though failure to march straight on Beijing probably cost the Taipings eventual victory, their control of the populous southern provinces led to a long and bitter struggle, which was ended only by an alliance between the British and Qing governments. The price exacted for putting down the Christian revolutionaries in 1866 was the concessions contained in the Treaty of Tianjin and the Convention of Beijing. These humiliating agreements had been wrung from a frightened emperor in 1858 and 1860. Once again gunboats had humbled China. Not slow to take advantage of this débâcle, the Russians seized vast territories along the Pacific coast in return for an offer of mediation. Thereafter the dismemberment of the late empire's sphere of influence proceeded apace: in 1885 Burma passed to Britain, and Vietnam to France, and after a short campaign Japan claimed a decade later Korea and Taiwan.

The crushing victories achieved by a modernised Japan on land and sea in the Sino-Japanese War of 1894–5 should have been enough to convince the Qing dynasty that change was overdue. In a deplorable state, the Chinese fleet sailed for Korea: engines were ill maintained, ammunition was in short supply, and ships were so damp that the crews stored their rice supply in the gun barrels to keep it dry. When in September 1894 the inefficient ironclads encountered the Imperial Japanese Navy at the mouth of the Yalu river, they were battered at close range by devastating fire.

Chinese scholars quickly recognised Japan's newly acquired strength and offered their own constructive ideas for improvement. When the Treaty of Shimonoseki was signed in 1895, Kang Youwei (1858–1927) led 1200 candidates, then in Beijing for the palace examinations, to submit a memorial to emperor Guang Xu (1875–1908), opposing the concessions to the Japanese and requesting immediate reforms. Kang Youwei, reinterpreting Confucius to justify innovation, proposed a gradual transition from traditional autocracy to democratic government – a utopian ideal anticipating the programmes of Dr Sun Yatsen and Mao Zedong. Recommending constitutional rule, in imitation of Europe and Japan, the would-be reformer received strong support in his native south China, where greater familiarity with foreign goods and ideas merely increased the exasperation felt at the dilatoriness of the imperial government. Five months before the famous Hundred Days of Reform in 1898, Kang Youwei made the following proposal to Guang Xu:

I humbly beg Your Majesty . . . to summon talented men for consultation with a view to extending Your Majesty's knowledge, to encourage loyal subjects to voice their opinions so that they may be known, and to announce formally a policy of reform, thereby inaugurating a new era for the empire. Then these counsellors can advise Your Majesty on the setting up of a parliament charged with the duty of deliberating all affairs of state and making decisions.

Convinced at last that change was imperative, the young emperor expressed his confidence in Kang Youwei and a series of edicts announced the modernisation of the state in a Meiji-like programme of reforms. But Guang Xi, who had just come of age and assumed imperial authority, reckoned without the empress dowager Ci Xi (1835–1908), who rallied the conservatives and staged a palace coup with the aid of the Chinese general Yuan Shikai. Her annulment of the governmental structure decreed by the emperor set the scene for the outburst of xenophobia known as the Boxer rebellion. For reasons of his own, Yuan Shikai (1859–1916) restricted the emperor to one of the islands in the palace gardens, a sentence that Ci Xi did not dare to convert to execution until she was on her own deathbed.

Her second great folly was to encourage the Boxers in 1900. Originating in Shandong province, the scene of the recent concessions of Qingdao to Germany and Weihaiwei to Britain, the sacred boxing undertaken by this sect was enlarged to include attacks on Christian missions and foreign importations such as telegraph lines. Their assault on the Legation Quarter in Beijing, abetted by detachments of the imperial guard, brought to the capital a punitive expedition of soldiers drawn from all the countries with diplomatic staff in China. Surrender might have had more serious consequences for China's integrity without the diplomatic intervention of the United States. President McKinley bypassed Congress and sent 5000 US troops from Manila on the understanding that they were to guarantee the right of access to all. As it was, the Russians tried to carve out of Manchuria another eastern province, till defeat during the Russo-Japanese War (1904–5) persuaded St Petersburg that Washington was right in advocating an 'open door' policy. Nothing could now save the late empire, which in 1911 disappeared amid the beginnings of the Chinese revolution.

7

CONFUCIAN KOREA

The Yi Dynasty
(1392–1910)

THE FOUNDING OF THE LAST KOREAN DYNASTY

Conscious of the need for a stable dynasty, and refusing to respond to a threatened invasion by Chinese troops, Yi Songgye in 1389 marched his own army on the Korean capital at Kaesong and deposed the king. In his stead Konyang (1390–92) was enthroned as the last Koryo ruler. The Chinese emperor Ming Hong Wu was swiftly appraised of this change, which satisfactorily removed a pro-Mongol king from his north-eastern frontier. Then Yi Songgye carried out overdue land reform that took back into public owner-ship many of the large estates belonging to the provincial aristocracy and the Buddhist monasteries. As a general, Yi Songgye had been constantly harassed by the problem of supplies, which an impover-ished throne could never guarantee. Strong support for the land measure came from Confucian officials, who understood the finan-cial difficulties facing the nation and opposed the exemption of the Buddhist clergy from the payment of tax.

Their settled dislike of Buddhism must have assisted the later offensive against the great monasteries under Yi Songgye's son, T'aejong (1401–18). A Neo-Confucian ring can be heard in accusa-tions such as the one that religion was merely a bundle of supersti-tions that 'deluded the world and deceived the people'. Argument raged both within the court and without, the outcome largely decided by the assassination of Chong Mongju (1337–92), who was opposed to Yi Songgye's policies of friendship with Ming China and the curtailment of the Buddhist faith.

117

Fig. 29. Founder of the Yi dynasty, the Korean general Yi Songgye. Quick acknowledgcment of the Ming dynasty in China preserved his country's independence

The forcible removal of this eminent minister, and the natural death of Kongyang later in 1392, left the throne open to the reforming general. That a non-aristocratic soldier was elevated shows how suited Yi Songgye was to his times. Even the Koryo dynasty in the person of the dowager queen had to acknowledge his fitness to succeed a house that had ruled for 475 years. Yi Songgye's quiet strength indeed recalled the character of the first Koryo king, Wang Kon, who was also enthroned by his supporters. The dynasty that Yi Songgye founded was to last for 518 years, its fall coincident with the end of national independence through the Japanese annexation in 1910. From the Ming emperor Hong Wu the tributary kingdom of Korea received the old name of Choson, although Yi, the dynastic title, is the usual name for this Confucian age.

A consequence of the close relationship with China was renewed interest in Confucianism, then at its zenith in the Ming encyclopedia movement. The antiquarian tenor of contemporary Chinese thought, concerned with the recovery of a cultural heritage blighted during the Mongol occupation, appealed to Korean scholars facing not dissimilar problems themselves. The royal order in 1403 for several thousand moveable copper types greatly stimulated book production. It was the first of fourteen court-sponsored typecasting initiatives undertaken before the close of the sixteenth century. In contrast to the Koryo dynasty, Yi kings were interested in the printing of Confucian, not Buddhist, literature. They commissioned nothing similar to the *Lives of Eminent Korean Monks*, a work composed at royal request in 1215 by a leading Buddhist cleric, Kakhun, preferring instead books on history, geography, farming and medicine. Following Chinese practice, Yŏng Songgye also began the composition of an official history of the preceding dynasty, the completed work only appearing in 1451. Most enterprising of all the Confucian scholarship in the early Yi period was the *Comprehensive Mirror for the Eastern Kingdom (Tongguk t'onggam)*, the first overall history of Korea. Patterned again on a Chinese model, the Korean history brought the narrative down to recent times as a comprehensive reference for the ruler. But its author could not resist the inclusion of ancient figures long banished as legendary from Chinese historiography. Possibly a growing ethnic consciousness explains the presence of Tan'gun, the semi-divine ancestor of the Korean people and the supposed founder of the original Choson in distant 233 BC. The offspring of a bear-woman and the god Ug, who changed into human form to marry her, Tan'gun was believed to have ruled in Pyongyang for the incredible period of 1500 years.

Supporting this literary activity was an expansion in the education system that witnessed the spread of the private primary school, the *sodang* or 'hall of books'. After the village *sodang*, children moved on to government schools in provincial towns, before graduation to senior institutions in the capital. At the apex was still the national university, whose student body of 200 first-degree holders were candidates for the highest Korean qualifications. Theoretically available to all children, the examination ladder was scaled by the offspring of landowners, the hereditary ruling class, the so-called *yangban* (the term means 'two orders' and refers to the civil and military officials in the state bureaucracy). The senior members of this privileged class were the *kongsin*, 'meritorious subjects', whom Yi Songgye rewarded with land and slaves on his enthronement. In dealing with crises the Yi kings subsequently used this measure to widen their base of power, so that by the eighteenth century over 1000 meritorious subjects had been created.

As wealth was still vested in land, the creation of so many meritorious subjects tended to weaken the financial position of the throne, with the result that a vigorous policy of reclamation was implemented to balance the royal budget. There was probably a threefold increase in the area under cultivation. Much of the new land was added to existing estates, but improved agricultural techniques were of benefit to small farmers as well.

In 1394 Yi Songgye had moved his court to a new capital at Hansong, the site of modern Seoul, a name in Silla speech meaning chief city. Its city walls were built in six months by 200,000 conscript labourers. But Yi Songgye lived in the splendid new palace only till 1398, when illness and conflict over the succession led to his retirement to a Buddhist monastery. The bitter squabble amongst his sons would have boded ill for the future of the dynasty had the restraint of Confucian ministers been absent. The winner, the forceful T'aejong, was wise enough to accept their advice and pour his energies into finishing the capital, which received under his direction a proper drainage system. He was astute enough, too, in abdicating in favour of Sejong (1418–50), not his original choice of successor. The thirty-one year reign of this king is thought to be a brilliant period in Korean history.

Though T'aejong's confiscation of land and slaves in 1406 had reduced the Buddhist establishment, the faith was not without its influential adherents, including Sejong himself. Ignoring the opposition of his Confucian officials, and a strike among university students, the king installed a shrine within the palace and checked the introduction of further anti-Buddhist measures. Nevertheless, Sejong had to accept the limit on buildings imposed in 1406 and forgo the sponsorship of any new foundations elsewhere. His devotion gave the Buddhist clergy respite for half a century, but it was not sufficient to arrest the steady decline in the popularity of the faith. Renewed persecution after Sejong's death snuffed out the final flickers of enthusiasm, and left Buddhism as a religion practised almost exclusively by Korean women.

Despite this difference of religious viewpoint, Sejong gathered round him a group of talented and loyal Confucian scholars. Perhaps its most valuable invention was the Korean writing system (*han'gul*), which gave expression to the everyday speech conveyed so inconveniently in Chinese characters. In 1446 Sejong officially adopted the twenty-eight letter script as a means of spreading literacy. It was initially used for the translation of Chinese texts, Confucian and Buddhist, but in time ordinary people borrowed its easier form for their own compositions. Yet the number of senior officials who strongly opposed the introduction of *han'gul* took Sejong by surprise.

Another instance of Sejong's earnest desire to promote the welfare of the Korean people was experimentation in agriculture, the fruits of which were published in 1430 as *Practical Advice for Farmers (Nongsa Chiksol)*. Whilst an improvement in productivity was of immediate benefit to state revenues, this timely royal initiative did much to adapt Chinese knowledge to the specific conditions of Korea. It also encouraged landowners to exercise more care over the use of their estates, their growing interest in the effect of the weather on productivity led to the invention of a rain gauge made of iron, and after 1442 the rainfall in each province was regularly recorded.

FACTIONAL CONFLICT AT COURT

The early death of Sejong's successor unfortunately left in 1455 a ten year old on the throne. Soon the stability of the kingdom was lost in a coup staged by the young king's uncle, who ruled as Sejo (1455–68). His massacre of officials ended the early peace of the Yi dynasty, as an abortive counter-coup only added to the chaos of a series of peasant rebellions in the provinces. But Sejo's determination overcame all resistance, even to the extent of moving large numbers of peasants to land adjacent to the northern frontier, where they were provided with houses, seed, animals and implements, and the title to the fields they were to reclaim. In order to strengthen this vulnerable land border Sejo gave estates near the Yalu river to prominent families too.

Sejo's later remorse for the bloodshed involved in his coup did nothing to resolve the usurpation crisis. On the contrary, the repentant king's devotion to Buddhism tended to make the political situation worse. Confucian officials simply bided their time, awaiting the enthronement of a malleable monarch, who appeared in the form of Songjong (1469–94). Placed conveniently under the dowager queen's care during his minority, this seven-year period of restoration was called 'listening to government behind a screen', because a woman was not allowed to assume authority openly in such a strictly Confucian world. The increasing influence of Neo-Confucianism during the Yi dynasty accounts for the lowering of the status of Korean women. In 1477 widows were forbidden to marry again, and it was not unusual for noble women to commit suicide after their husbands had died, rather than die in poverty themselves.

To the delight of the Confucian officials, Songjong was so inclined to their outlook that his reign witnessed the final consolidation of a Confucian system of government and society. Yet the triumph did not automatically guarantee tranquillity, for with a comparatively weakened throne there was more scope for official intrigue, and factions were formed within the court and the civil service. One faction was led by a royal tutor named Kim Chongjik (1431–92), whose followers introduced a more rigorous approach to government, once Kim Chongjik's access to Songjong secured their appointment and promotion. These radicals challenged conservative officialdom until in 1498 Songjong's son, Yonsan'gun (1494–1506), was persuaded to purge forty radical officials and brand the deceased Kim Chongjik as a villain: at royal command, the tutor's body was even exhumed and beheaded. In the sudden purge Yonsan'gun had accidentally discovered a convenient method of control over a powerful civil service.

The appointment of over one hundred meritorious subjects was found advisable on the accession of Chungjong (1507–44). Gradually the capital recovered from the blood-letting that preceded the fall of Yonsan'gun, and the more tolerant atmosphere again drew to court austere scholars, one of whom was Cho Kwangjo (1482–1519), an idealist who exercised great influence over the new king. Holding an impressive range of senior posts, Cho Kwangjo sought to re-establish in Korea the ideal Confucian state of Chinese antiquity, when at every level in society virtuous conduct was believed to have been the pattern of daily life. In the countryside a degree of self-government was intended to stimulate community spirit, a new village code outlawing among other things impiety, lack of respect for teachers, wife-beating, quarrels with neighbours, drunkenness, and gambling. Local officials were expected to oversee the administration of the village code, resolving disputes as they arose, but the real intention of Cho Kwangjo's reforms was the dawning of a utopian society that followed virtue for its own sake.

This radical transformation was terminated by Chungjong's meritorious subjects, however. Once Cho Kwangjo campaigned against the elevation of so many individuals, they all felt that their privileges were under threat, and joined together with the out-manoeuvred conservative officials. The inevitable repetition of 1498 was engineered in 1519, when in a purge Cho Kwangjo and his closest associates were sentenced to death. Factional strife in the capital was a lasting feature of the Yi dynasty, although from the late sixteenth century onwards the contest was between groups consisting of hereditary courtiers rather than a constant rivalry between the radical and conservative wings of officialdom. Wearied by the prolonged in-fighting, the philosopher Yi Hwang (1501–70) longed for a simple life out of office. The Korean thinker closest to Zhu Xi, the father of Neo-Confucianism in China, Yi Hwang held that personal experience grounded in morality was the sole source of learning. He was able to spend most of his life in moral self-cultivation by the expedient of declining royal offers of promotion, since a lowly provincial appointment was adequate for his own purposes.

THE JAPANESE INVASION OF 1592-8

While factional strife continued to paralyse the government in Seoul, an ominous threat to Korean independence was taking shape in Japan, now firmly reunited under the warlord Toyotomi Hideyoshi. Though of peasant stock, this military commander had risen to power by sheer ability and courage. In 1558 the warlord Oda Nobunaga had first noticed his talent, and Toyotomi Hideyoshi's rapid progress up the ranks fully justified his confidence. After the assassination of Oda Nobunaga in 1582 by a treacherous vassal, Toyotomi Hideyoshi had cut his own way to the top and thereby ended a century of civil war. His plans for conquest abroad were not then new, as he had already told Oda Nobunaga that one day he would defeat both Korea and China 'like a man who rolls up a piece of matting and carries it under his arm'. But with no opposition left to his authority at home, the time for action abroad was at hand.

Having beheaded his first envoys on their return to Japan for failing to gain an audience with the Korean king Sonjo (1567-1608), Toyotomi Hideyoshi was gratified to open diplomatic relations on the second attempt. In 1590 he dispatched a third mission to Seoul with an ultimatum: either join Japan in an attack on Ming China or be attacked first. The scornful reply from Sonjo nettled him, especially the comparison of his proposed attack on China to that of a bee trying to sting a tortoise through its shell. It is obvious that, as a tributary ally of the Ming emperors, Sonjo fully expected Chinese soldiers to bear the brunt of any blows delivered by the Japanese invaders. Once the Japanese landed, however, the Korean people were so angry about the country's unreadiness for war that Sonjo and his ministers met abuse when they abandoned the capital. To general surprise, the salvation of the Yi dynasty owed more to the activity of the Korean navy than to that of the Ming armies rushed into the peninsula. For admiral Yi Sunsin (1548-98) effectively isolated the Japanese invasion force by breaking its sea communications. The campaign dragged on for five years because the Koreans adopted guerrilla tactics and a scorched-earth policy.

In the spring of 1592 Pusan fell to the invaders, whereupon the Japanese launched a two-pronged attack on the capital. Little more than several thousand horsemen stood between an invasion force of 160,000 and Seoul, because everywhere the Japanese had slain or put to flight the Korean garrisons they encountered on their march northwards. Once Seoul was taken in early summer, the Japanese generals divided their forces again in order to subdue the whole peninsula. They were also awaiting a reinforcement of 52,000 men from Japan before marching upon the Ming emperor in Beijing. That this force never arrived was the result of Yi Sunsin's masterly handling of the Korean navy.

This energetic strategist had decided to add iron plates to some of the ships in his fleet, along the lines previously developed in the Chinese navy. His 'turtle' ships were small and swift vessels, propelled by a square sail and twenty oars. Where they advanced the design of the warship was in having an armoured top to give complete protection for the crew. The first turtle ship came into service just a few days before the Japanese landed, but soon Yi Sunsin had built enough vessels, and trained their crews, to sweep the seas of enemy craft. The greatest victory took place off Hansan Island, south-west of Pusan, and crippled Hideyoshi's fleet. In order to

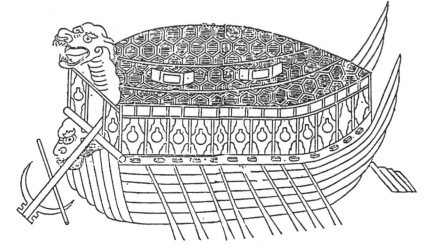

Fig. 30. A contemporary drawing of a turtle boat, the armoured vessel invented by the Korean admiral Yi Sunsin to defeat the Japanese invaders

encircle the Japanese ships Yi Sunsin ordered his own vessels into a newly devised formation, which resembled the outstretched wings of a great bird. With the envelopment completed, the turtle ships drove straight at the crowded Japanese fleet, discharging with impunity guns and firearms from all sides. 'Annihilation was complete within a matter of hours,' reported Yi Sunsin with satisfaction. 'Many of the Japanese leaders present died as a result of wounds inflicted by their own swords.' By the autumn of 1592 the enemy had lost hundreds of vessels.

With the invasion force spread thin and control of the sea in jeopardy, the Japanese generals were concerned at signs of mounting Korean resistance. The rugged interior was excellent terrain for guerrilla warfare, and a potential danger when combined with an approaching Chinese relief army. To thwart such co-operation the Japanese commander at Pyongyang, Konishi Yukinaga, strengthened the defences of the city with earthworks and a wooden palisade. He intended to halt the Chinese forces there with concentrated fire, but was overrun in early 1593 by a force 50,000 strong. Pyongyang had to be evacuated by the samurai, who retreated southwards to Seoul. A full-scale engagement could no longer be avoided, and the battle at Pyokchegwan, to the north of the Korean capital, was the bloodiest of the entire invasion. The Chinese army, enlarged by thousands of Korean volunteers, pressed the Japanese hard, until 10,000 of them fell in a ferocious counter-attack. Yet the great victory could not save the Japanese from another withdrawal and by the end of the year the territory under their control comprised a series of fortified camps along the southern coast of the peninsula.

Stung into action by the attitude of the Chinese ambassadors who arrived in Kyoto to negotiate a peace settlement, by 1597 Hideyoshi was ready to try another assault. Many Japanese military leaders were against a second campaign but the warlord was beyond reason and, with a renewed call to arms swiftly drawing volunteers, the project went ahead under the same generals. Improved ships, and the temporary demotion of the Korean admiral Yi Sunsin through court factionalism, gave the invaders the upper hand, at least until the gradual build-up of Chinese forces in the peninsula brought about a stalemate. Infuriated at this repeated state of affairs, Toyotomi Hideyoshi demanded without delay visible proof of samurai courage. After the battle of Sochon in autumn 1598, the ears from 38,700 Chinese and Korean heads were therefore cut off, pickled in salt, and sent back to Kyoto as a token of the earnestness of the invaders. The death of the warlord shortly after the receipt of this grisly prize relieved the Japanese generals in Korea of a thankless task. Harassed at sea and checked on land, they quit the devastated peninsula and returned in 1598 all their men to Japan – though not before a combined Korean and Chinese fleet dealt the Japanese rearguard a shattering blow at the battle of Noryang. Though mortally wounded by a stray bullet, Yi Sunsin ordered his own condition to be kept a secret until victory was secured. Less than fifty Japanese vessels managed to escape.

THE DECLINE OF THE YI DYNASTY

The effect of Toyotomi Hideyoshi's intervention in Korea was dreadful. Systematic destruction of towns and villages by the Japanese invaders, coupled with the denial of succour by the defenders, left the peninsula in an exhausted state that was difficult to alleviate. It was almost as if the tragedy of 1592–8 permanently crippled the will of the Yi dynasty, for later kings chose to ignore the outside world completely. Their policy of seclusion represents an extreme instance of a common tendency in late East Asian history, for which Korea was rightly dubbed the 'Hermit Kingdom'.

Recovery from the Japanese invasion was made all the more difficult by another onslaught from the north, the Manchu attack of 1627. The balance of power on mainland East Asia had been irrevocably changed by the Manchu leader Nurhachi (1559–1626), when he defeated the Ming army responsible for the defence of what today is Liaodong province at the battle of Sardu in 1619. Chinese forces were thereafter on the defensive along the northern frontier, while the confidence that Nurhachi's leadership gave to the Manchus not only signalled the decline of China as a military power, it also exposed Korea to new pressures at a time of chronic weakness. 'The year 1627,' Chinese records state, 'was spent by the Manchus in an invasion of Korea, which ended in the submission to an enemy of a country that had always been faithful to the Ming emperors.'

The Manchu entry to China occurred in 1644 as part of arrangements made by a frontier general to gain support during a civil war. Peaceful though the passage through the Great Wall was, the Manchus had not come to save the Ming dynasty but act in their own interests: the setting up of the Qing dynasty and the conquest of the late Chinese empire, was achieved with the fall of the last centre of resistance on Taiwan in 1683. As a result of Manchu success, the Korean king once again found himself the subordinate of an emperor of China, albeit a Manchu one, with good relations lasting almost to the end of the Yi dynasty in 1910.

Apart from a limited exchange with China and Japan, no foreign trade was conducted by the 'Hermit Kingdom'. Shipwrecked sailors were forbidden ever to leave Korea, or were put to death, if no use could be found for their skills. In 1628 a Dutchman, Jan Janse Weltevree, was lucky to be experienced in casting cannon. A second Dutch survivor of a shipwreck in 1653, Hendrik Hamel, also avoided execution. After many years of captivity, he escaped to Nagaski and returned home, giving the West its first detailed account of Korea. The closure of the peninsula to outside influence had unfortunate consequences. No commercial sector rose to challenge the authority of the great landowners, whose domination of the bureaucracy gradually rendered the throne impotent. In contrast with feudal Japan, where the shogunate was content to tax merchants but leave them alone, the Korean aristocracy severely regulated internal trade on the Confucian assumption that it was merely a necessary evil.

Korean culture began to ossify, as taste was dictated by a nobility uninterested in change. All the more extraordinary, therefore, that a minister such as Kim Manjung (1637–92) should be tempted by the richness of everyday language to write novels. Even so, his *Nine-Cloud Dream* (*Kuun mong*), written in political exile in 1689, still deals with the rarefied world of fine houses, official residences and military camps; nowhere is there a portrayal of life outside a privileged circle. Yet the final realisation of the hero may have touched a raw nerve, since at the pinnacle of social and personal success, he is made to understand how life is as insubstantial as a dream.

The year 1694 saw the take-over of the government by the most conservative faction, the advocates of the Old Doctrine (*Noron*). This group of officials was able to manipulate the examination and appointment process to assure the subsequent preferment of its own candidates, and thus hold on to power. Thereafter political conflict along factional lines was less intense, and more scholars were willing to emulate the example of the philosopher Yi Hwang, remaining in the provinces where a network of academies had sprung up. The new equilibrium was evident in the long and peaceful reigns of Yongjo (1724–76) and Chongjo (1776–1800), despite a personal tragedy separating the grandfather and the grandson.

An insight into the events of 1762 can be derived from a distinctive memoir written by Chongjo's mother, the Lady Hong. To set the record straight in the final years of her life, she detailed the

Fig. 31. King Yongjo (1724–76). At the insistence of his queen, he ordered the suffocation of his own deranged heir, Sado

mental breakdown and death of Sado, her own husband and the crown prince. Sado was always ill at ease in the presence of his father, so he would prostrate himself before Yongjo like any official rather than look him in the face. As the crown prince's mental illness started to manifest itself in erratic behaviour, relations between father and son deteriorated even more. Lady Hong's delivery in 1752 of Chongjo appeased the king until a memorandum from concerned officials criticising Sado's actions rekindled his ire. In desperation

the crown prince prostrated himself at the palace gate, but received a strong rebuke from the king. It was severe winter, and it snowed while he was waiting for a royal decision on his punishment. He lay prostrated in the snow, covered by snow flakes until people could hardly distinguish his outline on the ground. Still he refused to heed all pleas to get up, and he did not rise from the ice until the king's fury was spent.

Public penances like this, including some in which Sado beat his head savagely with a stone, kept the relationship of father and son on an even keel for a decade. Later Sado took to drink in almost open defiance of Yongjo, who forbade the use of alcohol at court. The crown prince also started to indulge his love of killing servants, besides the late-night parties that made his quarters as scandalous as they were dangerous. In 1762 Sado's own mother advised the king to kill him and fix the succession on Chongjo, his grandson. When Lady Hong realised that Sado had been suffocated by royal command in a grain box, her attempts at suicide were only just thwarted. She found peace in the thought that her husband, the crown prince, had at least left a son to succeed him.

Although Sado failed so miserably in his duties, the emphasis Yongjo placed on good administration was assisted by the movement for *Sirhak*, or 'practical learning'. Putting aside the ceremonial features of Confucianism, scholars gradually turned their attention to improvements in administration, justice, agriculture, technology and medicine. An outstanding advocate of the practical approach was Chong Yagyong (1762–1836), who was banished to an offshore island for his sympathetic reception of Catholicism. The faith was proscribed in 1785 and persecuted in 1801. Banishment could not stop Chong Yagyong's prolific brush, his ideas for reform being contained in over 2000 poems and 300 essays.

Even though Catholicism, known as 'Western learning' (*Sohak*), worried the government of Korea as an imported faith, it was *Tonghak*, or 'Eastern learning', that really brought trouble. The turmoil that each system stirred up can be taken as an indicator of dynastic decline. While tiny in comparison with the contemporary Taiping revolutionary movement in China, the Tonghak was imbued with the same sense of frustration at a remote and corrupt government. Its founder, Ch'oe Che'u (1824–64), was another Confucian scholar denied an official career. But, unlike the Taiping leader Hong Xiuquan, he did not resort to arms and lead a rebellion, possibly because the dynasty was a native one of great age and not a foreign house like the Manchu Qing.

From the start Ch'oe Che'u disdained the formalities of Confucianism. Having burned his books and left his well-to-do home in quest of personal understanding, he was convinced after wandering the peninsula for a decade that the end of the traditional world was at hand. Mystical experiences added to a conviction of his own destiny in remaking society, as the appointed agent of the supreme deity on earth. In all probability shamanism moulded Ch'oe Che'u's basic view of god and man as inseparably linked. 'Man and Heaven are the same,' he said. The idea of an inner union appealed to a downtrodden peasantry for the reason that it proclaimed an equality for all people as part of the oneness of being. Slogans such as 'all men are sages and princes', was bound to frighten an entrenched aristocratic order, especially when Ch'oe Che'u confidently predicted that 1864 would bring 'good news'. Foreseeing his trial and

death, the visionary handed the leadership of the movement to
Ch'oe Sihyong (1829–98), his closest follower. After the execution
of Ch'oe Che'u for 'deluding the world and deceiving the people',
the Tonghak went underground but membership continued to rise
till it felt strong enough openly to demand tolerance. Before the
gates of the royal palace several thousand members petitioned in
1893 for an end to suppression and a posthumous exoneration of
Ch'oe Che'u.

Fig. 32. Cho'oe Che'u, the martyr of the Tonghak, or 'Eastern learning' movement. He was executed by the Korean authorities in 1864

Initial government moves against Tonghak forces were foiled by
wholesale desertion among its own troops. In desperation ministers
let it be known that they were willing to listen to grievances, and the
hostilities ceased on the understanding that official misrule would
end. The Tonghak programme of social reform, however, was too
radical for acceptance. It demanded the punishment of corrupt
officials, the ending of noble immunity for misconduct, the abolition of slavery, the right of young widows to remarry, fair examinations for recruitment to the civil service, a cancellation of debts,
redistribution of land and, not least, the imprisonment of those
who collaborated with the Japanese. This last demand turned out to
be the critical one, because it branded the Tonghak as an anti-
Japanese organisation at the very moment Japan and China were
concerned to assert their suzerainty over Korea. The upshot was a

contingent of Japanese troops to stiffen the government force sent to crush the Tonghak army. In the south-west at T'aein the rebellion was harshly put down, and its leaders killed with the exception of Ch'oe Sihyong himself, who maintained throughout that armed struggle was a betrayal of the teachings of Tonghak's founder as well as treason.

AN END TO KOREAN INDEPENDENCE

The Tonghak rebellion of 1893–4 was nothing less than a revolutionary movement of the peasantry against an aristocratic order already in its death throes. The cry to expel the Japanese indicated the extent to which Seoul was already dominated economically from Tokyo. In 1875 a Japanese navy vessel had shelled a fortress on an offshore island, near the capital. Claiming that the captain had been fired on first, a larger Japanese force arrived later with instructions to conclude a trade agreement, which gave to Japan the advantages usually wrung from East Asian countries by Western powers. The Treaty of Kanghwa (1876) additionally sought to further Japanese political aims through the recognition of Korean autonomy. It was asserted that this acknowledgement of Korea's status as an independent nation was proof that Japan harboured no aggressive designs, though the real purpose was the prevention of Chinese interference with Japanese commercial and military activities in the peninsula.

The signing of the Treaty of Kanghwa marked a turning-point in Japan's foreign policy, for its renewed interest in Korea was the first step in the acquisition of an empire. Previously the modern leaders of the Meiji government had contented themselves with taking possession of small island chains and the development of the northern island of Hokkaido. From the late 1870s, however, an increasingly aggressive Japanese policy in Korea was aimed at outright control. A military mutiny in Seoul justified a second intervention in 1882, but the presence of a larger Chinese force brought the Japanese commander up short. Having watched developments in Korea with alarm, Qing China quickly sent troops at the request of its vassal. The reassertion of Chinese influence temporarily checked Japan, but hostilities in 1884 between France and China over Vietnam drew the attention of Beijing elsewhere. An agreed withdrawal of both Chinese and Japanese forces was then scuppered by Russia, a power with its own ambitions in the region. King Konjong (1864–1907) was so pro-Russian that it was rumoured a secret treaty had been signed. The Chinese general Yuan Shikai, a military adviser in Seoul, even thought of deposing the Korean monarch. With the full knowledge of China, a British force occupied from 1885 to 1887 an offshore island as a warning to Russia.

With the delicate balance of forces in the peninsula needing very little for a major upset, the widespread disorder caused by the Tonghak rebellion was sufficient to precipitate a major Sino-Japanese conflict. The war began with a surprise attack in July 1894 by Japanese warships at Asan Bay, close to Seoul, and ended in the

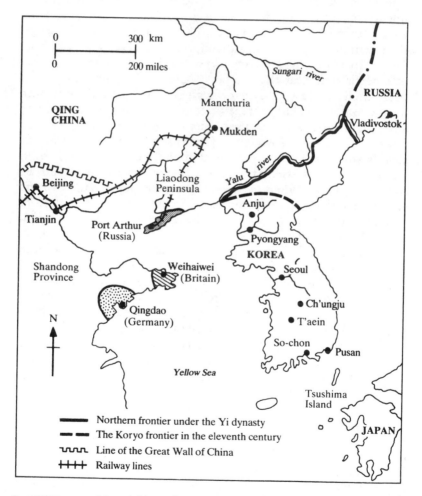

Late Yi Korea and its neighbours in 1900

utter defeat of China in early 1895. At the end of hostilities, the
Japanese had advanced beyond the borders of Korea to occupy the
Liaodong peninsula, including the naval fortress and dockyard of
Port Arthur at its southern tip. Finding the multilated remains
of Japanese prisoners within the defences, the captors rampaged
through the nearby city, killing and wounding hundreds of civilians. This incident was regarded by many of Japan's admirers in the
West as an aberration, a naïve response to the brutality for which
over time the Imperial Japanese Army was to become renowned.

It fell to Li Hongzhang, the commander of the defeated Chinese
forces, to sue for peace in Tokyo and obtain the best terms possible
for the tottering Qing dynasty. Fearful of the international repercussions of further conquest on the East Asian mainland, the Japanese
government ignored the army commanders' plea for an immediate
advance on Beijing and backed instead the southern expansion
then being advocated by the Imperial Japanese Navy. The Treaty of
Shimonoseki therefore accorded Korea full independence, while
requiring China to cede to Japan the strategically important Liaodong peninsula, plus the island of Taiwan. Even then, France,
Germany and Russia put pressure on Tokyo to return this peninsula
to Qing rule. When in 1898 the Russians instead of the Japanese
gained a twenty-five-year lease on the area, and extended the naval
facilities at Port Arthur, it became clear that Russia and Japan were
headed for war.

Opposition from Russia slowed down the Japanese seizure of
Korea, which retained a degree of freedom till the outbreak of
the Russo-Japanese War (1904–5). Although Korea formally proclaimed its neutrality, the Japanese occupied Seoul in 1904 and
filled government departments with advisers. Both Britain and the
United States acquiesced in this tightening of control, for they
regarded the expansion of the Russian empire as the most serious
threat to their interests. Contrary to all expectations, a string of
victories humiliated Russia and left Japan as the dominant East
Asian power. The 1905 Treaty of Portsmouth acknowledged this
far-reaching change of circumstances by transferring Russian rights
in China to Japan, accepting a Japanese protectorate over Korea,
and ceding the southern half of Sakhalin island. The Liaodong concession, renamed the Kwantung Leased Territory, was made the
headquarters of the Kwantung Army. It remained there until 1928,
when a move northwards to Mukden occurred as part of a general
Japanese advance into Manchuria.

As the Anglo-Japanese Alliance of 1902 was still regarded in

London as a guarantee of peace, Britain let Japan have a free hand in Korea. No protest was lodged at the methods used to reduce the country to subjection. When the Korean court refused to accede to the demand for a protectorate, Japanese troops occupied the palace and themselves affixed the Korean government seal to the desired treaty.

King Kojong's appeal for international protection against Japan received no response, in spite of the world press making the unsavoury events in Korea headline news. The Japanese resident general, Ito Hirobumi, actually used the furore as a pretext to replace Kojong with his son, Sunjong. Between 1908 and 1910 there was open rebellion that the Japanese had to extinguish by the most brutal methods. At the time of the formal annexation of Korea in 1910 more than 17,600 guerrillas were already casualties in over 2000 clashes, according to official Japanese statistics. The most important casualty on the Japanese side was Ito Hirobumi, shot down in 1909. His successor was the first governor-general, Terauchi Masatake (1852–1919), a hardened soldier who later became prime minister of Japan.

The passing of the Yi dynasty in 1910 resulted in the loss of Korean independence for over thirty-five years. The Japanese occupation was harsh throughout this period because the Koreans never really accepted their subjection. After the initial reign of terror, the colony settled down to effective and sustained passive resistance which hoped to gain from the 'self-determination' that President Wilson had proposed in 1918 should replace the 'immoral' reliance on an imperial balance of power. It was on the basis of this doctrine that the old empire of Austria-Hungary was broken up and new countries such as Czechoslovakia, Hungary, Bulgaria and Romania came into existence, 'along clearly recognisable lines of nationality'. Even though defeat for the Democrats in the 1920 presidential election turned the United States towards isolationism, Woodrow Wilson's ideas were never quite forgotten, either at home or abroad. The Japanese could go on crushing with apparent impunity peaceful Korean demonstrations, in 1919 burning protestors alive in a church near Sunron, south of Seoul; but the logic of this aggression would lead in turn to the nemesis that streamed from Pearl Harbor. In the fullness of time it liberated the Korean peninsula from Japan, but as two states rather than one country. For in 1945 international politics returned Korea to the age of division that existed prior to the founding of the Yoryo dynasty a millennium earlier.

8

FEUDAL JAPAN

From the Ashikaga Shogunate to the
Meiji Restoration
(1338–1868)

THE ASHIKAGA PERIOD (1338–1568)

An unforeseen consequence of the Mongol intervention in Japan was the breakdown of the feudal order established under the Kamakura shogunate. The fourteenth and fifteenth centuries experienced little effective government because no shogun was sufficiently strong to impose his will on distant provinces. In Kyoto the Ashikaga, the new shoguns, presided over a luxurious court noted for its achievements in literature and the arts, but the capital was often the scene of destruction by fire and sword. The worst violence occurred in 1441, when the peasants vented their fury at the introduction of new taxes. Raids on the outskirts developed into an assault on the city centre, where the pawnbrokers and moneylenders had their premises. Only a timely debt-cancelling edict dispersed the rebels.

Another disturbance in 1457 saw a pitched battle between samurai hired by the moneylenders and armed peasants. At this period the rigid distinction between warrior and farmer did not exist, and the advent of the foot-soldier opened up war as a career for discontented countrymen. Although the samurai preference for fighting on horseback had yet to pass away, the new conditions of street fighting required the use of infantry. Local lords also welcomed new recruits for their own quarrels, and the temporary organisation involved in these intermittent struggles made it easy for a peasant to join up. Not until the rise of all-powerful military leaders in the sixteenth century, and the professional armies on which they relied, would the place of the samurai become fixed in the feudal system. It still remains a peculiar Jaspanese decision that after his final victory over all his rivals at Sekigahara in 1600 Tokugawa Ieyasu chose not to abolish feudalism but, on the contrary, to reform and perfect its social distinctions. Thousands of samurai were thus guaranteed privileged status without the necessity of any exercise of their skill in arms. Unlike the battle of Bosworth, at the close of the War of the Roses in Britain, the outcome of Sekigahara was not the eclipse of the feudal system so much as its detachment from warfare. Thereafter, the great acts of *bushido*, 'the way of the warrior', concentrated on the redress of injured honour.

The feudal order was already in trouble within thirty years of the samurai triumph over Kublai Khan, not least because of the Hojo regents' financial embarrassment. The continued maintenance of coastal defences, the gifts bestowed on temples as a thank-offering for the storm that sank the Mongol fleet, and the rewards for service demanded by samurai, together placed an intolerable strain on their coffers. Several edicts were issued from Kamakura cancelling the debts of retainers, but they had no lasting effect, because money-lenders only raised the rate of interest on new loans.

Real difficulty came for the Hojo regents in a most unexpected quarter, the imperial palace. In 1318 Go-Daigo became emperor, and to the amazement of Japan indicated a desire to rule as well as reign. He issued edicts aimed at strengthening imperial authority. The lack of response by Hojo Takatoki (1316–26) provided Go-

Fig. 33. Wooden statuette of Go-Daigo, traditionally supposed to have been carved by the emperor himself during his years of exile. He was the last emperor who, in 1334, tried to rule as well as reign

Daigo with his chance to persuade some of the nobles to throw off their vassalage. Little respect could be accorded to a regent who devoted his energies to dog-fighting, dancing and women.

Go-Daigo's plans, however, were betrayed in 1331, forcing the emperor to seek refuge first at the Todaiji Buddhist complex in Nara, then at a remote monastery on the top of Mt Kasagi. When troops arrived from Kamakura, the Hojo stronghold, Go-Daigo escaped the siege but was soon captured and sent into exile. Although firm repression in Kyoto temporarily restored the prestige of the Hojo regency, there were samurai who preferred to continue in active opposition, chief among them being Kusunoki Masashige (1294–1336), a warrior from Akasaka, a fortress north-west of Nara. His daring rebellion against Kamakura and his constant support for Go-Daigo eventually converted Masashige into the archetypal loyalist. In the 1920s and 1930s he topped the list of heroes admired by Japanese youth, far outstripping Nogi Maresuke, the best general of the Russo-Japanese War.

Go-Daigo enjoyed in Kusunoki Masashige the service of a selfless samurai, a rare phenomenon in the confusion of the fourteenth century. The loyalty of his other followers was less certain, for the would-be ruler found that the great nobles were unenthusiastic about the restoration of a powerful monarchy. Not even the destruction of Kamakura in 1333 and the suicide of the last Hojo regent were enough for the realisation of Go-Daigo's absolutist dream. Already Ashikaga Takauji, supposed ally of Go-Daigo, moved with quiet determination towards the establishment of the next shogunate.

When Go-Daigo sided with Ashikaga Takauji's rivals, the latter marched against Kyoto and in one of the engagements Kusunoki Masashige was killed. To rid himself of the stigma of rebellion and rally supporters to his cause, Ashikaga Takauji then set up a new emperor, from another line of the imperial family, and in 1338 he was duly named as shogun. Yet again Go-Daigo escaped and established a second imperial court at Yoshino in the mountains south of Nara. The existence between 1336 and 1392 of a rival southern emperor led to a bitter civil war, which was ended only by the third Ashikaga shogun, Yoshimitsu (1358–1408). He promised the descendants of Go-Daigo that, if they returned voluntarily to the capital, they could alternate the throne with the northern line; the shogun, needless to say, broke the promise.

The shift in political power from the imperial palace to the shogun's tent was paralleled by a gradual transformation in religious belief. Despite the active support given to Go-Daigo by several of the larger monasteries, the old link between the court aristocracy and the Buddhist clergy counted for little in a world dominated by hardy warriors. The Chinese-inspired culture of the Heian period had already given place to more native forms at Kamakura, where a rejection of artificiality in art and literature ran alongside the growth of popular Buddhist sects. With the advent of a feudal society and the loss of court patronage, monks were obliged to consider the spiritual needs of the lesser nobility as well as the common people. In the process their new movements developed on characteristically Japanese lines and were attractive to all classes.

The first of the new sects was named Jodo, the Pure Land, after the Western Paradise ruled by Amitabha, the Buddha of infinite light. Its advocate was Honen (1173–1212), a novice at Enryakuji on Mt Hiei, who later became the disciple of an itinerant holy man named Eiku. Belief, he preached, should concentrate upon the power of Amitabha to effect salvation rather than one's own effort. Because an individual could not succeed alone, either Buddha or a bodhisattva would have to lend a hand for a devotee to achieve bliss. Not surprisingly the great monasteries opposed the Jodo sect. Its downgrading of the role played by the clergy they thought dangerous as only the old forms of worship ensured Buddha's protection of the country.

Honen's most influential disciple, Shinran (1173–1262), took his own dependence on divine aid to what he considered to be a logical conclusion. Having abandoned traditional methods of worship completely, he married and had children. Shinran never ceased to defy the authorities and carry his gospel of personal hope direct to both warriors and peasants. After his death, Shinshu, the True Sect, grew into a quasi-political organisation powerful enough to resist the attentions of the warlord Oda Nobunaga. They fought him under a banner which read: 'The mercy of Buddha should be recompensed even by rending flesh. One's duty to the Sage should be recompensed even by smashing bones!'

Equally charismatic was Nichiren (1222–82). In 1260 he prophesied the collapse of Japan from natural calamity and foreign invasion, and persecution was his lot until the envoy of Kublai Khan arrived in 1268, demanding submission from the emperor. Nichiren's warning may have been proved correct, but the regent Hojo Tokimune was tired of his attacks on the conduct of the monasteries, contaminated in Nichiren's view by the appointment of abbots for political reasons. Given the military might of the monasteries, the purging of worldly persons from high office could not be a priority for a busy regent preparing to meet a powerful foreign invader.

Of other sects Nichiren said: 'Those who call on Amitabha are due for hell; Zen is the very devil; Shingon ruins the country.' Yet he shared with the first belief in the superiority of faith over knowledge, and with the last the possibility of becoming enlightened during one's earthly lifetime.

Zen, the most enduring of all the new sects, was first brought to Japan in 1191 by Eisai, a monk of humble origins like Nichiren. Eisai (1141–1215) had twice visited China and studied there various sects, including Chan, the Chinese name for Zen. Eisai introduced tea as well. In China the beverage had long been recognised as an aid to meditation. Tea was grown on estates around monasteries so that its drinking would keep monks awake and their brains clear. A cult arose amongst scholars, but the Chinese tea party never approached the ritual extreme of the tea ceremony in Japan. Similarly, Chan doctrines of individual perception were exaggerated by the Zen sect into a way of belief that was eminently suited to men of action. Zen monks enjoyed the favour of the feudal nobility for the reason that they eschewed sectarian disputes, their aloofness from the quarrels that exercised the monasteries allowing them to become trusted scribes and advisers.

With the death of Ashikaga Yoshimitsu in 1408, the fragile hold of the shogunate on Japan gradually became apparent. Pressures connected with population growth and the expansion of trade unbalanced the network of feudal obligations, especially when smaller landholders chose to ignore the authority of older families and organise for themselves advantageous local alliances. The repeated cancellation of debts, the peasant risings, the smashing of toll-barriers, and the formation of guilds all testify to a decline in shogunal power. The Onin War (1467–77) saw fighting on a scale more widespread and terrible than Japan had ever experienced.

While the samurai were engaged in a protracted civil war that drew in large numbers of the peasantry as foot-soldiers, new classes were forming in the country markets and the coastal towns engaged in commerce. In order to shore up their financial position the Ashikaga shoguns had actively encouraged trade with China, then resurgent under the native Ming dynasty. One shipment of cargo is known to have been exchanged for a large sum in cash in 1342, some sixteen years before the final expulsion of the Mongols by the Ming emperor Hong Wu, while the subsequent import of copper and silver coinage helped to sustain shogunal rule. Amicable relations between China and Japan were properly established by the Ming emperor Yong Le, who wished to reassert Chinese influence in East Asia. A mission he sent to Japan in 1405 carried to Ashikaga Yoshimitsu a crown, robes of state and a seal of solid gold, which was too heavy to be lifted with one hand. As far as Ming Yong Le was concerned, the shogun was a tributary king and a useful ally in combating piracy, since Ashikaga Yoshimitsu agreed to attack the bases of Japanese pirates in return for the Chinese emperor's encouragement of trade.

The acceptance of the gifts has annoyed Japanese historians as an unnecessary admission of Chinese suzerainty. Yet, like other rulers, the shogun was able to join a privileged system of trade through the nominal acknowledgement of the Son of Heaven. Official trade continued until the early sixteenth century, although by then unofficial trade accounted probably for the bulk of the exchange between China and Japan.

THE ASCENDANCY OF THE WARLORDS (1568–98)

The century of conflict that began with the Onin War witnessed a redistribution of power throughout the country. Shogunal weakness facilitated the rise of new families as daimyo, great territorial lords, and in the growing confusion of the late sixteenth century reached a climax in the successive domination of Japan by two mighty warlords, Oda Nobunaga and Toyotomi Hideyoshi. Both were relatively humble men, although no other Japanese leader ever matched in a single lifetime the phenomenal rise of the latter from the peasantry to supreme power.

By 1551, when Nobunaga inherited the ancestral estates situated to the east of Kyoto, the family was quite strong and recognised by the imperial court. At seventeen he faced opposition from other members of the family, against whom he moved ruthlessly. His determination was soon put to the test, when an army of 25,000 men invaded his lands under the command of Imagawa Yoshimoto, a powerful neighbour. To defend his inheritance Nobunaga probably had no more than 2000 men, but his surprise attack on the enemy at the battle of Okehazama was one of the decisive victories in Japanese history. Taking advantage of close knowledge of the terrain, he caught Imagawa Yoshimoto's troops sheltering from a heavy downpour in a gorge. The appearance of a large blocking force on one side of the gorge – no more than an array of dummy flags and soldiers made of straw – unnerved the invaders and led to headlong flight once Nobunaga ordered his men to open an attack from the other side. An unexpected bonus was the allegiance of Tokugawa Ieyasu, who was freed from his obligation to Imagawa Yoshimoto. This able strategist would acquire in the end the territorial gains of Oda Nobunaga as well as Toyotomi Hideyoshi.

The death from leprosy of the only rival lord close to Kyoto enabled Nobunaga to seize the capital in 1568 on the pretext of restoring Ashikaga Yoshiaki to the shogunate and returning stolen property to the emperor. The destitution of the throne had surprised Francis Xavier (1506–52) on a visit a decade earlier. The missionary found the principal houses of Kyoto in ruins, the imperial court dispersed in nearby villages, and the emperor living in a cottage because he could not afford to rebuild the palace. When Francis Xavier was unable to pay the fee charged for an imperial audience, he quit the city in bewilderment.

In a characteristic display of munificence Nobunaga built a new palace for the shogun, and also one for the emperor, whom he treated with respect. Toyotomi Hideyoshi, his successor as chief warlord, continued this policy of subsidy for the imperial court, even though he seems to have been quite indifferent to the views of the throne. By avoiding politics altogether the imperial family survived the era of military dictatorship to remain the lasting symbol of national unity. Ashikaga Yoshiaki was less prudent, though, and his distaste for a puppet's role forced Nobunaga to expel him in 1573 from Kyoto. The shogun moved from place to place in search of support until his death in 1597, when the title lapsed. There was no shogun till 1603, the year Tokugawa Ieyasu filled the post.

Oda Nobunaga's task in reunifying Japan was immense. Ranged against his army were the considerable forces of the provincial daimyo, now equipped with imported Portuguese firearms, while the capital was threatened by the warrior-monks of Enryakuji. In 1569 Nobunaga forbade representatives from the great monastery access to the shogunal palace, and he licensed the Jesuits to preach openly in Kyoto. These measures were soon followed up with a surprise attack on Ashikaga Yoshiaki's would-be allies at Mt Hiei. Neither in Kyoto, nor elsewhere in Japan, could Nobunaga afford to face an alliance between militant Buddhists and dissident aristocrats. The notorious assault on the monastic complex of Enryakuji was meant to quell once and for all opposition from the Buddhist church. In 1571 a force of 30,000 men suddenly overran the hundreds of temples belonging to Enryakuji on the slopes of Mt Hiei,

long the paramount monastery. Every building was burned to the
ground, and every person killed. The destruction astounded Japan,
for the cruelty shown to men, women and children was a sign that a
new kind of authority had emerged. It gave a grim warning to both
allies and enemies, samurai and monks alike, that Nobunaga placed
the unification of the country above all else.

Luis Frois, a licensed Jesuit, described the event in a letter to his
superiors in Europe as an act of divine providence. Christian missionaries were ready to play on the dictator's enmity towards Buddhism, and on occasions they acted as ambassadors on his behalf.
Yet the willingness of Jesuits to become involved in affairs of state
led to their undoing; it was soon apparent that the teachings of the
gospels were in conflict with the way of the warrior. Refusal by a
Japanese convert to follow the pattern of loyalties prescribed in
bushido could be construed only as treason. In 1612 an edict of
Tokugawa Ieyasu prevented samurai from professing the Christian
faith, and two years later the Jesuits and other missionaries were
expelled. Dutch traders had conveniently arrived to replace the
zealous Portuguese.

One reason for the relish felt by Luis Frois at the desruction
of Enryakuji may have been the homosexuality known to flourish
there. According to legend, its founder Saicho had met on Mt Hiei
an angelic boy who explained the sacred and fortunate character of
the place. Possibly an ancient Shinto deity associated with homosexual love, the apparition was absorbed in Buddhist worship as a
boddhisattva, and later became identified with the young boy upon
whom an older monk poured his affection. Another tradition,
which claims homosexuality as an import from China, is less histori-
cally convincing. This would make Kukai, the importer of the
esoteric doctrines of Shingon, the first homosexual monk. The
problem is that the legend ignores the overwhelming emphasis on
heterosexual relations inherent in Chinese ancestor worship.

From the outset of his own mission Francis Xavier was conscious
of sodomy. 'There are monks who love the sin abhorred by Nature,'
he noted with anger. 'And nobody, neither man nor woman, young
nor old, regards the sin as abnormal or abominable.' As an Iberian
with a feudal background of his own, Xavier eagerly responded to
the samurai sense of honour. 'The Japanese are the best of the
peoples discovered up to now,' he wrote. But he could never learn
to tolerate the widespread homosexuality amongst monks and
samurai.

In 1587 the followers of a treacherous commander surprised the

Fig. 34. A *chigo* prepares. From a scroll celebrating homosexual love in Buddhist monasteries. The young man warms his bottom at a charcoal fire

residence of Nobunaga early one morning in Kyoto. With courage a young page fought off the attackers, until the entire house was enveloped by flames. The rebels seem to have lacked a plan of action. Apart from capturing the dictator's stronghold on the outskirts of the capital, and putting to death his next of kin, nothing was done to prepare for the inevitable counter-attack by the warlord's own generals.

Within a year Toyotomi Hideyoshi had avenged Oda Nobunaga's death and reasserted control over his territories, and within eighteen years he had reduced all Japan to obedience. Like Nobunaga, Hideyoshi made no claim to be shogun, and never received the title. He was content to rely on military power alone. Unlike Nobunaga though, he dealt generously even with those he had overcome in battle and did not tolerate the unnecessary slaughter of prisoners, at least until the frustration of the Korean campaigns of his later years. Instead of using an all-powerful position forcibly to integrate the country, and at the same time permanently weaken the feudal nobility, Hideyoshi chose to divert the restless energies of the samurai into conquest abroad, starting with Korea as the first stage of an invasion of China.

Although the idea of conquering China did not belong to Hideyoshi, his self-confidence in 1592 was such that few dared to suggest otherwise. His rage in 1596, when Chinese ambassadors offered him recognition as king of Japan in return for peace in Korea, reputedly caused 'vapour to rise from his head'. Whatever the ambition of Hideyoshi on mainland East Asia, Nobunaga had looked upon a war with China as desirable, even inevitable. While Japanese merchants were divided over the value of foreign conquest, they agreed with him about the need to stimulate foreign trade, still a victim of the restrictions being placed on sea-borne commerce by the Ming dynasty.

The choice of Osaka for his own stronghold cannot but have opened Hideyoshi's eyes to the condition of trade and industry too. The population of the busy port was already well on its way to the 350,000 inhabitants recorded in 1700. 'It is the best trading city in Japan,' Engelbert Kaempfer, a Dutch visitor, noted some years earlier, 'being extraordinarily well suited for carrying on commerce both by land and water. This is the reason why citizens include rich merchants and artisans.' Situated near the head of the Inland Sea, Osaka was ideally placed for Hideyoshi to deal with trouble either in outlying provinces or the capital. His enormous castle, completed there in 1586, was built with granite blocks so as to give protection against new weapons such as cannon. The might of its owner was manifest in the permanent barracks that it provided for armed and uniformed retainers.

To reinforce social distinctions, as well as disarm the peasantry, an edict of 1588 forbade the possession of 'swords, bows, spears and firearms'. Hideyoshi would not allow another peasant to repeat his own singular self-promotion. An extensive survey of land-holdings, conducted between 1582 and 1595, also served to end disorder and establish the basis for samurai stipends. Moves against Christian

Fig. 35. Toyotomi Hideyoshi shortly before his death in 1598

missionaries, combined with a discreet encouragement of the Buddhist church, can be seen to form part of Hideyoshi's traditionalism. He could afford to relax his guard as far as the monasteries were concerned: after the destruction of Enrayakuji most of the Buddhist monks had given up their arms, turning to study and charitable works.

For all the efforts of Hideyoshi on behalf of the samurai, their fate in later centuries was to become increasingly anachronistic. He would have been very surprised that the new world of urban Japan was to find its voice first in his own Osaka. The plays and novels of Ihara Saikaku (1642–93), for example, reflect the feelings of townspeople who were in the process of creating new opportunities for themselves. A novel such as *Five Women Who Loved Love* (*Koshoku Gonin Onna*) celebrates the success of one woman in winning her samurai lover from a desire for young boys. The cult of homosexuality may have been already in decline, as the prohibitions of the early Tokugawa shogunate clearly intended it should, but in the theatre, at least, male impersonation of female characters ensured its survival.

THE TOKUGAWA PERIOD (1603–1868)

Like Oda Nobunaga, Toyotomi Hideyoshi left only an infant heir, whom he was obliged to place under a joint regency that included Tokugawa Ieyasu. Since the fifty-six-year-old Ieyasu was the most powerful military leader in Japan, it was not long before most of the daimyo came to look upon him as the natural leader. There were lords who opposed this development, and until the battle of Sekigahara was won in 1600 the Tokugawa shogunate was no foregone conclusion.

The turmoil that followed the deaths of Oda Nobunaga and Toyotomi Hideyoshi presented many samurai with difficult choices. Shifting alliances could often lead to the betrayal of old friends or their killing in battle. Suicide offered an honourable solution to divided loyalties, and the poet Kinoshita Choshoshi (1569–1649) was in part dispossessed after Sekigahara for failing to commit harakiri. Sworn to serve the Toyotomi family, Kinoshita Choshoshi found himself in an impossible position in early 1600, when he received conflicting orders from its members and Ieyasu concerning the fortress he held. Instead of fighting to the death, or committing suicide, he fled the castle and went into retirement in Kyoto.

Another samurai who renounced his rank to become a poet was

Fig. 36. Tokugawa Ieyasu, the eventual winner of the warlord struggle at the battle of Sekigahara in 1600

Basho (1644–94). He lived as a commoner and had nothing to do either with the imperial palace in Kyoto or the shogun's court in Edo, the old name for Tokyo. His friends and followers included members of all classes, even criminals. It was a range of acquaintances that exactly reflects the accessibility of his own compositions. Particularly favoured by Basho were *haikai*, epigrammatic verses of seventeen syllables, frequently linked by one or more persons into long poems. The genesis of his most famous haiku is fortunately preserved. Sitting with friends one spring in his riverside house in Edo, listening intently to the cooing of a pigeon in the gentle rain, Basho was startled by the sudden splash of a frog. The poem runs:

> Breaking the silence
> Of an ancient pond,
> A frog jumped into the water –
> A deep resonance.

Although Basho never became a Buddhist monk, like many Japanese poets, there remains in his work a sense of mystery that puts him at odds with Ihara Saikaka, another prolific haiku writer. Whereas the world of Oranda Saikaka – 'Dutch' Saikaka as he was known for his delight in everything new – was epitomised by the bustle and dust of the city, Basho's vision acquired its quiet clarity in the countryside, through which he regularly passed to collect material for his renowned travel sketches.

Basho's personal solution to the problem of peace could not suit the temperament of all the samurai. As Tokugawa Ieyasu appreciated the dangers of renewed conflict between idle lords, he swiftly adopted measures that were intended to secure the victory won at Sekigahara. Apart from the revival of the shogunate to legitimise his rule, the land-holdings of less loyal daimyo were redistributed to his own strategic advantage; all daimyo were required to alternate their residence every year between their domains and Edo, where the shogun's castle stood; and finally, a seclusion policy was introduced to cut off outlying territories from the military and economic benefits of foreign trade. Commerce with European countries was ended, except for a limited exchange with the Dutch, who were allowed a single factory on the tiny island of Deshima in the harbour of Nagasaki. This outpost was the only channel through which the Tokugawa shogunate kept itself informed of events in Europe, and through which it received the Dutch books that a few Nagasaki interpreters could read. *Rangaku*, 'Dutch learning', tended to be practical because of the obvious skills displayed by the Dutch as navigators, ship-builders and gunners. Japanese scholars attracted to Dutch learning were concerned mostly with astronomy and medicine, although Hiraga Gennai (1728–79) also evinced an interest in Western art as well as electricity. A controversial figure, he petitioned the Tokugawa shogunate to develop an export trade in pottery, and wrote an official report on iron-ore mining, before his death in prison awaiting trial for the murder of a follower. Relations between the Dutch and the Japanese at Deshima were rarely harmonious, as the Dutch colonial authorities in Java admitted in 1670, since the 'recklessness and thoughtlessness' of many naval officers offended the sensitivities of the local population.

The power base of Ieyasu remained his own estates, in total one-quarter of Japan. Within their boundaries lay all the important mines, the chief ports including Osaka and Nagasaki, and the capital city of Kyoto. In these territories the shogun raised his funds, ruled directly, and maintained his armed forces.

Such domination left no room for fighting by others than those samurai commanded to action by the shogun himself. Not even duelling was permissible after 1650, and in 1694 pacification had gone so far that a reminder was felt necessary to ensure the practice of arms. The decline in military skills led to a concentration on ceremony and display, which the alternate attendance system at Edo inevitably fostered. By the mid-eighteenth century samurai were preoccupied with the problem of remaining financially solvent rather than with the finer points of swordplay, as fixed stipends of rice could never provide a reliable income in a money economy. Although samurai might carry two swords, and have the right to behead a peasant on the spot for an insult, the town-dwellers progressively owned the wealth of the country.

Several scholars turned their attention to the problem of the prolonged inactivity of the samurai under the Tokugawa peace. Almost from the start it was realised that, in the words of an edict of 1615, 'the study of literature and the practice of military arts must be pursued side by side'. A Neo-Confucian thinker such as Hayashi Razan (1583–1657) had no doubt about the urgent need to emphasise the virtues of loyalty, filial piety, and decorum. It has been argued that Ieyasu's search for a principle to justify his authority led to Hayashi Razan gaining his ear. The shogun must have been pleased to learn how Neo-Confucianism held that the universal law was the obedience owed by a son to a father, and a subject to a ruler.

China in fact remained the moral point of reference for Japan during all but the last years of the Tokugawa shogunate, not least because Japanese scholars made the study of Chinese synonymous with that of Confucius. The pioneer Yamaga Soko (1622–85), disdaining the metaphysics so dear to Hayashi Razan, preferred the ideal picture of ancient Zhou feudalism as described in the original teachings of Confucius, since it provided a model for the application of Confucian morality in the paramilitary world of feudal Japan. Thus a samurai was seen to combine martial and civil virtues in his person, and through example in war and peace he earned the respect of peasants, artisans and merchants. The warrior's code had indeed come of age.

The second half of the eighteenth century saw the beginnings of shogunal decline. Its financial troubles were first exposed in the writings of the historian and novelist Arai Hakuseki (1698–1725), who, as a minister under two Tokugawa shoguns, had urged monetary reforms. A good Confucianist, Arai Hakuseki was unable to abandon the principle of self-sufficiency and even consider an increase in external trade as a means of balancing the economy. Despite the persistent problem with finance, Arai Hakuseki had no doubts concerning the historical significance of the Tokugawa shogunate, for he saw the battle of Sekigahara as the culmination of samurai power. According to his *Survey of History*, (*Dokushi Yoron*), there were nine epochs of imperial rule, during five of which the nobles gradually expanded the military authority passed to them by an increasingly decadent throne, a process which allowed in theory Tokugawa Ieyasu to become the heir to a heavenly

1. A section of the terracotta army buried close to the tomb of the first emperor of China at Mount Li. It dates from 210 BC

2. Kiyomizu temple in Kyoto. This Buddhist foundation was burned down in 1113 by its great rival Enryakuji during a dispute over the election of an abbot

3. Ananda temple at Pagan, the capital of Burma until the Mongol invasion of 1278

4. The great Javanese temple of Borobodur, a Buddhist monument three and a half centuries older than Angkor Wat

5. The colossal four-faced towers of the Bayon, near Angkor Wat, the chief monument of Jayavarman VII, the last Khmer warrior-king. The face is that of the Hindu god Siva, probably modelled on the king himself

6. A Sumatran mosque. The tank indicates the earlier influence of Hindu and Buddhist beliefs prior to the arrival of Islam

7. Official Manzhouguo picture of Pu Yi, the last Chinese emperor, flanked by ministers, New Year's Day, 1933. Note the strong Japanese military presence

8. Dr Sun Yatsen in 1923. Standing is his successor as leader of the Guomindang, Jiang Jieshi

9. Guomindang troops in a skirmish with Japanese forces prior to the outbreak of the Sino-Japanese war in 1937

10. Churchill's gunboat bluff. The arrival of HMS *Prince of Wales* at Singapore on 2 December 1941 did not deter Japan: eight days later the battleship was sunk off Malaya by Japanese aircraft

11. Symbolic march past. Japanese soldiers celebrate the capture of Singapore from the British in February 1942

12. Aung San, the wartime Burmese leader whom General Slim judged to be a potential Smuts. Today Aung San's daughter, Suu Kyi, is under house arrest in Rangoon for her opposition to military rule

13. Mao Zedong in Yan'an, a northern base area from which he directed Communist resistance to the Imperial Japanese Army

14. Kamikazes inflicted heavy losses on American warships during the assault on Okinawa. Here USS *Bunker Hill* is forced to retire in March 1945

15. The Gloucester regiment moving up in April 1951 to Imjin river, where their stand helped to stem the Chinese advance down the Korean peninsula

16. The end of the road for Japan's imperial pretensions. The media witness unconditional surrender to General MacArthur aboard USS *Missouri*, 2 September 1945

17. Premier Yoshida Shigeru in 1954 at the Arc de Triomphe in Paris. He had opposed the Japanese attack on European colonies in South-East Asia

18. US aerial destruction of Vietnam in the 1960s included spraying toxic defoliants, like Agent Orange

19. Marcos using his undoubted political skills in 1986 to retain US support for his beleaguered presidency, with (left) US Presidential envoy Philip Habib and (centre) US Ambassador to the Philippines, Steven Bosworth

20. A student casualty of the bloody June 1989 confrontation in Tiananmen Square, Beijing. Reuter's photograph catches the weakness of the young demonstrators

21. South Korean riot police firing tear gas at protestors in Seoul, May 1990

22. Old Singapore giving way in the 1980s to high-rise development

23. Modern Tokyo, the present pace-setter of the Pacific Rim

mandate to rule Japan. Arai Hakuseki's singular attempt to invest the shogun with Confucian legitimacy was to founder in the nineteenth century, when a combination of internal and external pressures undermined the office of the shogun, and led to the restoration of the throne under the Meiji emperor.

Yet Tokugawa rule produced at least one effective leader in Yoshimune, shogun from 1716 till 1745, and might have been better placed to face the challenge of modern times if his successors were less feeble and incompetent. Yoshimune's favourite grandson, Ieharu, was so lazy that during his period of office (1760–86) ambitious and unscrupulous officials almost took over the running of the government. Such a man was Tanuma Okitsugu (1719–88), a soldier's son, who manipulated the palace ladies to influence Ieharu's judgement and to provide adequate scope for his own pursuit of bribes. No aristocrat was above gratifying his avarice when an important appointment was at stake.

The death of Tokugawa Ieharu in 1786 was followed by Tanuma Okitsugu's disgrace and a movement, known as the Kansei reforms, aimed at restoring the old ways. Their formulator, Matsudaira Sadanobu (1758–1829), was intent on bringing about financial stability through the curtailment of luxury, the restriction of commerce, and the revival of samurai virtues. Because of his family connections with the Tokugawa house, he was able to force his policies on the shogunal administration, although only the obviously corrupt suffered the indignity of being driven from office. Risings in the countryside and the towns became less violent and less frequent, but the abandonment of Sadanobu's reforms in 1793 once again left the national

Fig. 37. Tokugawa Yoshimune, the last effective shogun (1716–45). He initiated a programme of financial retrenchment, which slowed for a while the decline of the shogunate

economy to continue on its steady decline. Unseasonal weather merely added to the misery of the peasants, whose rebellions reached a zenith in 1837, when Osaka's citizens burned the commercial quarter and came close to destroying the Tokugawa garrison.

It was in these circumstances that the refusal of the shogun to countenance external trade led to a national crisis. From 1825 onwards foreign ships which approached the coast of Japan were fired upon, and their crews, if they landed, captured and put to death. This tightening of the exclusion policy, and a parallel persecution of scholars of 'Dutch learning', served to galvanise forces for change. The bold adoption of Western ways after the Meiji restoration of 1868, and the consequent foundation of the present-day Japanese state, should be seen therefore as a spontaneous effort at renewal, albeit under the catalyst of foreign pressure.

Contacts with the Russians, French and British seemed steadily harder to avoid, and after the easy defeat of China in the Anglo-Chinese War of 1839–42 there were Japanese who felt that Tokugawa isolationism could end in a similar disaster for Japan. But it was concern in Washington for the safety of American sailors involved in whaling that brought in 1846 the first foreign warship on a diplomatic mission to Japan. Eight years later a complete United States squadron under the command of Matthew Perry arrived with a request for the opening of ports, the protection of shipwrecked sailors, and the start of trade. To avoid war a treaty was signed in 1854, and isolation abandoned. This reversal encouraged open criticism of all shogunal policies so that renewed difficulties with foreign powers weakened feudal loyalties that were already stretched close to breaking-point.

The last shogun committed the fatal error of physically threatening his noble critics, thereby encouraging a general alliance against him. Tokugawa authority had evaporated by 1868, the year in which the shogun surrendered his office to the boy emperor Mutsuhito (1852–1912), later known as the Meiji emperor. After centuries of military rule, Japan once again had an imperial government.

9

SOUTH-EAST ASIA

The Medieval Kingdoms
(1287 onwards)

THE RISE OF THAILAND (1351–1932)

Political disintegration on mainland South-East Asia after the intervention of the Mongols provided the Thai with their chance for power. The Indianised states based on Pagan in Burma and Angkor in Cambodia were already in eclipse by the close of the thirteenth century. Although Cambodian authority did not collapse with the dramatic suddenness of the Burmese kingdom in 1278, there was a noticeable lack of dynamism at Angkor that no amount of ceremony could disguise. That the later decline in Mongol strength happened to coincide with even greater Thai pressure on Angkor meant simply that in the fourteenth century the Cambodians were left to wage a losing battle on their own. Angkor was captured three times before the Cambodian court abandoned the city altogether and moved downriver to present-day Phnom Penh.

Yet Thai migration long predated the coming of the Mongols. Moving southwards they encountered their cousins in the Shan of Burma and the Lao of present-day Laos, Thailand and Vietnam. A memory of such widespread migration is contained in the Lao legend of Khun Borom, the divine bringer of agriculture, handicrafts, manners, learning, and ritual. After a prosperous reign of twenty-five years on the plain around Dien Bien Phu, in the north of Vietnam, Khun Borom sent his seven sons to rule over the various Thai groups spread across mainland South-East Asia.

The story could well reflect the diffusion of power at the beginning of the fourteenth century. In place of the far-flung territories

151

of the Burmese and Khmer empires, there was a patchwork of Thai principalities stretching continuously from the Vietnamese border across the Mekong and Chaophraya rivers to the Gulf of Martaban. None of these petty kingdoms attained enough power to dominate their neighbours, and it was not until the foundation of Ayudhya in 1351 by the adventurer U Thong that any sign of regional strength reappeared. Following ancient precedent, the new ruler moved his subjects from a smallpox-afflicted city, most likely Lopburi, down the Chaophraya river to establish another capital at Ayudhya, named after Rama's stronghold in the Indian epic *Ramayana*. Possibly the son of an influential Chinese merchant, U Thong took the title of Ramathibodi (1351–69) and consolidated his grip on the lower river valley by installing client rulers in the main cities of Suphanburi, Lopburi and Ratburi. The international contacts of the flourishing port of Ayudhya may have stimulated further expansion down the Malay peninsula and along the coast of Cambodia. Proximity to what was left of the Khmer empire at Angkor undoubtedly inspired imperial ambitions in Ramathibodi, who took the city in 1352. Between 1351 and 1431 there was an almost permanent state of war between Angkor and Ayudhya. But armed rivalry did not preclude admiration for Khmer kingship and the court of Ayudhya adopted wholesale its protocol, thereby inaugurating the process by which Thailand came to absorb so much of Cambodian tradition.

The two enduring monuments of Ramathibodi are said to have been a large Buddhist temple and a law code. From his laws it can be deduced that Ayudhya was dependent in some measure on slavery, not least because there were very severe penalties for slaves attempting to escape. The rest of society was divided into a strict hierarchy, presided over by royal officials appointed from leading families. The administrative responsibilities of these officials were finally established by Trailok, or Borommatrailokanat (1448–88). Inheriting an empire which included new territories won from the Cambodians as

Fig. 38. The royal barge of Ayudhya

well as the Thai-speaking states of Lan Na and Lan Sang, Trailok sought order through a Khmer-like system of government. He centralised the administration, drew a distinction between civil and military officials, defined social position in terms of land-holding, amalgamated the separate military forces into a single army, and replaced local chieftains with princely governors. The outcome of this reform for Thailand was a stability unsurpassed anywhere in medieval South-East Asia. The system lasted with only minor modifications until in the nineteenth century Western-style reforms were introduced to modernise the country. Even then the government remained, prior to the constitutional revolution of 1932 which abolished absolute monarchy, largely the preserve of the nobles. The traditional resilience of Thai society helped Chulalongkorn (1868–1910) to contain Western imperialism by the timely sacrifice of outlying territories in Laos, Cambodia and Malaya – a conciliatory policy that acted as a sure protection for the Thai heartland.

The language spoken by the various groups of people who founded the kingdoms of Ayudhya, Lan Na and Lan Sang was once widespread in the present-day Chinese provinces of Yunnan, Guizhou and Guangxi. Another concentration of its speakers used to dwell in north Vietnam; hence the dispersal legend located at Dien Bien Phu. Pressure from successive Chinese and Vietnamese governments must account for migration and the development of dialects.

The wars conducted by Ayudhya against Lan Na and Lan Sang can therefore be viewed as a struggle for the leadership of migrant Thai. Fighting is never absent from the chronicles of all three kingdoms, with the founder of Chiang Mai setting an early example in 1281 through his cunning seizure of the Mon city of Lamphun. Chiang Mai, the 'new city', was capital of Lan Na, which translates as 'a million rice-fields'. Its wealth is demonstrated in the building activities of its kings, and especially Tilokaracha (1441–87), whose most interesting monument is perhaps the Mahabodharma, a temple with seven spires modelled after a large Burmese one in Pagan. The construction of Buddhist temples, however, failed to cool Tilokaracha's ardour for war, just as becoming a monk had little affect on his great opponent's expansionist plans in Ayudhya. Although in 1464 Trailok abdicated in favour of his son and entered a monastery, the former king was easily persuaded to resume power in Ayudhya when foreign affairs took a promising turn. Difficulties beset Lan Na on its eastern frontier when in 1478 a Vietnamese army captured Luang Prabang, the capital of Lan Sang. Threatened by this western drive, Tilokaracha arranged a defensive alliance with China, whose Ming emperors were still wary of Vietnam some fifty years after the withdrawal of their own troops from the country. The timely submission of Lan Na to Beijing represents the return of Chinese influence to the interior of mainland South-East Asia.

Yet it was upon Ayudhya that the full force of foreign invasion was to fall. The unexpected foe was the empire of Toungoo, named

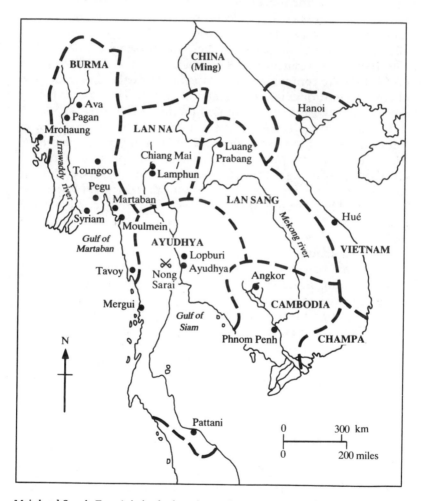

Mainland South-East Asia in the late sixteenth century, showing the advent of the Thai kingdoms of Ayudhya, Lan Na and Lan Sang

after the refuge of the Burmans following the fall of Pagan. From this stronghold, situated in the valley of the Sittong river, arose a dynasty capable not only of reuniting Burma but also carrying on campaigns beyond its borders. Its second king, Tabinshweti (1531–50), wisely conciliated the Mon people of the Irrawaddy river delta before embarking on conquest abroad. He patronised Mon culture and used the wealth of Pegu, the chief Mon city, to acquire Portuguese matchlocks and cannon as well as engage Portuguese mercenaries. An unsuccessful attack on Ayudhya precipitated a Mon rebellion and his own death in 1550, but Bayinnaung (1551–81), his successor, twice overran the Thai kingdom in 1564 and 1569.

The official Burmese justification for the attacks on Ayudhya was the refusal of its ruler to part with some white elephants, creatures highly regarded among South-East Asian royalty. The Portuguese trader Mendez Pinto had the good fortune to see one of them. The great beast, he writes,

was being taken to bathe in the river. It was shaded from the sun by twenty-four servants carrying white parasols. Its guard numbered three thousand men. It had a chain of beaten gold on its back, and silver chains hanging from the neck. They told me that on feast days it wore gold chains, but silver chains when it was going to have a bath. In its trunk it carried a golden globe, about twice the size of a man's head.

(That the last incarnation of Buddha prior to his ministry was a white elephant made the royal stable at Ayudhya a very tempting prize.)

When the Portuguese captured Malacca in 1511, they immediately sent a mission to Ayudhya in the belief that Malacca was its vassal. Later embassies confirmed peaceful relations and secured the right of residence for Portuguese traders. The Thai were very pleased to adopt modern firearms, till they discovered the military advantage that they expected to gain had been neutralised by Portuguese willingness to trade with the Burmese as well. Not even the presence of a company of Portuguese mercenaries inside newly built brick ramparts could avert disaster in 1569, when the Burmese king Bayinnaung stormed Ayudhya after a siege. Liberation from Burma had to await the manhood of Naresuen (1555–1605), a Thai prince. A hostage at the Burmese court in Pegu and married to Bayinnaung's sister, he was allowed to return to Ayudhya and under supervision hold a series of military commands. By 1585 he felt strong enough to defy his Burmese masters and five years later ascended the throne. The decisive moment came in 1593 at the battle of Nong Sarai.

Although outnumbered by the Burmese invasion force, Naresuen found comfort in the appearance of auspicious signs like the relics of Buddha, which glowed orange in the sky as they moved slowly northwards. But he placed his hope of victory in the effectiveness of the lotus array, a military formation using a vanguard supported by powerful wings. His army was thus stationed when a small force he had sent forward to reconnoitre the invader's positions was driven back in disorder. Instead of moving up to its aid, Naresuen decided to stand firm and let the Burmese come on in the belief that the whole army of Ayudhya was retreating before them. The uncoordinated approach of Burmese units gave Naresuen's soldiers the edge in the general engagement that ensued, even though they had to fight hard to avoid envelopment. Their determination won the day as the Burmese broke and fled on the news of their commander's death. Naresuen had slain this prince with his long-handled sword from the top of his favourite war elephant. In the rout the Burmese lost many troops, elephants and horses.

Not only did Naresuen roundly defeat the Burmese, he followed up his victory with an invasion of Burma itself, reoccupying on the way the ports of Moulmein and Tavoy. The Thai had shown how they could deal with their neighbours effectively, but fears arising from European infiltration were to provoke a sharp reaction. Trouble with the English East India Company caused blood to be shed at Mergui, an important port to the south of the Gulf of Martaban. It also drew in troops from France, a new ally welcomed by Narai (1656–88). The reaction on this king's death was a general expulsion of foreigners, though not a complete rejection of the outside world. It is something of a paradox that the first ruler to cause alarm by actively cultivating the European powers should have reigned during the golden age of Thai poetry. Ayudhya enjoyed peace until the 1760s, when, after a bitter siege by the Burmese army, the last king offered to surrender and become a vassal of Burma, but terms were refused. Then in 1767 the attackers breached the walls and conducted a ruthless sack. Tens of thousands were transported to Burma, where they died in captivity.

Disastrous though the Burmese invasion was at the time, its long-term result was the unification of Thailand, for the territories covered by the kingdoms of Ayudhya, Lan Na and Lan Sang were to be incorporated into an empire under the subsequent Chakri dynasty. The present Thai king, Bhumipol Adulyadej, who ascended the throne in 1946, is the ninth member of this dynasty to reign, his title being Rama IX. The first ruler to be titled Rama was Chaophraya

Chakri, a soldier of fortune during the confused period immediately following Ayudhya's fall. Of half-Chinese origin, he received financial aid from the local Chinese merchant community and, further afield, an unsought-after military diversion in a Chinese attack on northern Burma. The Qing emperor Qianlong seems to have been concerned to restore the balance of power on mainland South-East Asia by forcibly reminding Burma of its age-old submission to China. After the previous capture of Ayudhya in 1569, a Thai delegation had travelled to Beijing in order to request a new seal of office to replace that destroyed by the Burmese. The Chinese advance in 1769 on Ava, then the capital of Burma, gave a similar boost to Thai independence, not least because the Burmese withdrew the bulk of their troops, leaving only small garrisons behind.

By 1782 Chaophraya Chakri was ready to establish his own dynasty at Bangkok, where he first moved the capital across the river to the east bank so as to make it less vulnerable to Burmese attack. Modern Bangkok has grown around the splendid buildings raised during his reign as Rama I, which lasted until 1809. In the physical reconstruction of Siam, the name of the country till 1939, as in the reform of religious and cultural life, the new king claimed that what he was doing was restoring the traditions of Ayudhya. Yet the presence of high officials of Indian, Persian, Cham, Malay and Chinese descent among the sons of old Thai families who ran Rama I's administration helps to account for the cosmopolitan literature of early nineenth-century Siam. Stories from Java, Persia and India were translated into Thai, along with the Chinese historical novel *Romance of the Three Kingdoms*.

Siam was tested in the massive Burmese invasion of 1785, when successful resistance to the Burmese left Rama I a powerful ruler and his authority accepted by all the courts outside the borders of Vietnam and Burma. Even Cambodia was drawn into the Siamese sphere of influence from 1802 onwards, as a precaution against recently reunited Vietnam.

Bangkok seems hardly to have noticed the sultan of Kedah's tactical cession of Penang to the English East India Company until the death of Rama III, whose last words warned his successor Mongkut that 'there will be no more wars with Vietnam and Burma. We will have them only with the West.' In his opinion the British defeat of China in the 1839–42 war had signalled the end of an era, and the start of a new international order. That as Rama IV (1851–68) the former monk was able to steer his country on an independent course remains one of the surprising achievements of nineteenth-century history. The position of Siam was precarious, with Burma and Malaya being steadily absorbed by the British, and Vietnam and Cambodia coming under increasing French domination. Rama IV believed that for his people to survive in the modern world it was necessary for them to understand the newly arrived European powers. Treaties signed with Britain in 1855, and France the year after, regularised relations with Siam, although, never missing an opportunity for trade, Britain also gained for its infamous Indian export, opium, the waiving of import duty. The policy of playing off Britain against France was continued by Mongkut's son, Chulalongkorn, or Rama V, who was probably assisted in this dangerous game by the unstated desire of both countries to avoid having a common border between their colonial possessions in South-East Asia.

Chulalongkorn also followed his father's lead in the Westernisation of Siamese society and government. The kingdom became progressively more modern in matters of law, finance, communications, and military equipment. Nor did debt-bondage or slavery escape abolition in 1905, as the last vestiges of medieval custom were cleared away by a still absolute monarch. The reigns of the father and son preserved national independence and in 1932 facilitated a bloodless transfer to a constitutional monarchy. But the survival of Siam was not without its price. In 1867 Cambodia was placed under French protection; in 1888 the area around Dien Bien Phu was added to recently conquered Vietnam; in 1893 and 1905 the territories that became the protectorate of Laos were also ceded to France; then in 1907 followed the Cambodian provinces of Battambang, Siem Reap and Sisophon; and finally in 1909, all rights were abandoned over the sultanates of Kelantan, Trengganau and Perlis, by that date firmly within the British sphere of influence.

CAMBODIAN ECLIPSE (1431–1863)

With the final capture of Angkor in 1431 a dark age descended on Cambodia. A Thai prince was installed briefly as a vassal of Ayudhya, but soon the city was evacuated, the heir of the last Cambodian king fleeing south-eastwards to found a new kingdom at Phnom Penh. Apart from the greater distance from Ayudhya, the suitability of the new site for a capital lay in its location at the confluence of two rivers, the Mekong and Tongle Sap, thus enabling a diminished Cambodia at least to maintain itself as a commercial state. An intensification of trade with China had occurred in the half-century prior to 1431. More tributary missions were sent there under the late

Mongol and early Ming emperors than at any other time during the existence of the Khmer empire. It is not unlikely, therefore, that the shift of the Cambodian capital downriver had some connection with the expansion of Chinese maritime influence in South-East Asia.

Despite the loss of great ceremonial buildings, the position of the throne was not fundamentally altered through the abandonment of Angkor. Powerful families might combine to oppose the ruler's wishes on particular occasions, but the loyalty of the people was never in doubt. But so desperate did the threat from Ayudhya become in 1593 that one ruler seriously contemplated Christianity as a means of securing military aid. An appeal was made to the Spanish authorities in the Philippines, promising the adoption of the faith if sufficient assistance was forthcoming. In the event the king fled from Phnom Penh before the Spaniards could intervene and halt the invasion force of Naresuen, the Ayudhya king. Spanish mercenaries were subsequently on active service with the Cambodian army, and their introduction of firearms brought about a revolution in warfare. Useful though this foreign support may have been to an embattled Cambodia, the strategic weakness of the kingdom was its position, harried on two flanks by Thai and Vietnamese arms.

The practice of taking Siamese and Vietnamese princesses as royal brides in Phnom Penh inevitably produced two factions – one pro-Siamese, the other pro-Vietnamese. The loss of the western provinces of Battambang and Siem Reap can be attributed to their scheming, for Ang Eng was forced to take refuge in Bangkok because of internal strife. His accession to the Cambodian throne was confirmed by the Siamese king, Rama I, who sent him home in 1794 under the protection of an army. The commander of this Siamese force eventually withdrew from Phnom Penh, but on his master's instructions he continued to occupy the two western provinces. A second territorial loss to Vietnam in the south was brought about by factionalism after Ang Eng's death. No matter a Bangkok coronation in 1806, his son had to turn in 1811 and 1832 to the Vietnamese for help against Siamese-backed contenders. A Vietnamese force, stationed in Phnom Penh from 1833 onwards, even placed a Cambodian princess on the vacant throne two years later. From 1835 to 1841, she reigned over a Vietnamisation programme which aimed at reducing the country to a cultural satellite.

A full-scale war between Siam and Vietnam fought on Cambodian soil ended Vietnamisation through the accession of Ang Duong (1848–60). Concerned over the survival of his kingdom between these two rival powers, Ang Duong wrote to Napoleon III in 1853 seeking intervention and assistance, imagining in his innocence that France had no colonial designs of its own. Within a decade Cambodia was a protectorate attached to the expanding French empire on mainland South-East Asia. It was a subjection that lasted until the general French withdrawal in 1954, after the vain attempt to recover control following the Second World War.

THE SOUTHERN EXPANSION OF VIETNAM (1010–1885)

The Vietnamese 'march to the south' was very similar to that of the Chinese expansion within what are now the southern provinces of China. In both cases pressure on land, together with disturbances in the north, propelled people in a southerly direction. The Later Li dynasty (1010–1225) had formally begun the movement by annexing all Cham lands down to the 17th parallel, the border between the two Vietnams prior to the fall of Saigon in 1975. The equally long Tran dynasty which followed (1225–1400) kept up a steady pressure on Champa, despite suffering three Mongol invasions in the late thirteenth century. In 1306 the southern border had reached Danang, and further advance was halted only by a Cham counter-attack, which in 1371 sacked Hanoi. An unexpected consequence of this reverse was the brief reconquest of the Red river valley by the Ming emperor Yong Le. Resistance to this reimposition of Chinese rule was so fierce that in 1428 the existence of a separate state of Vietnam was recognised by Beijing in exchange for the acceptance of suzerainty.

The leader of the resistance, Le Loi, established the Later Le dynasty, which lasted from 1418 to 1789 and in its administration closely imitated that of imperial China. Even the official history of the dynasty was compiled as a chronicle in the Chinese language. Whenever envoys were dispatched to Beijing, the Vietnamese emperor was polite enough to refer to himself as a mere king but, at home, a ruler such as Le Thanh-ton (1460–97) was as absolute in his commands as the Son of Heaven himself.

During the period of the Chinese reoccupation of Vietnam the Chams had seized the chance to retake their lost territories. In 1441 they were pushed south again, and in 1471 the army of emperor Le Thanh-ton overran the whole of Champa, except for a few principalities which survived in the Mekong delta till the early eighteenth century. Pleased as the Vietnamese were to have beaten their old southern enemy, the acquisition of lands so distant from Hanoi brought with them serious problems of control, once migrants from the north discovered that by moving south they could largely escape government regulation. The long and narrow coastal strip, backed by an almost continuous chain of mountains, also worked against the maintenance of national unity. The situation was, futhermore, exacerbated through the contest between two great official families – the Trinh and the Nguyen. While the Trinh were powerful in the north, and especially around Hanoi, the Nguyen had carved out for themselves a power base in the south, with Hué as their headquarters. A line of feeble Vietnamese emperors would have given the Trinh unlimited scope for action had not the Manchu conquest of China brought a powerful new dynasty to the northern frontier. Emperor Qing Kangxi forcibly asserted his authority over south China, and then in 1683 he captured Taiwan, an island never before part of the Chinese empire. The Nguyen were less concerned about the displeasure of Qing Kangxi, and they welcomed Chinese refugees from the Manchus as settlers at Saigon, which was taken from the Chams in 1691. This unusual defiance of Beijing was possible for the Nguyen because of the distance overland from the Chinese border.

As neither the Trinh nor the Nguyen could win their dispute by the force of arms, the country was from 1674 onwards divided between two governments, both of which in theory owed allegiance to the powerless Le emperors. The division of Vietnam in almost the same manner as from 1954 to 1975 was confirmed by the building of two great walls just north of Hué. Both the Trinh and the Nguyen continued Chinese-style administrations in their separate territories, each adopting a calligraphy for the Vietnamese language based upon Chinese characters. Yet in the south, where scholars were far less numerous, Confucianism did not go unchallenged by the Buddhist church, which drew on Hinayana traditions inherited from Cham and Cambodian elements in the population.

The less regimented outlook of the southern Vietnamese was evident, too, in their earlier response to European contacts. Christianity was able to make headway in the seventeenth century with the arrival of Jesuit missionaries, looking for new fields of endeavour after the Tokugawa shogunate barred them from Japan. A later benefit of missionary activity was to be the adoption of *quoc-ngu*, the transliteration of Vietnamese in the Roman alphabet. This system of writing did not gain currency outside Catholic circles until the arrival of French colonial rule in 1862, when through translation it had the effect of opening Vietnamese literature up to outside influences. The masterpieces of Sino-Vietnamese literature date from the seventeenth and eighteenth centuries, and include adaptations of Chinese classics as well as original native works. The most prolific author was Le Qui Don (1726–83), an expert on every aspect of Chinese literature, who went as an envoy to Beijing in 1759 and wrote an interesting account of the visit.

The reunification of Vietnam under one ruler was indirectly abetted in 1771 by the Tayson rebellion, named after a district inland from Hué. Three brothers – Nguyen Van Nhac, Nguyen Van Lu, and Nguyen Van Hue – raised the standard of revolt, to which hundreds of thousands of discontented Vietnamese flocked. The rebels captured Saigon in 1776, and after wresting power from the Nguyen family in the south, they attacked the Trinh family in the north and by 1786 were masters of Hanoi. The Trinh appealed to the Qing emperor Qianlong for military assistance, but Tayson forces routed in 1789 the Chinese army he sent southwards on the Vietnamese frontier. Hardly more fortunate in his appeal for foreign aid was Nguyen Anh, the surviving heir of the Nguyen family. He asked a French missionary to arrange an alliance with Louis XVI, but events in France prevented its ratification. The Revolution did not prevent, however, volunteers from the French Navy from helping Nguyen Anh to defeat the rebels: Hué was retaken in 1801, Hanoi itself in the next year, so that in 1803 once again China gave its recognition to a reunited Vietnam. Four Nguyen emperors effectively reigned from 1802 to 1883, the year in which the French ended Vietnamese independence. Subsequently puppet rulers were sometimes placed on the throne by the French and the Japanese, till the dynasty expired with the dismissal of Bao Dai in 1955.

The second Nguyen emperor, Minh-Mang (1820–41), pursued an anti-Catholic policy and managed to keep at bay a France still exhausted from the Napoleonic Wars. He also intervened directly in Cambodian affairs, trying from 1832 onwards to impose a Vietnamisation programme on that country. His ultimate intention seems to have been the settlement of the country with Vietnamese colonists. Fortunately for the Cambodians Siam frustrated this arrogant scheme, even though like the Vietnamese they too were soon to suffer a not dissimilar fate from a resurgent France.

The government of Napoleon III used reports of the persecution of Catholics as a pretext for action, since French business interests were not averse to the establishment at Saigon of a port capable of serious competition with the British possessions of Singapore and Hong Kong. In 1858 a joint Franco-Spanish expedition attacked

Danang, and in the next year the French themselves occupied Saigon. A Vietnamese siege of the city was too good an excuse to miss, and French forces returning in 1861 from victorious operations alongside the British in the Second Opium War against China were diverted to southern Vietnam. As a result Hué was compelled to cede to France three southern provinces in 1862, shortly after which a French protectorate was declared over Cambodia. Further pressure in the north led in 1874 to a second treaty, announcing Vietnam's complete independence from any foreign power and granting it French protection. China naturally protested, pointing out that Vietnam had been in its sphere of influence for two millenniums. In 1885 the Chinese statesman Li Hongzhang and a French minister confirmed the loss of suzerainty over Vietnam, in part because at that time China had bigger fears about Korea, where a modernised Japan was putting together the beginnings of a mainland empire. The fate of distant Vietnam was less crucial to imperial defence, yet Beijing could not but sigh at the passing of yet another East Asian kingdom into European hands.

BURMESE SUCCESS AND FAILURE (1287-1886)

The perennial instability of states in Burma derives in large measure from its heterogeneous population. Geography has combined with a number of different ethnic groups to weaken the periodic attempts to secure national unity. The Burmans first became dominant by establishing Pagan, a kingdom which united the country from 1044 to the Mongol sack of 1287. Foreign intervention shattered Burman supremacy, but the fall of Pagan allowed the Mon people in the south at Pegu to reassert briefly their independence too. Not until the Toungoo dynasty (1486–1752) arose could the Burmans recover their once dominant position as rulers of a single Burmese state.

After the Mongol attack, Thai adventurers took control of much of Burma, even in the Mon homeland where at Martaban a strong kingdom came into existence on the coast. One of its early rulers reduced Pegu to dependence, and another moved the capital there in 1369. But the reunification of Burma commenced when the second Toungoo king, Tabinshweti (1531–50), conquered the whole of southern Burma and was in 1541 crowned at Pegu. That year he had taken Martaban, after a long siege, and occupied the coast as far south as Tavoy. The real strength of Tabinshweti's army lay in his ruthless mercenaries, companies of hard-bitten Portuguese who fought alongside equally tough Muslims from Java and India. Criticism of the Portuguese by Burman officers resentful of their royal favour could not obscure the advantage of adding up-to-date weaponry to traditional South-East Asian battle tactics. The range and accuracy of the matchlock was to prove most effective against the Shans, the Thai-speaking people of northern Burma, whose containment was essential to any Burman attempt at domination once more.

Having marched as far south as the port of Tavoy, Tabinshweti turned northwards against Prome, which surrendered after another siege. By 1546 he had extended his authority from the fortified city of Toungoo, in the Sittang river valley, to encompass all of Burma except the Arakan, where after the fall of Pagan a separate kingdom had emerged. A move against its capital, Mrohaung, was foiled by a clever defensive campaign and news of an Ayudhya attack on Tavoy. Tabinshweti's own counter-attack on Ayudhya in 1548 failed, despite an expeditionary force which included 500 war-elephants, an artillery train, and a crack unit of 500 Portuguese armed with matchlocks. The unexpected reverse encouraged Tabinshweti's Mon guards to assassinate him, and lead a general rising by non-Burman peoples.

Bayinnaung (1551–81), the brother-in-law of the dead king, had to rebuild the Toungoo empire by conquest, a process he accelerated through supplementing his forces with Thai-speaking auxiliaries, who joined his army in large numbers after Ava fell in 1555. Then, augmented by this extra Shan manpower, Bayinnaung twice conquered Ayudhya, in 1564 and 1569.

The protracted struggle between Burma and Thailand, in its earlier incarnations of Ayudhya and Siam, had a definite economic cause. Apart from the prisoners of war who became useful slaves, military dominance gave access to the manpower of the Thai-speaking states of Lan Na and Lan Sang. Bayinnaung conquered Lan Na and threatened Lan Sang: he also challenged Ayudhya commerce at sea with the construction of a navy. But the revival of Ayudhya under Naresuen spelt disaster for Bayinnaung's son, Nandabayin (1581–99), when his invasion force was soundly beaten in 1593 at Nong Sarai. As soon as Nandabayin sought to raise fresh troops to renew the attack, able-bodied men joined Buddhist monasteries, hid in the jungle, or fled to neighbouring states. Their flight underlined a fundamental weakness of the Toungoo empire, for its ruler exercised only indirect control over conquered territories.

Another intractible problem was the composition of the imperial

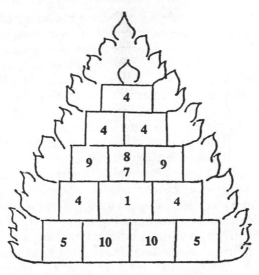

Fig. 39. Lotus battle array. This formation gave the Thai victory over the invading Burmese in 1593 at the battle of Nong Sarai

1. Commander-in-chief
2. Main army
3. Foot guards
4. Infantry, lightly armed
5. Spearmen
6. Infantry, with shields and swords
7. Archers
8. Cavalry
9. Elephants
10. Reserve troops

army, especially since the percentage of Mon soldiers in the ranks rose as replacements for casualties were hurriedly enlisted. In desperation Nandabayin reviewed the numbers of the Buddhist clergy and scrutinised the lay census records. To ensure an accurate count, he even ordered that all men were to be tattooed. But these emergency measures did little to stop the movement of people, or inhibit the spread of rebellion. The port of Moulmein rose and, with the aid of Ayudhya troops, repulsed a counter-attack from Pegu. The destruction of the imperial capital followed, and Nandabayin died a rebel prisoner in 1599.

The period of disorder ended in 1613 with the capture of Tavoy, then in alliance with Ayudhya. Another coastal city retaken by Nandabayin's grandson, Anaukpetlun, was Syriam, downstream from modern Rangoon. There, sometime before 1604, the Portuguese adventurer Filippe de Brito y Nicote had set up a fortified base in order to conduct raids on the interior and coastal traffic. As a punishment for looting Buddhist temples, de Brito was impaled on an iron stake. However, Anaukpetlun decided to spare his soldiers skilled in the use of cannon and firearms, and for 150 years their descendants were to be responsible for Burma's artillery.

Anaukpetlun's restoration of the Toungoo empire was safe-guarded by his successor Thalun (1629–48), who seems to have recognised the need for consolidation. He accepted the independence of Ayudhya and sensibly chose to ignore the sanctuary it offered to Mon refugees. External relations were endangered in 1662 only when a Manchu army crossed from the Chinese province of Yunnan in pursuit of a Ming pretender. The invaders soon withdrew, and friendship between Beijing and Ava was normal at least till the 1760s. Then the Qing emperor Qianlong sent four expeditions against Burma, and others against Nepal and Vietnam. Freed from military action on the northern frontier, he determined to assert the influence of the Chinese empire again in the far south.

But Toungoo authority had already disappeared prior to the renewed attacks from China. The fall of the dynasty in 1752 was due to a combination of forces inside and outside Burma. From 1724 onwards the Indian state of Manipur, which had been a vassal of Bayinnaung, raided the western frontier, weakening Ava at a time of acute unrest among the Mons of Pegu. Although the Mons took the capital in 1752, the garrison they left behind was weak, and Alaungpaya, a local Burman leader, reoccupied it in the name of the old dynasty. By 1755 his army of reunification had penetrated southern Burma, where he announced the imminent end to fighting in the name he gave Rangoon, which means 'the enemy is consumed'. Alaungpaya went on to invade Manipur and Ayudhya before he died on campaign in 1760.

The Konbaung dynasty that Alaungpaya finally founded continued on a belligerent course. His second son, Hsinbyushin (1763–76), led a well-planned attack on Ayudhya, which totally devastated the city in 1767. Hsinbyushin's brother, Bodawpaya (1781–1819), sent armies against the Thai on four more occasions, but under the Chakri dynasty Siam effectively parried these Burmese thrusts. Western expansion at the expense of Arakan, Manipur and Assam brought the Konbaung dynasty into conflict with the English East India Company, which was well entrenched in nearby Bengal. The First Anglo-Burmese War of 1824–6 began with a surprise seizure of Rangoon. It was ended, as were the subsequent wars of 1852 and 1885, with the cession of territory. Fear of French encroachment in northern Burma eventually led to the British imposition of colony status in 1886. An aggressive policy to help trade and industry was the work of Lord Salisbury, who had informed the Governor-General of India that he should let 'no other European power insert itself between British Burmah and China. Our influence in that country ought to be paramount. The country itself is of no great importance, but an easy communication with the multitudes who inhabit Western China is an object of national importance.' Thus Burma was incidentally annexed to the Indian empire.

THE COMING OF ISLAM (1292-1515)

For the inhabitants of what today are the states of Malaysia and Indonesia the great medieval event was the spread eastwards of the Muslim faith. Despite the significance of this conversion, documentary evidence of its progress remains scarce, and Islamic inscriptions on tombstones have to be supplemented with travellers' tales, few of which can be judged as entirely reliable. The oldest surviving inscription, which dates from 1082, was found in eastern Java, but there is doubt about its provenance because the deceased person appears to have been a foreign Muslim. The earliest Muslim ruler in the Indonesian archipelago may have been Malik as-Salih, the sultan of Semudera, a trading state in northern Sumatra: his gravestone offers the date of 1297 as the close of his reign.

Propagation of Islam in South-East Asia probably had to await its firm establishment in India, where in 1208 a Muslim dynasty came to power in Delhi. Headway in the conversion of South-East Asian peoples was made only when the new religion was introduced to them by Indian believers, previous contact with Arab merchants having scarcely any effect at all. The permanent settlement of Indian traders in Sumatra would have encouraged the spread of Islam, if only because their children were raised as Muslims. By the visit of the Moroccan traveller Ibn Battuta in the 1340s, the court of Semudera was thoroughly versed in Islamic law.

The development of Malacca as the major entrepôt for South-East Asian trade in the fifteenth century did much to diffuse Islam throughout the Indonesian archipelago. Situated in present-day Malaysia, the port of Malacca enjoyed a better location for international commerce than Majapahit, the Hindu-Buddhist kingdom of eastern Java. During the century following the abortive Mongol attack of 1292, Majapahit had held sway over most of the islands, an empire compared in extent by Javanese chroniclers of the day to that of China. Its architect was Gajah Mada, prime minister of Majapahit from 1331 to 1364, who formalised Javanese control of the spice trade by means of a system of annual tribute. Vassals who failed to present their quota of gifts to Majapahit were visited by a naval squadron. Until the twelfth century the Moluccas, the volcanic islands which produced mainly clove and nutmeg, had taken practically no part in political affairs, for the inhabitants were unaware of the market value of their natural resources. They were eventually drawn into the Javanese sphere of influence, which expanded in the Indonesian archipelago at the expense of Srivijaya, after that Sumatran kingdom was weakened through a combination of outside attack and internal revolt.

A war of succession weakened the kingdom of Majapahit at the very time Malacca was founded in 1402. Threats from either the Thai or the Javanese were negligible though, once the ruler of Malacca sought and received Chinese protection. To protect themselves when they called there, the Chinese constructed a double stockade around their warehouses and granaries, strengthened with towers at four main gates. Though politically immature, Malacca was rapidly becoming a focal point for East-West commerce, with routes extending to India, Persia, Arabia and Europe, to the Indonesian archipelago, and to China and Japan. Such an economic prize was bound to attract other powers after the Ming emperors decided on the rundown of the Chinese navy. An anti-maritime policy in Beijing from 1433 onwards removed East Asian power from the southern and the eastern seas, and gave the Portuguese, the Spaniards, the Dutch, and finally the English, the false impression that they were the first sailors to reach the Indonesian archipelago.

10

EUROPEAN COLONIAL INTERLUDE

From the Arrival of the Portuguese
to the Pacific War
(1511–1941)

In the course of the sixteenth century Europeans arrived in East Asia to found trading colonies, prompting a change in man's perception of the world. Prior to the circumnavigation of the globe, contact between the peoples at the extremities of the Old World had been indirect. Spices were believed in medieval Europe to come from the Earthly Paradise, a fabulous land credited by contemporary geographers to be the source of four great rivers – the Ganges, Tigris, Euphrates, and Nile. Marco Polo's account of his journey to and from the court of Kublai Khan whetted the appetite of merchants for direct contact with China and the East Indies, but only with the arrival of Portuguese and Spanish vessels in eastern waters could any coherent map of the world be drawn.

How dramatic was the alteration in outlook caused by maritime exploration can be glimpsed in the effect of Ferdinand Magellan's arrival off the Moluccas in 1521. By sailing to the Indonesian archipelago in a westerly direction, he violated the papal bull of 1493 that had divided the world between Spain and Portugal along a line west of the Azores. Assuming the earth to be flat, the Pope had no reason to expect that Spanish vessels headed westwards and Portuguese eastwards would ever meet on the other side of the globe. Circumnavigation proved him wrong and forced a revision of the papal bull in 1529, when the Spaniards gave up their position in the Moluccas in exchange for the Portuguese undertaking to allow the Spanish conquest of the Philippines.

Although Magellan lost his life in a violent encounter in the Philippines, his ship, *Victoria*, brought the first cargo of cloves directly from the Moluccas to Europe, where it was sold at a profit of 2500 per cent. This transaction made the Portuguese realise that it was essential to tighten their grip on the spice trade through an agreement with the sultan of Ternate, one of the smaller clove-producing islands. But the attempt to regulate spice production was largely a failure, as rising demand only encouraged the spread of cultivation to other islands. Another reason for Portuguese ineffectiveness was the rapacious behaviour of the adventurers who manned the semi-official strongholds.

The Portuguese intrusion in East Asia began, as did the British later on, with establishments in India. Vasco da Gama made landfall at Calicut on the west coast of the subcontinent in 1498, and declared that he had come 'to seek Christians and spices'. It was believed erroneously at the time that one of the apostles, Saint Thomas, had converted many Indians to Christianity. Trade and religion were two sides of the same coin, the untold wealth of the Orient so desired by the conquistadores. Attacking Muslim merchant ships, sacking ports and seizing strongholds could be justified in terms of the old argument between the Cross and the Crescent in the Ibernian peninsula: for Granada, the last Muslim stronghold there, had been conquered by Christian arms as recently as 1492.

The task of wresting control of the Indian Ocean from the Muslims was completed by the greatest of all the conquistadores, Alfonso de Albuquerque (1459–1515), who occupied Goa in 1510, Malacca in 1511, and Ormuz, the island at the mouth of the Persian Gulf, in 1515. He arrived in India at the very moment when the first Portuguese ship that had been sent to Malacca returned with news of its hostile reception. Setting sail with 1200 men in seventeen ships, Albuquerque invested Malacca in June 1511, only to discover its ruler was well supplied with cannon and Muslim mercenaries. Two attacks miscarried, with a heavy loss of life, and the defenders were overwhelmed only through a surprise assault at night. Critical assistance in this risky stratagem was forthcoming from Chinese and non-Muslim residents, whose property Albuquerque scrupulously spared. The victorious viceroy told his men:

We shall perform a great service for our Lord in casting out the Moors from this place and quenching the fire of the sect of Muhammad so that it may never be rekindled. As for trade, I am certain that if we take Malacca away from the Muslims, Cairo and Mecca will be made bankrupt and Venice will receive no spices unless her merchants go and buy them in Portugal.

Courage and fanaticism aside, Portuguese success depended upon their advantage in firepower. Their cannon outgunned all opponents, including the Chinese, who for centuries had led the world in the use of gunpowder. Portuguese muzzle-loaders were less likely to burst, their trajectories were longer and more accurate, and their shot was heavier than those of East Asian cannon of equivalent weight. The first Portuguese ships put into the southern Chinese port of Guangzhou in 1514, but the violent and ungovernable behaviour of their crews soon led to serious clashes, which were not contained until nearby Macao was leased in 1557 as a trading base.

Portugal's strategy of dominating the seaborne trade of East Asia by establishing bases at crucial points was dictated as much by its own weakness in manpower as by the strength of the states that its forces encountered. With a population of one million, there were never sufficient replacements to be sent out to cover losses from shipwreck, disease and war.

The Portuguese could expect to make little permanent progress, unless local antagonisms offered allies as a counterbalance in the wars they waged. In fact, they steadily lost ground while the authority of the Spaniards was extended further south from the Philippines, where in 1571 they declared Manila a Christian city. They would have taken over direct control of the Moluccas had not an event in the Iberian peninsula rendered the move unnecessary: in 1580 Philip II of Spain united Portugal to his throne.

Fig. 40. A Chinese picture of a European taking aim with a musket. The advent of this weapon, often in the hands of Portuguese and Spanish mercenaries, marked the beginnings of colonial expansion from Europe

An unforeseen consequence of Portuguese activity was the further spread of Islam, not least for the reason that the local population worked to keep the spice trade from falling into Christian hands. Equally unexpected was the impact of Portuguese weaponry, once local manufacturers learned to copy reliably for their own use. Just as lethal were the interventions of Portuguese mercenaries in the wars between the Burmese and the Thai.

More effective, and lasting in effect, was the Spanish conquest of the Philippines, the only Asian country today with a Christian majority. Dreadful though the brutality of its Spanish conquerors undoubtedly was, they mitigated their oppression of the indigenous peoples by intermarrying with converts. The effect of conversion in lowering the barriers between rulers and ruled would have been even greater had not the Spanish authorities decreed in the eighteenth century that only priests were allowed to live in the countryside.

From the start of colonial rule in the Philippines the propagation of Christian faith was cited as justification for annexation to the Spanish empire. In 1571 Manila became the centre of government and the headquarters of missionary enterprise, an event that arrested the further spread of Islam northward. The fiercest opponents of colonial rule were always the Filipino Muslims, the so-called Moros of the southern islands of Mindanao and Sulu. Christian settlements were planted there to deter Muslim raids on Luzon, the island on which Manila stands, but not until the 1830s did the Spaniards halt them completely.

On the arrival of the Spaniards the inhabitants of the Philippine archipelago lived in widely scattered communities, a circumstance that explains the many dialects still in existence. Lacking the natural commodities sought by Arab, Chinese and Indian merchants, the Philippines had remained isolated from international trade, while after the imposition of colonial rule commercial links were closer with Spanish possessions in the Americas than with East Asia. Their loss in the early nineteenth century made the Philippines even more of an economic backwater, as a colony so remote from Spain was a drain on its dwindling resources. Yet export business had never been very buoyant: the first shipment to Spain of tobacco and indigo dates from as late as 1784, and represents a transfer of tribute in kind rather than the beginnings of commercial agriculture. Most trading activities were conducted by Chinese immigrants, who weathered periodic Spanish persecutions to maintain a limited exchange overseas. The last serious attack on the Chinese community occurred during the Spanish recovery of Manila in 1762, when the merchants were blamed for their co-operation with the British, who had occupied the city for two years.

Perhaps it was fitting that an English visitor, Sir John Bowring, should sum up Spanish rule by recording in 1859 the opinion of a Filipino: 'The governor-general is in Manila (far away); the king is in Spain (farther still); and God is in heaven (farthest of all), but the priest is everywhere.'

DUTCH MARITIME SUPREMACY

Between 1580 and 1640, when Portugal was under the Spanish crown, the dispersed territories belonging to the Portuguese were neglected, in part because Philip II had decided that the two colonial empires of Spain and Portugal should remain separately administered entities. A satisfactory outcome to the wars that he, and his successors, waged in Europe would have freed ships and men for overseas service, but the naval disasters against the English in 1558 and the Dutch in 1639 seriously undermined Iberian seapower, and left ample scope for any European power intent on securing a major share of long-distance world trade.

The colonial war began in 1598 with Dutch attacks on Portuguese strongholds in Africa. Seven years later Dutch warships had reached the Moluccas, from which they expelled the Portuguese. A Spanish counter-offensive from the Philippines had to be repulsed by the Dutch, before they could gain the upper hand in the Indonesian archipelago over intruding English vessels and in 1641 take the greatest prize of all, Malacca, from the Portuguese. Through these hard-fought campaigns the Dutch East India Company, which had been founded in 1602, assumed almost complete control of the spice trade. But the war did not remain confined to South-East Asia, as the Dutch East India Company successfully challenged Portuguese merchants in Japan too. They achieved this goal by eschewing all missionary activity, a calculated policy that was condemned by their enemies as a cynical accommodation with Japanese superstition. Tired of religious conflict and suspicious of foreign interference, the Tokugawa shogunate welcomed Dutch circumspection, expelling in a short time both the Spaniards and the Portuguese. Under Japanese pressure the English had already shut down their factory in 1623.

On the island of Taiwan the Dutch East India Company set up a fortified trading post, where silks, porcelain and drugs could be stored. Interference from the Spaniards in the Philippines was halted by an energetic blockade of Manila, but a similar move against the Portuguese in Macao failed miserably. The governor-general, Jan Pieterszoon Coen, dispatched in 1622 sixteen ships and 1300 men to capture this Portuguese base in southern China. They were driven off with heavy losses, and resorted to piracy against Chinese coastal vessels, until the Ming emperor acceded to a request for a Dutch factory at the nearby port of Guangzhou. The savage treatment meted out to crews of Chinese trading craft taken by the Dutch served only to confirm prejudices in Beijing about the uncivilised character of Europeans. As a contemporary Chinese wrote: ·

The Dutch are Ocean Devils. They are greedy and cunning, knowledgeable about commerce, and clever in striking a bargain. They will risk their lives, and sail anywhere, in the pursuit of profit . . . If one has the misfortune of meeting them at sea, one is certain to be robbed by them.

The forcefulness of Coen's governorship of the Indies derived from his sense of the precarious position of the Dutch. His naval strength was insufficient to stamp out smuggling in spices and, more dangerous still, there was competition to be faced from the English, whose anti-Spanish sentiments could not be expected to encompass the transfer of a trade monopoly from Iberia to the Low Countries. The governor-general's advice was to guarantee the interests of the Company by the foundation of Dutch settlements, and the sending out of a large fleet to capture Manila and Macao.

Despite the promise of Japanese mercenaries, the Dutch East India Company decided to reject his mailed-fist approach and consolidate its authority in the Indonesian archipelago and Taiwan. The reluctance of Dutchmen to settle permanently in East Asia thwarted Coen's ambitions, and he even considered the wholesale abduction of Chinese settlers, since they were both industrious and unwarlike.

But the prime objective of the Dutch East India Company was trade rather than territory. Direct administrative responsibility was to be avoided at all costs unless the territory was of strategic importance. Occupation of the Javanese city of Jakarta, restyled Batavia after the ancient name for Holland, provided a good enough centre for operations after 1619: its fortifications were proof against the Muslim state of Bantam in western Java, so that ships sailing direct from the Cape of Good Hope found safe anchorage on first landfall. This route from the station at Cape Town remained the preferred one, even though the Straits of Malacca were soon in Dutch hands.

Fig. 41. A heavily armed Dutch vessel as seen in the seventeenth century in Chinese waters

With the English involved in their Civil War, the Dutch East India Company faced no effective rival in East Asia, an opportunity its warships exploited to acquire a supremacy in international trade that lasted for over a century. As one English commentator remarked at the time:

For it seems a wonder to the world that such a small country, not fully so big as two of our shires, having little natural wealth, victuals, timber or other necessary ammunitions, either for war or peace, should notwithstanding possess them all in such extraordinary plenty . . . by their industrious trading . . . from all the quarters of the world.

Although the Javanese states of Bantam and Mataram both resisted the rise of Dutch power, their mutual distrust ruled out concerted opposition, and by the beginning of the eighteenth century their sultans were Company nominees. Other rulers found themselves drawn into the same system of indirect rule, until the only free state was fanatically Muslim Atjeh in northern Sumatra.

The Napoleonic Wars could have ended Dutch authority overseas. When Holland was occupied by the French, the head of the Dutch state took refuge in England and ordered his colonial authorities to accept British control for the duration of the war. The order was resisted in Java and the island fell to sixty British warships in 1811. The British governor, Thomas Stamford Raffles, did much to reform the administration during his period of office, but the inflexibility of one of his officers in Yogyakarta precipitated a conflict that altered fundamentally colonial relations in the Indonesian archipelago. The destruction of the Yogyakarta court by force of arms deeply humiliated the Javanese aristocracy, and encouraged its more discontented members to lead the later popular uprising against the Dutch, whose return was confirmed by the Anglo-Dutch Treaty of 1824.

Resentment at changes in taxation and land law erupted at Yogyakarta the following year and engulfed Java in a bloody war. Before the rebel leader, Dipanagara, was overcome in 1830 at least 200,000 Javanese had died, against a loss of 8000 Dutch soldiers. Shaken by the war, and heavily in debt through its unexpected length, the colonial government that had replaced the Dutch East India Company determined to raise extra money by the introduction of the *cultuurstelsel*, or 'culture system'. The invention of Johannes van den Bosch (governor-general, 1830–3), the system required the Javanese peasant to devote one-fifth of his land or sixty-six working days each year for the cultivation of export crops for the Dutch authorities. The island thus became a huge estate on which the indigenous people toiled for the benefit of the colonial government. Between 1831 and 1877 the profit amounted to 825 million guilders, the bulk of which was remitted to Holland to pay for debts arising from the revolt of Belgium. In rejecting what he termed the 'perverted liberalism' of Raffles, van den Bosch renewed the segregation policy that had always underpinned Dutch rule in South-East Asia. Settlers who took local wives were not allowed to return to Holland, other than in a few exceptional cases. By 1716 the ban had been extended to Dutchmen who used female slaves as concubines, although the Dutch East India Company was not averse to training their children as artisans – in the relentless pursuit of profit.

Voices were raised on behalf of the oppressed Indonesians, but the horrors of the culture system were not properly exposed in Holland until the publication of Eduard Dekker's *Max Havelaar*. The author of this novel had served as an official in Java and, if we accept his own version of the story, was dismissed from his post because he defended the ordinary people against official extortions. In 1860 he wrote that he wanted to be read 'by members of the House of Representatives, who ought to know what is going on in the great Empire beyond the seas which belongs to the Realm of the Netherlands'. In 1864 liberal politicians began to abolish the culture system, although the valuable coffee crop was still grown this way as late as 1917.

The Dutch conscience gradually awoke, and gave birth to the

so-called ethical policy, which included improvements in health, education and agriculture. Its impact was greatly reduced by population growth: from 6 million in 1825, the number of Javanese had risen by 1900 to 28 million. Dutch businessmen were not deterred, however, from investment in Indonesia, since they saw that any rise in living standards would open up a new market. Between the British doctrine, which aimed ostensibly at the political education of the colonies in preparation for eventual self-government, and the French notion of assimilation, the Dutch persisted in their middle way of commercial exploitation. But the colonial government in Batavia could not ignore the American take-over of the Philippines, and the belief expressed by President McKinley in 1900 that Filipinos had a right 'to enjoy the blessings of freedom, of religious and civil liberty, of education, of homes'. The fact that the Filipinos then felt themselves ready for independence, and proclaimed as much in Manila, the United States was unable to accept immediately, doubtless to the profound relief of all the other colonial powers in East Asia. Imperial Japan was particularly fascinated by the spectacle of the Americans, the acknowledged advocates of national liberty, assuming a colonial role in the Philippines.

The idea that Asian nationalism would soon arise to prove far more formidable than the old pre-colonial states was beyond the ken of European officials and traders. Until the fiasco of the Second World War shattered the edifice of empire in East Asia, the position of the colonial ruler seemed unassailable, notwithstanding a rising murmur of dissent at the prolongation of imperialism in France and Britain. Yet the modernisation of the colonies was bound in itself to release new forces of opposition. In 1922 the Dutch may have tactfully replaced the term 'colony' with 'overseas territory', but the Indonesians were not deceived and within five years they had established the Perserikatan Nasional Indonesia, a party headed from the start by a young engineer named Sukarno (1901–70).

BRITISH EXPANSION (1786–1941)

When the French invaded Holland in 1795, Britain occupied Malacca and then Ambiona to keep these Dutch possessions out of French hands. But a blockade of Java could not be converted into a full-scale assault till after the fall of the main French base on Mauritius late in 1810. Governor-General Minto led the successful invasion and left Thomas Stamford Raffles (1781–1826) in complete charge of the island's defence and administration. Raffles's distaste for the oppressive rule of the Dutch, and his belief in the advantages to British trade of a less unjust administration, made it inevitable that his governorship of Java (1811–16) would be marked by a programme of reforms. For instance, the lifting of restrictions on the cultivation of crops quickly raised the standard of living of the Javanese peasant, who for the first time had enough cash to purchase British cottons.

Finding the Dutch in 1818 exercising once again their trade monopoly after the return of Java and Malacca, Raffles persuaded the English East India Company to annex a port 'possibly on the coast of the district of Johore at the eastern extremity of the Malay peninsula'. By its use as a staging post from India ships belonging to the Company, he argued, could proceed to China without crossing the Equator, the line dividing Dutch and British interests. The choice was inspired, for Raffles was right when he concluded that 'one free port in these seas must eventually destroy the spell of Dutch monopoly; and what Malta is in the West, that may Singapore be in the East.' Under the Anglo-Dutch Treaty of 1824 his planning received formal recognition in that Holland ceded Malacca and recognised the British claim to Singapore, while the British agreed not to enter into any treaties with rulers in the 'islands south of the Straits of Singapore.'

Intervention in the Malay states was slow and undertaken reluctantly. The end in 1833 of the English East India Company's privileged position in the China trade caused its officials in Calcutta to lose interest in the Straits Settlements of Penang, Malacca and Singapore. They continued to govern them, but without any wish to extend their responsibilities. This arm's-length policy allowed a private individual such as James Brooke (1803–68) to carve out a kingdom for himself in Borneo, an enormous island largely beyond the Dutch sphere of influence as delimited by the 1824 treaty. Fired by Raffles's *History of Java*, Brooke arrived at Kuching in his own ship in 1839 and offered his services to the local Malay ruler, the heir apparent to the sultanate of Brunei. These were welcomed in dealing with widespread disorder and in 1841 Brooke was appointed as governor of Sarawak. Support from HMS *Dido* and other British warships enabled the 'White Rajah' to suppress piracy and overawe the sultan of Brunei, who was obliged to offer in 1844 the island of Labuan as a port and coaling station. A permanent garrison was installed by Britain within two years. Brooke's own lucky survival of an uprising by Chinese tin miners in 1857 allowed the continuation of his dynasty, which steadily encroached on Brunei.

British interests were further secured in East Asia through the audacity of merchants dealing with China, who took full advantage of the English East India Company's loss of authority in Guangzhou. Because the Chinese government had ignored successive British trade missions, beginning with the polite rejection of Lord Macartney's embassy of 1793 and ending in an exchange of fire with Lord Napier's frigates in 1834, London disclaimed all responsibility for the transaction of trade, now entirely in private hands. The point at issue was the dumping of opium. So enormous had the imports of this drug become that the Qing emperor Dao Guang (1821–50) decided that something must be done – to save the economy from the export of silver and the population from the spread of addiction.

The resulting humiliation of the late Chinese empire in the conflict of 1839–42 sent a tremor round the world, and still casts a shadow over China's relations with Europe. The later pillage of Beijing in 1860 by an Anglo-French force under the command of Lord Elgin shocked all East Asia, and convinced the Japanese of their urgent need for modern technology.

The bullying tactics of Britain were skilfully used by Townsend Harris (1804–78), the first American minister in Tokyo, to persuade Japan to sign its first commercial treaty. Harris warned of the imminent arrival of British warships, and in the summer of 1858 agreement was reached prior to Lord Elgin dispatching a single gunboat from Tianjin. By the end of the year similar treaties had been signed with Holland, Russia, Britain and France. The Tokugawa shogunate was deeply embarrassed by this capitulation to foreign pressure, but it pointed the way to future policies under the Meiji restoration, when after 1868 the Japanese emperor presided over a systematic modernisation of the country. Although Japan still mistrusted Britain, the strongest naval power in East Asia, it was ready to accept British loans for its own industrial development. The British were also invited to assist in the organisation and training of the Japanese navy, a programme of co-operation that eventually resulted in the Anglo-Japanese Alliance of 1902. Admiral Togo Heihachiro (1847–1934), the victor over the Russians at Tsushima, studied at Greenwich Naval College in the 1870s. In that decisive battle most of the battleships he commanded came from British yards. But by 1922 Japan was able to build its own capital ships, including the first ship in the world to be built from the keel up as an aircraft-carrier.

The British choice of Japan as an ally was dictated by considerations for the balance of power on the East Asian mainland. Not only was a tottering Chinese empire falling under Russian sway in Manchuria, but in Shandong province even the Germans had won a naval base in 1898 at Qingdao, an acquisition that set off another series of demands for concessions. The new holding at Weihaiwei, on the northern tip of the Shandong peninsula, was Britain's response. It was made redundant by the defeat of the Tsar's ambitions in the Russo-Japanese War of 1904–5. Thereafter the British, and later the Americans, found themselves at a growing military and naval disadvantage to Japan. Both sought to maintain by diplomatic means the integrity of China as a republic, although it was hard to deny the territorial aims of the Imperial Japanese Army. The 1930 naval conference in London, which aimed at the limitation of navies, not only angered the military faction in Tokyo but set it on a course of extra-legal ventures in China which culminated in the entry of Japan into the Second World War.

With the previously friendly Japanese emerging as an enemy, the British government strengthened the defences of Singapore, as a bastion to be held until reinforcements arrived from Europe with the main fleet. Apart from Australia and New Zealand, the fortress at Singapore was needed for the protection of northern Borneo, Malaya, and Burma. The Colonial Office had taken over responsibility for these British territories after the dissolution of the English East India Company in 1858. Fear of imperial competitors and the requirement of peaceful conditions for trade produced this last advance of British power in South-East Asia. In the Malay states the resident system, established by Sir Andrew Clarke in 1874, formed a model for indirect rule. The sultans were obliged to accept as a permanent resident in their courts a British official, whose 'advice must be asked for and acted upon in all questions other than those touching Malay religion and custom'.

The wealth of Malaya was based on primary products such as tin and rubber, after the planting of rubber seeds, brought from Brazil via Kew Gardens, transformed the landscape and drew in labour from southern India. Tin was also dug by immigrants from China, who had moved into every South-East Asian country during the nineteenth century. Immigration to Malaya continued as late as 1936, when economic stagnation compelled the colonial government to close its borders. By 1942 the Brooke family in Sarawak ruled over 236,000 Chinese out of a total population of 750,000, which included several indigenous peoples. Conservative in outlook and uninterested in trade, the Malays were slow to develop a nationalist movement in comparison with their cousins in Dutch-ruled Indonesia.

Economic discontent, however, drove Burma into an early anti-colonial stance. The depression of the 1930s hit the rice industry severely and exacerbated tensions among its different peoples. Agitation became so violent that in 1935 the British separated the country from India and granted a degree of home rule. Japanese agents played upon the nationalist fervour of Burmese students, and in 1940 a group of thirty was secretly trained on the occupied Chinese island of Hainan as the nucleus of the Burma Indepen-

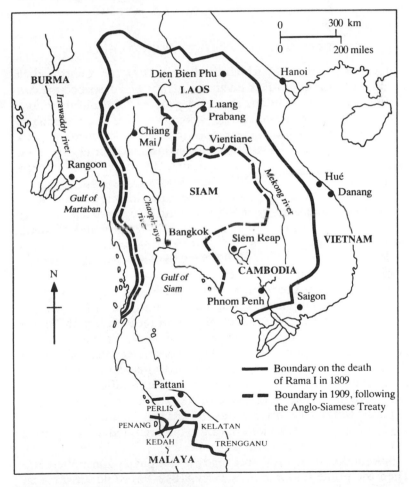

The shrinking of Siam, 1809–1909

dence Army. But its leading member, Maung Aung San (1915–47) was never impressed by fascism, and in 1944 he publicly criticised the behaviour of the Imperial Japanese Army in Burma. The good impression he made on William Slim, then in command of the British Fourteenth Army, caused the general to reflect that 'with proper treatment, Aung San would have proved a Burmese Smuts'. Japan was only interested in Burma because of the recently constructed road to China, a supply line for the Guomindang government besieged at Chongqing. As one of Aung San's followers told Slim: 'If the British sucked our blood, the Japanese ground our bones!'

THE FRENCH OCCUPATION OF INDO-CHINA

Indochine, the name by which the French knew the countries they occupied on the South-East Asian mainland, well described the two distinct historical traditions they endeavoured to amalgamate in a single empire. At its two extremes were Vietnam and Cambodia: the former, despite its long resistance to Chinese domination, was a country strongly influenced by Confucianism; the latter, though a shadow of its early glory, the lineal descendant of an Indian-inspired kingdom.

The French empire in Indo-China began with the annexation of the southernmost portion of Vietnam, the Mekong delta, in 1862. The treaty agreed between the emperors of France and Vietnam gave the French the right to navigate the Mekong, which was believed to rise in south-western China. Explorers had barely started to chart its course in 1863, when a French protectorate was declared over Cambodia at the request of its hard-pressed king. When the Second French Empire was toppled by Prussia in 1870 plans for expansion faltered, in spite of the continued efforts of Francis Garnier, an adventurer in the mould of James Brooke. News in London of his explorations on the Mekong river forced a forward British policy in Burma, while his armed intervention in the Red river valley opened northern Vietnam to French influence. Garnier was killed in action at the end of 1873 and, though the Third Republic was conciliatory towards the last real Vietnamese emperor Tu Duc (1847–83), Garnier's daring exploit resulted in the opening of the Red river to international commerce.

Not till the 1880s was France ready to completely annex Vietnam. Then the prime minister Jules Ferry (1832–92) could affirm 'that colonies in the present state of the world are best for business, as the place for investing the capital of an old and wealthy nation'. No satisfactory explanation has been given for this radical republican's espousal of imperialism, other than a blind belief in the value of long-term investment as 'the inheritance of our children'. Ferry chose to ignore the unpopularity of colonial expansion with French public opinion and the fact that profitable returns were more likely to come from capital invested in the newly independent countries of South America.

Unlike in Cambodia and Laos, where nationalism remained dormant until the end of the Second World War, a mass movement against the imposition of colonial rule grew steadily in Vietnam after its final conquest in 1885. A brutal campaign had crushed all outward sign of protest by 1913, but opposition was already taking on non-traditional forms, if only because resistance to all things French because they were foreign had ceased to be a practical option in a modern world.

Already Chinese-educated Vietnamese had responded positively to the reform programme in 1898 of Kang Youwei, an abortive attempt to salvage the Confucian empire in China; and showed sympathy for his more successful rival, the republican Dr Sun Yatsen. Japan's victory over Russia in 1905 drew among others to Tokyo the young Vietnamese scholar Phan Boi Chau (1867–1940), where he published his *History of the Loss of Vietnam (Viet Nam vong quoc su)*, which was circulated clandestinely throughout Vietnam. Having attained a first-class result in the civil service examinations, Phan Boi Chau rejected out of hand a French offer of an administrative post. His mission in life was not, he told his friends, to serve France: on the contrary, he aimed to end its colonial rule. Unfortunately, the desire of imperial Japan for European approval caused his expulsion, like that of Dr Sun Yatsen earlier, from Tokyo in 1910. Imprisonment at home subsequently dented the anti-French movement Phan Boi Chau hoped to lead and gave the colonial government a welcome respite. A fundamental weakness of his strategy was reliance on external help rather than on decisive action from the Vietnamese themselves.

A man who galvanised this irresistible force into action half a century later, Nguyen Sinh Cung (1890–1969), was in Europe protesting about the terms of the Versailles peace conference. Better known later as Ho Chi Minh, the placard-carrying nationalist decried the selective anti-imperialism that applied a doctrine of self-determination to East European nations, but no one else. Disillusioned by the double standards of colonialism, Ho Chi Minh, like other Vietnamese who travelled abroad, turned to Communism for the salvation of his country. Sent as a French delegate to the Moscow Peasant International in 1923, he quickly gained attention from the Soviet leadership and in 1924 was sent to Guangzhou, to organise a Communist movement from southern China. In 1930 he managed to unite three competing groups in Vietnam as the Indochina Communist Party, although there were hardly any members from Laos and Cambodia.

Since the acquisition by the Third Republic of a colonial empire, there had been advocates of an assimilation policy based on the long-established tradition of the unity and indivisibility of France. *La mission civilisatrice* was expected to overcome local sentiment through the admission of colonial peoples to the higher culture of metropolitan France, a notion more suited to the period of the French Revolution than the international rivalries of the late nineteenth and early twentieth centuries. As its critics were pleased to point out, the granting to all territories of the right, enjoyed only by the oldest among them, to send deputies to the French parliament would have incalculable results for politics in France. The result was an uneasy compromise: individual colonials could be assimilated, but for the majority the benefits of colonial rule would be limited to French protection. Even this was by no means certain, for in 1925 the governor-general of Indo-China used the death of the Nguyen emperor to reduce the throne to a cipher. His twelve-year-old successor, Bao Dai, was deprived of authority over justice, the cabinet, and the appointment of officials.

The turning-point in French-Vietnamese relations was reached in 1930, the year of nationwide protests against taxation, government monolopies, and the exploitation of labour. The French Foreign Legion put down the uprisings, strikes and demonstrations with such severity that only a tense truce could exist afterwards. Ngo Dinh Diem (1901–63), a moderate nationalist who later agreed to serve under a reformed monarchy as interior minister, resigned as soon as it became clear that the French were not prepared to share power. Colonial rule in Indo-China from 1933 onwards rested on naked force alone.

THE US COLONY IN THE PHILIPPINES

American domination in the Philippines was from the first intended to be a temporary phenomenon. Being an imperial power did not sit easy on the conscience of many Americans, themselves the first people to escape the clutches of European colonialism. The excitement of the Spanish-American War of 1898 quickly wore thin as the economic unimportance of the new colony became apparent. The Philippines offered neither an entry to the China trade, nor an exciting prospect for American investment. Administration costs were high, and the United States sustained the Filipino economy only by importing vast quantities of protected agricultural products such as sugar and coconut oil. American missionaries were equally disconcerted to discover that the Filipinos were Christians already, having been forcibly converted to Catholicism by Spain. The campaign to terminate colonial rule therefore succeeded in 1934, when Congress passed the Philippines Independence Act, which prescribed a preparatory period during which the colony was to be a semi-autonomous commonwealth under a government of Filipinos. The date for independence was scheduled for 4 July 1946.

The unease felt in the United States about imperialism may account for the significant failure to develop military and naval installations in the Philippines adequate to meet the threat from Japanese imperial expansion. Accidental though American policy in the Pacific may have been in its development, the potential enemy was long understood to be Japan. According to the Foreign Relations Committee's report at the time Hawaii was annexed, 'the present Hawaiian-Japanese controversy is the preliminary skirmish in the coming struggle between the civilisation and the awakening of the East and the civilisation of the West. The issue is whether, in that inevitable struggle, Asia or America shall have the vantage ground of the control of the naval "Key of the Pacific", the commercial "Crossroads of the Pacific".'

As if acknowledging in turn the truth of this statement, the Imperial Japanese Navy from 1909 onwards made the US Navy its sole imaginary enemy. Its planners concentrated on the main naval base at Pearl Harbor, which the United States had snatched from under the noses of the Japanese in 1897. With 20,000 Japanese already settled in Hawaii, Tokyo sent the cruiser *Naniwa* on regular visits to Honolulu in order to look after their interests. President McKinley was not to be denied such a strategic prize, however. He moved first and annexed Hawaii the year before the war with Spain brought American arms further east to the Philippines.

While the United States justified its annexation of the Philippines in terms of the maintenance of law and order as well as protection from foreign intervention, the Filipinos felt cheated, and early in 1899 American forces came under fire in Manila. An experienced insurgent against the Spaniards, Emilio Aguinaldo (1869–1964) declared national independence and took charge of the rebellion with guerrilla resistance continuing until 1902, shortly after Aguinaldo's capture. The cost of victory, 4200 US troops killed, enabled the Democrats to block the Rupublicans' expansionist policies. Almost discounted in the inter-party warfare were the 600,000 Filipinos estimated to have died in action or in prison on the main island of Luzon alone.

PART III

The Rise of the Pacific Rim

On 23 October 1868 the young emperor of Japan selected a slip of paper from among others placed before him. It bore the two characters 'bright' and 'rule', and thus gave his reign its name – Meiji. Although the characters were taken from an ancient Chinese book, the reformers who organised the Meiji restoration of imperial rule, after a lapse of more than a millennium, were not conservatives. They were anxious to modernise Japan as an urgent means of self-defence. Japanese weakness, even against the diminutive US Navy, led them to legitimise massive social and economic change. In its course their programme of borrowing from the West facilitated the formation of the Japanese empire, the outbreak of world war in East Asia, and the rise of what has become known as the Pacific Rim.

Japan's orderly transformation impressed would-be reformers in China. But the hopes of Kang Youwei for reform of the Chinese empire were to be frustrated as much by Japan as the forces of reaction at court, where a Manchu dynasty obstinately clung to power. A complication of modern East Asian affairs, by no means over today, is the aggressiveness of the Japanese. China was under siege until 1945 from both the West and a Western-style Japan. The subsequent triumph of the Chinese Communist Party can be attributed in part to the experience of the Japanese occupation. As Mao Zedong succinctly commented: 'The history of modern China is the history of imperialist aggression.'

If the period leading up to the Pacific War (1941–5) saw an accommodation with modern times, then East Asia's response to post-war opportunities indicates a fundamental renewal. Despite divisions introduced by US-Soviet rivalry during the Cold War, there has been a steady movement towards independence within a buoyant economic grouping. Hurt though the British were by the coldness of Malaysia during the 1980s, its premier had a point when he told London that his country had more to learn from Japan, South Korea and Taiwan. He might have added Singapore, had not that star of the Pacific Rim been too close to Kuala Lumpur for a Malaysian leader to mention without embarrassment. That the United States was indirectly responsible for much economic progress outside of the People's Republic of China there can be little doubt. The Korean War gave Japan its critical boost in the early 1950s, just as a decade later the conflict in Vietnam enriched Thailand, Singapore, South Korea and the Philippines. American expenditure in these two wars represented one of the greatest transfers of wealth from one part of the world to another in history.

The architect of Japan's post-war recovery, premier Yoshida Shigeru, referred to US military procurement during the Korean War as 'a gift from the gods'. An opponent of the Japanese attack on the United States and Britain, Yoshida Shigeru was wise enough to recognise the luck of his defeated country in having to bear only an American occupation. An episode of September 1945, recorded in his memoirs, is revealing:

My car was passing through a deserted avenue . . . when two GIs suddenly appeared and signalled my driver. I imagined them to be on some kind of marauding expedition, but they turned out to be soldiers returning to Tokyo who had lost their way, and they politely requested a lift . . . we had not proceeded far before they were pressing chocolates, then chewing-gum, and finally cigarettes upon me. The incident surprised and pleased me . . . I recall thinking at the time that it was this natural way of acting on their part, and the inherent good nature of the American, which enabled the Occupation of Japan to be completed without a shot being fired.

Another advantage bestowed by the Americans on Japan was a centralised planning system that continues on a lesser scale in the economic direction of MITI, the Ministry of International Trade and Industry. This engine of growth is a unique feature in an advanced industrial economy.

Mao Zedong agreed with Yoshida Shigeru's assessment of the ordinary American. Between the peoples of China and the United States, he maintained, there were 'strong ties of sympathy, understanding and mutual interest. Both are by nature peace-loving, non-aggressive and non-imperialistic'. (No doubt Ho Chi Minh took a different view.) But Washington's commitment to the Guomindang prevented dialogue from taking place, and East Asia was divided in 1949 on the lines it still is today.

11

IMPERIAL JAPAN

From the Meiji Restoration
to the Pacific War
(1868–1941)

The second half of the nineteenth century in Japan witnessed great changes. In the 1860s the country still was divided politically into numerous feudal domains under the ebbing authority of the Tokugawa shogun in Edo (Tokyo). By 1900 imperial Japan was the only modern state in East Asia, having abolished feudalism and imported from the West the institutions, finance and technology necessary for the establishment of an industrialised economy. Recognition of this new international status led Lord Salisbury to commit his government in 1902 to an Anglo-Japanese alliance. During the Boer War (1899–1902), the British Army in India was short of 11,000 men and the defence of its north-west frontier seemed perilous in the event of a Russian attack. Should this happen, Britain hoped for relief through a Japanese invasion of the Tsar's Pacific province.

The Japanese government welcomed the British initiative as an admission of its rightful place in East Asian affairs, although the refusal of Salisbury's cabinet to accept any demands over China had to be kept secret from the public. The enthusiasm of the Japanese press for an alliance with the world's leading naval power stemmed from memories of the humbling of the Tokugawa shogunate by American warships. Although Royal Navy vessels had visited Japanese waters in search of Dutch ships under Napoleonic control, the task of opening up the country to international commerce fell not to Britain, but to the United States. In 1853 a quarter of the

189

US fleet, eight frigates in all, sailed to establish relations with the Japanese government. Commodore Matthew Perry (1794–1858) forced the Japanese to accept a letter from the President of the United States to the Japanese emperor and then weighed anchor, promising to return in one year for an answer.

No sooner had the smoke cleared from Perry's departing 'black ships' than argument broke out as to the course of action that the shogun should adopt. Almost all agreed on the need for strengthening defences to meet the threat of foreign attack. On the question of foreign policy, however, opinion was sharply divided between those who believed in national isolation and those who considered it wise to open the country to outside influences. An advocate of the open policy was Sakuma Shozan (1811–64), a gunner who saw no other way of building up a modern navy. Having completed his study of the Confucian classics at Edo, the young samurai had with the aid of translated Dutch books taught himself how to cast cannon. Sakuma Shozan's advocacy of 'Eastern ethics and Western technology' was later echoed by the Chinese moderniser Li Hongzhang, a stalwart supporter of the declining Qing dynasty.

On Perry's return in 1854, the unusual method that Sakuma Shozan adopted to realise his ambition of a modern Japanese navy landed him in prison. It is likely that his punishment would have been execution had not influential members of the shogun's court interceded for Sakuma Shozan and his disciple, Yoshida Shoin (1830–59). With Sakuma Shozan's encouragement, Yoshida Shoin

Fig. 42. Commodore Perry. After a Japanese portrait painted in 1854

had tried to stow away on one of the American warships, only to be
handed over to the shogunal authorities before the vessel sailed. In
the book he wrote on release from prison, *Reflections on My Errors*
(*Seiken-roku*), Sakuma Shozan defended the attempt to reach the
United States by underlining the wretchedness of Japan's military
position: 'Should a national emergency arise, there is no one who
could command the respect of the samurai and halt the enemy's
attack. . . Now I propose the use of armoured warships to inter-
cept and destroy an enemy fleet before it can reach our shores.'

Sakuma Shozan was assassinated in 1864. His views had enraged
samurai who were opposed to an open policy. He was doubtless
associated by them with the pro-emperor teachings of Yoshida
Shoin, who accused the feudal hierarchy of treating their domains
like private kingdoms. The execution of Yoshida Shoin in 1859 on a
charge of plotting against the shogunate was inevitable. Yet his
death could not halt the movement for radical change; when the
shogunate was unable to determine a response to Perry's mission,
the question of foreign trade was referred to its vassals. This invitation to comment on policy was unprecedented, and the disagreements which ensued did more than anything else to undermine the
shogun's position. The majority of the daimyo urged outright rejection, an opinion shared with the imperial court at Kyoto. In despair,
the shogun concluded a treaty with Perry and compelled the
emperor to give it formal sanction, another unprecedented request.

The continued mismanagement of the economy by the shogunate, as well as the new expenses incurred through the construction of coastal defences and the purchase of foreign military
equipment, had to be met by imposing higher taxes on the peasant-
farmers and by demanding forced loans from merchants. Foreign
trade, regularised by commercial treaties with the United States,
Holland, Russia, France and Britain, was soon found to be unprofitable for Japan as well as a serious financial drain. The burden of
increased taxes and higher prices became intolerable, with the result
that a series of revolts broke out in the towns and the countryside.

The prestige of the shogunate was further lowered in 1863 by the
visit of Tokugawa Iemochi to Kyoto. A cavalcade of 3000 retainers
could not conceal the fact that this was the first time since the
seventeenth century that a shogun had been obliged to attend the
imperial court. So necessary did imperial sanction become for any
major decision that the last shogun of all lived in Kyoto for the
whole period of his office and felt he could not risk returning to
Edo. After a few months of frustration, he resigned his office in

November 1867, hoping by this conciliatory gesture that a reform movement would emerge to create a modern Japan. It did: first as an imperial competitor in East Asia, until its defeat in the Second World War; and then as the industrial superpower we know today.

The significance of the events that led to the shogun's resignation was not missed by foreigners. The British minister was convinced of the need for a resolution of the emperor-shogun relationship before Japan could attain stable government. Given the shogun's intractible difficulties with the daimyo, he cultivated these rebellious nobles as possible future power holders under imperial rule. It was even suggested that they should be members of a council of great lords, but the uncertainty of late 1867 caused only sixteen daimyo to arrive in Kyoto in response to a request for attendance. The French saw this failure as an opportunity to gain influence by backing the former shogun, whose supporters in Edo were pressing for military action against rebellious nobles, and especially those of Choshu and Satsuma. But these nationalistic western domains had already recovered from earlier attacks by shogunal forces and, armed with imported rifles, they struck first by seizing Kyoto in January 1868. An irregular imperial edict obtained from friendly elements at court justified the coup in terms of a restoration of imperial rule. The boy emperor Mutsuhito, or Meiji, was persuaded to proclaim the event as such, and in the ensuing weeks the 'imperial forces' of Choshu and Satsuma, augmented by large numbers of non-samurai volunteers, put all opposition to flight.

THE MEIJI RESTORATION (1868)

It is something of a paradox that the anti-foreign stance of Choshu and Satsuma should combine with the conservative imperial house to produce a government dedicated to the fullest extension of foreign exchange. At the time of the imperial restoration the coup seemed little more than a shift of power from one section of the aristocracy to another. Accustomed to figurehead emperors and shoguns, Japan hardly expected the events of 1867–8 to inaugurate a complete transformation of its economy and society. The motive power for change was the group of young samurai who took the initiative in formulating policy immediately after the collapse of Tokugawa power. Their programme is evident in the five articles of the Charter Oath announced in the name of the emperor:

1 Deliberative assemblies shall be widely set up and all issues decided by public discussion.
2 Everyone, high and low, shall actively unite in the administration of the state.
3 The common people, no less than the civil and military officials, shall be free to pursue whatever calling they chose so that harmony prevails.
4 Evil customs of the past shall be discarded and everything based on the just laws of Heaven and Earth.
5 Knowledge shall be sought throughout the world in order to strengthen the foundations of imperial rule.

The final article accounts for the long-range vision of Okubo Toshimichi (1830–78), one of the strongest of the Meiji leaders. A visit to Europe in 1871 confirmed his belief in the importance of internal order and systematic progress. So impressed was he with industrial Britain that on his return home he became the first Japanese to appear at court with Western clothes and hairstyle. Such enthusiasm for change led to the introduction of modern schools, a postal system, a census, military conscription, the telegraph, railways, banks, courts of law, steamships, income tax, electricity, a cabinet system, a constitution and, finally in 1890, a parliament. An international dividend was to be a revision of the unequal treaties imposed on Japan, and an escape from the semi-colonial status implicit in Western insistence on extra-territoriality and tariff control.

When after a lapse of nearly a millennium the Meiji emperor reassumed political authority in 1868, there were only 400 government soldiers in the imperial guard. The rest of its military strength was derived from Choshu and Satsuma samurai, as well as the irregulars who had rallied to the throne's defence. In 1873 the first Western-style conscript army was raised by the emperor. Uprisings protesting against conscription occurred at first amongst the peasantry, but within a decade all men in the armed forces were conscripts. As time passed and imperial Japan entered upon its phase of expansion overseas, military service became a useful channel for upward social mobility, so that in times of crisis the peasantry usually supported the military establishment rather than civilian leaders. The samurai, who had lost all their privileges by 1876, also came to accept the new system, playing an important role as officers in the army, which was designed after the Prussian model. The Imperial Japanese Navy made a slower start, for as late as 1889 its capital vessels comprised three British-made ironclads and three other ships made from a combination of wood and iron. It was modelled, however, on the Royal Navy and dominated by Satsuma men.

Preoccupied with material progress through national prosperity and defence, the Meiji government strove to develop the strategic industries on which modern military power depended. It took the lead, too, in developing modern communications, the extraction of raw materials, and the mechanisation of textile manufacture. By 1880 silk accounted for nearly half of Japanese exports, a welcome reversal of the deficit in textiles experienced during the years that followed the opening of the country to international trade. But the strain on the imperial exchequer proved too great, and in the financial retrenchment of the early 1880s most of government holdings were sold cheaply to supporters in the business community, even to officials. Once the initial difficulties of industrialisation were overcome, and the national economy put back on a steady course, the few Japanese who had been able to buy these government-sponsored enterprises exercised a powerful influence on affairs of state. By the 1920s they had evolved into financial combines (*zaibatsu*), such as Mitsui and Mitsubishi, each of which encompassed a great variety of enterprises, including banking, extractive industries, manufacturing companies, transportation, and trading firms. Mitsui began as provincial brewers in the early seventeenth century, turned to money-lending and became the official banker for the Tokugawa, besides establishing shops in Edo, Kyoto and Osaka. The successful transition to modern capitalism was achieved by Minomura Rizaemon (1821–77), the first non-family appointment to the post of general manager. He sent people to the United States in order to study modern business methods and then used their newly acquired knowledge to reorganise Mitsui into the largest zaibatsu company.

In contrast to historical development in the West, the Japanese experience of economic as well as constitutional change was not one of a rising bourgeoisie bent on enhancing its social and political rights. Rather, the sweeping transformation under the Meiji government was the work of an élite that had woken up to the danger confronting feudal Japan in the modern world. The promulgation of the constitution in February 1889 shows exactly how change was instituted from above. In a ceremony held in the audience chamber of the imperial palace, the emperor, the empress, courtiers, officials, and a few politicians all dressed in Western-style clothes, together with foreign diplomats, listened to the reading of the imperial decree of 'the present immutable fundamental law', which was promulgated in the name of the imperial ancestors. Afterwards the national anthem was sung, bells rang and cannon fired: the proceedings, which lasted barely ten minutes, gave Japan the 'Constitution of the Great Empire'.

An oligarchy had decided that the country was ready for an imperial constitution. The public neither knew, nor were allowed to know, what discussion had led to the choice. All they had to do was live within its framework, pay their taxes, develop the country, and serve in the armed forces. Although in 1881 public interest in a nationally elected assembly had caused the emperor to announce that he would grant a constitution, the length of time between the announcement and the promulgation is an indicator of the tight control exercised by the Meiji reformers over political development. They made no pretence that modernisation would lead to democracy. As Ito Hirobumi (1841–1909), the person responsible for selecting a German model, told presidents of prefectural assemblies in February 1889, a constitution by imperial edict

means that it was initiated by the Sovereign himself and that it was sanctioned and granted by the Sovereign. It is my hope that you will always remember this fact, and inscribe it on your hearts . . . Remember, too, that the nature of our government . . . its control and operation rests on sovereignty, which . . . is united in the august person of the Emperor.

Because cordial relations existed between the throne and the people, Ito Hirobumi later asserted, the constitutional position of Japan was totally different from that of England, whose Magna Carta was elicited from a tyrannous king by barons at the point of a sword.

What Ito Hirobumi chose not to mention was the closeness of conditions in contemporary Germany and Japan. Arising from the defeat of France in the war of 1870, Bismark's empire was an autocratic government thinly disguised with some democratic institutions of no real power. For like the Japanese, the Germans were a warlike people who valued might and held their soldiers in the highest esteem. The similarity was not lost on the American press, which otherwise praised the Japanese as 'Asiatic Yankees'.

Prior to the reading of the imperial edict in 1889 the emperor participated in a private Shinto ritual. Designed ostensibly to reassure the imperial ancestors and the gods that the new constitutional arrangements about to be announced were going to preserve the ancient form of government bequeathed by them to the country, this ritual was part of the making of a modern myth concerning the unbroken ancestral tradition of the imperial house. Even the day itself made a contribution as the anniversary of the accession of the first emperor, a legendary event which had been miraculously pushed back to a date 2,549 years earlier. Ito Hirobumi was an advocate of this mythology because he looked upon the imperial house as the 'cornerstone' of Japan. Without religion, Ito Hirobumi felt, 'politics will fall into the hands of the uncontrollable masses'. Since Buddhism was in decline and Shinto too weak on its own, the elevation of the emperor's divine descent was desirable. The Meiji government had established in 1868 a department for Shinto and separated this native belief from Buddhism. In 1870 all households were required to register with a local Shinto shrine, whose purpose was worship of Japanese gods and the showing of respect to the emperor. A year later lands belonging to Buddhist temples were confiscated, and all Buddhist ceremonies banished from the imperial palace. Then, in 1872, by government order, the custom of celebrating the emperor's birthday as a religious festival was finally instituted. Meiji was no longer only head of state: he was revered as a living god, the direct descendant of the sun goddess Amaterasu. Hardly noticed in this religious revolution was the transfer of his residence to Tokyo, where a new imperial palace rose on the site of the last shogun's stronghold. Divine though the ruler might be in the eyes of the people, his authority was not considered to be powerful enough for him to reside at any great distance from Japan's largest city.

The emperor's presence was indeed an asset for the Meiji oligarchs. The new parliament, named the Diet in imitation of Germany, had two equally powerful houses, of Peers and Commons. In the event of a disagreement between both of them, the matter was referred to the emperor, who was guided by a cabinet responsible to him alone. This meant that the old tradition of government behind the scenes prevailed. Yet the political life of Tokyo was never calm, for the reason that rivalry among the surviving Meiji reformers opened up avenues of advancement for party politicians, who scrambled for the financial rewards of office. Already the involvement of big business in political parties could be seen through the backing provided for increasingly expensive election campaigns. This large-scale injection of funds only tended to encourage malpractice, the number of bribery cases rising year by year.

To protect the interests of the armed forces an amendment to the constitution laid down that ministers for the Army and the Navy had to be serving officers. In 1878 an army general staff was established on German lines, which also had the privilege of reporting directly to the throne. This was to have unforeseen consequences for Japanese politics. The Imperial Japanese Army's cabinet nominee could safely disagree with the premier of the day, when there was a direct line of authorisation from the emperor for the policies of his military superiors.

Beneath the modern appearance of Japan in 1902, the year of the Anglo-Japanese Alliance, much of the traditional heritage remained untouched. The revival of Shintoism had already brought about the persecution of Christian academics and clergymen, especially when they expressed reservations about the unbridled nationalism inherent in emperor worship. Although the Sino-Japanese War of 1894–5 diverted patriotic fervour elsewhere, the traditional disdain for individualism that informed the assault on the Christian conscience was still very strong. As the early American expounder of things Japanese, Lafcadio Hearn, noted in 1913, 'the inhabitants of Japan continue to think and act in groups, even by groups of industrial companies'.

THE DRIVE TO EMPIRE (1874–1931)

The Sino-Japanese War of 1894–5 was of major importance because it revealed the full extent of the Qing dynasty's collapse and set off a scramble among the European powers for territory and markets on mainland East Asia. Within three years Germany, Russia, France and Britain had obtained leases and concessions from China, producing fear in Tokyo of an impending break-up of the Chinese empire. To secure its own position Japan was inevitably drawn into this imperial race, and within a decade had fought and won a first encounter with a European power, Russia.

The tentative start of the Japanese drive for empire dates from 1874, when Okubo Toshimichi persuaded the Meiji reformers to extend Tokyo's control over Okinawa and the rest of the Ryukyu Islands, instead of backing an alternative plan for an invasion of Korea. To mollify samurai discontent still further, the example of Perry was followed in Korea and a show of strength led in 1876 to the Treaty of Kanghwa; two ports were subsequently opened to Japanese trade in addition to Pusan, the traditional Korean trading port. Anxiety over Russian expansion in Manchuria persuaded Tokyo of the need to dominate Korea, in order to prevent the peninsula from being used as a springboard for an attack on the Japanese islands themselves. The Imperial Japanese Army always took the view that Korea could not be held without control of the nearby

Liaodong peninsula, where on territory leased from China the Russians from 1898 were to build at Port Arthur a major naval base.

The Japanese intervention in Korea in 1894–5 ended in the utter defeat of China. The Treaty of Shimonoseki ceded the Pescadores, Formosa, and the Liaodong peninsula to Japan, recognised Korean independence, and obliged the Qing dynasty to pay a large indemnity. Within a week of reaching this agreement, however, Germany, Russia and France forced Japan to renounce possession of the Liaodong peninsula, an intervention which increased Tokyo's sense of isolation in world affairs. The brush with the United States over Hawaii in 1897, as well as the American annexation of the Philippines two years later, served only to strengthen Japan's determination to guard its own interests. Even more frustrating were the restrictions placed by the US colonial authorities in the Philippines on foreign trade and immigration. American racial prejudice was to be one of the few effective propaganda weapons used by the Japanese in the Philippines during their period of occupation in the Second World War. Attitudes towards East Asian immigrants, and especially Japanese settlers, hardened in the United States from the 1920s onwards. As the radical writer Kotoku Shusui (1871–1911) put the problem at the beginning of the twentieth century:

The fashion of imperialism is spreading like a prairie fire . . . Not even the United States seems incapable of copying it. As for Japan, after the great victory in the Sino-Japanese War the people, both high and low, have fanatically turned toward it like a wild horse attempting to discard its yoke.

Everywhere patriotism was being replaced by militarism and colonialism. 'If the United States truly fought for freedom and independence in Cuba,' Kotoku Shusui pondered, 'why does it try to deny the freedom and independence of the Philippines?' Although he was correct in anticipating that a conflict between the United States and Japan would have to precede the emergence of his own country as an economic superpower, Kotoku Shusui failed to foresee how this industrial surge might occur in post-colonial East Asia.

The initial challenge to European supremacy came with the Japanese defeat of Russia in 1905. Relations between the Russians and the Japanese had deteriorated badly after the Boxer crisis of 1900, since the Tsar had been encouraged by his advisers to use the anti-Christian movement in China as an excuse to overrun the whole of Manchuria. With Japanese diplomatic support, China compelled the Tsar to agree to a three-stage withdrawal of his troops, at the very moment the Anglo-Japanese Alliance was signed as a way of strengthening Tokyo's position in case war should break out. The guarantee of British neutrality was not the sole advantage of the alliance for Japan; apart from denying the Russian fleet assistance from the ubiquitous facilities of the Royal Navy, there could be no question of a British loan to finance St Petersburg's war effort.

Despite the difficulty of supplying an army on a war footing by means of the single-track Trans-Siberian railway, and the tremendous voyage that any naval reinforcement would have to undertake in order to sail from the Baltic or the Black Sea, the Tsar allowed events to drift towards war. In frustration at Russian duplicity Tokyo broke off negotiations and announced its intention of taking such independent action as was necessary for national defence. Early in 1904 Japanese torpedo boats attacked Russian warships off the Korean coast, and then followed up this action with a surprise bombardment of Port Arthur, before formally issuing a declaration of hostilities. Within months the Imperial Japanese Army had an expeditionary force of 300,000 men operating against the Russians, who were soon besieged at Port Arthur. By the spring of 1905 when the battle of Mukden was fought, the Japanese had almost one million soldiers in the field, a total somewhat below the Russian strength. Casualties at Mukden were 85,000 Russians killed as against 70,000 Japanese. The courage of the Imperial Japanese Army impressed military observers who flocked to this first 'modern' war. Losses at Port Arthur were proportionally higher because of the determination of the Japanese commander, Nogi Maresuke, (1859–1912), who underestimated the tactical advantage of prepared positions; enemy fire had cost the Japanese nearly 57,780 dead and wounded out of a total force of 90,000 when in January 1905 the Russian general surrendered Port Arthur.

The surrender was blamed on bureaucratic muddle in Russia, although Lenin correctly saw it as 'the prologue to the capitulation of Tsarism'. But no matter the repercussions in St Petersburg, the skill with which the Russian soldiers defended their positions could not deter an attacker who recklessly charged in close formation. In the last action before the surrender the Japanese lost 11,000 men, the Russians only 1200.

The final effort of the Tsar to wrest victory from Japan failed at the battle of Tsushima, where in an action lasting twenty-four hours his Baltic Fleet was annihilated. After sailing right round Africa, because the British refused permission to pass through the Suez Canal, the Russian vessels were engaged in the straits between Korea and Japan in May 1905. The resounding victory at Tsushima was won by battleships built outside Japan. Yet the alacrity with which zaibatsu firms responded to the tide of patriotic fervour that flowed from Russia's defeat can be seen in subsequent figures for naval construction. Over 235 major units were built before August 1945, including in 1922 Japan's first aircraft-carrier, *Hosho*.

The mediation of the United States brought the Russo-Japanese War to a close. By the Treaty of Portsmouth, signed in September 1905, Russia allowed Japan to occupy the Liaodong peninsula, assume its railway rights in Manchuria, take over the southern half of the island of Sakhalin, and act as the protector of Korea. Modern Japan had arrived on the world stage. Not only did the victory over Russia confer the Chinese territory the European powers had denied Japan in 1895, but more important it demonstrated that a properly equipped oriental country could beat an occidental one.

The victory over Russia probably represented the zenith of the Meiji period. As the emperor was held responsible for this matching of Western power, the throne came to symbolise both the might of modern Japan and its traditional values. Had Japan stopped its drive for possessions at this point, it is possible that the Japanese empire might have remained intact and avoided the military domination of its government. But the imperialist spirit was already in command of the Japanese consciousness, the riots in many cities after the announcement of the peace terms of the Treaty of Portsmouth showing how high had been Japanese expectations. Significantly, protest never encompassed the throne: the emperor was always separated from the failures and credited with the successes of the nation.

With the end of hostilities and the elimination of Japan's rival to the control of Korea, it was not long before Korea was formally annexed into the Japanese empire. In 1910 the last Yi monarch was removed to Japan, and the country placed under a governor-general, the iron-fisted soldier Terauchi Masatake (1852–1919), whose repressive techniques shocked world opinion. In the Japanese quest of modernisation Koreans were deprived of their freedom, and even their identity. The earlier esteem for Korea as the superior exponent of Chinese culture was effectively relaced by outright contempt, which has continued to the present day when half a million people of Korean origin who live in Japan continue to suffer discrimination in spite of their absorption of Japanese culture and language.

The outbreak of the First World War gave Japan a chance to

strengthen its grip on Manchuria and acquire, as an ally of Britain, other parts of China, such as the German concession of Qingdao in Shandong province. The overthrow of the Qing dynasty in 1912 had left China in the hands of warlords, notwithstanding Dr Sun Yatsen's declaration of a republic. The chief warlord, Yuan Shikai, became a Japanese target in 1915, when as president of China he was presented with the 'Twenty-One Demands'. Amounting to a virtual protectorate over the country, Yuan Shikai tried to reject as many demands as possible, while quietly acknowledging Japan's supremacy in Manchuria and its privileges elsewhere in China. His refusal to stand up to Tokyo ended his dynastic ambitions, but there was little in reality that the Chinese could do to oppose the presence of the Kwantung Army.

Japan's unwillingness to curb militarism in the 1920s and 1930s appears to have been connected with a gnawing sense of insecurity. What is striking about this period is how it remained beset by a notion of precarious deficiency, of living on the very edge. National resources were certainly stretched by imperial commitments as successive governments struggled with an acute economic crisis, although Japan suffered nothing akin to the runaway inflation of 1922–3 in Germany. In both countries, however, single-minded patriotism and the use of terror by right-wing groups contributed to the rise of authoritarian rule. The assassination of Hara Takashi (1856–1921) did much to undermine parliamentary democracy by removing an adroit politician from the complicated workings of the Japanese party system. The prime minister's death also ended any hope of amelioration in colonial rule, for Hara Takashi had promised a modest series of reforms aimed at greater opportunities for Koreans in government, education and commerce.

But Japanese expansion, however, was arousing the fears of the West. The Washington Naval Treaty (1921) compelled Tokyo to accept a ratio of 5:5:3 in battleships to the United States and Britain; it also wound up the Anglo-Japanese Alliance. The Nine Power Pact (1922) attempted to maintain the status quo in East Asia by providing a guarantee for China's territorial and administrative integrity. These treaties were resented in Japan, where many believed that they had been made by civilian leaders who did not understand the imperatives of imperial defence. A subsequent conference of the signatories of the naval treaty held in London in 1930 extended limitations to all types of naval vessels, much to the anger of the Imperial Japanese Navy. When a direct appeal to the emperor failed to prevent ratification, senior army officers began to take the direction of foreign policy into their own hands. The assassination of the prime minister of the day at Tokyo railway station by another right-wing extremist simply increased the furore that preceded the Mukden Incident in the following year.

Yet the Imperial Japanese Army, rather than the Imperial Japanese Navy, saw itself as the arbiter of the empire's fate. Failure to check this role in the 1930s practically left the politicians with no alternative than to accept military domination of cabinet decisions in the years prior to the outbreak of World War Two. From the Mukden Incident onwards Japan was set on a pre-determined collision course with the United States, the chief guarantor of China's independence.

By the late 1920s Tokyo had come to accept the leadership of Jiang Jieshi (Chiang Kai-shek) in China. Japanese politicians were delighted over his bloody break with the Chinese Communist Party in 1927, and hints may have been dropped concerning a joint campaign against it at a future date. But Jiang Jieshi was favoured in China, not Manchuria. North of the Great Wall, Tokyo wanted to back a pro-Japanese government under the control of Zhang Zoulin, a Manchurian warlord. The Chinese leader would not agree to co-operate in such an arrangement, his forces in 1928 moving on Zhang Zoulin's headquarters in Beijing. This final stage of the Northern Expedition worried the Kwantung Army, because the Guomindang force received help from several northern warlords, some of whom were believed to be in league with the Russians. When Zhang Zoulin began to show undue independence himself, the Kwantung Army blew up his train *en route* from Beijing to Mukden. The expectation that this act would create disorder and give a pretext for a take-over of Manchuria failed to materialise, but the failure of Tokyo to punish any of the officers involved encouraged an even more aggressive military outlook. Too young to remember Japan's former weakness in the face of Perry's threats, and frustrated by the stalemate on mainland East Asia following the First World War, a new breed of army officer arose to demand that a bulwark against Russia be built in Manchuria in preparation for the struggle to be fought between Japan and the West.

In 1930 a typical group, the Cherry Blossom Society (*Sakurakai*), met in a Tokyo suburb. One of its supporters, a major at the time, recalled that 'we were concerned not only over the Manchuria-Mongolia problem but also over domestic reform . . . We were fed up.' Deepening world depression and the slow development of Manchuria made the 'open door' policy advocated by the United

States seem bankrupt. Between 1929 and 1931 Japanese exports fell by half, with disastrous effect on both factory workers and farmers. The Cherry Blossom Society believed that only Japan had the capability to modernise Manchuria as a means of relief for its own pressing economic problems. The search for self-sufficiency had lain behind Japanese foreign policy since 1868, but in the aftermath of the Wall Street crash it assumed a greater urgency.

If anything, the assassination of Zhang Zoulin reduced Japanese freedom of action. Zhang Xueliang, the warlord's son and successor, rapidly came to an understanding with Jiang Jieshi. He also blocked Japanese plans to build further railways in Manchuria, starting in direct competition a network of his own. By September 1931 the Kwantung Army, with the tacit agreement of army general staff, was ready to provoke a crisis in Manchuria. Spurred on by the threat of financial retrenchment, several of its field commanders caused an explosion on the tracks of the Japanese railway line close to Mukden, then used the incident as a pretext for attacking Chinese troops in the area. Once the commander-in-chief of the Kwantung Army heard of these developments at his headquarters in Port Arthur, he was faced with a dilemma. Not privy to the plot, he had either to terminate the action or allow the spread of hostilities: the second option could be interpreted as a capital office, because no commander was allowed to move his troops in a foreign country without the emperor's consent. After much persuasion by his staff officers, he agreed to the dispatch of troops both from the Kwantung Leased Territory and Korea. In Tokyo the main concern was the possible reaction of Russia, an anxiety that proved groundless. By the end of 1931 the whole of Manchuria had fallen under Japanese military control, and the Kwantung Army began to plan with the South Manchurian Railway the establishment there of a new state, Manzhouguo.

The independent action of the Kwantung Army brought down the Japanese government, the last one in which politicians predominated until after the Second World War. Assassinations of ex-ministers in early 1932 underscored the loss of civilian authority in a country gripped by ultra-nationalism. Nothing that the Kwantung Army did in China was thereafter considered to be wrong, not even its spread of fighting to Shanghai. Before the take-over of Manchuria, this commercial city had been the centre of anti-Japanese agitation. A boycott of Japanese goods had hit trade, while strikes in Japanese-owned factories almost stopped production completely. To divert international attention from Manchuria

and humiliate Jiang Jieshi, an incident was touched off there. But it
soon expanded into a full-scale engagement, which took 30,000
soldiers to settle satisfactorily. The Japanese army general staff was
more than relieved that fighting had remained localised, for it was
realised that at least half of the men then under arms would have
been necessary for a general showdown with Jiang Jieshi. Although
Guomindang forces stationed in Shanghai fought with unexpected
tenacity, the Guomindang government was then out of sympathy
with this demonstration of nationalism. Ammunition and supplies
were denied to the combatants and, as soon as all resistance ceased,
an agreement was reached with the Japanese over the creation of a
demilitarised zone around Shanghai. Jiang Jieshi preferred to concentrate his forces against the Chinese Communist Party.

The truce in Shanghai had been preceeded by the creation in
Manchuria of the new state of Manzhouguo. Despite warnings from
Tokyo the Kwantung Army installed the former Qing emperor,
Puyi, as the head of this puppet state, deliberately giving the
impression that his elevation was a restoration of the old
Manchu dynasty. Accepting the inevitable, Tokyo announced that
Manzhouguo would be 'an essential part of the empire', function-
ing as a state 'under Japanese power and influence'. In 1934 Puyi
exchanged the title of president for emperor, a dignity conferred
upon him by the emperor of Japan. The League of Nations was not
fooled by these trappings of power, and in 1933 Japan quit the
organisation, choosing to ignore international condemnation and to
go it alone.

ENTANGLEMENT IN CHINA (1931–45)

The Mukden Incident, the overture to the Pacific dimension of the
Second World War, was for Japan the beginning of fifteen years'
conflict. The Kwantung Army remained the chief protagonist till
military deadlock in China widened the scope of hostilities to
encompass the whole of East Asia. That final phase began in
December 1941 with the surprise attack on the US naval base at
Pearl Harbor.

The Japanese challenge to the United States in the Pacific Ocean
seems now to have been a reckless gamble. However, its unreality
was obscured by initial Japanese successes, just as the hopeless task
of subduing a country the size of China failed to register in time
for any limitation of war aims. The temper of the Kwantung Army
allowed little scope for compromise, especially when its officers were

wedded to a plan of detaching Chinese provinces and warlords piecemeal from the Guomindang side. They failed to notice how Chinese resistance gradually stiffened and, like Jiang Jieshi, they underrated the guerrilla strength of the Chinese Communist Party. Reluctance to negotiate truces was a symptom of the unbridled spirit of the Kwantung Army.

Perhaps the emphasis on harshness and endurance was in part a consequence of Japan's limited economic strength. From the earliest days of colonial expansion, Japan compensated for its weakness by a ruthless policy of plunder. Land was seized for the settlement of Japanese immigrants in Korea, Taiwan and Manchuria; in China proper businesses were confiscated and workers kept on starvation wages; and the Imperial Japanese Army on active service always lived off the land. The very drabness of the Japanese uniform was a constant reminder of the need for personal sacrifice in the service of the emperor. Whenever human flesh and will-power failed, there was always *gyokusai*, 'glorious self-destruction', to preserve national honour. Thus the armed forces of imperial Japan never shook off entirely the character of being the ruler's army of personal retainers.

The Tangku Truce (1933) brought about military disengagement in north China, the Kwantung Army pulling back its units to approximately the line of the Great Wall. But its simultaneous removal of concentrations of Chinese troops from the same area created a power vacuum in which Japanese agents could foster autonomy movements. Their schemes involved various provinces either side of the Great Wall. The Kwantung Army also had its eye on the iron ore of Shanxi province, whose quality was vastly superior to that mined in Manzhouguo.

It was a good moment, according to Itagaki Seishiro (1885–1948), while Europe and the United States were preoccupied by internal problems, 'to get northern China into the hands of Japan'. The senior staff officer of the Kwantung Army, Itagaki Seishiro had been the ringleader of the Mukden Incident. His readiness to exploit every clash, real or devised, was to earn him in 1939 an imperial rebuke. Officers more concerned with the Soviet threat decided to engage the Soviet forces stationed on the boundary of Manzhouguo. The first action in the summer of 1938 at Chengfukeng, south-west of Vladivostok, entailed a small-scale Japanese reverse. When, in the ensuing year, the Kwantung Army committed 56,000 men at Nomonhan, on the border between Manzhouguo and the newly independent Mongolian People's Republic, Russian and Mongol troops launched a powerful mechanised counter-offensive, supported by aircraft. The unexpected effectiveness of 'fire bottles' (*kaenbin*) against Soviet armour provided only temporary relief for Japanese infantry units without any artillery support. Even a bottle with an unlit wick was found to ignite on striking a tank because of the heat of the vehicle and the sun. Despite these heroic efforts, which accounted in the course of the battle for over 100 tanks, a soft drink bottle filled with petroleum and sand could never be a substitute for an anti-tank gun, and Nomonhan ended as a Russian victory. The losses of over 8000 men dead and nearly 9000 wounded had to be concealed from the Japanese public.

The desperate series of infantry attacks foreshadowed the suicidal handling of troops during Japanese reverses towards the end of the Pacific War. Officers of the Imperial Japanese Army were just as slow against the Americans at Guadalcanal and the British at Imphal/Kohima in appreciating that bravery was not sufficient to win an engagement. Lack of flexibility in tactics became in the end a more serious handicap than either inferior equipment or shortage of supplies.

Emperor Hirohito (1926–89) rebuked Itagaki Seishiro for allowing the ill-fated operation to take place, as the Army minister knew that the advance into foreign territory had not been sanctioned by the throne. The Kwantung Army was told firmly to desist from embroiling itself in such unnecessary incidents, an order that was swiftly communicated to a grateful Stalin by his secret agent in Tokyo, Richard Sorge. The implication of the audience was transparent: the conquest of China must remain the top military priority. The defeat at Nomonhan confirmed the Soviet Union as Japan's most feared antagonist on mainland East Asia, and caused the transfer of its own strategic emphasis permanently to the south.

This southern campaign had begun in earnest two years before, following yet another incident at the Marco Polo bridge, south-west of Beijing. A skirmish between Chinese and Japanese soldiers in July 1937 developed into an advance by the Kwantung Army. To all intents and purposes China and Japan were at war and remained locked in combat till 1945. The extension of fighting in China was by no means a unanimous decision, the magnitude of the task dawning on officers who realised that three divisions would not be sufficient to compel Jiang Jieshi to sue for terms.

For much had changed in China during the four years since the signing of the Tangku Truce. Separatist movements in the demilitarised northern provinces proved hard to sponsor as the true intentions of the Japanese became apparent. But the breaking point had come in 1936 with the Japanese demand to grant diplomatic recognition of Manzhouguo's independence. This split the Guomindang military command when Zhang Xueliang found that Jiang Jieshi was unwilling to countenance action in the field to recover his homeland. The young Manchurian commander forced Jiang Jieshi at gunpoint to end hostilities against the Chinese Communist Party and prepare for a united front against the Japanese. Known as the Xi'an Incident, the impromptu agreement laid the foundation of the unexpected national resistance encountered by the Kwantung Army after the exchange of fire at the Marco Polo bridge.

In Japan, too, the mood had changed dramatically. The abortive military coup in February 1936 encouraged the ultra-nationalists, although the person most responsible for crushing the insurgents was the emperor himself. Military leaders became even more aggressive in their demands for financial support, while cowed politicians and civilian advisers to the throne thought twice before opposing their will. But a climate of opinion in favour of war arose as much from schools and colleges as the foreign adventures of the Kwantung Army. Starting in 1925 active-duty army officers were assigned to educational institutions, and military training became part of the curriculum. Some 600,000 students were drawn into this scheme of training and indoctrination. The Imperial Japanese Army's strength rose from twenty-four divisions in 1937, to fifty-one by the summer of 1941. Whereas there were over 2 million soldiers under arms at the time of Pearl Harbor, the Imperial Japanese Navy had 311,000 sailors on active duty. Another 4½ million men were on the reserve list. The cost of such phenomenal growth was the development of a wartime economy in which the military and the zaibatsu firms worked closely together. The emphasis on arms production resulted in the expansion of heavy industries as companies such as Mitsubishi built warships and produced the Zero fighter. In 1937 Japan's total army and navy budget was 60 per cent of annual government expenditure, in 1944 it was 85 per cent. The changeover to a wartime economy created hardship in the countryside as men were drafted into the armed forces or went to work in factories. The fall in agricultural output that resulted only worsened the lot of ordinary people: rice became expensive, wages remained artificially low, and diet suffered. After 1944 the Japanese health authorities stopped announcing the rising number of deaths from tuberculosis.

When the Kwantung Army advanced in 1937, most of its officers believed that Jiang Jieshi would not really resist: that northern

China at least would be yielded to them, and that another truce agreement could be enforced which left the Guomindang government in a dependent position. By the spring of 1938 Jiang Jieshi was still fighting. Angered by this refusal to submit, Japanese soldiers embarked on a series of atrocities that only their Nazi allies were to surpass. In the rape of Nanjing, the Guomindang capital, more than 200,000 men, women and children were slaughtered. Some officers felt revulsion at the news of the killings, but the ferocity of the foot soldiers soon became a commonplace of operations in the Imperial Japanese Army. The world was appalled, even though at first no tangible aid was forthcoming. In Tokyo the outrage was censored, but the cabinet may have sensed that the country had embarked on a conflict already out of control.

The full extent of Japanese brutality towards the Chinese is still not squarely faced today. When in 1988 *The Last Emperor* was screened in Japan, the film's distributor arranged for the scenes of rape and murder at Nanjing to be cut, lest they annoy Japanese audiences. Facing up to past aggression has also spoilt relations between Korea and Japan during the post-war period. The South Korean president was not entirely satisfied in 1990, when at an imperial banquet in Tokyo the son of Hirohito used an obscure Japanese noun to express his regret for the colonial administration imposed on Korea. But he did express his pleasure at a promise to improve the legal status and treatment of third-generation Koreans living in Japan.

The lack of practical aid given to Jiang Jieshi was a disappointment. Except for a certain amount of military equipment from the Soviet Union, the West contented itself merely with a public condemnation of Japan. President Franklin D. Roosevelt spoke of a need to quarantine aggression, but he was prepared to accept prompt apologies and reparations in December 1937, when Japanese aircraft sank USS *Panay* near Shanghai. With a war imminent in Europe, the British also had to tolerate damage inflicted on HMS *Ladybird* and HMS *Bee*, when the Americans made it clear that they would not agree to concerted naval action against Japan. Even Germany, a member with Italy and Japan of the Anti-Comintern Pact, was unenthusiastic about the Sino-Japanese War, not least because it felt that involvement in China might prevent Japan from serving as an effective ally against the Soviet Union and other European powers.

After the capture of Nanjing the chance of a truce disappeared altogether. Abandoning Shanghai and the coastal provinces, Jiang

Jieshi retreated inland, first to Wuhan on the middle course of the Yangzi, then to remote Chongqing in Sichuan province. There the Guomindang government was cut off from the outside world, its only overland communication routes being two earth roads: one ran through the huge province of Xinjiang to Russia, while the other zigzagged across mountainous terrain to connect Yunnan province with the British colony of Burma.

The first shipment of war materials to pass up the Burma road arrived at Jiang Jieshi's headquarters in December 1938. The value of the arms and ammunition was more symbolic than real, for a stalemate had already been in existence on the battlefield for some months. Japan possessed insufficient men to prosecute the advance on Chongqing as well as deal with the partisan activities of Communist irregulars behind its lines. The fighters of Mao Zedong (1893–1976) were able to bring to bear long experience of guerrilla warfare against an enemy with superior weapons and to offer the enraged peasantry the advantages of a co-ordinated approach to armed resistance.

By 1939 Japan seemed to have reached the limits of its military power in China. No gains were made in the Yangzi valley, where the bulk of Jiang Jieshi's forces stood guard, and the southern swoop on the island of Hainan could hardly be called an outflanking movement. The unopposed seizure of the island frightened the

THE DRAGON MOVES AGAIN

Fig. 43. Dunkirk persuaded the Japanese to demand the closure of Jiang Jieshi's supply route, the Burma road. The British duly obliged during the rainy season, but in October 1940 they let military supplies flow again as this *Daily Express* cartoon was pleased to note

French colonial authorities in nearby Indo-China, but it drew Japanese attention away from the basic question: how to end the Sino-Japanese War?

The same inability of army leaders to set realistic strategic goals in China was about to bring to South-East Asia its share of the havoc of the Second World War. The Imperial Japanese Navy strenuously objected to the southern thrust under consideration, even though it was confident of achieving superiority at sea. The author of the surprise attack on Pearl Harbor, Yamamoto Isoroku, was under no illusions about the fate of his country in an extended contest with the United States. After success at the outset of hostilities, Japan simply would be overwhelmed by American industrial power. If war came, the only hope would be a peace negotiated from a position of strength. It was with reluctance, therefore, that senior naval officers accepted an alliance with Germany, which was signed in September 1940. The agreement provided for Japan's recognition of the leadership of Germany in Europe and Italy in Africa, while those countries in turn recognised the role Japan wished to play in establishing a new order in East Asia.

Not even an American embargo on strategic exports in retaliation to the pact could dent official Japanese optimism. The fall of Holland and France offered too tempting an opportunity in South-East Asia, especially when Britain stood alone in Europe. Having in 1941 pushed into French Indo-China and settled imperiously a border dispute in Thailand's favour, Japan was ready to seize the oil, rubber and tin supplies of the Dutch and British colonies farther south. All that was required first was the destruction of the American Pacific Fleet.

12

REPUBLIC OF CHINA

From its Founding to the
Triumph of Communism
(1912–49)

American intervention during the Boxer rebellion in 1900 had prevented any dismemberment of China. President McKinley's determination to preserve 'Chinese territorial and administrative integrity' was accomplished not through US military force, but by playing one European power against another. Japan quickly adopted the same bluff against the United States, when McKinley was forced to disavow an attempt by the US War Department to acquire a Chinese naval base. An 'open door' policy, Washington had to agree with some embarrassment, applied to all nations. The clever Japanese challenge touched a raw nerve in American foreign relations. In 1882 Congress had passed the first anti-immigration measure in US history when it barred Chinese immigrants for a decade. Yet at the same time popular pressure increased for discriminatory legislation at home, US missionaries abroad looked to their government for help and protection, especially as European powers crowded into China.

Saved though China was from immediate colonisation, US goodwill was insufficient to prevent internal breakdown following the overthrow in 1911 of the Qing dynasty. In a sense, American moral concern added to the problem of post-imperial government, for revolutionaries such as Dr Sun Yatsen (1866–1925), while seeking to emulate the United States, imagined erroneously that a liberal regime could take root in a country without liberals. Dr Sun Yatsen was indeed a new type of rebel in Chinese history; neither a

211

Fig. 44. An American view of President McKinley's military intervention during the Boxer rebellion of 1900. It reveals the ambivalence of Washington's policy towards China – part protective, part imperialist

disappointed candidate for the imperial civil service, nor a military commander who had once been a bandit, he was an overseas Chinese in education and outlook. Although born of humble stock in Guandong province, he was sent to live with his elder brother in Hawaii, where he attended a Christian boarding school. Later he studied at the Medical College in Hong Kong, the forerunner of the present university there. This foreign experience convinced him of the need for a republic, for only with the adoption of democratic government could China hope to recover from its backwardness. The flaw in his argument was a fundamental lack of understanding of what was involved in the working of democratic institutions, a circumstance necessarily depriving his fellow advocates of republicanism of widespread support. As a British observer of the 1913 election remarked:

The election of members, whether of the National Parliament or of provincial assemblies, is absolutely unreal . . . In Newchang, which is a town of 100,000 inhabitants, the election of a parliamentary representative took place while I was there. Thirty-five voters recorded their votes, and of those thirty-five the majority were the employees of the local administrator. The public took no part and exhibited no interest in the proceedings.

Between the republicans and the majority of the Chinese people there was only one point of agreement: the correctness of overthrowing the Qing dynasty.

Thus the swiftness of the anti-Manchu rising of late 1911 left a power vacuum in the country. As news spread of its successful start in Wuhan, the capital of Heibei province, rebellions occurred throughout south China. By the fall of Nanjing in December two-thirds of the empire had already repudiated the Qing dynasty. At first Beijing underestimated the extent of the rising, but as soon as reports showed its true proportions a desperate expedient was adopted. In November Yuan Shikai was recalled and given full powers to deal with the situation. It was an invitation the forcibly retired general had patiently waited for three years.

While he assumed command of the imperial forces confronting the rebels, Yuan Shikai also dispatched a truce delegation to meet with leaders of the revolutionary forces. The deal that was eventually struck with the provisional government at Nanjing, where in January 1912 Sun Yatsen had been sworn in as the first president, entailed the abolition of the imperial system in return for Yuan Shikai's own appointment as president of the new republic. Without the support of the general, and especially his ability to control the modernized northern armies, the republicans feared that China would suffer partition.

On 15 February Sun Yatsen therefore made way for Yuan Shikai, who three days earlier had secured the abdication of the last Qing emperor Xuan Tong (1909–12). The six-year-old former ruler was granted a generous annuity for the maintenance of his family within the imperial palace. Better known as Puyi, he remained there until warlord politics engulfed Beijing in 1924. Shortly afterwards he took refuge in the Japanese concession at Tianjin, where his hosts persuaded him to head later the puppet state of Manzhouguo.

With the ending of Manchu power, Yuan Shikai started his own bid for the throne, which realistically seems to have recognised that his title might need to be king rather than emperor. His initial move was to weaken the influence of the Guomindang, or National People's Party, as Sun Yatsen's followers became known in 1912. In spite of banning military involvement in politics, he chose to ignore soldiers' harassment of provincial assemblymen that made a mockery of local self-government. Against local commanders, the warlords who taxed the provinces for the benefit of themselves and their troops, Yuan Shikai had to move cautiously. His overriding difficulty was finance, which a consortium of British, French, German and American banks exploited for its own advantage. Although Woodrow Wilson pulled out US bankers, he made no protest when Yuan Shikai set about destroying republicanism in the need for 'stability'. Except for reservations in Tokyo, there was in 1913 no international comment on the outlawing of the Guomindang as a political party and the substitution of presidential dictatorship for parliamentary rule.

All was not going according to Yuan Shikai's plan, however. The outbreak of the First World War removed Europe's restraining hand on the Japanese, who occupied the German-leased territory of Qingdao in Shandong province. Then, in January 1915, Japan presented the 'Twenty-one Demands', the purpose of which was to reduce China to a virtual protectorate. Since it had become obvious that Yuan Shikai intended to strengthen his administration still further by founding a new dynasty, Tokyo was determined to thwart his ambitions, lest they block Japanese expansion on mainland East Asia. With no hope of European or American support, Yuan Shikai was compelled to accept the least offensive demands. 'This is both sad and humiliating,' he said, 'but let us remember it and do our best to wipe out this disgrace.'

The unfavourable public reaction in China did nothing to advance Yuan Shikai's own dynastic plans, which became known at the end of 1915. At dawn on the winter solstice the president had driven in an armoured car to the Temple of Heaven on the southern outskirts of Beijing. The entire route was covered with yellow sand, as was customary for an imperial progress, and at the ninety-minute ceremony Yuan Shikai changed his military uniform for a robe embroidered with dragons. The purpose of this revival of ancient ritual was made clear six days later in the announcement of a new dynasty entitled the Great Constitution. The would-be emperor was on the throne less than three months before opposition from republicans and warlords alike 'demoted' him to president. But the abandonment of imperial pretensions were not enough to save him politically, not least because Japanese agents egged on his military rivals. Five provinces immediately declared independence from the Beijing government, whose desperate ministers stripped the presidency of executive power in order to halt the separatist movement. Asylum in the United States was still being considered when Yuan Shikai died following a collapse brought on by nervous exhaustion.

THE WARLORD PERIOD (1916–28)

Although Yuan Shikai's death lifted the threat of disunity, the protestations of loyalty made by military commanders to his successor were really a cover for the pursuit of provincial autonomy. Between 1916 and 1928 China was divided among various local warlords who fought each other for the resources they needed to obtain modern weaponry. Their troops were ruffians in uniform, former bandits and the dregs of society. Not even the remnant of Yuan Shikai's modern, trained forces could claim the distinction of having seen action against a foreign foe; they were garrison troops whose commanders turned their garrison areas into private estates. The most common methods of extortion included a squeeze on central government taxes, local trade, and the rents due from the peasantry. Government deteriorated, the economy languished, and Chinese society after a century of decline reached its lowest ebb. Only in the Treaty Ports could any material progress be seen to take place, and this profitable development remained largely in foreign hands.

Throughout the warlord period the Beijing regime continued to function as the legitimate government, for the reason that European powers with financial interests at stake refused diplomatic recognition to any other. Their loans were recovered by customs duties which they collected in its name. As it was so valuable a prize, the northern general Zhang Shun attempted to assume power in the capital by restoring the ex-Manchu emperor, until the intervention of another warlord sent the eleven-year-old swiftly back into retirement. Of the brief restoration in July 1917 Puyi recalled:

After Yuan Shikai's death, the Forbidden City became lively again and, with Zhang Shun's audience with me in 1917, the first restoration movement reached a climax . . . After the general had kowtowed, I pointed to a chair and asked him to sit down. At this time the court had abandoned the custom of having high officials report while in a kneeling position . . . I followed my tutor's instructions in asking about the situation of the army under his command, but I did not pay much attention to his reply. I was somewhat disappointed in his looks. He wore lightweight summer clothes, his face was red, he had very thick eyebrows and was fat. Had he not worn a moustache he could have passed for one of the eunuchs in charge of the palace kitchens. I noticed, however, that he did wear a pigtail.

The retention of this distinctive way of dressing the hair was taken as a sign of loyalty to the throne by Puyi's tutors, since those Chinese who supported republicanism always shaved it off. Mao Zedong's pigtail, for example, had disappeared as soon as the city of Changsha rose in the 1911 rebellion.

'But it all lasted', Puyi noted with surprise, 'little more than five days. Everything changed when an aeroplane from the forces stationed at Tianjin dropped some bombs on the palace. Then there were no longer people who came to pay their respects or kowtow to me and there were no more imperial edicts to read.' Court officials hurriedly disappeared, and Zhang Shun sought refuge in the Dutch legation.

The confusion in Beijing was made even worse through the growing dependence on Japanese loans. After China declared war on Germany in August 1917, the Beijing government financed its own internal quarrels by borrowing enormous sums from Japan, on the pretext of fighting the Germans. The new privileges demanded in return for this financial support, coming so hard on the heels of the 'Twenty-one Demands', made the Japanese hated throughout the country. Such was Chinese anxiety about the steady growth of Japan's influence that in 1919 a surge of patriotic protest compelled the Beijing government to withdraw its delegation from Versailles without signing the peace treaty. The May Fourth Movement, spearheaded by Beijing University students, was a spontaneous reaction to the news that Japan had been awarded the former German holding of Qingdao. Ignoring official warnings, 3000 students demonstrated in Tiananmen Square, expressed their concern at the American legation, and then burned down the houses of pro-Japanese ministers. The impact of the demonstration upon China was out of all proportion to its size: in towns and cities meetings were held and a boycott of Japanese goods inaugurated.

The May Fourth Movement was a watershed in the history of modern China. It raised political consciousness in urban areas, thereby stimulating discussion about the problems facing the republic. Dr Sun Yatsen had always argued that three stages were necessary in its development: struggle against the late empire, educative rule, and democratic government. In the Beijing student demonstration the republic at last had found educators capable of advancing understanding under an authoritarian regime. The lightning effect their views had on public opinion also indicated that the traditional role of the scholar as the upholder of public morality was by no means dead. But the massed assembly of students in Tiananmen Square was a new kind of event. Huge blue and white national flags, placards and posters were held aloof in denunciation of ministers, who dared not disperse the protestors by force. The great open space, in the very centre of the capital, was transformed into an arena for political dissent.

Repression of student activities, however, was not long following the Fourth May Movement. In the port of Tianjin Zhou Enlai (1898–1976) was imprisoned for six months along with other graduates. Even before Zhou Enlai set out for France in 1920, he had become deeply interested in Marxism and pondered the possibility that it might provide a solution to China's ills. But it was another young activist who perceived how the brutality of military rule was preparing the conditions for the next stage of rebellion, that of the peasants. This was Mao Zedong, one of the twelve founding delegates of the Communist Party of China in Shanghai in July 1921.

South China held aloof from the actions of the Beijing government. Dr Sun Yatsen had gone in 1917 to Guangzhou with Guomindang colleagues and most of the Chinese Navy. There he convened in the city an alternative parliament and headed a military government with the title of generalissimo. The Beijing government could not physically remove the challenge to its legitimacy, but this hardly mattered because even in the northern provinces it no longer counted. As Sun Yatsen was to learn painfully himself, the warlords were the real power holders. The murder of his closest followers by soldiers forced him to retire in 1918 to Shanghai. The move was not without significance, for there he met a senior Russian emissary, Adolph Joffe, who explained that Soviet policy towards China was based on the abrogation of the treaties which the tsarist government had imposed on the weakened Qing dynasty.

The Bolsheviks had recently taken power in the full expectation that they were part of a wave of revolution sweeping Europe, and in 1919 the Soviet government renounced the conquests and special privileges obtained under the Tsars. This admission of past unfairness so impressed Sun Yatsen that he began to wonder if Western democracy could ever rebuild China, when Britain, France and Japan were only too willing to exploit its internal weaknesses. 'The one real and genuine friend of the Chinese Revolution', the disillusioned democrat concluded, 'is Soviet Russia.' It was unfortunate for the republic that the Beijing government preferred to rebuff in 1922 Joffe's offer of negotiation on the tsarist treaties. A sticking point was Mongolia, from the previous year a Soviet protectorate but then (as now) claimed by the Chinese to be within their sphere of influence. Unable to make headway in Beijing, Joffe went on to see Sun Yatsen in Shanghai, where as a result of their meeting members of the Chinese Communist Party were allowed to join the Guomindang as 'individuals' and plans were laid for a revolution to crush the warlords and reunite the country as a socialist state.

The government and the army were to be left in the hands of the Guomindang, while the Communists concentrated on propaganda and mass organisation. To increase military efficiency Jiang Jieshi (1897–1975) was sent to the Soviet Union for training and on his return became the first commandant of Huangpu Military Academy, near newly regained Guangzhou. The course of advanced studies with the Red Army enabled Jiang Jieshi to train a generation of famous generals – Guomindang and Communist. His appointment also gave him a chance to build up a military following within the Guomindang, so that after the death of Sun Yatsen in 1925 he assumed the leadership of the Northern Expedition against the warlords.

At Huangpu the relations between the Communist advisers and the Guomindang military experts were generally amicable. The diplomatic skills of Zhou Enlai may have contributed to this unity of purpose, since in 1924 he was recalled from Europe and appointed its political director. His return was timely as events moved swiftly after Sun Yatsen's death. In May 1925 a crowd of students was fired upon with some fatal casualties by a British-officered police detachment belonging to the International Settlement in Shanghai; the students had taken to the streets in protest at brutalities already perpetrated on striking workers in a Japanese-owned mill. That these young people could be shot down without any redress aroused indignation at the freedom of action foreigners claimed in China under treaties signed by the Qing emperors. Extra-territoriality became the focus of widespread agitation and early in 1926 Jiang Jieshi judged that the moment for moving against the compliant warlords had come. By the summer his forces had reached the Yangzi river and the great cities of Wuhan, Nanjing and Shanghai were all occupied, but the victorious march forward brought the Communists and the Guomindang into open conflict, as the landlords and businessmen backing Jiang Jieshi were terrified over the bitter social conflict being stirred up by Mao Zedong in the countryside and Zhou Enlai in the towns.

In April 1927 Guomindang troops were ordered to co-operate with underworld toughs in attacking rebellious Shanghai workers. Zhou Enlai was lucky to escape the massacre, which in subsequent days engulfed thousands of activists. Henceforth the Chinese Communist Party and the Guomindang were enemies, despite the Japanese invasion of China which produced in the late 1930s a second united front.

GUOMINDANG RULE (1928-37)

The Shanghai massacre stalled the Chinese revolution for two decades. Yet it made Jiang Jieshi the premier warlord, because in 1928 his soldiers reached Beijing and gained for him the diplomatic recognition that had always eluded Sun Yatsen. Although Japan tried to obstruct the final stage of the Northern Expedition, the Guomindang army bypassed Japanese units stationed in Shandong province and easily drove out of the capital forces belonging to the Manchurian warlord Zhang Zoulin. His assassination by the Japanese, who blew up the armoured train in which he fled, may not have been so opportune for the Guomindang as at first appeared.

Eight years later it was his son, Zhang Xueliang, commander of the anti-Communist expedition in Shaanxi province, who devised the Xi'an Incident, when at the point of a gun Jiang Jieshi agreed to a truce with the Communists and the formation of a united front against the Japanese. The 'Young Marshal' Zhang Xueliang was assisted in the conspiracy by another Guomindang general, Yang Hucheng. Later Zhou Enlai, the Communist negotiator at Xi'an in 1936, unofficially adopted Yang Hucheng's son after Jiang Jieshi had the general executed during the final days of his power on the Chinese mainland. Zhang Xueliang remained in prison on Taiwan until 1962.

The kindness shown by Zhou Enlai after the Communist victory in 1949 was unknown in top Guomindang circles, where a legacy of warlord rivalry still lingers on today. For Jiang Jieshi's success in 1928 had depended on other powerful military commanders, with whom the new generalissimo had to accept alliance. Not only were these northern warlords always concerned to free themselves from Jiang Jieshi's ever-growing influence and to assert greater independence, but other military adventurers tried also to take advantage of their intrigues, even in the southern provinces. Jiang Jieshi outwitted them all, with the assistance of the Shanghai financiers who raised his foreign loans, but there was no peace: from the early 1930s the Communists emerged as a real threat in the south, and after the death of Zhang Zoulin the Japanese tightened their grip on large parts of north China. In 1931 the latter were able to take over the whole of Manchuria and rename it Manzhouguo, the 'Manchu homeland'.

Although the capture of Beijing had obliged foreign powers to acknowledge Guomindang rule, policy towards China never really advanced beyond the gunboat era. The British were quite typical in their insistence that the Yangzi was an international waterway, the last vessel in their Yangzi river flotilla, HMS *Sandpiper*, being launched as late as 1933. To overawe the Chinese it was customary for such gunboats to salute each other by firing salvoes. Live ammunition was fired, however, on Chinese targets whenever passport holders were deemed to be in jeopardy, or labour troubles required a show of force. Britain's ambivalence about the republic was used adroitly by Japan to lend a degree of respectability to its own aggression.

Whilst Jiang Jieshi was ready to press the European nations on the vexed issue of extra-territoriality, which the Foreign Office in London thought it advisable to concede, he avoided offering direct resistance to the increasing Japanese threat. In part his reluctance to fight Japan stemmed from the Guomindang leadership's appreciation of the strength of its modernised neighbour.

Japanese-educated Wang Jinwei (1883-1944), China's future Pétain, was firmly convinced, on the other hand, that the liberation of East Asia depended upon an alliance between Japan and China. Even after the heavy bout of fighting in Shanghai at the beginning of 1932, Wang Jinwei could not be persuaded that the Japanese were unnatural allies against the West. Fortified by Wang Jinwei's foreign policy line, Jiang Jieshi was able to concentrate on internal order, if only because the other reason for not immediately standing up to Japanese pressure was his firm belief that the beneficiaries of a Sino-Japanese conflict would be the Communists.

So Jiang Jieshi concentrated on extermination drives against the Chinese Communist Party which, after a number of abortive urban risings in the late 1920s, had moved its operations into the countryside. In 1928 Mao Zedong and Zhu De (1886-1976) first withdrew to the hinterland in order to secure an effective base on the Hunan/Jiangxi provincial borders. There Mao Zedong came to the conclusion that the impoverished peasantry could wage protracted war from revolutionary bases situated in remote areas, as it was at places where the control of the Guomindang was weakest that the spark of revolution could be ignited.

More than any other Communist leader Mao Zedong recognised that China's plight was unique. The country differed from outright colonies in that it was controlled not just by one foreign power but by several who could never adopt a common approach. The lack of any strong central authority, together with the concentration of foreign power in the larger cities and along the coast, made the vast spaces of the countryside a promising area for sustained uprisings. Unauthorised by Comintern, the rural 'soviets' of Mao Zedong were condemned by the Central Committee of the Chinese Communist Party in Shanghai as 'rightist', especially as by implication they appeared to regard industrial workers, the sacred proletariat, as auxiliaries of the peasantry. The disastrous urban uprisings of 1930 finally persuaded Mao Zedong that the only strategy was 'encircling the cities with the countryside'. Looking back on these difficult years in 1939 he said,

the ruthless economic exploitation and political oppression of the peasants by the landlord class forced them into numerous rebellions against its rule . . . It was the class struggle of the peasant uprisings and the peasant wars that constituted the real motive force of historical development in Chinese feudal society.

What the Chinese Communist Party had to do was lead the peasantry in its historic mission: the democratic forces of the countryside would rise to overthrow the bureaucratic feudalism supported by the cities, be it imperialist or republican.

Skilful though Jiang Jieshi was in balancing the various forces within Guomindang politics, he failed to match the ideology of the Communists with any programme of popular appeal. The three principles of Sun Yatsen – nationalism, democracy and socialism – never became a clarion call for the Guomindang, whose membership was expected to offer Jiang Jieshi uncritical obedience. To many foreign observers he ended the chaotic conditions of the warlord period, a return to which business interests argued would bring irrevocable ruin to trade and endanger the substantial investments already made in the Chinese economy. They chose to overlook the uglier aspects of Guomindang rule. Scant notice was taken of the political activities of the Blue Shirt Society, a parallel of the Italian Black Shirts and the German Brown Shirts, while the spoils of office, the vast fortunes amassed by senior members of the Guomindang, went almost unremarked, even though it was known that Jiang Jieshi personally used the craft of the Opium Suppression Superintendence Bureau to traffic in the drug.

That the Guomindang never achieved a tight discipline over its members is not hard to understand. With no alternative political organisation allowed to exist, the party admitted to its membership everyone of importance, however dubious their social credentials. The tone had been set during the Shanghai massacre, when Jiang Jieshi relied on assistance from underworld bosses. Contrary to later report, the Guomindang in the 1930s was never the creature of big commercial and industrial interests. Its own militarism was sufficiently ingrained to encourage the leadership to regard these interests simply as a source of revenue, even if funds had to be extracted at the point of a bayonet. Having dispensed with Russian military advisers, Jiang Jieshi copied the Japanese and looked to Germany for support in building up his army.

Great effort went into the five offensives Jiang Jieshi launched against the Communist base areas in the southern provinces of Hebei, Hunan, Jiangxi and Fujian; the first two, in 1930 and early 1932, were repulsed by guerrilla tactics then being developed by Zhu De and Lin Biao (1907–71). The third encirclement, directed by Jiang Jieshi himself, was interrupted by the Mukden Incident in September 1931. The actual cause of Japanese intervention was Zhang Xueliang, who made no secret of his desire to check further encroachment in his homeland. There was nothing for it but to drive him south of the Great Wall.

Although fighting spread to Shanghai, where a heroic stand was made in early 1932 by Chinese forces stationed in the city, the Guomindang government quickly came to terms with Japan. Then Jiang Jieshi again turned on the Communists, but with such effect that by the end of 1934 total defeat stared them in the face. The only hope was to break through the encirclement and regroup elsewhere. In October the Long March began, an epic of human endurance lasting 370 days and covering 8000 kilometres. Of the 100,000 men who fought their way through the Guomindang network of forts and blockade lines only 20,000 survived the ordeal. It was force of circumstances rather than deliberate planning that made the march so long. Withdrawal to the north-east corner of Guizhou province was the first objective, a move covered through a rearguard action mounted by scattered guerrilla bands, largely comprising men unable to travel a great distance because of wounds. But continued harassment from Guomindang forces made it plain that the Communists needed an overall plan. This was devised at the Zunyi conference in January 1935, when Mao Zedong was acknowledged as the leader of the Chinese Communist Party. Taking up his slogan 'Go north and fight the Japanese', the conference endorsed a strategy of rural conflict and agreed that they should head northwards to Yan'an, the only remaining base area in Shaanxi province.

It was no accident that Mao Zedong came to power at the very moment Japanese forces readied themselves for action. The possibility that in order to avoid war the Guomindang might reach a general settlement with Japan was a daunting prospect for the Communists, against whom joint action by the Imperial Japanese Army and Jiang Jieshi's forces had been suggested by Tokyo. When the Guomindang indicated no great reluctance over extending diplomatic recognition to Manzhouguo or granting 'autonomy' to Hebei and Chahaer provinces, the Chinese Communist Party became very alarmed and embraced Mao Zedong's nationalist approach.

Jiang Jieshi felt he had no need of foreign allies against Yan'an. The expeditionary commander was less enthusiastic about the 'final encirclement'. Zhang Xueliang and his Manchurian troops could not understand the reason for the Guomindang's willingness to appease Japan, while their native provinces remained occupied and, by contrast, were very susceptible to a Communist slogan such as 'Fight back to Manchuria'. When in late 1936 the signing of the Anti-Comintern pact between Germany, Italy and Japan led Mussolini to establish diplomatic relations with Manzhouguo, Zhang Xueliang told his officers: 'This is absolutely the end of the Fascist movement in China!' Apparently unaware of the strength of feeling amongst all ranks of the northern armies, Jiang Jieshi arrived to expedite the campaign but found himself the prisoner of Zhang Xueliang and Yang Hucheng, commander of the Shaanxi army. At their insistence he concluded a truce with the Communists, who were represented at the negotiations by Zhou Enlai. Then an agreement was signed by which the Chinese Communist Party acknowledged the Guomindang government, but was allowed to establish its own autonomous regime in Yan'an. Both parties pledged themselves to resist Japan.

THE SINO-JAPANESE WAR (1937–45)

The pledge was soon to be honoured: in July 1937 an exchange of shots between Japanese and Chinese soldiers at the Marco Polo bridge, south-west of Beijing, gave Tokyo a pretext for war. The local Chinese commanders were willing to make concessions in order to reach a settlement but, confident of meeting little serious opposition from the Guomindang government, the Japanese war minister informed Hirohito that the conflict would be over within a month. His prediction to the emperor at first seemed correct, with the encirclement and surrender of Beijing in less than twenty days. Few Japanese army leaders expected a major campaign to ensue, and none foresaw how a military stalemate in China would lead to

Japan's fateful entry into the Second World War. Punishing a disorderly China was to prove no easy task.

For the Chinese Communist Party the clamour of public opinion that compelled Jiang Jieshi to respond forcibly to the fall of Beijing was a welcome relief. It was agreed that Guomindang armies would meet the enemy in positional warfare, while Communist forces infiltrated behind Japanese lines, waging a guerrilla campaign and organising local resistance. By the time Jiang Jieshi in late 1938 had made his wartime capital the city of Chongqing, in remote Sichuan province, Mao Zedong's guerrillas were operating on the shores of the Yellow Sea, nearly 1000 kilometres from Yan'an. The growth of national self-awareness, rudely stimulated by Japanese atrocity, can be judged in the increased numbers joining Communist units. That the great welling up of national consciousness took on a revolutionary vigour is a tribute to Mao Zedong's vision of the Sino-Japanese conflict as part of a larger struggle against Fascism.

Jiang Jieshi, too, held the view that China might benefit from an extension of war. If a Japanese victory could be prevented, he was sure that changes in the international situation would eventually create a climate favourable to the Guomindang government. The regime based in Chongqing therefore began to regard the United States as its most likely future ally against Japan. The outbreak of the Second World War in Europe, and Japan's subsequent alignment with the Axis powers, further convinced Jiang Jieshi of the rightness of his resistance. But a recurrent problem for him was the deep division inside the Guomindang hierarchy, especially after the defection of Wang Jinwei to the Japanese cause at the close of 1939.

In August 1937, however, Jiang Jieshi threw his crack units into battle at Shanghai as fighting erupted in the city. This move represented an attempt to force a stand in the southern provinces, for it was realised that Japanese strategy could be upset by compelling the Imperial Japanese Army to reinforce its troops in Shanghai against the numerically superior Guomindang forces. A bloodier repeat of the clash following the Mukden Incident, the second battle of Shanghai lasted for seven weeks and cost the lives of 250,000 Chinese soldiers. At such a price did Jiang Jieshi buy time for continued resistance in the interior, as a steady withdrawal towards Chongqing soon became a military necessity. *En route* a temporary respite was won at Tai'erzhuang, near the border of Shandong and Jiangsu provinces, where a Guomindang force not only inflicted 30,000 casualties on the over-confident Japanese, but afterwards executed a skilful retreat without losing any heavy equipment.

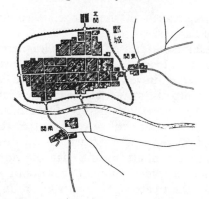

Fig. 45. The old walled city of Yancheng, Henan province. It is one of the military maps prepared for the Imperial Japanese Army for its war in China

Chongqing was well beyond the scope of a Japanese advance. Lines of communication were already overstretched and supplies hardly met the daily needs of the troops at the front. With bankruptcy in sight, Tokyo desperately tried to implement a new policy of supporting the Sino-Japanese War from local Chinese resources. To facilitate this policy, the Imperial Japanese Army seized the most important rivers, canals and railways which formed China's economic arteries. From a distance the military situation appeared to reflect an overwhelming Japanese victory. Little of China worth conquering was apparently left at the end of 1938: it was only a matter of time before Jiang Jieshi succumbed to an economic blockade. Yet from the viewpoint of Tokyo all was uncertain, with an economy crippled by expenditure on war, threatened by international trade embargoes, even armed intervention. The Soviet blows at Chengkufeng and Nomonhan merely served to underline Japan's weakness in 1938–9, when confronted by forces using modern equipment. Despite the commitment of half the Imperial Japanese Army to the Chinese theatre, there were insufficient soldiers to engage in the conventional battles required to reach Jiang Jieshi's refuge at Chongqing, and deal with the partisan activities of Communist regulars behind the lines. The latter eventually became standard tactics for the Chinese resistance and caused Japanese garrisons much difficulty. On the eve of the Pacific War twenty-seven Japanese divisions were still tied down by poorly equipped Chinese combatants: only one-fifth of the Imperial Japanese Army actually took part in operations in South-East Asia and the Pacific. It was as if the Japanese equivalent of the Panzerarmee Afrika drove the Europeans out of East Asia.

Once Jiang Jieshi had indicated his unwillingness to make peace, the Japanese turned instead to a puppet Chinese government under the leadership of Wang Jinwei. Expelled from the Guomindang for his pro-Japanese sympathies, Wang Jinwei had secretly travelled to Tokyo in order to discuss terms before. On a rainy day in March 1940 he declared his 'reformed' government established in Nanjing. His promise to rejuvinate China fell on deaf ears and the lack of any popular support meant that the administration he headed could not survive a single day without the backing of Japanese arms. In the treaty signed with Japan on 30 November, Wang Jinwei accepted terms far more severe than those imposed by Hitler on the Vichy regime in France. Its chief stipulation was Chinese recognition of Manzhougou, cold comfort for the restored Puyi. So frightened had the ex-Qing emperor become of the Japanese that he took his irritation out on servants by frequent floggings.

The focus of events in East Asia, however, moved elsewhere after the December 1941 attack on Pearl Harbor, despite President Roosevelt's unexpected broadcast of Jiang Jieshi's acceptance of 'supreme command over all land and air forces of the nations which are now, or may in the future, be operating in the Chinese theatre, including such portion of Indo-China and Thailand as may become available to the troops of the United Nations,' as the Allies were then known. This announcement was in accord with Roosevelt's decision to treat China as a Great Power: he intended to oust at the very least the French from their colonial holdings, at the end of hostilities. Although Jiang Jieshi was prepared to commit under American generalship a substantial part of his forces to the Burma campaign, he proved intractable when offensives were urged upon him in China. By 1944 it was obvious to Washington that the supreme commander intended to save his strength for a showdown with Mao Zedong. The best Guomindang troops, furnished with the latest American equipment, were deployed near the Yan'an base area. Rather sadly the same conclusion had already been reached by the Communists, who reconciled themselves to an armed struggle once Japan was defeated. Because of his warlord outlook, Jiang Jieshi was unable to perceive that building up a modern army was not enough to hold China. Idleness after 1940 weakened the morale of Guomindang soldiers just as energetic resistance to the Japanese strengthened the resolve of Communist irregulars. As the latter received virtually no outside supplies and had to survive on captured guns and ammunition, their successful actions indicated an iron will that was not likely to be bent by imported fire-power.

The defection of so many Guomindang generals to the Japanese side, and the use of their troops against Communist guerrillas, aroused the suspicion that Jiang Jieshi was merely awaiting the outcome of the war. According to popular rumour in 1944, Chongqing and Tokyo had come to an agreement by which Jiang Jieshi would not be attacked in his Sichuan stronghold, provided Guomindang forces offered no resistance to Japanese advances elsewhere. This patent double-dealing made the triumph of Communism in China almost unavoidable. At the very least it ensured that on the surrender of Japan in August 1945 the Chinese Communist Party alone could make a patriotic appeal.

THE TRIUMPH OF COMMUNISM (1946-9)

The shaky Guomindang foundations were not apparent outside China. The Chinese Communist Party had waged an unknown campaign in the northern provinces, while the generalissimo had been praised by Allied propaganda as a determined opponent of the Japanese, bravely holding out in beleaguered Chongqing. American diplomats and military advisers could not be unaware of the ramshackle administration and army that Jiang Jieshi led, but the reports they sent back to Washington were not intended for general consumption and, anyway, their criticisms would not have squared with accepted attitudes towards China in the United States.

Ever since President Roosevelt had elevated China to Great Power status, American public opinion looked upon the fate of the country as being synonymous with that of the Guomindang government. The near collapse before the final Japanese offensive in 1944 was not generally advertised, although Mao Zedong pointed out the reason for Jiang Jieshi's military failure: 'For five years and six months the Guomindang have been standing by with folded arms, completely deprived of fighting capacity.' But the comments of a Soviet puppet could be safely ignored in Washington, where the powerful 'China Lobby' ruled the roost. Once the weakness of the Guomindang armies could no longer be disguised in the civil war of 1947-9, lobby members stepped up their pressure on the administration to succour Jiang Jieshi and prevent a 'Red China'. By temperament they were unable to accept the fact of Mao Zedong's victory, an inability to face reality that Senator Joseph McCarthy was about to exploit for his own purposes.

Civil war could not be avoided as long as Jiang Jieshi thought that he would win. Initially he had expected American forces to land on the southern coast and move northwards against the Japanese. Behind the shield of the US Army he would have been able to consolidate his own position, before striking against the Chinese Communist Party. It was, therefore, a bitter disappointment to him when the success of the campaigns in the Pacific caused the United States to alter its strategy from a landing on the Chinese mainland to one of island-hopping until the Japanese islands themselves were reached. This change relegated Jiang Jieshi to the periphery of the war and made available to the Guomindang far fewer military supplies than he anticipated. In the event, the dropping of atomic bombs on Hiroshima and Nagasaki in early August 1945 caught everyone by surprise.

The war in East Asia was suddenly over, but the problems created by the Sino-Japanese conflict remained unsolved. The Guomindang were bottled up in western China; Chinese puppet troops were spread throughout the Japanese-dominated areas; and Communist guerrillas controlled the northern provinces apart from the cities and towns with Japanese garrisons. To whom these soldiers should surrender proved an immediate point of dispute.

With Soviet forces moving into Manchuria to disarm Japanese troops and to seize industrial plant for use in Russia, Washington decided that swift action was required. Roosevelt's successor, Harry Truman, ordered the Japanese to stay and maintain order until they could be replaced by Guomindang or US forces. 'It was perfectly clear to us,' he wrote in his *Memoirs*, 'if we told the Japanese to lay down their arms and march to the seaboard the entire country would be taken over by the Communists.' Airlifting Guomindang units to relieve the hated Japanese ranks was one of the worst decisions taken at the end of the Second World War. The returning troops of Jiang Jieshi were seen as the allies of the Japanese and the puppet troops who had sided with the invaders. 'In Nanjing,' an American diplomat noted with bewilderment, 'the high Japanese generals are bosom buddies of the Chinese. In the north tens of thousands of Japanese soldiers are used to guard railroads and warehouses and to fight the Communists.' The political mistake was to prove just as disastrous in terms of strategy. With the Communists in effective control of the countryside, Jiang Jieshi simply inherited the military difficulties of the Imperial Japanese Army. Had he chosen to secure south China first, and at the same time tried to reassure the peasants by introducing a measure of land reform, then he might have been able to push northwards without peril. Not even the presence of 143,000 American troops in the northern provinces during 1946–7 could guarantee Guomindang success.

The withdrawal of Soviet forces in April 1946 from Manchuria set the scene for the outbreak of civil war in the northern provinces. Whilst Jiang Jieshi garrisoned the larger towns and cities with his best troops, the tactics of the People's Liberation Army, as the Communists now styled their forces, were quite different: units were pulled out of urban areas, including Yan'an, and efforts were directed at consolidating its position in the countryside, from which attacks could be delivered at Guomindang concentrations without the risk of large-scale engagements. Despite an overwhelming superiority in men and fire-power, the Guomindang forces were badly overextended. Yet nothing could deter Jiang Jieshi from seeking a final contest with Mao Zedong. Washington was obliged to stand by and watch in horror as both the Guomindang army and the Chinese economy dissolved. Official corruption, rampant inflation, and unchecked military expenditure on the civil war assisted the Communists to power almost as much as their own actions in the field.

The end was in sight in April 1949, when Communist field artillery trapped between Shanghai and Nanjing the Royal Navy frigate HMS *Amethyst*. For three months the vessel remained a prisoner of the People's Liberation Army, which refused to let the ship weigh anchor until her captain signed a document admitting British responsibility for 'a criminal invasion of Chinese waters'. Although the frigate's daring escape upheld the honour of the Royal Navy, the incident unequivocally marked the end of the gunboat era in China. But this reassertion of Chinese sovereignty belonged to the countryside, where as an American diplomat also noted, 'the Communists, perhaps as much through necessity as wisdom, are penetrating the villages and finding a response where for a long time no one has cared what happened . . .'.

13

END OF EMPIRE

The Pacific War
and Its Consequences
(1941–7)

By the end of 1939 Japan was living beyond its means. The impact
of the European war on the price of key commodities proved disastrous for the Japanese economy, already struggling to keep pace
with rising military consumption in China. Planned increases in
Japanese output were hit by the doubling in price of scrap iron, and
the shortage of good-quality coal for making steel. Perhaps the
most worrying aspect of the situation, though, was the growing
dependence of Japan on imports from the United States. In scrap
iron, aluminium, nickel and oil products American dominance
was so great that Tokyo could not withstand any economic pressure
from Washington for more than a few months. But the Imperial
Japanese Army held that withdrawal from China was an unreasonable price to pay for such essential items, even though President
Roosevelt made no secret of his anger at its actions against the
Chinese.

To forestall any US demands the Imperial Japanese Army
launched a new offensive in early 1940, but this attempt to breach
the Yangzi gorges and advance on Jiang Jieshi's headquarters at
Chongqing ground to a halt at Ichang in late summer. While this
operation was in progress, army leaders learned of the German
conquest of the Low Countries and France, and they resolved to
capture the oil, tin and rubber available from their weakened
colonies in South-East Asia.

Vichy France was unable to resist Japanese demands: the Imperial

Japanese Army chose Saigon as the headquarters for a southern thrust against Malaya, Borneo, the Philippines and Indonesia. An ally was made of Thailand by supporting claims for territory appropriated in the nineteenth century by France. An admirer of Mussolini and Hitler, the prime minister, Luang Phibunsongkhram (1879–1990), or Phibun for short, had changed the country's name from Siam to Thailand in 1939 as a token of its rebirth as an authoritarian power. Phibun was rewarded with Japanese planes, guns and ammunition in the Franco-Thai War of 1940–1. Although French colonial forces won a major naval victory in January 1941 at Ko Chuang Island, the Thai had better luck on land along the Cambodian border where the French could not easily replace their losses. By May it was agreed that parts of Laos and Cambodia should be ceded to Thailand. In January 1942, when the Japanese were pressing down the Malayan peninsula towards Singapore, Phibun's government declared war on the United States and Britain. The Thai ambassador in Washington, however, refused to deliver the declaration of war and set about organising a Free Thai movement with American assistance.

The only power to which Vichy France could have looked for aid in South-East Asia was Britain, but after the Royal Navy bombarded French warships in North African ports during July 1940 to stop them from falling into German hands, all diplomatic relations had been severed. Even an attack on Gibraltar was launched in retaliation from Vichy airfields in Algeria. These international niceties were appreciated by Matsuoka Yosuke (1880–1946), the spokesman for the Imperial Japanese Army. Minister for foreign affairs after September 1940, he was not a man to hesitate over a confrontation with a Western state. Bitter experience of racial prejudice in the United States, where he graduated as a lawyer, scarcely prepared Matsuoka Yosuke for the role of diplomatic conciliator. He began his ministerial career instead by forming an alliance in September 1940 with Germany and Italy. It was directed primarily at the United States, since Hitler assured Japan that a concentration of German divisions on the Russian border would be enough to deter a move by the Soviet Union in East Asia. Germany wanted Japan to fall upon British and Dutch possessions in South-East Asia. With a rare understanding of American politics, Hitler calculated that Roosevelt would find it very difficult indeed to go to war for the sake of Singapore.

Britain's refusal to surrender in the winter of 1940–1 awakened new fears in Tokyo, as did the passing of the Lease-Lend Act in

"*SCRAM!*"

Fig. 46. This *Daily Mirror* cartoon of August 1940 welcomed the decision of the United States to restrict oil supplies to Japan. As yet, the Japanese threat was seen as a tiny irritant

March 1941. Because the United States was rapidly turning itself into a gigantic arms factory, and building up its own military strength in Hawaii and the Philippines, Matsuoka Yosuke reinsured his diplomacy by concluding a month later the Russo-Japanese neutrality pact, which remained in force almost to the end of the war in East Asia. But his fatal mistake was to ally Japan with countries too distant to offer direct military help. The move southward into South-East Asia not only ended in failure, but it also turned Britain and the United States into enemies of Japan. The German invasion of the Soviet Union in June 1941 added another opponent, although a state of belligerence between the Russians and the Japanese was not declared for another four more years.

The Japanese occupation of French Indo-China brought relations between Washington and Tokyo to a head. General Tojo Hideki (1884–1948) had recognised the dangers involved, but the government he headed could see no alternative: the resources of South-East Asia alone offered Japan a chance of concluding the Sino-Japanese War without falling under American domination.

Last-minute negotiations were conducted with Washington in case a peaceful solution could be reached. The task force sent against Pearl Harbor was ordered to leave room for calling off its surprise operation, so that it could return to Japan with peace preserved. In the event there was no agreement between Japan and the United States, and early on the morning of 7 December 1941 400 carrier-based Japanese planes attacked the American naval base in Hawaii.

The damage caused by the torpedo-bombers and dive-bombers to American battleships in the three-hour raid seemed impressive: seven sank at their moorings or went to the bottom of the harbour close by. American carelessness played its part. Radar reports of approaching aircraft were not acted upon, and even the detonation of the first bombs was taken to be nothing more than a practice drill. When Japanese planes were overhead there was no time to do more than limit the damage to ships and installations. That under 3000 American servicemen were killed came as a surprise when the action was over, just as the permanent loss of only one ship, the USS *Arizona*, showed how an encounter close to shore was less destructive than one fought at sea. The badly damaged battleships were rebuilt to modern standards, much to Japan's eventual disadvantage, with enough anti-aircraft guns to supplement the air cover that was recognised as essential for their safety. The absence of the three American aircraft carriers belonging to the Pacific Fleet also reduced the Japanese triumph.

Yamamoto Isoroku (1884–1943), who planned the air attack, was realistic about American capacity for recovery. He said, 'This war will give us much trouble in future. The fact that we have had a small success at Pearl Harbor is nothing.' But the immediate strategic consequences of Pearl Harbor blinded the Imperial Japanese Army to the basic weakness of Japan's position, not least because the easy southern sweep into South-East Asia, that a Pacific almost empty of enemy warships permitted, gave a false impression of its strength. In the United States the perspective on Japan was equally affected by its lightning successes on sea and land. The racial stereotype of the Japanese male as a slow-witted and short-sighted dwarf gave place to an exaggerated fear of his superhuman stamina and courage.

But Pearl Harbor brought the United States into the war as a determined belligerent, so fierce was American anger. President Roosevelt was not even certain that Congress would declare war on Germany, but on 11 December 1941 Hitler fortunately solved the dilemma by declaring war on the United States.

During the first six months of the Pacific War the Japanese advanced from victory to victory. The stunning blow at Pearl Harbor upset the strategies of both the Americans and the British in East Asia. As the United States expected that one of Japan's initial moves would be an invasion of the Philippines, the task of the American garrison at Manila Bay was to hold the naval facilities there until the Pacific Fleet could arrive from Hawaii. Likewise the British had

"WHEN ARE YOU COMING IN, MATSUOKA? I'VE ALREADY ENTERED MY THIRD WEEK
IN RUSSIA."
"WHAT'S THE HURRY, ADOLF? WE'VE JUST ENTERED OUR FIFTH YEAR IN CHINA."

Fig. 47. A *Daily Express* cartoon neatly pointing out the different problems of
Germany and Japan in 1941

always pinned their hopes on Singapore, where a powerful naval
base was sited. But Britain had never built a separate modern fleet
to operate east of India. To placate Australian and New Zealand
anxieties it was declared that in the event of trouble with Japan the
main British fleet could be sail to Singapore within seventy to ninety
days. This planning presupposed that Britain was not endangered
itself. In late 1941 the Royal Navy was tied down by German U-
boats in the Atlantic Ocean.

In November 1941 Churchill had written to his new ally Stalin
that 'with the object of keeping Japan quiet we are sending our
latest battleship, *Prince of Wales*, which can catch and kill any
Japanese ship, into the Indian Ocean'. It was a hurried gesture that
Churchill would have cause to rue. The original plan called for the
dispatch of the *Prince of Wales* and the battlecruiser *Repulse*, along
with the aircraft-carrier *Indomitable*. Unfortunately the latter ran
aground in the West Indies and was unable to sail eastwards. Thus
the two great warships arrived in Singapore, where they were
required to operate without air cover. Three days after Pearl Harbor
they were caught by Japanese aircraft off the east coast of Malaya and
in a few hours sent to the bottom. Only the presence of two destroy-
ers enabled as many as 2000 sailors to be rescued. As Terence
O'Brien, an RAF pilot who was later transferred to East Asia, wrote
of sending the battleships without air cover:

It was an incredible action. Around England even single merchantmen
had an air escort, convoys not only had a continuous patrol overhead but

were also covered by fighter contacts . . . the two battleships . . . were nothing more than sacrificial targets.

As a result of their loss, the way was opened for an unimpeded Japanese advance into South-East Asia.

Having captured Hong Kong in December 1941, the Imperial Japanese Army swept on to take the surrender of the British forces at Singapore in February 1942, and that of the Dutch in Java and the American in the Philippines in May. By then the Imperial Japanese Army had overrun Borneo, Burma, Timor, Guam and the eastern islands of the Solomons, besides landing in strength on New Guinea. Meanwhile the Imperial Japanese Navy cleared the seas of hostile craft, sinking a combined Allied squadron of eleven ships in the battle of the Java Sea. Forays into the Indian Ocean wrought havoc amongst British merchant shipping, the sinking of a number of Royal Navy vessels, and resulted in the bombardment of two coastal cities in Ceylon (present-day Sri Lanka). Had not British warships recourse to a secret base in the Maldives to the south, there is every reason to believe that losses could have been even worse. As it was, the Japanese destroyed one light aircraft-carrier, three cruisers, and one corvette for the loss of seventeen aircraft. Churchill feared the fall of Ceylon and the invasion of India, which would have severed all contact with Guomindang China, but to the relief of the Allies, the withdrawal of the Imperial Japanese Navy indicated that Tokyo had secured its immediate strategic objectives and was not planning to advance further westwards.

Although the Japanese whirlwind of late 1941 and early 1942 amazed the world, nothing in its irresistible path of destruction quite matched the unconditional surrender of 85,000 men at Singapore. The fall of this 'impregnable' fortress was a psychological shock from which the British empire never fully recovered. It heralded the liquidation of Western authority throughout East Asia. A mistaken confidence in a jungle shield militated against any preparation of landward defences for Singapore; its heavy guns faced the sea. Added to the difficulty was the untimely diversion of Hurricanes to Russia, then locked in titanic combat with Germany. The Royal Air Force estimated that over 500 planes would be needed to retain air superiority. Out of the 158 available only forty-one American-made Brewster Buffaloes offered any real threat and they were quickly downed by agile Zeros. Last-minute reinforcements of more modern aircraft from Britain were frittered away in uncoordinated actions.

Yet British blunders aside, Japanese tactics in the Malayan campaign deserve praise for sheer ingenuity. General Yamashita Tomoyuki (1885–1946) broke through the Jitra line, a strongly fortified position of wire entanglements and deep trenches astride the road to Alor Star. It was expected to be held for three months. An impromptu night attack by barely 500 Japanese soldiers drove off the bulk of the defenders in a matter of hours. Along with 3000 prisoners came large stores of ammunition, petrol and food. For the rest of the campaign, according to staff officer Masanobu Tsuji, these frequent bags of supplies were called 'Churchill's allowance'. To turn British positions baffling tactics were employed, such as night attacks, encirclement, sudden charges, and small boat operations. To maintain the momentum of the advance Japanese infantry commandeered bicycles. Masanobu Tsuji recalled how

a bicycle repair squad of at least two men was attached to every company . . . [but] repairs were only makeshift. When the enemy were being hotly pursued . . . punctured tyres were taken off and bicycles ridden on the rims . . . Numbers of bicycles, some with tyres and some without, when passing along the road, made a noise resembling that of tanks. At night when bicycle units advanced the enemy frequently retreated hurriedly, saying, 'Here come the tanks.'

When necessary the Japanese abandoned pedals and advanced through the jungle, a tactic the British found very disconcerting. Another was to be subject so often to an attack from the rear.

Yamashita Tomoyuki intended to capture Singapore by the anniversary of the first emperor's legendary accession. The intense battle for the bridge over the Slim river in January 1942, sealed the fate of Kuala Lumpur, capital of the Malayan Federation. Outflanking movements through the jungle, which lay behind the rubber planations on each side of the road, forced the British and Indian troops to fall back.

The casualty list for the Imperial Japanese Army on the eve of its final assault on Singapore was just over 4,500 killed and wounded. British losses were estimated at five brigades, or 25,000 men. With the island's population swollen with refugees and displaced troops, the last-minute arrival of raw British and Australian reinforcements can be regarded only as supreme folly. Few of them fired a shot in the confused defence of Singapore, which a force of 35,000 Japanese easily captured. Churchill was compelled to admit: 'The violence, fury, skill, and might of Japan far exceeded anything we had been led to expect.' Tomoyuki's men had outrun their supplies, and yet won a notable victory by bravery and bluff. They had also treated abominably captured soldiers and civilians, a recurrent trait that caused the observant Masanobu Tsuji some alarm.

JAPAN'S NEW ORDER IN EAST ASIA (1942–4)

With the retreat of shattered British and Chinese forces into Assam, the most westerly country in South-East Asia fell under Japanese control. The capture of Burma in May 1942 did more than close the Burma road, Jiang Jieshi's southern supply route; it made Japan, however briefly, the sole imperial power in East Asia. The Imperial Japanese Army lost no opportunity of humiliating Europeans before local populations. In Malaya British captives, stripped to the waist, were made to tackle manual work as a reminder that before the Japanese came Europeans never undertook such tasks. The sultans who controlled the various Malay states, the *Shonan Times*, (the renamed *Straits Times*) reported on 18 April 1942, paid their respects to the Japanese commander-in-chief, and were all looking forward to becoming leaders in the rebuilding of Malaya. They probably did not enjoy the decision of Tojo Hideki in May 1943 to hand over to Thailand the states of Perlis, Kedah, Kalantan and Trengganu, British acquisitions of 1909, because of rising Thai discontent. Turning Thailand into Japan's rice bowl had exacerbated food shortages in Bangkok and other Thai cities.

This move ran counter to a policy of favouring Malays. Necessity drove Japan to appease Thailand in the same way that it obliged an accommodation with the overseas Chinese communities scattered throughout South-East Asia. Denied reliable news from China, the overseas Chinese had to pin their hopes on an Allied counter-offensive. Individuals thus took great personal risks when they endeavoured to ease secretly the lot of European prisoners, who toiled under appalling conditions on such projects as the Burma railway. Over 100,000 indented coolies, mainly from Indonesia and Malaysia, are estimated to have died in its construction; and over 12,000 Allied prisoners of war are known to have perished at the rate of one death for every 25 metres of track.

The imperial edict of Hirohito which proclaimed a state of war with the United States and Britain announced the purpose of the conflict as being the independence of East Asia. Elimination of Western interests would allow the establishment of the Greater East Asia Co-Prosperity Sphere, in which East Asian peoples could develop together an unexploited and self-sufficient economic zone.

In January 1942 Tojo Hideki said that, since Hong Kong, Malaya and Singapore were strategically vital for East Asian defence, they would remain under the direct authority of the Imperial Japanese Army. Providing the peoples of the Philippines and Burma pledged their support, these two countries could expect to be granted independence. A less definite pledge was offered to the people of Indonesia, the former Dutch East Indies. Possibly the welcome received by the Japanese invasion force encouraged Tokyo to believe that a longer timescale was feasible. The passivity of the local population, except in Timor and Amboina, ruled out any attempt at guerrilla warfare by the Dutch. In Sumatra Dutch settlers had to be protected by Japanese soldiers during a foretaste of the anti-colonial agitation that was to engulf the restored Netherlands government after the surrender of Japan. The contrast between resistance in the Philippines and Indonesia was not missed by Roosevelt, who started to consider new political arrangements for a post-war settlement. With independence from American rule only five years hence Filipino soldiers fought shoulder to shoulder with US servicemen in the defence of the Bataan peninsula, south-west of Manila, necessitating heavy Japanese reinforcements to overcome its stubborn defenders.

President Roosevelt's intentions had to be concealed until the Allied landings took place in French North Africa during late 1942. Once the Vichyite authorities there were neutralised, the whole question of post-war East Asia could be discussed. Vichy collaboration with the Japanese in Indo-China still smarted, and Washington informed London of a plan for a trusteeship, possibly administered by the Guomindang government. Churchill was deeply shocked. If the United States succeeded in dismantling French colonial territories in South-East Asia, the British colonies would be next. Already American pressure for Indian independence had called forth his famous rejoinder: 'I have not become the King's First Minister to preside over the liquidation of the British Empire.' But this thorny problem was to be solved for Churchill by Jiang Jieshi, whom not even the 'China Lobby' in Washington could excuse for hoarding military supplies against a showdown with Mao Zedong. The point-blank refusal of Jiang Jieshi in 1944 to send American-equipped troops to aid the British in Burma marked the end of Washington's confidence in China as a guarantor of future peace.

The imperial settlement imposed by the Japanese was somewhat different. For the formation of the Greater East Asia Co-Prosperity Sphere meant not only the attainment of Japan's long-desired self-

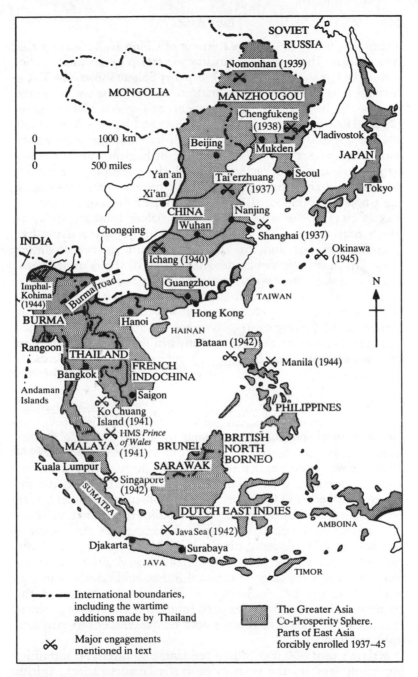

The Greater Asia Co-Prosperity Sphere

sufficiency, but more the replacement of China as the leading East Asian power. That a special ministry was set up to formulate policy within the Greater East Asia Co-Prosperity Sphere shows how Tokyo envisaged its complete subordination to the Japanese economy. A meeting of allegedly independent members – Manzhougou, China, Thailand, Burma, the Philippines and Japan – held in late 1943 simply dealt with cultural issues. Japanese language specialists had been sent out to eliminate the use of English and Dutch as a second language. The dependence of the assembled leaders on Japanese military support indicated the fundamental weakness of the whole organisation. Tojo Hideki himself did not assume the post of chief of the army general staff before February 1944, by which time the war was lost. The Imperial Japanese Army had created the empire and, till the Allies became an overwhelming threat, its harsh rule went unchallenged in all the occupied territories, including those with supposedly independent governments. From 1944 onwards, however, anti-Japanese nationalist movements began to emerge throughout the Greater East Asia Co-Prosperity Sphere, as the striking contrast between the ideal of a joint venture and everyday life destroyed all enthusiasm for Pan-Asianism. Had the Japanese empire not been torn apart by war, it would have surely succumbed to a bloody series of liberation struggles.

THE FALL OF THE JAPANESE EMPIRE (1944–5)

One liberation movement sponsored by Tokyo aimed at freeing India from British control. Its leader, Subhas Chandra Bose (1897–1945), rejected the attachment of Gandhi to non-violent protest and was impatient to have an Indian army fighting alongside the Japanese. Whether in Germany, where he broadcast and met Indian prisoners captured by the Panzerarmee Afrika, or in Japan, to which he travelled in German and Japanese submarines that made a rendezvous off Madagascar, his considerable energy was poured into the task of raising the Indian National Army. A prime target for recruitment was the large number of Indian soldiers who had surrendered on the fall of Singapore. With the permission of the Japanese authorities, Bose extracted funds from the Indian business community in Malaya to finance both his government-in-exile and its armed forces.

Malaya's own 800,000 Indian residents also offered possibilities for recruitment. In the years prior to the Japanese attack, British settlers were very concerned about preserving their prestige as 'minor gods'. In Singapore the two main clubs, the Tanglin Club and the Swimming Club, were both exclusively European in membership. The racism underlying this arrangement became very apparent in the months before the Japanese siege of the island, as Indian officers found themselves denied entry unlike fellow British officers from their regiments. Clubs frankly reflected and reinforced the political realities of empire in a way that for instance the cinema did not: a rigorous censorship of the films on show often failed to protect British prestige. Settlers were annoyed that film studios chose to portray Europeans as lascivious lovers, fools, criminals, and even tramps like Charlie Chaplin. It was because they believed that the war, the cinema, and other outside influences were undermining their privileged position that Europeans living in Malaya felt they should do all they could to maintain the status quo. They were naturally shocked to discover later that the strictness of club committees provided no protection from Yamashita Tomoyuki and his men.

Subhas Chandra Bose attended the 1943 meeting of the Greater East Asia Co-Prosperity Sphere in Tokyo as an observer. In 1944 he was allowed to administer the Andaman and Nicobar Islands, much to the alarm of the British government of India. But Bose's attempt to suborn Indian troops in the British Fourteenth Army failed miserably. One problem was the low morale of the Indian National Army, which the Japanese allowed to join their March 1944 attack across the Indian border. Units took little part in the heavy hand-to-hand fighting. Their role was to confuse and dismay the Indian soldiers helping to oppose the Japanese advance. After the Imperial Japanese Army fell back, and retreated into Burma, Bose's men found themselves largely abandoned to their fate. General Slim, commander of the Fourteenth Army, remembered how at Palel, south of Imphal, dispirited men belonging to the Gandhi Brigade of the Indian National Army just wandered about

without object or cohesion. They had suffered a good many casualties at the hands of our patrols and during May were surrendering in large numbers, but our Indian and Gurkha soldiers were at times not too ready to let them surrender, and orders had to be issued to give them a kinder welcome.

The march on Delhi, so proudly proclaimed by Bose at the start of the Japanese attack, was off.

The costly attempt to invade India had been doomed from the start by the Imperial Japanese Army's refusal to consider logistics.

Without adequate support from the air, Japanese soldiers ran short of supplies and had to eat pack oxen as well as grass for food. Their situation was made worse by the British Fourteenth Army, which stood firm and fought on whenever its positions were surrounded. No supplies were captured as in the Malayan campaign. The improved strength of the Royal Air Force was another factor, since it was able to sustain hard-pressed garrisons by parachute drops, a new tactic devised as a result of British activities behind Japanese lines. Food and ammunition were dropped from the skies, while at the height of the struggle in Kohima, when the Japanese gained possession of the defenders' water supply, planes flew in at tree-top level to deliver motor-car inner tubes filled with water.

The rout of the Japanese as they were pressed back in Burma had cost them 100,000 men by the fall of Rangoon in early May 1945. One of the worst defeats ever inflicted upon the Imperial Japanese Army, the retreat was characterised by inexplicable acts of valour and violence. To the amazement of their pursuers a cut-off group of Japanese, in full equipment and with closed ranks, marched into the Irrawaddy river until the water closed over their heads. As self-destructive, though more effective, were the human mines used to deal with British tanks. A Japanese soldier would crouch with an aircraft bomb between his knees in a foxhole, and strike the fuse with a stone as a tank passed overhead. Elsewhere unprovoked attacks on hospitals and the civilian population were signs of Japanese rage.

The attack on India was almost the last major operation launched by the Imperial Japanese Army. During 1943 the outer defences of the Greater East Asia Co-Prosperity Sphere began to crumble dramatically. The Solomon and Gilbert Islands were lost, then the Marshall Islands fell in February 1944, and the Japanese garrison on Truk, in the Caroline Islands, was the same month condemned to a fierce US air and naval bombardment.

Whereas the Japanese were unable to replace the four aircraft-carriers lost at Midway, American shipyards were turning out dozens of aircraft-carriers that became the core of task forces assaulting Japanese bastions across the Pacific. While the battle of the Coral Sea in May 1942, the first naval engagement to be decided by carrier-based planes, had stopped the Japanese capture of Port Moresby in New Guinea, the American victory was far from decisive. Only at Midway, a month later, could the United States seize the initiative by sinking with dive-bombers four Japanese aircraft-carriers. Three were destroyed in six minutes by a dozen pilots. In this epic battle the United States lost one aircraft carrier, one destroyer, and 147 planes.

After Midway Japan was on the defensive. American marines followed up with landings in the Solomons, which they soon controlled despite the unexpected naval reverse at Savo Island. An Allied offensive in 1943 also secured New Guinea, although many Japanese troops fled into the jungle, where a few die-hards were to remain for over twenty years. By mid-1944 Douglas MacArthur, (1880–1964), the Allied commander in the southern Pacific, had begun an island-hopping campaign towards Tokyo. In October the general was recorded by film cameras wading in knee-deep water as American troops returned to the Philippines. But a resolute Japanese defence left 100,000 Filipino civilians dead in the battle for Manila. The unexpected loss of the Philippines breached Japan's inner defences, and Tojo Hideki was forced to resign. His successor sought to carry on the war while losing no opportunity to secure a satisfactory peace.

The days of the Greater East Asia Co-Prosperity Sphere were numbered. In an unadvertised campaign as unrestricted as that waged by German U-boats, American submarines had sent Japanese merchantmen to the bottom by the hundred. Few ships were left afloat to transport oil, the very product for which Japan had begun hostilities. The last Japanese premier of the war said: 'The basic cause of defeat is the loss of shipping transport.' The drive for imperial self-sufficiency had obviously come to nothing.

Before the final capitulation, bloody engagements were fought by the United States for the capture of Iwo Jima and Okinawa, two heavily fortified islands on the doorstep of Japan. American losses of almost 27,000 killed on Iwo Jima were greater than the annihilated Japanese garrison. On Okinawa the Americans lost 40,000 men in order to kill 110,000 Japanese entrenched in caves and bunkers. These horrendous losses doubtless persuaded Roosevelt of the need for Russian intervention as soon as possible. The president had realised that Jiang Jieshi would never assist American interests in East Asia. The United States was later to appreciate that Stalin's support had more to do with the recovery in China of Russian concessions lost to Japan in 1906.

Once the Americans had landed on Okinawa, they realised that a suicidal foe awaited their every move. Japanese troops in skilfully constructed hideouts dogged any advance, while kamikaze pilots harassed the vast task force anchored off the island. Several thousand suicide air attacks surprised the Allied fleet, and snatched world headlines, in a futile sacrifice of brave young pilots that revealed the feebleness of Japan's defences against American technology.

The ferocity of the kamikazes struck terror in Allied hearts, but they had no real chance of halting the operation, despite sinking 36 ships and causing damage to 371 others. Japanese planes were no match for the improved American fighters in the last eighteen months of the Pacific War, and whole squadrons were often largely wiped out before they could reach their targets.

The surreal atmosphere surrounding the Okinawa campaign was enhanced by another Japanese sacrifice, the leviathan *Yamato*. The pride of the Imperial Japanese Navy, the *Yamato* with a displacement of over 68,000 tonnes was the largest battleship afloat. As the ultimate kamikaze, its mission was to wreak as much havoc as possible, firing its great guns until all ammunition was spent. On the way to Okinawa the battleship, entirely unprotected by Japanese aircraft, fell prey to waves of American bombers.

The fate of the *Yamato* on 7 April convinced the Allies that the Japanese government knew that defeat was imminent. The surrender of Germany exactly one month later could only add to the certainty, as Allied might was henceforth free to concentrate on the Pacific. Yet the lack of any Japanese move to end the fighting remained a worry for Harry S. Truman, the vice-president who succeeded to the presidency in April on Roosevelt's death. He was as convinced as his predecessor about the need for Stalin's help against a Japan determined to fight to the last. In the ruins of Berlin at the former German imperial palace at Potsdam, the United States, Britain and Russia issued in July a declaration calling upon Japan to cease hostilities or face 'prompt and utter destruction'. At this conference Truman had told Stalin that a new weapon had been exploded at a test site in New Mexico a few days before. The explosion was the climax of a research project that involved American, Canadian and British scientists, although during the final stages of development the United States chose to keep secret the method of the bomb's construction.

Disenchanted with Stalin and uncertain of the American casualties in an invasion of Japan, Truman decided that two of the new atomic bombs should be dropped to end the Pacific War. Several of the scientists involved in the project insisted that the United States warn Tokyo with a demonstration of the weapon on a deserted island, not on a Japanese city. The suggestion was rejected, and the bombing authorized. Truman later declared that he dropped the atomic bombs on Japan to save lives. With American planes already destroying entire Japanese cities by means of incendiary devices the president's explanation looks a very thin one indeed. But a quick end to the Pacific War would also conveniently avoid the need for a Russian occupation of Manchuria. Frostiness between the United States and the Soviet Union had already begun to affect the political climate of the world, in what was recognised later as the Cold War. Truman therefore rejected the Japanese wish to preserve the religious authority of the emperor – he wanted unconditional surrender. Stalin readily concurred because he wanted to declare war himself and lay claim on Japanese territory.

On 6 August a mushroom cloud spread above Hiroshima as the first atomic bomb devastated the city with a force 'brighter than a thousand suns'. In hours 80,000 of the inhabitants were dead, and 120,000 more suffered from terrible burns and from the effects of radiation. One survivor trying to help a woman took her 'by the hands but her skin slipped off in huge, glove-like pieces'. As the Japanese cabinet on 9 August was considering the Potsdam terms for surrender now that Russia had entered the war too, news came of a second atomic explosion at Nagasaki, where another 65,000 people immediately died. The next day Hirohito overruled prolonged resistance, and offered to surrender if the Allies accepted the continuation of the imperial house. Neither an abortive military coup nor the ritual suicide of senior officers could dent the emperor's resolve, with the result that a startled nation heard the voice of their ruler for the first time on 15 August broadcast the war's end. No one dared look at a radio during the brief statement, and afterwards Hirohito's message had to be translated from the arcane language of the imperial court into intelligible everyday Japanese. But the Pacific War was over.

THE POST-WAR SETTLEMENT (1945–7)

From a prisoner-of-war camp in Java Laurens van der Post welcomed the news of Hiroshima for a special reason. 'This cataclysm I was certain would make the Japanese feel that they could now withdraw from the war without dishonour, because it would strike them, as it had us in the silence of our prison night, as something supernatural.' His own study of Japan convinced him that the fireball would be associated with divine will, and allow the Imperial Japanese Army to surrender with honour to such an overwhelming force. Whether or not many Japanese reflected on the power of the sun goddess Amaterasu that August, they were swiftly back to earth on 2 September when USS *Missouri* sailed into Tokyo Bay. General MacArthur, yet another implacable Perry, was on board to oversee Japanese officials signing the surrender documents.

The post-war settlement in East Asia that stemmed from this ceremony did not accord with the liberal principles of the Atlantic Charter. Truman had to look the other way as the British, French and Dutch moved back into their colonies. Yet there was a significant difference in attitude between these three colonial powers. Having elected by a landslide a Labour government, Britain alone would be spared disastrous colonial wars. With a keen awareness of the economic and political changes wrought by Japan's temporary triumph, the British prime minister, Clement Attlee, took on the issue of decolonisation himself: 'The Commonwealth is a free association of free peoples,' he said in 1946. It would have been dishonest to keep peoples within its borders against their will.

The biggest problem facing Britain was India, for which Attlee cleverly chose Mountbatten as the viceroy responsible for the handover of power. Lord Louis Mountbatten (1900–79) had been supreme commander of the South-East Asia Allied Command when the Labour government was formed in July 1945. Within a few weeks of taking office, Attlee decided to give Mountbatten an unusual freedom of action on military grounds which he employed to bring about fundamental political changes. In early 1945, though the Japanese were in retreat, it was far from clear that their expulsion from Burma was at hand. With Attlee's support then as a member of the wartime coalition government, Mountbatten had absorbed the troops of the Burmese Independence Army into his own forces and admitted Maung Aung San, its commander and a former supporter of Japan, to a role in shaping affairs after the Japanese were driven out. He reminded the Burmese leader, however, that he had 'a lot of leeway to make up, in our eyes as well as those of their compatriots who have suffered at the hands of the enemy'.

The Japanese capitulation did not leave the same power vacuum in Burma that occurred elsewhere in French and Dutch South-East Asia, because Allied troops were already in occupation. But self-government, Mountbatten tried to tell London, would have to come much sooner than envisaged, and would be dominated by the nationalists led by Aung San. His advice was largely ignored by the Colonial Office, which seemed almost loath to return to the limited degree of home rule granted to Burma after its separation from

India in 1935. Once Attlee realised the mistake, he consulted Mountbatten, who recommended Hubert Rance, his chief civil affairs officer. After half an hour's talk with the prime minister, Rance found himself appointed as the last governor of Burma. The speed at which the colony then moved to independence was just as breathtaking. Not even the assassination of Aung San, by a political rival, caused Attlee to slow down the independence process: in October 1947 Burma became free, and left the Commonwealth three months later. Its withdrawal was not unexpected, Attlee noted, because murder had removed the one man who could have maintained Burmese membership.

The British decision to grant independence to Burma was an almost inevitable consequence of the Labour government's determination to quit India. This policy must be ranked as Attlee's original contribution to post-war East Asia, not least because the granting of independence to Britain's largest possession spelt the beginning of the end for European colonial rule.

Both the French and the Dutch refused to acknowledge the reality of post-war politics, however. Restoring some kind of imperial presence in South-East Asia was for them a psychological as well as an economic necessity. In 1945 de Gaulle had flatly rejected Roosevelt's proposal for a trusteeship in Indo-China. The American president was told that France would not only resent the loss of its most developed and prosperous territory; it would hold the United States solely responsible for the chain reaction of unrest that must follow throughout the remainder of the French empire. The Netherlands was keen to resume control, too, in what was soon to become independent Indonesia.

Neither France nor the Netherlands possessed the military strength to reimpose their colonial administrations once Japan surrendered. The first troops to arrive belonged to Mountbatten, who had been ordered to secure southern Indo-China, Java and Sumatra, besides Thailand, Malaya and Singapore. Indo-China was a priority because Saigon contained the headquarters of the Imperial Japanese Army in South-East Asia. Above the 16th parallel, virtually the border until 1975 between the two Vietnams, the Japanese were required to hand over their arms to Guomindang troops. Because Jiang Jieshi's forces were short of money for supplies, they sold or bartered many of the weapons to the Viet Minh, the 'Vietnamese League' set up in 1941 to further the cause of independence. Thus the revolutionary supporters of Ho Chi Minh acquired an arsenal of rifles and light machine-guns. Although in March 1945 the Japanese had wound up Vichy French rule and declared Laos, Cambodia and Vietnam independent kingdoms, the Communists refused to acknowledge the restored Vietnamese emperor and, when the Japanese surrendered, they seized Hanoi and declared a republic. Following the withdrawal of the occupying Guomindang army a year later, the returning French recognised with some reluctance Ho Chi Minh's Communist government as a state within the federation of Indo-China and the French Union.

The conditions facing Mountbatten in Saigon were just as confused. And such was the inadequacy of the troops available for the task he had been set that the local commander, Douglas Gracey, was allowed to enlist the aid of the surrendered Japanese. On arriving in Saigon an RAF pilot recorded how 'everyone is a little dazed with having Japanese chauffeurs and guards, the Japanese being fully armed'. The British commander of the Fifteenth Indian Corps made similar use of Japanese manpower in Indonesia. The decision was as bad a mistake in South-East Asia as it was in China, where Truman himself sanctioned co-operation between Guomindang and Japanese forces against the Chinese Communist Party. 'If there is one thing that makes my blood boil,' said MacArthur, 'it is to see our allies in Indo-China . . . deploying Japanese troops to reconquer these little people we have promised to liberate.'

But the events of 1945–7 in East Asia were probably moving too fast anyway for more than a piecemeal approach. With the urgent need to rebuild and settle relations in Europe, the United States could not be expected to regard it as an area high on the international agenda. Indeed, the advent of the Cold War seemed to confirm the central position of Europe through the formation of NATO, the North Atlantic Treaty Organisation. Yet the civil war in China, the partition of Korea, and the military occupation of Japan deserved more serious attention in Washington. Neglect of South-East Asia was to prove a costly omission too. Apart from Thailand and the Philippines, which returned quietly to their previous existences, the misguided attempts of the French and the Dutch to thwart nationalist movements served only to accelerate political change in Indo-China and the East Indies. Comparative calm marked the remaining British possessions, but even they experienced the first stirrings of discontent at the arrangements being made for their attainment of self-government within the Commonwealth.

14

PEOPLE'S REPUBLIC OF CHINA

The Modern Miracle
(1949 onwards)

Although President Truman came under harsh attack for the Communist triumph in China, he was himself reconciled to the collapse of the Guomindang. Jiang Jieshi's government, Truman said privately, 'was one of the most corrupt and inefficient that ever made an attempt to govern a country'. Not until the outbreak of the Korean War brought US troops back to mainland East Asia in 1950 would he offer any assistance to Taiwan, the island refuge to which Jiang Jieshi had retreated. That conflict dictated a policy change because of Taiwan's strategic importance to US forces in Korea. The 'China Lobby' also believed that the Guomindang offered a rallying point for opponents of the People's Republic.

American allies, led by Britain, condemned the deployment of the US Seventh Fleet as a defensive screen for Jiang Jieshi. They believed he was a lost cause and refused to offer any support for his regime. When comedians on BBC radio were later to mention General Cash My Cheque, their audience knew exactly who was meant. But the restarting of US economic aid to Jiang Jieshi effectively ended the Chinese civil war, despite the Communist shelling in 1954 of several offshore islands still held by the Guomindang. As long as Washington remained preoccupied with Soviet-US rivalry, then there was little scope for an improvement of relations between the United States and the People's Republic. Not even the unexpected split between Beijing and Moscow could dent American belief in a unified Communist bloc. It took major clashes between Chinese

249

and Russian troops in 1969 to bring an alteration in official attitudes. And only in 1972 did President Nixon make a state visit to China and reverse the whole of American post-Korean War policy in East Asia. In a joint communiqué issued at Shanghai the United States accepted in principle the future withdrawal of its forces from Taiwan.

Unperceived outside China were the strained relations between Beijing and Moscow, whose tensions long preceded the establishment of the People's Republic in October 1949. Apart from the heterodox theory of rural revolution he so fervently espoused, Mao Zedong exhibited an independence quite unacceptable to Stalin. The well-reported remark of 1936 that the Chinese Communist Party was 'certainly not fighting for an emancipated China in order to turn the country over to Moscow' still rankled with the Soviet leader. As late as April 1946, the date of the Soviet troop withdrawal from Manchuria, Stalin still believed that Mao Zedong was unlikely to win. Russian soldiers were ordered to dismantle and remove to Siberia the industries built up there by the Japanese before handing over the cities to Guomindang forces. What the Soviet leader failed to realise was the lack of appetite amongst the Chinese for a conflict waged on Jiang Jieshi's behalf. 'When marching through Shanghai,' an American consul noted in 1947, 'Guomindang recruits have to be roped together.'

If the meagre aid sent to Yan'an by Moscow during the Sino-Japanese War derived from a lack of confidence in Mao Zedong's ultimate prospects, then the reluctance of Stalin to offer any encouragement in 1945 was bolstered by his anxieties over American possession of the atomic bomb. 'Many were frightened,' Zhou Enlai clearly recalled, 'even Stalin was mentally shocked, and was concerned about the outbreak of the Third World War.'

It is difficult to recapture the uncertainties of the late 1940s, when neither the Soviet Union nor the United States could distinguish between genuine anxiety and political opportunism. In Washington, a city unscarred by war, few appreciated the devastation wrought by the Germans in Russia. Stalin became preoccupied with the defence of Eastern Europe, even to the extent of discouraging the Communist movement in China. The Russian leader totally misunderstood American intentions and, by adopting a tough line in negotiations, helped to justify anti-Soviet fundamentalism in the United States. Everything Churchill said of an 'iron curtain' descending across Europe in his celebrated speech at Fulton, Missouri, in March 1946, seemed to be confirmed. Its repressive

Communist regimes in Eastern Europe reinforced attitudes that were deftly manipulated by the 'China Lobby'. The Republicans, denied national power for over a decade, were not slow to take up the idea of Stalin as a controller of a monolithic world movement, a Communist threat to be met wherever his agents were at work. Doctrinal differences between Stalin and Mao Zedong were simply dismissed as no more than theoretical arguments as the Cold War began in 1948, and Truman committed the United States 'to support free peoples who are resisting subjugation by armed minorities or by outside pressures'.

So it was in December 1949 that Mao Zedong went to Moscow to sign with his lukewarm sponsor a thirty-year treaty of 'friendship, alliance, and mutual aid'. For Mao Zedong the visit to Moscow was not a happy event. No discussion was allowed of the tsarist borders and the financial aid offered was less than the loan granted a year earlier to Poland. Worst still, unlike the credits freely given by the United States to Taiwan, the Soviet Union expected to be repaid with interest over a short period of time. 'In signing the Sino-Soviet treaty,' a Russian observer said, 'the Chinese showed us mistrust and suspicion.' Yet for Washington the agreement was enough to justify in 1951 the US-Japan Security Treaty as a counterbalance to Communist power on mainland East Asia.

Soured though Sino-Soviet relations were from the very start, Mao Zedong had little choice when it came to seeking foreign aid for the daunting task of reconstruction. The People's Republic inherited a war-torn economy, burdened with chronic inflation, high unemployment and outmoded methods of production. That by 1956 the country largely overcame this impoverishment is sometimes overlooked because of subsequent turmoil. A strong centralised state existed once again after decades of disunity, a programme of modernisation was well in train and, not least, China's international position had been reasserted by fighting the world's greatest military power to a stalemate in Korea.

A factor making for the undoubted progress was the unity of leadership sustained throughout the 1949–57 period. With rare unanimity the Chinese Communist Party oversaw the growth of heavy industry as the initial stage of socialism. Following the Soviet model, heavy industry would be the key to the development of light industry and then agriculture, whose harvest levels could be raised only by extensive mechanisation. Although Mao Zedong's initiative to speed up the pace of agricultural co-operation in 1955 led directly to the commune movement two years later during the Great Leap

Forward, and the first serious rift in Sino-Soviet relations, this had
not been planned. It would appear that he expected co-operatives to
develop in time directly into state-owned farms rather than col-
lectively owned communes. What caused the change was the rapid
spread of co-operatives, far in advance of the most optimistic
projections.

The success here, as in other fields, seemed to demonstrate Mao
Zedong's insight. Thus it was a shock in 1959 for the People's
Republic to learn of major disagreements within the leadership over
the economic effects of the Great Leap Forward. Perhaps as startling
was the forthright criticism delivered by Peng Dehuai (1898–1974),
one of the commanders during the Korean War. But his dismissal
afterwards as Minister of Defence for meddling with Mao Zedong's
policies hardly tarnished the reputation he had gained on the battlefield. Intervention in Korea revived national pride in a way that
nobody could have imagined, prior to contingents of the People's
Liberation Army standing up to General MacArthur and other foreigners who talked of invading China.

THE GREAT LEAP FORWARD (1958–60)

The success of the co-operative movement in the countryside placed
most of the Chinese people under a socialist form of organisation.
The reform process was not only faster than Soviet collectivisation
but much less disruptive in its transformation of peasant life. Some
70 per cent of the land was worked by owners, the majority of whom
were persuaded without great violence to pool their resources:
approximately 2 million died out of a total population of 580 million in the redistribution of land. The change brought about an
immediate expansion in food production during the early 1950s,
but the improved diet of the peasant accounted for most of this
increase and the amount of grain collected by the state, through
taxes and compulsory purchase, remained stationary. When after
1955 the growth of agricultural co-operatives drove up production
levels in many provinces, the situation was judged right for another
step forward.

That this step became a great leap can in part be explained by
ideology. Mao Zedong seems to have decided a shake-up was
needed. In 1956–7 he lifted some of the restrictions on public
expression, urging the people to 'let the hundred flowers bloom, let
the hundred schools contend,' a reference to the contending
philosophical schools of the Warring States period. Through the

Fig. 48. A 1951 woodcut catches the upsurge for revolutionary change in the Chinese countryside. It is entitled 'A slacker being criticised'

expression of constructive criticism, he hoped, would come a tremendous release of latent energy that the Chinese Communist Party could harness to accelerate China's economic growth. This was the first occasion on which Mao Zedong demonstrated his belief in continuing revolution. For he insisted 'that which is correct always develops in the course of struggling against that which is wrong. As mankind in general rejects an untruth, a truth will be struggling with erroneous ideas. Such struggles will never end. This is the law of Marxism.' So the key to unlock a socialist utopia was psychological change, the perpetual renewal of enthusiasm amongst party members and people alike. Even Liu Shaoqi (1898–1969), the scapegoat of the Cultural Revolution of 1966, echoed this principle when he commented: 'The present task is to effect a thorough and systematic readjustment in the relationships between people, rooting out the capitalist and feudal survivals of bygone days and building new socialist relationships.' Along with other senior Communists, Liu Shaoqi disapproved of the Hundred Flowers episode and took advantage of the economic difficulties caused by the Great Leap of 1958–60 to reduce the power of Mao Zedong. It could be said that the cultural turmoil that raged between 1966 and 1969 was an attempt by Mao Zedong to regain control.

The differences between Mao Zedong and Liu Shaoqi were highlighted by the torrent of complaints that poured forth in 1956–7. Although Mao Zedong was taken aback at the depth of many educated people's dislike of the regime, withdrawing in June 1957 the licence to criticise, he was more disturbed by the general reluctance of the Communist bureaucracy itself to accept criticism. The officials were simply a modern version of the scholar-bureaucrats of the old imperial civil service. China's tradition was of public management by bureaucracy rather than of large-scale private enterprise, and there existed a real danger that these officials might revert to a Confucian scale of values, owing as much loyalty to their own prominent families as a people's state. The problem was connected with the size of the Chinese Communist Party, its membership having risen from 1.2 million in 1945 to 17 million in 1961. As a later slogan recalling simpler days put it, people needed to 'follow the Yan'an way'.

As the chief of the party apparatus, Liu Shaoqi could not be expected to take kindly to any view that placed the peasant on a pedestal, which was in essence Mao Zedong's reaction to the failure of the relaxation policy. For him the Chinese peasant personified the new spirit of China as a whole, soon to be expressed in the rejection of the Soviet economic model, and the determination to catch up and overtake the West by very different means. Possibly as a precaution against such headlong change, Liu Shaoqi agreed to the dropping of references to the thought of Mao Zedong in the newly adopted party constitution. Chairman Mao was praised for his leadership during the two decades since the Zunyi conference, but none of the delegates attending the equivalent gathering in late 1956 could doubt that this represented a downgrading of his importance in the history of Chinese Communism. Liu Shaoqi said candidly:

the amount of experience gained by the Party and the choice of leaders do have an important bearing on whether the Party makes mistakes, but what is more important is whether the rank-and-file Party members, and primarily the high-ranking cadres, can, in the various periods, apply the Marxist-Leninist stand, viewpoint and method to sum up experience in the struggle, hold fast to truth and correct mistakes.

A kinder interpretation might suggest a need to differentiate Mao Zedong from Stalin, whose reputation was then under assault in Moscow. But Nikita Khrushchev's denunciation of Stalinism as a way of modernising the Soviet system cut little ice in Beijing, when a direct result of this 'revisionism' was the hurried invasion of Hungary in order to prevent its abandonment of Communism.

What particularly annoyed Mao Zedong about Khrushchev's revision of Soviet policy was the advocacy of peaceful coexistence with the West. In East Asia the chief enemy of the People's Republic remained the United States, then underwriting any and all anti-Communist governments. Well might Khrushchev assert that capitalist countries would achieve a transition to socialism without undergoing a revolution: the 1954 military pact between Taiwan and the United States was bad enough, but Suez also cast doubt on the acquiescence of Britain and France in their diminished world roles, though Mao Zedong did not fail to notice that it was President Eisenhower who stopped the joint invasion of Egypt. Unless China made rapid strides on its own account, there was a distinct possibility of a return to the semi-colonial domination suffered prior to the Communist triumph. As the Americans and the Russians edged towards an arms control agreement, and Soviet aid to China was allowed to tail off, Mao Zedong decided that the time had come to push ahead alone.

The Great Leap, however, took shape gradually. In 1957 the Chinese leaders still faced the disillusionment caused by the Hundred Flowers episode. But there was a feeling that new methods were needed if China was ever to break out of its economic backwardness, which Mao Zedong exploited to abandon the Soviet model. Instead of a major programme of agricultural modernisation, as launched in the late 1970s, he attempted to expand output by the use of traditional methods. It was anticipated that rural backyard furnaces would provide China within fifteen years with an annual steel output larger than that of Britain.

No matter how disruptive the Great Leap Forward of 1958–60 was later recognised to have been by the Chinese themselves, there can be no denying that Mao Zedong's call for action evoked considerable support from the mass of the population. By late 1958 the agricultural cooperatives had been merged into 25,000 communes, each with around 20,000 members as compared with 3000 in the average co-operative. The initial surge of production was excellent, and in consequence targets were raised for 1959. Overlooked in the excitement of the campaign was the smelting of mostly useless steel in rural backyards and the exaggeration of many local officials when making agricultural returns. When the 1959 cereal harvest finally became known, the total was 30 million tonnes down on the 1958 figure of 200 million tonnes. Bad weather played its part as well as the dispersion of labour into too many projects. Instead of taking note of the warning signs and rethinking strategy accordingly, Mao Zedong pressed on with the campaign until famine forced a halt. Food shortages probably accounted for an extra 10 million deaths in 1960 and, though this figure is low in comparison with any of the bitter years of the 1920s and the 1930s, it was the first occasion since the founding of the People's Republic that so many people had died from diseases caused by malnutrition.

So in late 1960 and early 1961 the Great Leap Forward was abandoned, as the peasants engaged in industrial production or large-scale projects were sent back to the fields in a desperate attempt to alleviate the food shortage. Communes were reduced in size and rewards given according to the performance of a family or team; also private plots, which had been largely eliminated during the campaign, were restored. During the crisis Mao Zedong supported the far-reaching retreat from socialist goals, and in June 1961 he offered self-criticism (*ziwo piping*) at a meeting in Beijing.

CULTURAL REVOLUTION (1966–76)

Once conditions began to improve, however, tensions among the Communist leadership rose as Mao Zedong sought to regain his position as director of the continuing revolution. Although he was still chairman of the Chinese Communist Party and was consulted on policy matters, he found that he was often overruled by other senior members, usually at the behest of Liu Shaoqi and Deng Xiaoping (born 1904). Red Guards were to term them 'number one capitalist-roader' and 'number two capitalist-roader' respectively. Reflecting on this period during the Great Proletarian Cultural Revolution, Mao Zedong said that he felt like a revered ancestor to whom only polite gestures were made. Perhaps he ought to have compared himself to a temporarily neglected grandfather, for his method of regaining power was to urge on his seventy-third birthday a rebellion of the young. Sensing the frustration of young people in 1966, Mao Zedong guided their revolt into an attack on the complacency of the Chinese Communist Party itself.

Preparations for the Great Proletarian Cultural Revolution, which began in the spring of that year, had started four years earlier with an understanding between Mao Zedong and key members of the armed and security forces. His point-blank refusal to countenance the rehabilitation of Peng Dehuai, an outspoken critic of the Great Leap Forward, suited the man who had been appointed to replace him as Minister of Defence, the other Korean War veteran Lin Biao. Starting in 1963, Mao Zedong also increasingly promoted the People's Liberation Army as the model organisation for the country to follow. It had, under Lin Biao, won an impressive series of victories in the 1962 border war with India and two years later achieved the first detonation of an atom bomb. At the same time Lin Biao promoted political work among the troops that led in 1966 to the publication of a selection of Mao Zedong's thoughts as the infamous 'little red book'. Because the People's Liberation Army was able to combine so effectively action with politics Mao Zedong sought to expand its role in the political system, an objective the ambitious Lin Biao was pleased to foster.

Another reason for looking upon the People's Liberation Army as an ideal organisation was Mao Zedong's growing disenchantment with the Chinese Communist Party. Fearful of the emergence of a new form of privilege, he noted how

the children of our cadres are a cause of discouragement. They lack experience of life and of society, yet their airs are considerable and they have a great sense of superiority. They have to be educated not to rely on their parents or martyrs of the past but entirely on themselves.

His perspective was sharpened too, by the quarrel with Khrushchev, whom he accused of tolerating a privileged class of bureaucrats. 'Completely divorced from the working people of the Soviet Union,' Mao Zedong thundered, 'they live the parasitical and decadent life of the bourgeoisie.' Their self-interest would lead to a revision of Marxism-Leninism and eventually pave the way to a restoration of capitalism. The dangers of a similar tendency in China obliged Mao Zedong to rebuke in 1963 university lecturers who discussed the social teachings of Confucius. He told them that there should be less talk about personalities of the past and more about the contemporary situation. A year later, he advised a Nepalese delegation that China's education system was 'fraught with problems, the most important of which is dogmatism . . . The school years are long, courses too many, and various methods of teaching unsatisfactory. The children learn textbooks and concepts which merely remain textbooks and concepts; they know nothing else.' Educational reverence for the past was Mao Zedong's prime target, not least when an emphasis placed on calligraphy inevitably depressed the social standing of the people. China was a poor country without even universal primary education. Strenuous efforts were being made to train teachers and expand provision, but the in-built advantages enjoyed by the children of well-educated parents were very apparent, and a worrying phenomenon when graduation from a secondary school or a college was virtually the guarantee of a responsible position in Chinese society.

Thus the public debate about Wu Han's historical play *Hai Rui Dismissed from Office* was more than an academic wrangle. The argument arose when an article, published in November 1965, alleged that the dramatist intended a defence of the forcibly retired Peng Dehuai because, like the loyal official in the play, the former minister had not hesitated to say what was wrong with government policy. Underneath such an interpretation lay the whole issue of privilege: here was a member of the landlord class being presented as a hero. How could a person in such a privileged position ever be a true friend of the people? That the play might be more than a piece of 'bourgeois mentality' struck Mao Zedong when he found it difficult to arrange for the publication of his own criticism in Beijing. He had to use the connections of his third wife Jiang Qing (1914–91) in Shanghai to get an adverse review published. A Shanghai actress whom Mao Zedong married in Yan'an, Jiang Qing had until this time obeyed the prohibition on political activity imposed when the Chinese Communist Party gave permission for the marriage. Ill-health in the 1950s had involved her in prolonged periods of treatment in the Soviet Union, but she was sufficiently recovered by the mid-1960s to take a leading role in the Cultural Revolution, and to exercise even greater power in the last few years of Mao Zedong's life. In April 1975 Zhang Zhixin, a minor official, was executed as an 'active counter-revolutionary' for challenging Jiang Qing's right to speak on behalf of Mao Zedong. The rather impudent comparison that he liked to make between himself and the First Emperor, possibly to unsettle the learned establishment, proved to be no joke. It was as much a tragedy for Mao Zedong as it was for China that the Cultural Revolution appealed so strongly to Jiang Qing's thwarted theatrical talents.

Although Liu Shaoqi tried initially to control the campaign by putting advisory teams of cadres into the main universities and colleges, the students of Beijing University reacted against this supervision and in a wall poster, put up in May 1966, they demanded it should be a vigorous mass movement. Once Mao Zedong had the poster reprinted in the *People's Daily*, the challenge to Liu Shaoqi's handling of events was obvious and Beijing students responded in a manner worthy of the May Fourth Movement. Student agitation increased, wall posters attacking professors and officials appeared, links were made with factories and farms, and the first Red Guard organisation was formed. Within a fortnight of the display of Mao Zedong's own big-character wall poster, 'Bombard the Headquarters', Jiang Qing staged in August in Tiananmen Square the first of eight gigantic gatherings that brought, within three months, 11 million Red Guards to Beijing to exchange experiences.

'Bombard the Headquarters' charged that there were people in the Chinese Communist Party at all levels up to the very top who were following reactionary politics. Mao Zedong did not name the culprits, but it soon became clear that the chief ones were Liu Shaoqi and Deng Xiaoping. Lin Biao then joined in the attack and the two 'capitalist-roaders' were imprisoned. Only Deng Xiaoping survived incarceration, his recall in 1973 at Zhou Enlai's request eventually leading five years later to his own leadership of the Chinese Communist Party. The Great Proletarian Cultural Revolution caused greater economic dislocation than any of Mao Zedong's other radical shifts of policy. Production fell dramatically as pronouncements were made against specialisation of any kind: everyone was to be developed in 'an all-round way' so as to become 'a new Communist person with proletarian political consciousness'.

But by mid-1967 the radical challenge was submerged in a rising tide of disorder which compelled the intervention of the People's Liberation Army to restore public services, reopen schools and colleges and send large numbers of students to the countryside. Life in China did not return to something approaching normality till late 1969, but the Cultural Revolution was to all intents and purposes over, no matter the propaganda broadcast to an incredulous outside world. Even Jiang Qing had to modify her combative Red Guard slogan, 'Attack with words, but defend yourself with weapons.' She was forced to support Mao Zedong's call for a peaceful, not an armed, struggle. Captured weapons were surrendered and rival factions of the Red Guards urged to sink their differences, although continued street fighting in several cities in the spring of 1968 saw tanks in action. Casualties were still being reported as late as the summer, at the time when the movement to the countryside started in earnest. Going to the rural areas is estimated to have involved 17 million youngsters between 1968 and 1978, and one of the pressing demands Deng Xiaoping had to deal with in the 1980s was requests for the return of individuals and institutions to their original places of residence. In justification of this upheaval, Mao Zedong said: 'It is necessary for educated people to go to the countryside to be re-educated by the poor and lower-middle peasants. Party members and other people in the cities should be persuaded to send their sons and daughters who have finished junior or senior middle school, college or university to the countryside.'

Whilst this movement was enough to convince Mao Zedong that the continuing revolution was on course, the general confusion it helped to create increased the political influence of the People's Liberation Army, and Lin Biao enjoyed for a spell his designation as Mao Zedong's 'close comrade-in-arms and successor'. His sudden death in a crash on an unscheduled flight to Mongolia has never been satisfactorily explained. The accident is said to have occurred in September 1971 after the failure of a plot to kill Mao Zedong and seize power. Better relations with the United States may not have suited Lin Biao. The arrival of President Nixon in China the following year necessarily altered the balance of power from the armed forces a civil administration headed by Zhou Enlai. Mao Zedong seems to have been aware of the dubious quality of Lin Biao's support when launching the Cultural Revolution, but regarded it as a lesser evil than the Chinese Communist Party bureaucracy.

When in 1972 Mao Zedong said that Lin Biao had intended to overthrow the entire leadership, he also conceded the wrongful harassment of Liu Shaoqi and Deng Xiaoping, who were not counter-revolutionaries but belonged instead to a less serious category of dissidence. The admission facilitated the rehabilitation in 1973 of Deng Xiaoping, the ultimate survivor of what he has called a 'Ten-Year Catastrophe'. He was lucky enough to be untouched by the attack Jiang Qing launched on him in the last year of Mao Zedong's life. 'It is contrary to the will of the people to revise verdicts,' she alleged her ailing husband to have said. But it was already too late for the 'Gang of Four', as Jiang Qing and her closest associates were soon to be called. First Zhou Enlai died in January, then Mao Zedong in September, leaving the reins of government in the comparatively inexperienced hands of Hua Guofeng (born 1920), an administrator from Hunan province upon whom the succession had been settled.

CHINA AFTER CHAIRMAN MAO

Prior to the death of Mao Zedong a factional struggle had already broken out in which the issue of specialisation reappeared. In his last public appearance, Zhou Enlai outlined a set of policy guidelines for the whole country: after an immediate period of consolidation, there would be a programme to achieve 'comprehensive modern-isation in agriculture, industry, defence, and science and technology' by the year 2000. These 'four modernisations', more than anything else, have determined the shape of Chinese politics over the last two decades. From the outset Deng Xiaoping was not prepared to endorse their pursuit by means of ideological experiment. He had clashed with Jiang Qing in 1974 over the launching of the first 10,000-tonne ship built in China, because sticking to a policy of 'self-reliance' was no compensation for its poor performance. In 1975–6 Deng Xiaoping went further and said how far the People's Republic lagged behind the industrial nations of the world. The best Chinese scientists were 'red and expert' but those who were 'white and expert' also served the country. The colour of the cat, he said, did not matter as long as it caught the mouse. At least these people made a larger contribution to material progress than idle ideologues, who just 'sit on the lavatory and not do a shit'.

The argument about the best way ahead was raging in April 1976, when an unheard-of event took place in Tiananmen Square. At the time of the Qingming festival – the occasion on which filial duty used to be demonstrated by sweeping the ancestral graves but remembrance of one's forebears is now shown through flowers – wreaths in memory of Zhou Enlai started to appear on the Monument to the People's Heroes. Within a matter of days thousands of tributes were placed there, many of whose inscriptions implied dissatisfaction with the policies associated with Mao Zedong's name.

Overreaching themselves in dealing with this demonstration of public feeling, Jiang Qing and her close associates arranged for the police to remove the wreaths and cordon off Tiananmen Square one night. They blamed Deng Xiaoping for the disorder which erupted after these measures were taken, and he was relegated to the background for a couple of months. But Marshal Ye Jianying (1897–1986) stalked out of the disciplinary hearing in protest at Jiang Qing's actions. Deng Xiaoping seems to have obtained the backing of powerful military leaders well before the death of Mao Zedong so that he could afford to bide his time. He did not have to wait long, however. Within two months of the event, Jiang Qing and her closest associates were in custody. The exact circumstances of the arrest are unknown, despite rumours that an armed bodyguard resisted the troops sent to Jiang Qing's country residence near Beijing.

The 'Gang of Four', Mao Zedong's most fervent disciples, did not go on trial until the winter of 1980–1, along with the followers of Lin Biao. When the case opened, the government announced that the defendants were not on trial for having lost a power struggle, but for having used illegal means in trying to win it. The guilty verdicts handed down were intended to show that the People's Republic had returned to the rule of law and rejected their 'ultra-left' policies. The delay in bringing charges is explained in the time it took Deng Xiaoping to establish effective control.

The immediate cause of Jiang Qing's downfall was the desire of Hua Guofeng to weaken the influence of radical elements in the Chinese Communist Party. Although he subsequently advertised the smashing of the 'Gang of Four' as 'the triumphant conclusion of our first Great Proletarian Cultural Revolution', he was always careful to link future class struggle with the need to 'bring about great order across the land'. The crucial support of Marshal Ye Jianying was in effect gained through the tacit admission of the overriding importance of strong government. Party discipline must take precedence over any experimentation with democracy, a new outlook that was to cost many students their lives in Tiananmen Square in June 1989. Given such military assistance, Hua Guofeng ought to have been secure as Mao Zedong's chosen successor. That he was not, despite an attempt to project him as a similar cult figure, reflected the very different circumstances of the late 1970s. As leader of mainstream Maoism, Hua Guofeng remained vulnerable to attack from those who suffered in Jiang Qing's final crackdown, when the police cordoned off Tiananmen Square. Not only did he fail to rehabilitate any of them, but he allowed the arrest of many more activists. Their grievances, along with other protests at official injustice, surfaced in posters on the so-called Democracy Wall in central Beijing. The first to appear in 1978 was provocatively entitled 'Democracy: the fifth Modernisation'.

It suited Deng Xiaoping when the theme emerged that the mistakes of the past could not be blamed on a handful of wicked leaders. The main target of complaint was the policy line defended by Hua Guofeng, but Deng Xiaoping also received a share of the criticism. One man was arrested within days of putting up a poster calling upon the people to ensure that 'Deng Xiaoping does not degenerate into a dictator'; his sentence was fifteen years' imprisonment. The removal of the Democracy Wall from a main avenue to a small park dampened down the protest, which ended with a wave of arrests in 1980–1. But dissidence was not so readily dispersed and in 1987 Deng Xiaoping reluctantly sacrificed his heir-apparent Hu Yaobang (1915–89), following nationwide student demonstrations.

Hu Yaobang had replaced Hua Guofeng as chairman of the Chinese Communist Party in June 1981, four months after Jiang Qing was sentenced to death with a two-year stay of execution. Later the sentence was commuted to life imprisonment, and she remained in custody until 1984, after which she lived quietly at home. With the 'Gang of Four' removed from the scene, it was deemed safe to inform the people that cultural revolution had been a disaster. Unless the country was freed from such 'ultra-left' constraint China could never expect to modernise itself. During the late 1970s the 'politics first' approach was thus gradually discounted, as socialist goals were subordinated to economic objectives. Material incentives, autonomy for enterprises, the encouragement of competition, pricing goods according to the real cost of production, special investment zones, and similar proposals inaugurated a transformation that within a decade effectively privatised agriculture and made the profit motive respectable. Even the achievements of the Dazhai production brigade were publicly ridiculed in the early 1980s. Whilst the enterprise of this model brigade in transforming barren hillsides into terraced fields was still acknowledged as a tremendous feat, it was revealed that Dazhai's vaunted spirit of self-reliance had been secretly subsidised with government aid.

Although the countryside answered the relaxation of regulation with increased output, there were signs that the economy as a whole was becoming overheated, as complaints about inflation indicated. For a country that was previously isolated from worldwide inflation, the advent of price rises came as a shock and a reminder of the monetary horrors of Jiang Jieshi's last years. Particularly hard hit were the students, who could see their contemporaries earning large sums in street markets and through increased factory bonuses. Books were expensive, and from 1985 onwards most students had to pay for higher education.

Competition, nonetheless, remained fierce for entrance to colleges and universities, with less than 6 per cent of secondary school leavers going on to higher education. Pressures in this bottleneck for the ambitious probably account for some of the demands made by students in the steady build-up of protests that reached such a tragic climax in June 1989. That their supreme gesture of defiance was the placing of a statue to democracy next to the Monument to the People's Heroes was perhaps the saddest aspect of the final demonstration. For this improvised goddess, made from chunks of

polystyrene at the Central Institute of Fine Arts, derived her inspiration as much from Hu Yaobang's encouragement of freer expression
as from growing foreign influences. Its likeness to the Statue of
Liberty may have allowed Deng Xiaoping to blame the United States
afterwards for becoming too involved in the turmoil, but it remains
a fact that the Chinese leader at first indulged student urgings of
further reform. The 'fifth modernisation' of democracy was increasingly seen as a possible aid to progress, even if a democratic atmosphere in China never meant the end of strong central control. A
more pragmatic approach to the modern world was required, instead
of dogma, as Hu Yaobang indicated in December 1984:

> Marx's works were written more than a hundred years ago. Some were his
> tentative ideas at that time, and things have changed greatly since then.
> Some of his tentative ideas were not necessarily very appropriate. Many
> things have happened which Marx and Engels did not experience, and
> which even Lenin did not experience, so they had no contact with them.
> We cannot expect the writings of Marx and Lenin at that time to provide
> solutions to all our current problems.

To explain the implications to cadres, the Party journal *Red Flag*
quickly underlined the new thoughtfulness being advocated: 'We
must study Marxism in close connection with realities . . . and distinguish clearly what is still applicable from what is not.'

As long as Deng Xiaoping was able to convince the Chinese
Communist Party that his modernisation programme was working,
the general drift of government policy could continue to be a dis-
mantlement of Mao Zedong's cultural revolution. Deng Xiaoping
had told senior colleagues that 'utilisation of foreign investment
funds in a planned way and the promotion of a degree of individual
economy are both serving the development of a socialist economy'.
He conceded that certain 'evil things that had long been extinct
after the liberation have come to life again', but these problems
would attract 'firm steps to deal with them'. No one was going
to undermine the miraculous recovery the economy had already
achieved under Communism. To many observers the reported
speech appeared to be half-hearted capitalism, which it certainly
was not. All that Deng Xiaoping had meant to indicate was that
there were limits to private enterprise – not an unusual notion in a
country whose long experience under the imperial system had been
a high degree of state control. Just in case the inhabitants of Hong
Kong missed the message, or mistook student calls for popular
reform, he reminded them that they would never be able to use the

'cloak of democracy' to turn future discontent against China's interests.

Yet there was deep disquiet felt by conservative members of the Political Bureau about the affect that rapid modernisation was having on the young, who were criticised for being indifferent to social issues and over-preoccupied with personal interests. More hedonistic Chinese students undoubtedly were, but political apathy did not typify their widespread demonstrations. It was rather that the nature of protest had changed. Instead of any concerted campaign waged in support of a specific reform programme, student discontent tended to break out erratically whenever a new issue arose. The unsatisfactory radio tribute on Hu Yaobang's death was such a trigger for renewed demonstrations in Beijing.

THE TIANANMEN TRAGEDY (1989)

Not even his Long March credentials were enough to save Hu Yaobang in 1987 from the accusation that his sponsored reforms had weakened the People's Republic. His resignation was the price exacted for such unwelcome imports of capitalist behaviour as student agitation at the slowness of political change. Deng Xiaoping found himself in an awkward position when protesting students again took to the streets of Beijing and other cities in 1989. Calls for democracy, a free press, and an investigation of official corruption left him with little room for manoeuvre, once it became obvious that neither the Political Bureau nor the students were prepared to compromise. The protest began with the announcement by Radio Beijing on 15 April of Hu Yaobang's death. Discontent with government policy was shown from the moment tributes to the former reforming minister were stuck up on notice boards at Beijing University. An early one read: 'A true man has died, false men are living.' The students who had helped to cause Hu Yaobang's fall obviously considered it necessary to record their support for the modernisation programme he had tried to instigate.

Recalling the precedent set by Zhou Enlai's mourners, the Chinese Communist Party broadcast within four hours of the announcement of his death a radio tribute to Hu Yaobang, 'the great proletarian revolutionary and statesman'. But there was no mention of his fall from office. For the students of Beijing University this was tantamount to an insult to Hu Yaobang's memory, and they swiftly demanded his full rehabilitation, a course of action that would have obliged the Political Bureau to acknowledge its mistake in ejecting him. Wreaths were also placed on the Monument of the People's Heroes in Tiananmen Square, although it was not until two days later that the first demonstration took place.

Barely 400 students participated in the demonstration, but the slogans they shouted in Tiananmen Square that day formed the agenda for the mass movement of May and June. After placing their wreaths on the monument, they chanted: 'Long live Hu Yaobang. Long live democracy. Long live freedom. Down with corruption. Down with bureaucracy.' For those who were caught up in the subsequent demonstrations, these slogans incorporated a general sense of grievance at the lack of material progress. The renewal of the license to criticise under Hu Yaobang's successor, Zhao Ziyang (born 1919), seemed a poor substitute for the shortages caused by the change-over to market-determined prices. Inflation was running at its highest level since the foundation of the People's Republic, and hoarding only exacerbated the price spiral as city dwellers sought to beat the queues. Although Zhao Ziyang might extol the virtues of short-term pain, the Political Bureau had backed away from the problem and restored a degree of price control. Thus few people were satisfied in mid-1989 with the state of affairs in the cities.

That limits to discussion still existed had become apparent in February, when the astrophysicist Fang Lizhi (born 1936) was barred from attending a barbecue hosted by President Bush. His error, according to official sources, was of 'instigating trouble by saying that Chinese intellectuals . . . ought to constitute an independent force'. There was indeed a challenge to established views in his belief that 'intellectuals, who own and create information and knowledge, are the most dynamic component of the productive forces'. Though Fang Lizhi was eventually cast as the chief villain behind the 'counter-revolution rebellion' of 1989, the Political Bureau cannot have been unaware that he played no direct role in the protests once they had started. Probably his comments to foreign newspaper correspondents caused the greatest annoyance. 'This is not just for Hu Yaobang,' Fang Lizhi said. 'This is a chance for students to let the government know how unhappy they are with the present situation.' His flight to the United States embassy, the day after the People's Liberation Army moved into Tiananmen Square, merely confirmed suspicion of American manipulation of the student movement.

Any explanation that blames an outside instigator for the tragic events of June ignores the spontaneous outburst of protest that followed the announcement of Hu Yaobang's death. Furthermore, it overlooks the general support shown for student protestors in Beijing and other major cities. Rallies and hunger strikes were reported from Guangdong, Hubei, Hunan, Shaanxi and Sichuan provinces, while in Shanghai protest ended with the firing of a train after it had ploughed into crowds blocking the railway tracks. In Beijing itself the ordinary citizens also suffered at the hands of the People's Liberation Army. The shooting-up of a crowd of pedestrians and cyclists outside the Beijing Hotel, on the main avenue leading to Tiananmen Square, shocked even seasoned reporters. But it was the savagery of the attack of 3–4 June on students in the square itself that was immediately dubbed a massacre. Officially few were killed in the night clearance, but eyewitnesses say that they saw numerous corpses strewn across the flagstones. The total death toll for the city may have run into several thousands.

The tragedy was watched by millions outside China, because foreign television crews were still in Beijing following the visit of Mikhail Gorbachev, then President of the Soviet Union. His arrival in the middle of May, and the attention it received from world media, gave the students a unique opportunity to embarrass the Chinese authorities, already on the defensive through foreign reports about riots in Tibet.

At first, foreign viewers were surprised at the restraint of both the Political Bureau and the student leaders. Zhao Ziyang, moreover, seemed to balance effectively the need to restore order with a fair hearing of the students' complaints. Conscious of the unpredictable forces which the originator of *glasnost* could unleash in Beijing, Zhao Ziyang was anxious that the first visit by a Soviet leader for thirty years should be a diplomatic triumph equal to the coming of President Nixon in 1972. It was unfortunate that his efforts to diffuse the confrontation in Tiananmen Square failed so miserably. The student leaders disregarded his warnings about repressive measures, and the Political Bureau lost patience with his visits to hunger strikers and his public appeals. At a meeting with President Gorbachev, which was to constitute his last official engagement, Zhao Ziyang confessed to his own impotence: on all important issues, he said, 'we still need Deng Xiaoping as the helmsman'. This off-the-cuff remark was taken by his rivals to be an attempt to shrug off the blame, but Zhao Ziyang had no need to direct public criticism at the elder statesman. Students already paraded with banners which read 'Deng Xiaoping should retire' and 'It doesn't matter if the cat is black or white as long as it resigns.' They knew who was really running the country.

On 18 May Deng Xiaoping decided that things had gone far enough, and he ordered soldiers to the capital. In one account of the decision, Deng Xiaoping shouted, 'I have the army behind me.' When Zhao Ziyang countered by shouting, 'But I have the people behind me,' he rudely was told, 'You have nothing.' That power resided in the barrels of the People's Liberation Army proved correct. The military backers of Deng Xiaoping, fearing perhaps a return to the chaos of cultural revolution, bloodily put down the student protest shortly after the declaration of martial law. Li Peng (born 1928) made an attempt to reason with the student leaders, who were in no mood to heed his blunt warning.

It is impossible for us to sit idly by doing nothing. It is impossible for us not to protect the safety and lives of students, not to protect our socialist system.

Nor would they listen to Zhao Ziyang, when choked with emotion he spoke to them in Tiananmen Square, the day of his resignation. Some students, sensing an imminent crackdown, urged a pullout from the square. They were, however, unable to secure any change of tactics among the reduced numbers encamped there.

'Only evil-doers were killed' was the first official comment. Later on, the 47 million members of the Chinese Communist Party were told to unite against the 'counter-revolution', which had been quelled with a minimum loss of life. Whilst the government's authority was reasserted in a way to deter outright challenges in future, the issues behind student discontent remain to be solved. But not even the pointless carnage in Tiananmen Square can permanently reverse the changes Deng Xiaoping has overseen, both internally and externally. The settlements regarding the future of Macao and Hong Kong ought to allow a more relaxed approach to the world at large, just as improved relations with Taiwan clear away any obstacle to mutually beneficial trade and investment. Even the Guomindang response to the events of June 1989 was muted. A spokesman in Taibei commented that the chief mistake of the Beijing students was that they demanded too much. They gave Deng Xiaoping no face at all.

This restrained comment shows the extent to which the People's Republic has become accepted as a Great Power, even on Taiwan. But if the siege of China has been lifted by the Chinese people themselves, then the People's Liberation Army deserves credit since 1949 for its effective defence of the country's borders. Providing it is not weakened by embroilment with politics at home, there is little reason to suppose China will endure another period of disunity or miss playing a key role in the development of the Pacific Rim. Economically powerful Japan might be today, but China has the military muscle to block any backdoor attempt to revive the Greater Asia Co-Prosperity Sphere.

15

TWO AMERICAN SETBACKS

The Wars in Korea (1950–3)
and Vietnam (1954–75)

AN UNNECESSARY PARTITION (1945–50)

In the thirty-five years which followed the Japanese annexation in 1910, Korean nationalists did what they could to free their country from an oppressive colonial administration. Resistance groups waged open warfare until 1925, when Japan's increasing influence in Manchuria was used to deny them a base from which to operate. Exiles driven to China usually adopted terrorist tactics in their fight against Japan, killing with bombs high-ranking officials and army officers. The leading Korean exile Syngman Rhee (1875–1965) tried to put a stop to such bomb-throwings, by arguing that Japanese propaganda represented Koreans as fanatics. He advocated that Korea be made a League of Nations mandated territory, and worked hard to gain Chinese and American recognition for a government-in-exile. Following the Japanese invasion of China, this group of exiles moved with Jiang Jieshi to Chongqing, while Syngman Rhee was based in the United States.

Until the Cairo Conference of 1943 there was no sign of Allied interest in the fate of Korea, then suffering badly as its resources were exploited to sustain the Japanese war effort. But at Cairo Roosevelt, Churchill and Jiang Jieshi issued a statement declaring 'that in due course Korea shall become free and independent'. Syngman Rhee was puzzled by the phrase 'in due course', but the meaning of this qualification was never explained. Possibly Roosevelt had in mind a trusteeship along the same lines as he proposed for Indo-China. Whatever the reason for the delay of

270

independence, the United States had inadvertently created the conditions for a partition of Korea.

Situated between China, Russia and Japan, the strategic position of the Korean peninsula went unnoticed in Washington. Forgotten were the old rivalries between Russia and Japan for dominance, once the Chinese empire was in its final decline. The Japanese annexation had been justified, according to Tokyo, because Korea formed 'a dagger pointed at the heart of Japan'. Yet Roosevelt and Truman both overlooked the Russian interest in their desire for military assistance on mainland East Asia. As late as the Potsdam Conference of July 1945, Washington was preoccupied with the projected casualties of an invasion of Japan. It regarded the Japanese armies still in occupation of China, Manchuria and Korea as a formidable foe, and was only too pleased to leave their defeat to Russian troops. A limit to the operations that Stalin would have to mount to achieve this victory was agreed at Potsdam: the line between the Russian and American zones was to be the 38th parallel, almost exactly the boundary between the two Koreas today.

The dropping of atomic bombs on Hiroshima and Nagasaki ended Japanese resistance at the very moment Russian forces swept through Manchuria and northern Korea. Suddenly, the United States was able to occupy Korea south of the 38th parallel without military action. Suspicious that the Russians might attempt to seize the whole peninsula, the Americans made an ill-planned and rushed move from Okinawa in September. The American commander thought that, like Douglas MacArthur in Japan, he could act through the Japanese authorities. The Koreans naturally found intolerable the continuance in office of a colonial government which had oppressed them for decades and from which the Allies were supposed to be liberating them. General MacArthur quickly ordered that Japanese officials must be removed from office, but the damage had been done. It was, a US officer concluded, 'one of the most expensive mistakes we ever made there'.

The Russian treatment of the Japanese was quite different. North of the 38th parallel – where to the relief of Washington they halted their advance – the Russians disarmed Japanese soldiers and arrested colonial officials, including the policemen from whom American military administrators were so ready to receive information and advice in South Korea. They entrusted day-to-day administration to Korean politicians, including liberal nationalists, but formed in February 1946 a provisional government under the chairmanship of Kim Il-song (born 1912). More than anyone else

Kim Il Sung, as he is known to the West, converted North Korea into a model Communist state. To Koreans living south of the 38th parallel the behaviour of the Russians seemed reasonable, since they did not interfere directly with politics. The Americans, on the other hand, replaced the Japanese with their long-serving collaborators, Koreans detested by the general public. Criticism of this move was again misunderstood by the US military authorities, who branded the objectors as dangerous subversives. With the struggle for political control of China entering a critical stage, it was easy to believe that anti-American comment was orchestrated by the Russians. Even groups of Koreans most sympathetic to the ideals of the United States came under surveillance because of their insistence on the immediate independence of the entire peninsula as a single country.

At a conference held in Moscow in December 1945, the United States, Britain and the Soviet Union adopted a trusteeship plan as a means of solving the Korean problem. They decided that during a five-year period a provisional democratic government should work with a joint commission of the occupying military forces to develop the framework for independence. When the plan was received with anger in Seoul, the Americans simply hastened into existence a national council which excluded Korean Communists. Elected its president, Syngman Rhee was a conservative who distrusted the intentions of the United States as well as those of the Soviet Union. Conflict between the joint commission and the national council could not be avoided, and the separation of Korea hardened until it became absolute, with a Soviet-backed government under Kim Il Sung in the north, and Syngman Rhee's right-wing administration in the south. The United Nations supervised an election south of the 38th parallel in July 1948, when Syngman Rhee was confirmed as president. In December of the same year the Republic of Korea was acknowledged by the UN General Assembly as the lawful government, although in the north there already existed the Democratic People's Republic of Korea.

Washington's view of the importance of Korea had not changed: it still lay outside the US defence perimeter in East Asia. And the reverses then being suffered by the Guomindang government in China were properly regarded as a separate issue. By early 1949 Truman was almost reconciled to the fact that Jiang Jieshi's position had become untenable. His close associate, Dean Acheson, was preparing American public opinion for the probable fall of the last Guomindang bastion, the island of Taiwan.

The implicit denial of a Russian role in Mao Zedong's defeat of Jiang Jieshi was not accepted by all Americans. Giving up the Guomindang because it was a spent force did not mean embracing the 'Reds', however, for the opening up of diplomatic relations with the People's Republic of China remained only a possibility, not a likelihood. Mao Zedong had been rebuffed by Washington once before, and he had also to reach an understanding with his powerful neighbour, the Soviet Union. It suited neither Beijing nor Washington to hurry over recognition.

The climate of uncertainty and despair created by the unscrupulous politician Senator McCarthy not only stiffened American foreign policy in East Asia, but drew the United States into military alliance with a number of governments unworthy of support. The first was to be that of Syngman Rhee, whose corruption and tyrannical methods became widely known. McCarthy's accusation that over 200 Communists infested the State Department could not have come at a worse moment: foreign policy experts were disinclined to criticise the conduct of the South Korean regime and run the risk of being labelled pro-Soviet.

What must have concerned Washington most was Syngman Rhee's insistent clamour for the unification of Korea by force. Although the Russians had withdrawn their troops, they continued to train and supply Kim Il Sung's army, which at 135,000 men was larger and better equipped than South Korea's own force. The bellicose pronouncements of the South Korean president were not unconnected with his political unpopularity; at the second general election of May 1950 for the National Assembly Syngman Rhee's party secured only 56 seats out of the 310 contested. The following month Kim Il Sung decided to exploit Syngman Rhee's political problems by invading South Korea. He believed that he could move so fast that no American reinforcement would be able to arrive in time to save his opponent.

THE KOREAN WAR (1950–3)

Prior to regular North Korean troops crossing the 38th parallel, there had been sporadic fighting in South Korea between government troops and Communist insurgents. Casualties were numbered in thousands, but these figures remain tiny in comparison with the huge losses sustained in the Korean War. The South Korean army would lose 350,000 killed or missing, and 250,000 wounded; another 100,000 civilians would be forcibly removed to North

Korea. 33,000 Americans would lose their lives, and 106,000 be wounded. Against this, North Korea is estimated to have lost over half a million men, and China a staggering 900,000. By the end of the conflict in 1953 few in the West would believe any more that it had been a necessary war.

Worried by McCarthyism, Truman determined to reverse US policy in Korea and declared his firm intention to resist what he saw as Soviet-sponsored aggression. As had happened only too often in the past, Korea became a battlefield, and its people by their mutual antagonisms were hopelessly entangled in the struggle. To this day, there is no certainty that Truman's judgement was correct in 1950. Kim Il Sung may have had Stalin's blessing over the attack, but he was expected to manage its consequences on his own. Britain disliked the new American commitment to Taiwan and steadfastly maintained its own recognition of the People's Republic, but it was drawn into the Korean War as part of the United Nations force.

The North Koreans achieved complete stategic and tactical surprise. They drove southwards almost unopposed, once the overwhelmed South Korean units stationed on the border broke and ran. The US troops they encountered also fell back in a confused retreat. Within little more than a month all resistance to the North Koreans was concentrated around Pusan in the south-east of the peninsula. A mixed UN and South Korean force of 95,000 men was all that was left to defend this last, unconquered portion of the Republic of Korea. For six weeks it was subject to attack by day and night, until at last the effort to break through the hastily dug defences exhausted North Korean strength. Gradually the number of assaults diminished and the defenders were able to push back Kim Il Sung's tired soldiers. The battle cost many lives on both sides, but for North Korea the failure at Pusan was most damaging because through this port the UN commander-in-chief, Douglas MacArthur, could supplement his forces with fresh troops as they arrived by sea.

General MacArthur was concerned to turn the North Korean flank too. This he achieved by recapturing Seoul on 28 September, following a brilliant amphibious landing at Inchon. Two days later UN troops crossed the 38th parallel, invaded North Korea, and moved towards the borders of China. Thus Washington abruptly switched from a policy of containment to one of rollback, much to the anxiety of its allies, especially Britain. On 7 October, the UN passed at American request a resolution which sanctioned the general advance northwards. General MacArthur was so full of confidence that he issued a surrender ultimatum. Although he felt that neither Stalin nor Mao Zedong would dare to intervene, Truman flew to meet MacArthur on Wake Island to check on the military situation. Apparently satisfied with the meeting, the president seems to have given the UN commander-in-chief his head, providing Chinese forces stayed out of the conflict. In order to minimise such a possibility MacArthur was strictly instructed to remain at a distance from the Yalu river, the border between North Korea and the People's Republic.

Had the UN commander not been so contemptuous of the idea of a buffer zone along the Chinese border there is no reason to suppose that Beijing would have opted for war. Conventional conflict was not a method that Mao Zedong would have willingly chosen to solve the problem of a divided peninsula, because it could prove exhausting and dangerous with active American support for South Korea. There was also a chance that Washington might be tempted to back Jiang Jieshi in a bid to reconquer China, perhaps through an invasion overland via Korea. Mao Zedong had always made it perfectly clear that he could accept the reconquest of South Korea, but not the loss of North Korea, any more than Truman had been able to tolerate the original invasion.

Brushing aside all restraint, however, MacArthur ordered his forces to continue the advance northwards. A clash with Chinese troops in October had no influence on him, although they withdrew across the Yalu river after catching a couple of UN units by surprise. Their swift disengagement lends weight to Beijing's contention that this action was intended to warn Washington of the possibility that a full-scale Chinese attack was possible.

That attack fell on MacArthur's soldiers with devastating violence on 26 November, less than a month after Syngman Rhee had ceremoniously received a bottle of water from the Yalu river. At least 300,000 Chinese 'volunteers' stormed UN positions in waves, then harried the broken formations as they struggled to retreat. Everywhere carefully laid ambushes awaited their columns, as Chinese thrusts were delivered from the mountainous interior. This supposedly impassable terrain had provided the Chinese commander Lin Biao with a means of entering North Korea unnoticed by air reconnaissance. But the mountainous interior's great strategic advantage was as a protected operational base situated directly between the two UN routes of advance. The division of the UN forces into two separate commands proved to be a fatal military error. At Chosin reservoir, on the eastern side of the central mountain spine, 40,000 men were quickly surrounded by Chinese troops as winter set in. It took over a month for a fighting retreat to bring the frost-bitten UN survivors out to waiting ships at the port of Hungam, barely 100 kilometres south. The First US Marine Division alone suffered 11,731 casualties during the withdrawal.

On the western side of the peninsula the UN collapse was more far-reaching. A trail of ditched vehicles, discarded weapons, and deserted supply dumps marked the ten-day retreat back across the 38th parallel. It was painfully apparent that MacArthur had been routed by the Chinese intervention. Mobility had saved the bulk of his forces, but at the cost of a tremendous drop in morale.

The winter of 1950 was a desperate period in Korea. President Truman hinted at the use of the atomic bomb, a statement that brought the British prime minister post-haste to Washington. Clement Attlee at once damped down any American enthusiasm there might have been for an atomic strike on China. He also encouraged the president to curb MacArthur's insubordination, the principal cause of the Korean disaster. Meetings took place over four days in December, and by the end Attlee had explained through the American media that neither opposition to the extension of war in Korea nor Britain's recognition of the People's Republic of China was a form of appeasement. When in early 1951 Truman took steps to open negotiations with North Korea for a truce, MacArthur openly criticised the move. The president at first remained silent, but finally he replaced his outspoken commander-in-chief with Matthew Ridgway. Given the Republican surge in popularity because of McCarthyism, Truman took a calculated political risk when he sacked MacArthur. General Ridgway, however, never compromised the president. And his firmness as a commander put a much-needed sense of purpose back into an army henceforth committed to defensive action.

There were heavy casualties in the spring and summer of 1951, as UN firepower slowly got the better of the Chinese method of mass attack. One of the actions that helped to halt the last major Chinese offensive, the three-day battle at the Imjin river in which the Gloucesters played a key part, allowed the new commander-in-chief to stabilise a front close to the 38th parallel. Truce talks began three months later in July at Panmunjon in the no man's land between the armies. They were used by the North Koreans and the Chinese to gain time in which deep defences could be prepared to cope with the increasing UN barrage from the air and heavy artillery. When, in July 1953, the armistice was signed, the agreed ceasefire line followed, with minor variations, the line of the positions dug immediately after the Imjin engagement.

THE TWO KOREAS (1953 ONWARDS)

With the war's end it was not only the political division of Korea that remained. The Korean peninsula was divided physically by one of the most heavily fortified frontiers in the world. In 1953 there seemed no likelihood of its breach, but today the situation is less certain. The Korean people are a nation with a strong sense of unity, which produced in the Yi dynasty a ruling house capable of maintaining a united state for half a millennium down to 1910. A by-product of the relaxation in the former Soviet Union under Mikhail Gorbachev has been a hope of reunification at least among South Koreans, although demonstrations in its support are reported too from Pyongyang, the North Korean capital. South Korean police in late 1989 were ordered to halt large numbers of people on their way to a unification rally at Panmunjon. One of their demands was the right of free travel in the two Koreas.

Post-armistice experience has been very different north and south of the fortified frontier, except in terms of government repression. Neither administration can be said to have governed with a light touch. The first political convulsion in South Korea ended with Syngman Rhee's resignation in 1960 as president and his exile to Hawaii, where he died five years later. The ensuing experiment in parliamentary democracy was not a success: the financial chaos inherited from Syngman Rhee was exacerbated through severe industrial unrest and student demonstrations aimed at securing Korea's neutrality in the Cold War. In May 1961 the South Korean army took charge at the instigation of Park Chung Hee, a general originally commissioned in the Japanese-led forces of Manzhouguo. The coup appears to have been planned well before the student demonstrations of April 1960 brought down Syngman Rhee. Until his assassination in 1979 at a dinner in Seoul, Park Chung Hee was the dominant political figure. The general was elected president in 1963 as a token of the return to civilian government, but the military always remained powerful in the background.

President Park Chung Hee's real achievement was the normalisation of relations with Japan, a reversal of previous policy which channelled substantial financial aid and investment to South Korea's expanding industrial sector. The scene was thus set for the country to become one of the booming economies of the Pacific

Rim, in 1989 its annual growth rate nearly topped 7 per cent. With an export-led industrial economy similar to the Japanese model, South Korea has ceased to be primarily an agricultural country, although the best farming land is concentrated in the southern half of the peninsula. Like Japan, too, during the Korean War, it derived great benefit from US military expenditure: between 1965 and 1970 Seoul was also rewarded with substantial American subsidies for its deployment of combat troops in South Vietnam.

The South Korean government met the quadrupling of oil prices in 1973 through a programme of intensive development of certain strategic industries such as steel, petrochemicals, machine tools, shipbuilding and motor cars. This boosted exports, and helped the country to pay for its imported oil. An extension of Syngman Rhee's earlier special treatment of new industrial enterprises, the effect of the programme was to enrich a few privileged entrepreneurs rather than the people as a whole. Labour disputes arising from this uneven spread of wealth still periodically disrupt production, closing companies and discouraging foreign investment. The Daewoo Shipbuilding and Heavy Machinery Company shut down in 1988 its shipyard on Koje Island, off Pusan, after a strike, while two years later police raided in Ulsan factories belonging to the car manufacturer Hyundai, South Korea's biggest exporter. The 1990 raid on the Hyundai Motor Company was directed against workers protesting over the arrest of trade union leaders. With political stability heavily dependent on a rapidly expanding but fragile export-oriented economy, South Korea could face serious difficulties in the event of any sustained international trade recession. President Roh Tae Woo, former commander of South Korean forces in South Vietnam, appears to be more conscious of the need for conciliation, though, since he came to power in 1987.

North Korea has remained under the personal rule of one man, Kim Il Sung. Besides seeking to secure the succession for his own son, he has spent his energies on turning the country into a powerful military force, despite a population which is barely half South Korea's 42 million. The attempt at reunification by force of arms dies hard in Pyongyang. In 1968 a specially trained commando team was sent to assassinate Park Chung Hee in Seoul, an unsuccessful start to a long campaign of terrorist activity. The violent act that caught world attention happened in November 1987 when a bomb exploded on a Korean Air flight bound for Seoul; all the passengers and crew were killed.

Until 1991 North Korea and South Korea were still technically in a state of war. Right down to the signing of a non-aggression pact at the end of that year, North Korean radio continued to call for a South Korean revolution as a means of national unification. Removal of American troops from South Korea remains a prime objective of Pyongyang, but with the passing of the Cold War era, the North Korean government has found its militancy hard to sustain. During 1991 both North and South Koreans actually engaged in negotiations aimed at making the peninsula a nuclear-free zone.

THE COLLAPSE OF FRENCH INDO-CHINA (1945–54)

The origins of the second setback for the United States in post-war East Asia go back to the collaboration of the Vichy authorities with the Japanese in Indo-China. After the fall of France in 1940 they were obliged to give way to Japanese demands. First, the Imperial Japanese Army occupied airfields, railways and port installations in northern Vietnam so as to deny Jiang Jieshi the shipment of war materials; second, pressure was applied to cede border territories in Laos and Cambodia in settlement of the Franco-Thai War of 1940–1; third, Saigon became the Japanese headquarters for the push against British and Dutch colonies farther south. Although the French governor-general might point out how Indo-China remained a tranquil haven in the midst of a storm, the ignominious position of the colonial administration as a Japanese hostage hardly impressed subject populations.

While the Dutch were to misjudge the post-war situation in South-East Asia almost as badly as the French, they returned to their island empire in 1945 with none of the shame which attaches to a collaborator. Nor had they earned the enmity of a revolutionary general such as Vo Nguyen Giap (born 1912), one of the century's most astute strategists. He had been embittered by the death of his young wife, also an ardent nationalist, who died in a French prison in 1941, along with their baby. Her sister was guillotined in Saigon about the same time. In contrast to Vo Nguyen Giap, Ho Chi Minh was a 'moderate' with a steady preference for negotiation.

In the mountains north of Hanoi Vo Nguyen Giap organised a military base area for the Viet Minh, the independence movement founded in May 1941. He had selected the place for its proximity to the Chinese border, over which arms and other supplies could easily pass. Jiang Jieshi disliked the presence of a communist stronghold on his southern frontier, but from 1943 onwards he acquiesced in the flow of American aid to its active forces. Gradually they pushed back the Japanese, who could have received aid from Vichyite soldiers had not Tokyo decided to instal a puppet government. In March 1945 the last Vietnamese emperor Bao Dai was restored to the throne as the legitimate ruler. The Viet Minh welcomed the disarming of the French, but had no sympathy for a Japanese-sponsored emperor in Hué. Bao Dai himself may have hoped that an American landing in Vietnam would prevent a long period of collaboration.

The surrender of Japan caught Bao Dai as well as the Viet Minh short. The latter was organised only in the northern provinces. Ho Chi Minh was nevertheless determined to seize Hanoi, which Vo Nguyen Giap's men occupied without opposition. When, in August, Bao Dai's viceroy there resigned in favour of a citizens' committee, the emperor declared his willingness to have Ho Chi Minh form a government, an invitation that the Viet Minh leader probably would have liked to accept. Popular opinion dissuaded him from this compromise: as the Japanese stood passively by, an independent republic was announced, and Bao Dai abdicated in favour of the Viet Minh regime. The former ruler also wrote an appeal to de Gaulle on behalf of Vietnamese independence, which de Gaulle ignored, and in March 1946 Bao Dai went to live in Hong Kong as a playboy. Ten years later Ngo Dinh Diem, with American support, arranged a referendum in South Vietnam to abolish the imperial throne forever and establish a presidency – for himself. The Nguyen dynasty, founded in 1802, was no more.

It was the Potsdam Conference decision to divide Indo-China at the 16th parallel, allowing the Guomindang to occupy the north and the British the south, that really weakened the Vietnamese independence movement. The British forces under Douglas Gracey, who occupied the southern provinces, were even weaker than the meagre strength the Viet Minh could field in the street fighting that occurred in Saigon. But convinced of his duty to preserve for the French their colony, the British general refused to have any dealings with nationalists. Obtaining the reluctant approval of his commander-in-chief Mountbatten, Gracey extensively deployed Japanese forces against rebellious Vietnamese, and allowed armed French civilians to sack the Viet Minh headquarters in the city. By early 1946 resistance in the south of Vietnam was broken. To escape the political consequences of a military involvement in Indo-China, the Labour government expedited the movement of French troops to Saigon to enable them to relieve Gracey.

Thwarted though the nationalists were in the south, France had to come to terms with Ho Chi Minh's government in the north of Vietnam. To the surprise of many Vietnamese, the Viet Minh leader signed an agreement with the French, allowing them to send troops to Hanoi to replace the Guomindang troops who had occupied the area during the Japanese surrender, in exchange for recognition of the Democratic Republic of Vietnam as 'a free state forming part of the Indo-Chinese Federation and the French Union'. Apprehension of China motivated Ho Chi Minh in 1946, when he commented: 'It is better to sniff France's dung for a while than eat China's all our lives.' With the March agreement he secured the withdrawal of Jiang Jieshi's troops and undermined the position of pro-Chinese nationalists in Vietnam. In return for Chinese recognition of French sovereignty over Indo-China, France surrendered its territorial rights and privileges in China.

A self-governed, united Vietnam was expected to emerge in which the French would hold much of their old economic power and cultural influence. Opinion in the southern provinces would be tested by a referendum. With a series of short-lived governments in Paris, however, the initiative passed by default to the colonial authorities in Indo-China. They had already reclaimed Laos and Cambodia with the assistance of British vehicles and boats. In the south of Vietnam they soon felt strong enough to sponsor a puppet regime and renege on the referendum. On 23 November the French cruiser *Suffren* shelled Haiphong, thus starting seven years of hostilities with the Viet Minh.

Landings by French reinforcements followed. Within a few weeks the Viet Minh had been expelled from Haiphong, Hanoi and the larger towns; sweeps through the countryside proved less successful. The Viet Minh ceased to be an open political party, but remained the focus of national calls for independence. As a guerrilla war dragged on, the French were forced to admit the strength of Viet Minh support and the unsettled military situation. To weaken Viet Minh popular appeal, France announced in 1949 the creation of the Republic of Vietnam as an associated state within the French Union, along with Laos and Cambodia. Brought back from Hong Kong, the jaded former emperor, Bao Dai, was proclaimed the Vietnamese head of state. Britain and the United States gave recognition, but not the Soviet Union.

The United States had ignored repeated appeals from Ho Chi Minh, who was believed at the time neither to be anti-American nor under Moscow's control. Needing France as a member of NATO,

Washington stood back from the conflict in Indo-China, at least till it was transparent in China that Mao Zedong would win. Attitudes changed rapidly in late 1949, when mistakenly it was thought that the People's Liberation Army might intervene in Vietnam. The outbreak of the Korean War in the ensuing year confirmed Cold War fears and the president gave substantial aid to the French. Viewed from McCarthyite Washington, resistance to the Viet Minh had become part of the free world's struggle against international communism.

However, little headway was made against the Viet Minh. In the northern provinces, French forces suffered successive defeats at the hands of Vo Nguyen Giap. Although a mixed force of 500,000 men was now available to fight the Viet Minh, no less than 350,000 were tied down, defending settlements, holding strong-points, escorting convoys, patrolling roads, and searching villages suspected of hiding and supporting guerrillas. By 1954 the French were heading for defeat, in spite of the United States bearing nearly 80 per cent of the war's cost. In a last gamble to bring the Viet Minh to a decisive battle, the French commanders allowed the garrison at Dien Bien Phu, a fortified base north-west of Hanoi, to be cut off by Vo Nguyen Giap. It was calculated that the Viet Minh supply system would not be able to match supplies flown into its landing strip. The French were wrong, for Viet Minh artillery hidden in the surrounding hills put the airstrip out of action.

The battle of Dien Bien Phu lasted from 13 March to 7 May, when the surrender of the French garrison pushed an international conference already in session at Geneva to recognise the complete independence of North Vietnam. The world watched as Vo Nguyen Giap's men gradually overcame the defenders, until a day before the final assault they were confined to a space the size of two football pitches. At the beginning of April France had requested the intervention of American carrier-based aircraft, but President Eisenhower was not prepared to act alone. Churchill, prime minister once again, flatly refused to commit Britain to a lost cause. When in desperation John Foster Dulles suggested the idea of saving the French by means of 'small' nuclear weapons, Eisenhower was just as unhelpful: 'We can't use those awful things against Asians for the second time in ten years.'

Thus the generalship of Vo Nguyen Giap destroyed French Indo-China. The Geneva agreement, which Dulles refused to sign on behalf of the United States, divided Vietnam at the 17th parallel, and provided that neither North nor South would join a military alliance or allow foreign bases. Laos and Cambodia were to be neutral.

AMERICAN INTERVENTION (1954–75)

Dulles immediately set to work to contain Ho Chi Minh. His first action was to commit the United States to Ngo Dinh Diem (1901–63), called by Bao Dai to form a government in South Vietnam. A would-be reformer in the 1930s under the French and a collaborator with the Japanese, Ngo Dinh Diem lacked Ho Chi Minh's charisma. His own Roman Catholic beliefs also set him apart from the Buddhists, who formed the majority of Vietnam's population. In Washington though, his faith made him popular with such influential politicians as John F. Kennedy.

Dulles next devised SEATO, the South-East Asia Treaty Organisation, whose members included the United States, France, Britain, the Philippines, Thailand, Pakistan, Australia and New Zealand. Whereas India, Burma and Indonesia opposed the pact, Laos, Cambodia and South Vietnam were excluded from membership because of the Geneva stipulation about military alliances. SEATO did not become an effective military organisation, and its main use for the United States was as a cover for its growing commitment to Ngo Dinh Diem's government. Only small contingents of Australian and New Zealand troops ever saw combat in South Vietnam, while the Philippines and Thailand contributed support units. The biggest East Asian contributor of combat soldiers was a non-SEATO member, South Korea. In 1966 at American expense some 48,000 South Koreans were sent to fight alongside the 277,000 US servicemen already committed to the defeat of the Viet Minh.

When with the approval of Dulles, Ngo Dinh Diem refused to hold in 1956 the elections agreed at the Geneva Conference because he feared Ho Chi Minh would win, the threat of large-scale US intervention alone stopped the Viet Minh overrunning South Vietnam. Having removed Bao Dai from the political scene by a rigged referendum, the new president of South Vietnam was free to enjoy the fruits of massive American aid. He distributed lucrative appointments among his family and ruled with an increasingly authoritarian manner. In 1956 emergency powers were used to arrest political opponents and establish what can only be called a police state. The much-vaunted aid programme hardly affected the Vietnamese people, since only 3 per cent of it went to the rural areas where 90 per cent of the population lived. Disgruntled peasants swelled the mounting criticism of the government, the tell-tale signs of unrest jolting the anxious South Vietnamese military into a coup attempt in November 1961. Ngo Dinh Diem survived, but as one US adviser wrote at the time, 'American aid has built a castle on sand.'

Having alienated the majority of South Vietnamese, Ngo Dinh Diem prepared the ground for revolutionary activities best suited to Viet Minh strategy. Opposition became organised and co-ordinated, even the Buddhists forming in 1963 a unified church. In May, Ngo Dinh Diem's brother and a Catholic archbishop, forbade the display of flags in Hué to commemorate the birthday of Buddha. In protest a crowd stormed the local radio station and demanded that a programme be broadcast in Buddha's honour. Government troops shot nine of the protesters dead, before tear gas dispersed the rest. No one gave credit to the government claim that the deaths were the work of the Vietcong, the name by which Ngo Dinh Diem termed the Viet Minh. A series of self-immolations by Buddhist monks soon exposed the excesses of his rule to the world. It also cost Washington's support, because no move was made to save him in early November when the South Vietnamese army finally took over power.

Between 1965 and 1967 the South Vietnamese military hierarchy played musical chairs for the political leadership of the country. Two strong men eventually emerged: Nguyen Cao Ky (born 1930), an admirer of Adolf Hitler, as vice-president and Nguyen Van Thieu (born 1923) as president. They were just as dependent as Ngo Dinh Diem on US support and such devices as ballot rigging. Nor was there any let-up in the corruption that typified all the military administrations sponsored by the Americans on the mainland of South-East Asia after the Second World War.

President Kennedy, Eisenhower's successor, had employed in 1962 carrier-based aircraft and troops to preserve the neutrality of Laos, but he could not deny the North Vietnamese the use of the Ho Chi Minh Trail, a supply route for guerrillas operating in the south. This trail was to be extensively bombed by US planes during the course of the war against the Viet Minh. Kennedy had in fact committed the American people to an undeclared conflict aimed at saving South Vietnam. Vice-President Lyndon B. Johnson was no less enthusiastic for Ngo Dinh Diem, whom he praised as the 'Churchill of today'. Johnson's own presidency (1963–9) turned largely covert operations into an open war. In August 1967 a total of 525,000 US troops were on active service in South Vietnam. But when, after the

Tet offensive of February 1968, the American commander William Westmoreland asked for 200,000 additional men, Johnson refused to continue the troop build-up, because he knew the war was lost.

How the United States came to meet this first defeat in its history has already passed into legend. The devastation of Vietnam by B-52 bombers carrying incendiaries and high explosives (more bombs were dropped on Vietnam than were used by the Allies during the Second World War); the endless raking of the countryside by fire from helicopter gunships, and its long-term pollution with toxic defoliants; the My Lai massacre of March 1968, when US troops indiscriminately killed 500 South Vietnamese villagers, including women and children; the ruin of Bangkok, and other South-East Asian cities, as continuous 'R & R' ('rest 'n' recreation') facilities for combat troops; anti-war protests in the United States, including such bizarre incidents as the shootings by Ohio National Guardsmen at Kent State University in May 1970; the temporary capture of the American embassy in Saigon during the 1968 Tet offensive; and the swift collapse of South Vietnam following the withdrawal of US troops.

At first Johnson's successor, Richard Nixon, showed a similar faith in military technology, until the truth gradually dawned on a politician who had pledged to 'end the war and win the peace'. He decided to withdraw therefore behind a protective programme of Vietnamisation on the ground, and a vigorous aerial bombing campaign. In May 1970 US troops were ordered to support a South Vietnamese invasion of Cambodia, a country hitherto spared the horrors of ground fighting, in order to cut the Ho Chi Minh Trail. This was a complete fiasco, delivering within four years the Cambodian people to the not so tender mercies of the Khmer Rouge. Equally futile was the attempt to make the ARVN (Army of the Republic of Vietnam) self-reliant. It proved no match for Vo Nguyen Giap's lightning campaign, once US troops had departed. Instead of an expected two years, he rolled back the ARVN in four months, capturing Saigon in April 1975. With Nixon forced to resign over the Watergate scandal, the Republicans were in no mood to contemplate further bombing. There was nothing to do but quit. Former president Nguyen Van Thieu had already made his own escape by US plane to Taiwan, taking his family with him, as well as 16 tonnes of gold and silver looted from the vaults of the national bank.

THE RECONSTRUCTION OF VIETNAM (1975 ONWARDS)

Although it singularly failed to crush the Viet Minh, the US war machine did succeed in devastating much of Vietnam and killing and maiming many of its people. In contrast with American casualties – 58,000 dead and 150,000 wounded – the Vietnamese losses were colossal: at least 2 million died and twice that number were wounded. Probably the full extent of the suffering will never be known. Just as damaged as its inhabitants was the land itself. Apart from the record tonnage of bombs dropped during the American intervention, more than 100,000 tonnes of toxic chemicals was sprayed on jungle, forest, swamp, plantation and orchard. As a result of the spraying of defoliants food production was put in jeopardy for several years, and Vietnam did not become an exporter of rice again till 1989. More worrying are the unseen effects of dioxin, the highly toxic constituent of notorious Agent Orange.

Reconstruction could never be easy in the wake of such wholesale destruction. The economy of South Vietnam had been dependent on American aid, while that of North Vietnam was crippled by destroyed roads, railways, bridges, and dams. The ancient irrigation system of the Red river valley was so badly disrupted that over 1000 of its waterways needed urgent repair. There was an immediate threat of famine, which natural calamities such as droughts and floods between 1976 and 1978 nearly made a dire reality. Since the Vietnam War had been felt by so many Americans to be a national humiliation, it was no wonder that their government used its vast economic and diplomatic strength to isolate and weaken its former antagonist. Barred from entry to the international community of nations, Vietnam turned to the Soviet Union for assistance, although at the unwelcome cost of a naval base for the Russian Pacific Fleet. Vietnam's military intervention in Laos and Cambodia (present-day Kampuchea) would not have been possible without Soviet assistance, but arguably this alliance served to divert resources from domestic projects and hasten a border clash with China. In February 1979 Beijing said its temporary border invasion was intended to warn Vietnam over military action in Kampuchea and the treatment of ethnic Chinese. What was left unsaid concerned China's own unease at the emergence of a difficult neighbour on its southern border.

16

POST-WAR JAPAN

The Rise of an Economic Superpower
(1945 onwards)

THE AMERICAN OCCUPATION (1945–52)

On 14 August 1945 Japan notified the Allied powers of its willingness to surrender. That morning in an underground bunker in the grounds of the imperial palace Hirohito at last persuaded the cabinet that 'the unendurable must be endured,' or 'the whole nation would be reduced to ashes'. The Japanese had planned to negotiate a peace when the Americans grew tired of fighting, but Tokyo was never in any position to dictate terms. For an empire schooled in the worship of its ruler the uncertainty of what would happen to the imperial house was insupportable. Hirohito alone could therefore respond to the dropping of the atomic bombs.

Hirohito understood that members of the Imperial Japanese Army and the Imperial Japanese Navy might be accused of war crimes. But he told the cabinet of his belief in 'the peaceful and friendly intentions of the enemy'. The subsequent economic recovery put in train by the American occupation of Japan was to prove him right. In August 1945, though, the country's first conquest by a foreign power did not augur well for the future. Memories of Pearl Harbor were fresh; the American public wanted Hirohito's head.

General Douglas MacArthur, the Allied viceroy of Japan, bucked public opinion and threw his energies into the 'world's great laboratory for an experiment in the liberation of a people from totalitarian military rule and for the liberation of government from within'. He was lucky in having a free hand. His staff comprised almost entirely US personnel dedicated to remaking Japan in America's image. An

287

important concession to Japanese sentiment was made over the imperial house: in return for Hirohito's renunciation of his own divinity, the emperor remained on the throne. The general and the emperor, moreover, hit it off from the first moment they met. Hirohito impressed MacArthur most by offering personally to shoulder the guilt for the Pacific conflict:

This courageous assumption of responsibility clearly belied the facts of which I was fully aware and moved me to the marrow of my bones. He was Emperor by inherent birth, but in that instant I knew I faced the First Gentleman of Japan in his own right.

With sole exception of the emperor, the institutions held responsible for Japanese militarism were removed, including Shinto as the state religion, and in their place democratic institutions installed. The amended imperial constitution was an entirely new one based on a set of fundamentally different principles. It transferred sovereignty from the throne to the people, established a parliamentary system of government, outlawed war, allowed trades unions and guaranteed civil liberties. At the same time MacArthur placed severe limits on the operations of the zaibatsu, the business combines which he regarded as warmongers. They had been partners of the Imperial Japanese Army in colonising Korea, Manchuria and other parts of China. The continuation of the practice of forcing employees to swear loyalty oaths to these companies was looked upon as a dangerous feudal relic. But the attempt made to dismember the zaibatsu was thwarted largely by conservative politicians in the United States, who agreed with Yoshida Shigeru (1878–1967) that this programme was likely to slow down Japan's economic recovery. Premier five times between 1946 and 1954, Yoshida Shigeru did much to thwart reform, successfully tempering the radical transformation of Japanese society. Annoyed at the arrest of war criminals, and even others held to be politically dangerous, Yoshida Shigeru later wrote of the occupation:

A purge was enforced which deprived our nation of a trained body of men at a crucial moment . . . the financial concerns were disintegrated through the complete break up of zaibatsu and by the institution of severe anti-monopoly measures, gravely retarding our economic recovery . . . notorious Communist leaders were released from prison and praised for their fanatical agitation, causing untold injury to our body politic . . . education was reformed, sapping the moral fibre of our bewildered youth. Besides, our politics were so disorganised that militant unions, heavily infiltrated by Communism, ran amok in defying the authority of the government.

Labour unrest seemed to support this view: in January 1947 MacArthur was forced to ban a general strike, which had brought 5 million workers on to the streets. This ban represented a watershed in the American occupation.

With China's conquest by Communism, Japan became the key to US policy in Asia. From 1949 onwards there was a purge of left-wing sympathisers among politicians, trade unionists, teachers and journalists. This tough American line delighted Yoshida Shigeru. Antagonism towards his government came to a head in 1952, when May Day celebrations ended with a series of violent confrontations between demonstrators and police. The government reaction was legislation aimed at eliminating politics from the state education system.

Yoshida Shigeru, like some Meiji oligarch, appreciated the new relation in which Japan stood to the post-war world. The outbreak of Korean War in 1950 had completely changed the economic outlook. Billions of dollars poured into the country, which served as the main base for UN forces fighting on the Korean peninsula. Few booms have ever matched the Japanese business expansion of 1950–2. Military procurement accounted for nearly 40 per cent of foreign currency earnings, and generated demand in a wide range of industries, which later switched production to exports. It was, Yoshida Shigeru commented, 'a gift from the gods'. No less opportune was the signing in 1951 of the US-Japan Security Treaty, a bilateral agreement through which the Japanese could have full independence if, in return, they created a small 'self-defence' force and allowed for at least a decade US bases on Okinawa and the main Japanese islands. It effectively returned Japan to the community of nations, and from 1952 onwards released the United States from the financial burden of the occupation. Cold War rivalry between Washington and Moscow was already straining superpower resources.

'THE BLESSINGS OF HARMONY AND PROGRESS' (1952–73)

In San Francisco Yoshida Shigeru expressed his hopes for the future at the signing of the US-Japan Security Treaty. What he chose not to mention during the moment of rehabilitation was the dependence of the Japanese economy on the UN campaign in Korea. When, prior to the San Francisco ceremony, the Japanese premier had indicated that he was thinking of reopening trade relations with China, Washington quickly intervened. Despite his private belief that East Asian geography would favour Mao Zedong, and not Jiang Jieshi, Yoshida Shigeru allowed Japan to be drawn into the US-sponsored blockade of the People's Republic, which was to last for two decades.

Instruments used by subsequent leaders to secure Japan's phenomenal economic development were the Ministry of Finance and the all-powerful Ministry of International Trade and Industry (MITI). The latter has consistently managed growth by means of subsidies, when they were necessary, and protection during times of trade difficulty, and has channelled investment into high-growth industries. The vision of MITI has remained true to that of the Meiji era – Japan must match the West. This continuity in policy had an interesting parallel in the continuity of staff, since senior MITI officials in the 1950s and 1960s had received their bureaucratic training in ministries devoted to the economic self-sufficiency of the Japanese empire. And their successors have retained the old sense of urgency about national survival, so much so that MITI's response to the oil crisis of the early 1970s was a plan to switch the economy from reliance on heavy industries towards electronics and robotics. The present-day lead enjoyed by Japan in many areas of new technology owes a great deal to this strategic foresight.

The sudden increase in oil price and the reduction in supply appeared as damaging a blow to the national economy as had been the US oil embargo just before Pearl Harbor. It shook Japan more than the West because Japan was the world's largest importer of oil, which met almost 80 per cent of its energy needs. Encouraged by a buyer's market during the 1960s, Japan had come to consume more and more oil, with the likelihood, according to Tanaka Kakuei (prime minister, 1972–4), that its consumption would triple over the next few years. His discovery following OPEC's move in 1973 that Japan had just four days' reserve supply, over and above what was already in the distribution system, was a startling revelation. The continued recovery of Japan's economy looked in doubt.

Dr Henry Kissinger, the newly appointed Secretary of State, visited Tokyo in order to keep Japanese and American policy aligned on the Arab-Israeli conflict. His meeting with Tanaka Kakuei was unproductive, since the United States would not guarantee Japan's supply of oil. Japan therefore modified its foreign policy: economic ties with Israel were replaced with a commitment to use Japanese industrial skills in the development of Arab states. The immediate diplomatic reward was exemption from cuts in supply – the cost of more expensive oil had still to be met.

Japan weathered the first oil crisis, and frosty trade relations with the United States, without the loss of too many companies. MITI initiatives in energy conservation and labour-saving methods actually made the survivors more prosperous. By the time of the Iranian revolution and the second oil crisis of 1979, Japan was less dependent on Arab supplies. Hydro-electric, nuclear and solar power then accounted for a third of energy used. That by the year 2000 possibly half of the national supply would be drawn from nuclear power stations was a popular aim at least until the Fukui accident in February 1991 sent a radioactive plume across the Inland Sea. Its passage over the city of Hiroshima was one of the ironies of the worst nuclear leak since Chernobyl.

The determination apparent in this notable turn-round of economic fortunes impressed observers in the West as well as in Japan. Overlooked at first in the search for an explanation was the centralised planning of the economy bequeathed by the American occupation. The desperate need to revive Japan had forged a tradition of government guidance more rigorous even than that during the darkest period of the Pacific War. Added to this central mechanism for the promotion of export-led investment was the windfall of foreign exchange accumulated as a result of the conflict in Korea. Driven by Japanese insecurity, a powerful modern trait since Perry first threatened war in 1853, the emergence of an economic superpower seems now almost inevitable, considering the international denial until 1992 of any military role. Like other advanced economies in the 1980s, Japan began to experience de-industrialisation as resources started to shift from the manufacturing to the service sector. Quite typical was the Japanese response to this fundamental change: MITI launched in 1981 an extensive research and development programme aimed at designing the fifth generation of computers. If the semi-conductor was to be the equivalent of oil in the next millennium, then Japan had to possess the technological edge over its competitors. The very same attitude had persuaded the Meiji reformers to encourage industry and commerce, as a defence against the West.

INTERNATIONAL AFFAIRS AFTER 1952

Underlying economic progress from the 1960s onwards was an extraordinarily stable society. Voting patterns reflected a new consensus that showed no sign of breaking down till the late 1980s, despite a number of notable political scandals. In July 1976 the former premier, Tanaka Kakuei, was arrested for receiving bribes from the Lockheed Corporation amounting to 500 million yen. Yet Tanaka Kakuei retained his parliamentary seat right up till conviction in 1983, and during the years of his unresolved appeal, he has continued to influence government policy behind the scenes like a latterday shogun.

The Recruit Cosmos scandal of 1988 indicated, too, how deeply corruption was ingrained in public life. An aggressive Japanese real-estate company, Recruit Cosmos's insider deals brought down several cabinet ministers, and gave to the Socialists the first chance in nearly three decades to challenge the established political order. In the 1990 general election they gained fifty-one seats, nearly 25 per cent of the vote. Perhaps more significant for Japanese society was that the Socialist leader was a sixty-year-old spinster, Doi Takako. It was apt that a woman academic should be chosen to lead the Socialist Party against the ruling Liberal Democrats, shortly after a former geisha had caused the resignation of the premier, Uno Sosuke. Although the American occupation established women's rights to inherit property, marry whom they pleased and file for divorce, the traditionalism of Yoshida Shigeru ensured that further progress was slowed down.

The Lockheed scandal occurred at a bad time for Japan, just as Tokyo was preparing to become a major force again in world affairs. Cutting loose from American foreign policy goals proved less easy than might otherwise have been expected. A certain cynicism was directed at Japanese protestations of goodwill for the Arab cause, rather in the manner that Tokyo's reluctance to actively participate in the United Nations military action against Saddam Hussein was more recently dismissed as diplomatic calculation, and not the constitutional matter it really happened to be.

Until 1952 Japan's foreign policy was actually in American hands. Pledged to the minimum use of force, the Japanese were willing to shelter behind American arms, even if it meant that regaining control over Okinawa had to wait another twenty years. There was great reluctance on the part of the Pentagon to surrender control over the bases built there, but the strength of Japanese anti-war feeling had to be recognised. Before a formal agreement in 1972, US forces had been at liberty to operate from them against an array of enemies: China, North Korea, Russia, Laos and North Vietnam. Thereafter Tokyo forbade nuclear weapons altogether, and insisted upon prior consultation before any other offensive action. Anger in Japan had been aroused by American intervention in Vietnam. Demonstra-

tions against American bases on Japanese soil and protests at government support for the war-effort were led by the Zengakuren students' federation.

The Vietnam War was a catalyst for student unrest in Japan, as in many countries. Other causes of dissatisfaction existed: the universities themselves, the pervasive influence of the examinations for entry, the increase in school tuition fees, and the problem of rapid urban growth. By the time USS *Enterprise*, a nuclear-powered aircraft-carrier, docked in January 1968 at Nagasaki there were few campuses undisturbed by student occupations or strikes. The ship's arrival rallied a strong anti-nuclear movement, which Zengakuren activists were delighted to spearhead. It seemed at the time that in international affairs the United States and Japan would be soon divided, but the Japanese government refused to budge from its support of American intervention in Vietnam, and was rewarded in late 1969 by Washington with the promised return of Okinawa. As the Vietnam War showed signs of coming to an end, through the slow withdrawal of US troops, this conciliatory gesture defused the political conflict in Japan and left continued student protest essentially a matter of academic discipline. Public support for the students evaporated and government pressure ensured that normal tuition resumed.

Some students remained active, but the subsequent rise of a middle-class majority drove them to extremes: for instance, in the United Red Army attack in 1972 at Tel Aviv airport, which left twenty-four people dead. Even in the 1980s sporadic disturbances occurred, although without loss of life. The imperial house became the main establishment target. Apart from firing the odd rocket into the palace grounds, there were disruptions at the ceremonies to mark the funeral of Hirohito in 1989 and the accession of his heir, Akihito. But these irritants had little affect on growing Japanese enthusiasm for education. Whereas only slightly over half of those finishing secondary school went on to sixth-form studies in high school in 1955, nearly 90 per cent did so in 1973; the proportion of high school leavers who entered further and higher education rose from 5 per cent to over 30 per cent in the same period. By 1985 the percentage of students staying in full-time study after the age of eighteen had reached the world record of 51 per cent, as Japan under the direction of MITI endeavoured to capitalise on its human resources.

One of the oddities of contemporary history has been Japanese resentment of US policy in East Asia. Tokyo may have been

prevented from trading with the People's Republic of China prior to Nixon's visit in 1972, but Washington more than compensated for this loss by facilitating the expansion of Japanese trade amongst its allies there. Waiving as a crippling burden the greater part of its reparations, the United States allowed Japan to compensate South-East Asian countries by means of manufacturing and services. By 1959 renewed economic ties with them had laid the basis of a growing sphere of commercial influence that eventually was to be recognised in the so-called Kaifu doctrine. Early in 1991 Kaifu Toshiki (prime minister, 1989–91) announced a series of meetings with East Asian heads of state intended to cement together a continental trading bloc which would rival the European Community and the United States. Whilst Tokyo was at pains to deny any attempt to recreate the Greater East Asia Co-Prosperity Sphere, this initiative was a break with Japan's post-war diplomacy. For the first time Japan decided to assert its role as the East Asian economic superpower.

Prior to his resignation Kaifu Toshiki also announced the ending of economic sanctions against China, thus giving notice to the West of the importance to Japan of its giant neighbour. The trade embargo, like those of other nations, had been imposed after the bloody repression of the Tiananmen Square demonstration in 1989. At the instance of MITI, Tokyo unfroze a package of development loans worth 810 billion yen so as to ensure Japanese companies had a head-start in the enormous Chinese market. With an economy already twice the size of the re-unified Germany, Japan has need of all East Asia for its products. MITI's new strategic plan for the region's development, nonetheless, may not be regarded with warmth in some of the former territories of the Japanese empire. Heavy investment in factories and property causes alarm, especially when accompanied by the bulk purchase of raw materials – oil, rubber, ore and timber. Accusations over the unnecessary destruction of tropical forests in Thailand and Malaysia are based not entirely on ecological concern: apprehension can be discerned at the way in which aid or investment is tailored to Japan's own industrial requirements. Memories of exploitation are not yet dead.

MODERNISATION OR WESTERNISATION?

Nostalgia today for a rural past ignores the chronic poverty of traditional village life, which was undoubtedly a factor in pushing Japan toward expansion overseas. The oppression and backwardness of the

countryside nurtured the violence that Japanese soldiers exhibited to conquered peoples during the Pacific War. Their embrace of a stern warrior ethic had as much to do with lack of opportunities for personal advancement at home as with any belief in Japan's imperial mission to drive the Western powers out of East Asia. Through the practice of primogeniture small farms persisted in Japan until the 1930s. Younger sons left the land to work in the modern industrial sector, or took up arms as a way of escape from hired agricultural labour. In order to curtail rural unrest during the American occupation, MacArthur sought to encourage smallholders at the expense of landlords. Misjudging the conservative tendency of rural Japan, he not only strengthened a social group opposed to his own programme of reform but he inadvertently preserved the village idyll as well. Present-day Japanese still enjoy the notion of themselves as a nation of farmers not quite sure what to do with their new affluence.

It is an exaggeration to say that the advent of an advanced industrial society in Japan has had no affect on tradition. Beneath the business suits and technological gadgetry a great deal of the old Japan survives, especially outside the growing conurbations, but modernisation is a fact of Japanese life which threatens to encompass even the paddy fields of the smallest rural community. Rice imports were banned between 1952 and the 1989 round of trade talks under the auspices of GATT, the General Agreement on Tariffs and Trade. Agriculture emerged as the key issue of the GATT talks when the US delegation objected to European Community farm subsidies and the Japanese ban on rice imports. With an export trade in manufactured goods vulnerable to American tariffs, Japan could not afford a trade war. Officially, Tokyo maintained that it would continue to protect the farmers. 'With regard to rice,' Kaifu Toshiki told the Diet in October 1989, 'and the special importance of rice and rice farmers, I intend to keep it as part of our basic policy of self-sufficiency from domestic production.' Yet an easing of import regulations was quietly put in hand, as the ruling Liberal Democrats realised how far the national economy had shifted away from agriculture.

Japan had changed from being primarily a rural society during the period of the American occupation, with nearly half of total employment in agriculture, into a country with a far stronger industrial and service-sector orientation. Only 7 per cent of Japan's workforce was engaged in agriculture at the end of the 1980s, roughly a seventh of the 1950 level. The building of new factories in the

Fig. 49. Japan's new economic position in the world, from a 1989 British cartoon

countryside and the extensive mechanisation of rice production were responsible for this major alteration in employment pattern. Government encouraged the trend, striving to wean farming families away from agriculture, without forcing them to leave their homes. A prime example is the deliberate concentration of nearly half of Japan's integrated circuit production in rural Kyushu.

Many farmers have not sold their land. As a result, the number of part-time farmers has increased, along with a rising surplus of rice. By the time Kaifu Toshiki addressed the Diet the rice mountain had reached 1.5 million tonnes. Intense lobbying by farmers, who remain politically significant, together with increased government revenues from a fast-growing economy, has discouraged the Liberal Democrats from doing anything radical to rectify the situation.

Another manifestation of traditional concern about the land is the Japanese reaction to pollution. In the headlong rush for economic growth, which a deep-seated pessimism about Japan's capacity for survival continues to fuel, the zaibatsu have been allowed to devastate the natural environment. Annual growth rates of around 10 per cent until 1973, and almost 4 per cent after the oil crisis, were far too high to be effectively managed. During the late 1980s Japanese growth rates remained double those of the European Community and usually greater than that of the United States. Today Japan is one of the most polluted countries in the world.

Although Tanaka Kakuei came to power in 1972 as a moderniser, his plan for remodelling the Japanese archipelago had put the quality of life on the political agenda. Tanaka Kakuei's aim was to reverse the urban sprawl blighting large areas of the country by means of an improved railway system and the development of high-tech industries in outlying areas. Unfortunately for Japan, the scheme triggered land speculation and runaway building in the areas favoured for development and industrial relocation. The oil crisis, and subsequent exposure of government corruption, destroyed public confidence in national planning on such a scale. In 1973 a ten-year court battle against the Chisso Corporation ended in favour of brain-damaged victims of methyl-mercury poisoning. The widely publicised case proved beyond any doubt that evidence of an effluent contaminating fish was overlooked by the Minamoto local authorities because of company intransigence. As the biggest employer, the Chisso Corporation had easily brushed aside complaints for twenty years.

An environmental issue that brought into alliance farmers and student activitists was Narita airport. The 1966 government decision to build a new international airport on farming land, some 45 kilometres east of Tokyo, incensed a large number of people who did not hesitate to support the direct tactics employed by Zengakuren students. Almost up to the moment Narita airport opened in 1978 there were pitched battles between protestors and the police. The bullet-train line from the capital has never materialised, and the single runway eventually built still restricts the number of flights handled each day. The impasse at Narita marks perhaps the first socially imposed limitation on Japanese growth.

Interwoven with the drive for modernisation is the strong commitment of Japanese employees to their companies, an attitude of mind unsuited to a serious appraisal of environmental issues. In Japan the traditional emphasis on the group has hardly been weakened by the post-Meiji transformation of society. Life is still judged by a social consensus that establishes standards of performance and behaviour. The network of obligations, duties and debts, largely Confucian in origin but thoroughly Japanised over time, embraces the home, school and workplace. Moreover, its insistence on loyalty is far more absolute than the original Chinese model. A beneficiary of such devotion has been the zaibatsu, whose internal structures in large measure resemble a feudal hierarchy. Executives join a combine for life and rise in rank by moving through its various companies. The system of lifelong careers has been extended to skilled workers, who remain loyal through the introduction of wage scales that increase with length of service. The firm has become another extended family, concerned to look after its own members as far as necessary in the battle for commercial success.

Despite the rapid growth of trade union membership during the American occupation, the power of organised labour has not yet been strong enough to challenge the feudal ethos of the zaibatsu. Once MacArthur clamped down on strikes, and company-sponsored unions appeared on the industrial scene, labour militancy ceased to be a political force. Trade unions have a role to play in the running of companies, although from a Western perspective it seems to be essentially co-operative. The line between management and union membership is easy to cross, since promotion for workers depends on length of service. A *tantosha*, or 'person responsible', can be someone who has entered management via the shop-floor or joined the company at a level above which the union recruits. Because employees identify themselves with a company, taking pride in its prestige and products, they are able to exercise quality control as a self-organising group. A corollary of this personal commitment is workaholism, a problem being tackled at present by MITI through the study of recreation. Victims of such anxiety are usually reported dying of heart attacks. On average a Japanese works 40 days more each year than his counterpart in Britain.

Yet pressure on children to acquire the qualifications needed for access to the most demanding jobs shows no sign of abatement, as mothers now have their children coached in order to obtain a place in a favoured kindergarten. In borrowing Western school models Japan did not borrow Western concepts of learning and childhood. Unlike their American and European colleagues, Japanese teachers see education as the moral key to social cohesion, economic growth and international political stature. It enforces the conformity upon which Japan depends. The MITI initiative in the management of human resources has tended only to intensify competition within the education system. Because education in Japan determines the occupational ladder a child will eventually climb, there is intense pressure at the selection points, such as entry to high school and university. Crammers offering *juku*, after-school tuition, are used by most Japanese children, while those experiencing trouble in a specific subject may have a home tutor as well. Students are told to persist in a spirit of self-discipline and sacrifice. Examination nerves regularly fell well-prepared candidates, and reduce caring parents to a deplorable state of neurosis.

Social pressures also remain strong for newly-weds to have children early in their marriage, though automatic dismissal of women upon pregnancy was made illegal in 1986. Ambivalence towards womanhood is a long-standing Japanese cultural trait, which can alternate between fearful repression and outright adulation.

THE NEW SUPERPOWER OF THE 1990s

The end of the Cold War has come as an unexpected bonus to Japan: the American/Russian nuclear stalemate appears to leave a world role for an economic superpower to play. Both nuclear superpowers have found it difficult to impose their wishes by military means – Afghanistan was for the Soviets a lesser Vietnam – while OPEC nations have even dared to use oil prices as a political weapon unimagined in simpler imperialist days. The mutual exhaustion of the Russians and the Americans was disguised to an extent by the UN action over the Iraqi annexation of Kuwait, but impressive though US military capability remains, the United States was still obliged to dispatch envoys to Tokyo and Bonn for financial assistance. Following the Gulf War, the Japanese were in 1992 even persuaded to amend their constitution so that soldiers could be sent overseas for the first time since the Second World War. Though Kiichi Miyazawa (prime minister, 1991 onwards) spoke reassuringly of Japan's military contribution to United Nations peace efforts, an opinion poll showed 55 per cent of the respondents were opposed to the change.

But perhaps Japanese influence will be most noticeable in Eastern Europe, following the abandonment of Marxist dogma. Investment in countries there could prove more profitable than in the United Kingdom, given lower labour costs and the likelihood of eventual admission to the European Community. Tokyo is not playing down this opportunity for its enormous balances of foreign exchange, but MITI seems to favour involvement with mainland East Asia. It is determined to exploit the trade potential of the People's Republic of China. Should Beijing respond favourably to Tokyo's blandishments, then Kaifu Toshiki's erstwhile vision of an East Asian economic community could still prove to be the basis of a potent political force in world affairs after the year 2000. Whatever course the Chinese choose to follow, and they may well adopt an exclusion policy as before in their long history, Japan is pivotal in the future development of the Pacific basin, an area already identified as next century's economic pace-setter. Not for nothing has Nomura Securities, Japan's leading stockbrokers, predicted that within two decades the country's gross national product will be even larger than that of the United States. With a population of 123 million, Japan possesses a strong home market for its products. In the late 1980s the Japanese economy began to break away from growth based on exports and move towards growth based on domestic demand, a

trend shaped not only by the adverse effect on export prices of a
strong currency, but the steady rise of consumerism in Japan itself,
as more and more people have started to enjoy for themselves the
new wealth.

How Japan will actually use its power in the world remains to be
seen. Its national identity has not been eroded either by the American occupation or its rise as an advanced industrial economy, notwithstanding the scandals threatening to engulf leading politicians.
As Yoshida Shigeru wrote in 1961: 'History attests to the fact that
we are a resilient nation, quick to recover. We have recovered rapidly from the disastrous defeat, thanks largely to the assistance of the
United States. We are convinced that our future lies in the fullest
co-operation with the free nations.' That the former premier drew
such a distinction between countries then is a reminder of conservative Japanese politicians' fear of Communism. Nonetheless, relations between the Chinese and the Japanese are probably now the
critical factor in determining the course of East Asian history over
the next fifty years.

17

SOUTH-EAST ASIAN INDEPENDENCE

The Nationalist Response to the Post-War Era
(1945 onwards)

THAILAND PRESERVED

By aligning with Japan in 1942 Thailand could have ceased to be the only South-East Asian country to avoid European colonial rule. The declaration of war on Britain and the United States was made by Phibun, a military dictator who exercised power as regent: throughout the Second World War the Thai king remained a schoolboy in Switzerland. One of the promoters of the 1932 coup that ended an absolute monarchy, Phibun had gradually assumed unlimited powers until, tempted by the opportunity for territorial gain, he brought his country into collaboration with Japan. The Franco-Thai War of 1940–1 had already recovered provinces lost to French Indo-China, but with Japanese assistance there was scope for acquiring once again those others incorporated into British holdings in Burma and Malaya.

During the first year of the Pacific War Thailand was enthusiastic about the conflict, and proud to be the only fully independent Asian state in alliance with imperial Japan. An economic agreement was reached for the exchange of rice, rubber and tin with goods from Japan which were no longer available from Britain and the United States. But Japan had nothing spare to export, and the Imperial Japanese Army brought on runaway inflation by printing Thai currency itself as a way out of the dilemma.

Before the war went against Japan in 1944, conditions in Thailand had already degenerated to the level of a black-market economy, with recurrent shortages of basic commodities. The fall of the

301

Japanese prime minister, Tojo Hideki, shortly after the American recapture of the Philippines, seems to have encouraged the National Assembly to vote Phibun out of office. The general stood aside and a civilian government took charge under the direction of his rival, the lawyer Pridi Phanomyong. The name of the country was changed back to Siam, and close contacts developed with the US-sponsored Free Thai movement. Unlike Britain, the United States had never offered a reciprocal declaration of war, considering Phibun's action to have been taken under constraint.

This was a relief to the new government, worried about Allied invasion, and a reported British desire to turn Thailand into a protectorate. To placate London it was indicated that the Malayan and Burmese annexations of 1942–3 would be restored. Relying on American support in the post-war settlement worked, although it did not prevent a return to a military regime in 1947. First, Phibun's escape from prosecution as a war criminal undermined the government's authority. The second crisis of 1946, again poorly handled, was the death of the young king in mysterious circumstances. He was found in bed, shot through the head with a pistol. The suspicion of regicide, rather than suicide, could not be dispelled, and rumours of revolution in the ensuing year gave the army its excuse to act. Phibun returned to power in April 1948. Elections were held every year until 1957, when another military strongman replaced him, but democracy withered away.

Exploiting the Thai desire for firm government and American fears of Communist subversion, Phibun was able to rebuild Thailand as he wished with foreign aid. Phibun's policy of state-sponsored enterprises owed more to traditional practices of royal monopoly than to the socialist programme his opponents had formerly advocated. Few of these enterprises were efficient but they provided employment and opportunities for peculation. The anti-Chinese policies Phibun pursued were justified after the founding of the People's Republic as measures aimed against Communism. At the same time, he encouraged greater Thai-Chinese assimilation through marriage. The substantial Chinese business community came to terms with the government by offering influential Thai positions on company boards, a practice to be greatly expanded under Sarit Thanarat (prime minister, 1957–63).

Phibun's premiership was an unsettled period for Thailand. The kingdom was more populous, and soon much more prosperous than it had been: American aid and international loans sustained the post-war recovery, but the reins of government were held by a small group of officers, who violently suppressed political opposition and settled their own quarrels with bullets. In June 1951 Phibun himself was lucky to escape one of the many coup attempts against him, when he was seized aboard a ship and had to swim ashore. His deposition in 1957 was peaceful, however. General Sarit Thanarat sent him into exile in Japan. On his own death six years later Sarit Thanarat was also succeeded without violence by his nominee, Thanom Kittikachorn.

Sarit Thanarat restored the monarchy to an active role in Thai society, reviving public ceremonies and making much of the king's support for military rule. King Bhumipol Adulyadej (1946 onwards) was ostentatiously placed at the apex of the social order as a symbol of national unity. While not allowed to interfere in politics, he has exercised great influence on decision making, and is reputed to have played a critical role in maintaining stability during the October revolution of 1973. Massive demonstrations then against official corruption, student repression, and the banning of political parties led to clashes with the police. Nearly half a million protestors, including students and professionals, challenged Thanom Kittikachorn's attempted re-imposition of direct military rule. When the army wavered and heeded the orders of more moderate officers supported by Bhumipol, the would-be dictator was forced into exile and a civilian government took over control. Among early policy changes were a demand for an immediate American troop withdrawal and negotiations for a resumption of diplomatic relations with the People's Republic of China.

The American build-up in Thailand had coincided with the war in Vietnam. As a member of SEATO, Thailand sent a token force to this conflict, but its chief contribution was the provision of bases for US aircraft. In return, the Thai government received a promise of American military support and US $1000 million in economic aid. On his death in 1963 Sarit Thanarat was discovered to have left a personal fortune approaching US $150 million. But for his fall, Thanom Kittikachorn would have followed his example.

The experiment in parliamentary democracy that followed the deposition lasted for three years, during which there were four governments, one of them lasting a single week. Students had articulated the general disgust with the web of corruption that entangled the state: their radical views briefly united the country in a desire for change, even though feuding politicians frustrated a legislative programme by continually dissolving coalitions. But abhorrence of the old regime was not the same thing as an endorsement for far-reaching reforms, especially at the very moment the 600-year-old monarchy in neighbouring Laos was abolished by the Pathet Lao, an ally of the Viet Minh. Communist advances in South Vietnam and Cambodia were an additional worry to the Thai monarchy, which along with its most ardent supporters came to see the student movement as either Communist directed or inspired. By early 1976 right-wing reaction aimed at preserving the status quo had reduced Thailand to chaos, thus opening the way for another military coup.

This occurred one year after a massive blood-letting perpetrated by right-wingers at Thammasat, the more recent of Bangkok's two universities and the centre of student agitation. Fears that an era of political violence was about to begin were allayed by the army, which stemmed the rising tide of violence. Realising the extent of public unease, the Thai military have been more circumspect in the last two decades, at least until early 1992. Then an attempt by an unelected general to form a government led to bloody clashes in the streets of Bangkok, which were ended by the intervention of the monarch. King Bhumipol Adulyadej was shown on television in audience with the leaders of the rival factions, whom he commanded 'to solve this problem'. Whether the compromise lasts, or military coups once again disrupt Thai politics, remains to be seen.

From a small state underpopulated before the Second World War, the Thai kingdom has become crowded and overpopulated relative to its present economic performance. The population rose from 18 million in 1947, through 44 million in 1980, to 57 million in 1990. Development of a tourist trade out of the 'rest 'n' recreation' facilities previously established for US serviceman has brought in plenty of foreign currency, but at a grave social cost. The most dramatic changes have happened in congested and air-polluted Bangkok, which has a skyline punctuated no longer by elegant pagodas but towering high-rise hotels and office blocks. In quite another league, however, is the newly developed seaside resort of Pattaya, reported to have in 1990 no less than 266 hotels catering for *farangs*, 'foreigners'. In what the British travel writer, Norman Lewis, has called 'a fun-fair reflection of the United States', a foreigner can partake there for a modest sum a bewildering range of sexual delights (and catch AIDS).

INDEPENDENT CAMBODIA AND LAOS

After the Communist victory in South Vietnam in 1975, Thailand endeavoured to improve its relations with China as well as Vietnam.

Diplomatic relations were established with the People's Republic and citizenship regulations eased in favour of ethnic Chinese living in Thailand. Getting on to friendly terms with Vietnam proved more difficult, because the Vietnamese would not agree to establish diplomatic relations until US forces had evacuated Thailand in July 1976. A further complication was the Vietnamese occupation of Cambodia (1978–89), which forced hundreds of thousands of refugees across the Thai border. In the mid-1980s the Thai army battled with Vietnamese units in hot pursuit of retreating Cambodian guerrilla bands. These guerrillas belonged to the Khmer Rouge, a Cambodian Communist movement originally assisted by Hanoi. On the Cambodian attainment of complete independence from France in 1954, the Khmer Rouge had split into two factions: one retired to North Vietnam, the other stayed on in Cambodia to resist the rule of Norodom Sihanouk (crowned 1941). The latter were fiercely anti-Vietnamese, for which they were eventually rewarded with Chinese aid.

King Sihanouk had declared Cambodia's independence first in March 1945, a month before the Laotian monarch was induced to follow suit by the Imperial Japanese Army. French colonial rule had been acceptable to both countries largely because it was less onerous than the alternative Thai or Vietnamese domination. The Japanese occupation, however, discredited France and encouraged a desire for national freedom. The returning French were obliged to agree to compromises over autonomy, until in late 1953 the country was virtually independent. The author of this triumph was the king himself, and perhaps the worst consequence for Cambodia was his belief that he had won the right to govern as he thought fit. 'I am the natural ruler,' he told a French reporter, 'and my authority has never been questioned.'

An apparent transition to constitutional rule was handled with considerable acumen. Following a French-style plebiscite, which confirmed his leadership, Sihanouk stepped down as king in favour of his father and assumed a political role. In the September 1955 elections his party won 85 per cent of the votes cast. When the first serious cabinet crisis developed in 1960, another plebiscite conveniently conferred on Sihanouk the position of head of state for life. Always excluded from playing a part in government, the Cambodian countryside accepted the rule of a modern prince, but educated townspeople hankered after a republic. Population was beginning to put pressure on traditional agricultural methods too. It increased from 1 million to 4 in the century before 1950, and then accelerated. Prince Sihanouk drew upon the age-old Khmer reverence for their rulers, but his popularity could not outlast the protection he had to provide the peasants if they were to bring in the harvest. In the late 1960s a revival of Khmer Rouge activities cast a doubt over his ability to perform this royal duty. Ignoring Hanoi's wishes, guerrilla activities were stepped up in the countryside. The North Vietnamese were contented to let Sihanouk remain in power, since he tolerated the transportation of war supplies through eastern Cambodia to guerrillas in South Vietnam. But a rising chorus of protest from the Cambodian army during 1969 obliged Sihanouk to appoint the anti-Communist general Lon Nol as prime minister, and set off for Moscow and Beijing to bring diplomatic pressure to bear on the North Vietnamese to end their support for the Khmer Rouge.

Throughout the conflict in Vietnam Sihanouk had tried every diplomatic gambit to preserve Cambodian neutrality. He said nothing when the United States bombed Communist bases, even though the 1969 raids were kept secret from the American public. All that these air strikes achieved was to drive the Communists further inside Cambodia, thus bringing even greater disruption to the country. While Sihanouk was on the diplomatic trail in Moscow, he learned that Lon Nol had deposed him. The United States then persuaded Lon Nol of the need for an invasion of eastern Cambodia. The ground action ordered by President Nixon against Communist camps was another unmitigated disaster: it enlarged the Vietnam War, encouraged the Khmer Rouge, and left 600,000 Cambodians dead. Intense bombing of the countryside crowded refugees into the cities under the control of the Lon Nol government. By the time the conflict ended in 1975 over 2 million people, or a third of the population, had become refugees, with a resulting breakdown of traditional agriculture and the social order.

American intervention undoubtedly enabled the Khmer Rouge to seize control. By early 1974, it dominated the countryside and threatened starving cities, which depended almost entirely on deliveries of rice by the Americans.

A similar, though slightly less sanguine, fate overtook Laos. In February 1971, Nixon tried to halt Communist gains with an invasion by South Vietnamese troops. But without American ground support, they hurriedly fell back in the face of North Vietnamese and Laotian counter-attacks. A reversion to saturation bombing was Washington's inevitable response, with the same flood of desperate refugees pouring into Laotian towns. As in Cambodia, there was nothing to suggest that military intervention in Laos would be effective. Ever since the Geneva Conference of 1954 Laos had also struggled to remain neutral. The American government secretly armed 15,000 Meo or Hmong tribesmen against Laotian Communists, who were supplied in turn by the Russians via North Vietnam. Harold Macmillan, the British prime minister, had told his SEATO ally Eisenhower how disturbed he was 'at the trouble we are both getting into over Laos.' To President Eisenhower's successor, Kennedy, he jokingly expressed his scepticism at the leverage any Western power could hope to exert in Laos. When in April 1961 the two leaders, on a yacht cruising down the Potomac river, passed a small flotilla from a local high school, struggling raggedly against the current, Macmillan quipped: 'Looks like the Laotian Navy!' Britain could not afford to waste resources on such a futile venture: unfortunately for mainland South-East Asia the new American president did believe that he possessed the necessary strength. Within two years, nonetheless, difficulties in Laos and Vietnam prompted Kennedy to restrict media coverage of the increasing US involvement.

Less than six months after the 1971 invasion, the Communists and their allies held more of Laos than before. The main group, the Pathet Lao, 'the land of the Lao', had to be brought into a coalition government, which lasted until the abolition of the Lao monarchy and the founding of the Lao People's Democratic Republic in late 1975. By this time the Khmer Rouge had taken over the running of Cambodia and begun its controversial policy of evacuating cities and towns When on 17 April Phnom Penh was surrounded, its population had reached 2 million. With surrender and the end of American deliveries of rice, the Khmer Rouge was forced to transfer the inhabitants of the capital to the countryside, where they could repair irrigation canals, plant rice, and undertake other tasks on collective farms. Yet this decision appears to have been anticipated in the emptying of towns already under Khmer Rouge control. Quite possibly the rank and file of the movement, recruited from the poorest sections of the peasantry, saw these measures as a just end to the parastic rule of an urban hierarchy. If so, then it was a deliberate removal of the immemorial gap between town and countryside upon which the Khmer kingdom had rested. The impoverished peasantry was not prepared to sustain by its toil a privileged modern capital like a latterday Angkor.

The leader of the Khmer Rouge, Pol Pot (born 1928), may have adopted the strategy of population transfer for security reasons as well. Despite the crushing defeat of the Lon Nol government, the organisation of the Khmer Rouge was still perhaps too rudimentary for the management of an urbanised Kampuchea, as Cambodia was renamed. Certainly the execution of opponents by the Khmer Rouge stands in contrast to the Viet Minh emphasis on re-education and rehabilitation. As many as 250,000 people were executed during the ascendancy of the Khmer Rouge (1975–8). Five or six times that number may have died in the resettlement programme. This is less than the claim of the Vietnamese-sponsored government which replaced Pol Pot's regime. According to its statement in 1979, genocide had accounted for some 3 million Cambodians. Sensitivity to Cambodian feelings about a Vietnamese occupation must account for the exaggeration, not least because it was remembered how in the 1830s the Vietnamese emperor Minh-mang had tried to remake Cambodia in his own country's image. Pol Pot's foreign policy was anti-Vietnamese, and a series of military actions designed to clear the Vietnamese out of border provinces culminated in the full-scale war of 1978. Like the warrior-king Jayavarman VII, the Khmer Rouge leader was interested in ideology and war, paying little attention to either the costs or consequences involved for his country. But unlike the twelfth century ruler, who decisively beat the Chams, Pol Pot was a loser in his struggle with the Vietnamese. Both men overstrained the Cambodian economy in the pursuit of their beliefs – the hereditary king as an ardent Buddhist, the revolutionary leader as an uncompromising Communist. It is somewhat ironic that, despite its hatred of religion, the Khmer Rouge should have spared Angkor Wat, whose reconstruction was Jayavarman VII's chief concern. Whereas Buddhist temples were systematically destroyed in the rest of the country, the damage there was restricted to the defacement of Buddha's portraits.

The practice of religion was strictly forbidden by the Khmer Rouge. As part of a policy directed at a return to the primitive virtues of subsistence agriculture, Cambodia was not only cut off from the spiritual realm but also the outside world. There was a single scheduled international flight into the country, a fortnightly connection between Beijing and Phnom Penh. Foreign trade was limited to the exchange of rice for essential goods, while consumer products were entirely homemade, since the economy aimed at self-sufficiency. To foster the spirit of self-reliance the use of money was banned too.

This extreme socialist experiment ended in late 1978 with the arrival of 160,000 Vietnamese troops. Pol Pot and his followers were pushed into the Thai borderlands, while in Phnom Penh the People's Republic of Kampuchea replaced the Democratic Republic of

Kampuchea set up by the Khmer Rouge. For China the change was a diplomatic blow. Regarding Vietnam's recent alliance with the Soviet Union as an attempt at Russian encirclement, Chinese forces had invaded northern Vietnam earlier in the year to prevent the toppling of Pol Pot. But the Vietnamese were not to be deterred, and they remained in Cambodia for a decade. Aware of its own colonial past in that country, Vietnam made efforts to keep its soldiers out of towns and station them in the battle zone along the Thai border. Their final withdrawal in 1989 caused mixed feelings among the Cambodians, who at first were left to meet any attempt to return by the Khmer Rouge themselves.

But a UN-sponsored peace plan officially ended fighting in late 1991, and allowed exiled Cambodian leaders like Sihanouk to return home. Less welcome were those of the Khmer Rouge, the spokesmen of Pol Pot, who preferred himself to stay hidden in southern Thailand. Under the peace plan the Khmer Rouge has had to agree that 70 per cent of its forces will be demobilised before elections take place in 1993. Prince Sihanouk, when asked about this promise, said: 'If the Khmer Rouge dared to try a coup, this time the international community would invite Vietnam to save the Cambodian people . . . Now the Khmer Rouge has to change its policy. Its members are cruel and tough, but fortunately they are intelligent as well.'

REUNITED VIETNAM

Being regarded by Beijing as 'Moscow's puppet in South-East Asia' was an unfortunate consequence of the diplomatic isolation imposed on Hanoi by the United States, following the fall of South Vietnam in 1975. There have been major clashes along the Sino-Vietnamese border in the 1980s, and the long occupation of Kampuchea can be seen essentially as a struggle between pro-Chinese and pro-Vietnamese forces. Vietnam was able to maintain its position only at a high cost – heavy expenditure on a million-strong army, shelving internal reconstruction schemes, and dependence on Russian aid. Arguably the dispute with Beijing was avoidable, but in the difficult years immediately after reunification no country other than the Soviet Union, then China's enemy, would offer any tangible assistance.

Vietnam's second five-year plan (1976–80) was practically scrapped. A massive Russian aid programme propped up the damaged economy, though until 1983 most of the money was still spent on arms. A symptom of internal collapse were the 'boat people', refugees who fled from Vietnam by sea. The exodus began in the summer of 1978 under the impact of a government decree nationalising industry and commerce, and other measures allegedly discriminating against the ethnic Chinese who ran businesses in southern Vietnam. By 1982, over a million people had taken to boats in order to reach other South-East Asian countries: around two-thirds were of Chinese extraction, representing almost half of the Vietnamese Chinese population. Hanoi was criticised for trying to destabilise the region by driving out these refugees, Malaysia feeling threatened enough to consider shooting boat people who landed on its shores.

Since 1986 the Vietnamese government has loosened central controls in order to stimulate economic growth. Local initiative is espoused by Nguyen Van Linh (born 1913), a revolutionary leader who was brought up in the more entrepreneurial southern provinces. Press though he might for a programme aimed at 'modernisation', the social and economic problems facing Vietnam remain formidable. There are encouraging signs: in 1989 the Vietnamese evacuated Kampuchea; they achieved in 1990 an estimated growth rate of 5.6 per cent, a figure not unworthy of the Pacific Rim; and in 1991 they re-established normal relations with the People's Republic of China. It will be some time, however, before an economically strong Vietnam emerges from the war-torn era through which the country has been so conspicuously dragged.

SOCIALIST BURMA

Choosing to emulate the British Labour government that granted independence rather than the Communist regime arising in neighbouring China, Burma borrowed parliamentary institutions and restricted the ownership of private property instead of confiscating it wholesale. Anti-Indian sentiment, the product of an influx of Indian merchants during British rule, was associated with anti-colonialism and anti-capitalism, and thus tended to reinforce the government's declared intention of controlling economic affairs. But the ruling Burmans were quite aware of the need to accommodate ethnic minority interests, especially the Karen, Shan and Mon. They tried to provide for a federal union of the various peoples living in Burma, although the Malaysian compromise of an all-embracing alliance dominated by the largest single group failed to evolve in time to save civilian government. The assassination in early

1947 of Aung San, along with six other senior politicians, gravely weakened independent Burma at the very moment political skills were required to secure national unity. Beginning in 1948, the Karen rose in rebellion. In pursuit of a demand for an independent state that would include the Irrawaddy river delta, they briefly threatened Rangoon itself until checked by a vigorous counter-attack under the command of Ne Win (born 1910), a general close to the murdered Aung San.

One of the lasting effects of the hard-fought campaign against the Imperial Japanese Army in Burma was the growth of military power, official and unofficial. In contrast to other South-East Asian countries, the Japanese occupation caused widespread dislocation of the economy: it also drew into the resistance movement the different hill peoples. In accordance with Allied planning Karen guerrillas fell on Japanese columns as they retreated southwards in 1945: they were led by British officers, who had been parachuted into the hills. Their excellent training in ambush and sabotage was put to good purpose then, and later against Burmese government forces, which included units of rival hillsmen. Today, the Karen still maintain an unsubdued guerrilla army, and account for a large portion of 40 per cent of the national budget that is spent on counter-insurgency. Much of the rest goes on containing a Chinese-sponsored Communist movement in northern Burma. When in 1958 the country was almost engulfed by civil strife, brought on by the collapse of a four-year economic plan, the civilian government was obliged to submit to temporary control by an emergency military regime, which continued for about eighteen months. That perennial liability of Burmese politics, factional fighting, allowed Ne Win to impose permanent military rule in 1962. Parliament was dissolved, politicians imprisoned, and criticism banned.

Ne Win's main motive was a nationalist desire to maintain Burma's territorial integrity, which seemed in danger of falling apart under an unstable democratic system of government. His coup met no effective resistance, and from the outset Ne Win carefully cultivated the image of successor to Aung San. Lasting longer than any Thai dictator, Ne Win was not forced into exile till August 1988, when demonstrations and riots forced the resignation of his chosen successor, Sein Lwin.

A unifying call among the protesters was for the restoration of a multi-party system. Burma had been given a new constitution in 1974, but periodic elections at local or national level meant nothing when only one political party could field candidates. Power was always concentrated in a revolutionary council, composed of members of the armed forces and chaired by Ne Win himself. Because many Burmese refused to co-operate with the military government, to run the economy Ne Win came increasingly to rely on left-wing, even Communist, army officers, who strove to eliminate foreign businessmen – Indian, Chinese and European. Under British colonial rule foreign investment had been concerned to exploit primary products such as oil, rubber and tin, a process that tended to enrich Burmese towns during a period of drastic rural decline.

In 1962 Ne Win declared that 'exploitative capitalism must give way to social justice in an effort to meet the people's essential needs for food, housing, clothing, and jobs'. Nationalisation of large sectors of the economy, together with the expulsion of foreign businessmen, deprived Burma of critical management skills from the outset of the socialist revolution. Even educated Burmans in sympathy with socialism refused to support a military domination, with the result that a breakdown in distribution soon caused chronic shortages of goods, and a thriving black-market. Ne Win faced multiple rebellions in the countryside and riots in the towns. The tenor of his government was set within two months of its coming to power, when in 1962 he authorised the shooting of student demonstrators, and the demolition of buildings belonging to Rangoon University. The oppression lasted for nearly a decade, in spite of popular hostility to continuing army rule bringing about the release of political prisoners from 1967 onwards. By the late 1970s, however, progress on the economic front had eased the lot of towns and villages alike. Once again Burma became an exporter of rice, the yield rising each year through the introduction of new strains of paddy seed.

Although in foreign policy Burma has chosen to remain non-aligned, like its more powerful neighbour India, the cost of self-imposed isolation until the 1970s was a distinct shortage of international aid and loans. Since then the level of borrowing has risen at an alarming rate, fuelling the black-market economy which handles extensive imports from India and Thailand. A government expedient in 1987 to deal with the rampant inflation this illegal haemorrhage caused was the abolition of certain currency notes. Overnight millions lost their savings. The protest movement eventually erupted in the riots of March 1988, which Sein Lwin, Ne Win's successor, crushed with utter ruthlessness. The Shwedagon Pagoda in Rangoon, as well as Buddhist shrines in other cities, became the subsequent rallying points of enraged protesters. But the Buddhist church in Burma did not play a role analogous to that of the Catholic one in the Philippines, possibly because Ne Win ruled with less ostentation than Ferdinand Marcos. The precious stones and metals the general salted away for his exile hardly compared with the US $220 million Marcos misappropriated during his presidency.

Disagreement among the military hierarchy as to the best method of dealing with the civil disorder ended the authority of Ne Win, and his tough protégé. There was above all the challenge posed by Daw Suu Kyi, the daughter of Aung San. An impromptu speech she made in Rangoon, during a visit from Britain, led to public demand for a return to constitutional government. Encouraged by the widespread support she received, Daw Suu Kyi (born 1945) decided to remain in Burma and fight for political reform, until house arrest in 1989 removed her from the campaign trail. To the embarrassment of the military hierarchy her supporters gained a landslide victory in the 1990 elections and a year later Daw Suu Kyi was awarded the Nobel Peace Prize in recognition of her 'non-violent struggle for democracy and human rights'. Yet the greatest challenge facing Burma today is not so much the constitution as the integration of its minority peoples: they number 13 million, one third of the country's entire population. The continued Karen rebellion is a symptom of this old sore.

FILIPINO DEMOCRACY

Unlike Indonesia, the other modern South-East Asian island state, the Philippines developed no indigenous anchor equivalent to medieval Java. Its archipelago remained without a stabilising political and cultural point until the Spaniards made the city of Manila their capital. Colonial rule left an indelible religious impression that provided some basis for national identity, but as the United States discovered on supplanting Spain in 1898, there were strong separatist tendencies at work beneath Filipino resistance to the imposition of an American administration. Besides the belligerent Muslims on the southern island of Mindanao, rivalry between Roman Catholics was marked by entrenched regional antagonisms. The two parties, the Nacionalista and the Liberals, that dominated Filipino politics after the attainment of full independence in July 1946, were in turn dominated by a landed oligarchy. The struggle of great families to gain office, and the lucrative opportunities thus opened up for relatives and friends, still gave expression to regional differences, not least because Filipinos nearly always voted for the local candidate. Whereas hard-working Ferdinand Marcos (1917–89) hailed from Ilocos Norte, the poor province at the northern tip of Luzon, his spendthrift wife Imelda descended from small landowners in the Visayans, a central island group associated by the Filipinos with unabashed hedonism. When the couple fled the country in 1986, Imelda Marcos was forced to leave behind a mountain of shopping, which included thousands of dresses and pairs of shoes.

Whilst the inspiration for the constitution of the Philippines was American, it provided for a unitary government whose authority was vested almost exclusively in the office of the president, who could invoke the extraordinary device of direct rule by placing 'the Philippines or any part thereof under martial law'. In September 1972 Marcos chose to deal with popular opposition to his own administration by such a declaration, and in order to overcome the prohibition on a president serving more than two terms, he redrafted the constitution. Prior to this, the Nacionalista and the Liberals had taken it in turns to provide presidents, Marcos having changed himself to the Nacionalista in 1965 so as to obtain nomination as presidential candidate. A switch like this was nothing unusual for a Filipino politician, nor was the lavish entertainment he showered on the convention delegates.

In the two decades before the Marcos presidency, the Philippines surmounted with American assistance several regional crises, underlying each of which was chronic agrarian unrest. In 1972 Marcos belatedly promised that he would use his martial law powers to break up the landed oligarchy. His failure to do anything at all accounts for the present-day strength of the New People's Army, a left-wing guerrilla force active in almost every province. When not engaged in open warfare, its members organise farmers and put pressure on landlords to reduce rents. In the late 1980s it also campaigned to reduce milling fees charged by merchants and increase the wages of agricultural labourers.

In these decades American aid and Japanese reparation payments kept the economy afloat, but there were already signs of the coming troubles of the 1980s, when the Philippines gained the unenviable fame of being the only East Asian country afflicted with the Latin American malaise of heavy and unserviceable foreign debts. The 1988 budget recognised the bleakness of the situation by allocating 40 per cent of its expenditure for debt service. President Corazon Aquino missed a unique opportunity to reduce the country's debt burden by challenging the legitimacy of the obligations contracted under Marcos's dictatorship on her own inauguration in 1986.

Until Ferdinand Marcos was elected president in 1965, the Philippines had been spared one-man rule. Having in 1969 become the only president to be re-elected and by a 2 million-vote margin, Marcos seems to have begun to envisage himself as a perennial leader, however. That ballot rigging and vote buying contributed to the second victory the citizens of Manila had no doubt. Their demonstrations in January 1970, after the president had delivered his state of the nation address, embarrassed Marcos particularly when they assumed an anti-American character. But the relative decline of US power in East Asia, with the growth of the post-war Japanese economy, meant that Washington needed help from its allies, including the Philippines. Having been the wealthiest country in the world for more than half a century, the United States discovered during the 1970s its economic power wasting away at such a rate that by 1984 it was the world's greatest debtor. This unexpected weakness was one reason why nothing was said after Marcos imposed a corrupt martial-law regime on the country in 1972. Another reason for the lack of condemnation was the dictator's own manipulative skills. As Raymond Bonner, a recent biographer, has written:

He was an absolute master of the American political system. He knew more about that system, its intricacies and nuances, and about the men who ran it than they ever did about his country and the man who ran it. He deployed his knowledge, ingenuity, and cunning to extract far more from Uncle Sam than he ever gave. At each turning point, each showdown, whether over Vietnam or human rights, Marcos stood his ground. It was always the powerful United States that blinked.

Confident of American acquiescence, Marcos proclaimed martial law and imprisoned his main opponent Beningno Aquino. After this suspension of democracy, the government progressively became the preserve of the Marcos family and its supporters: Imelda Marcos was appointed governor of Manila in 1975, cabinet minister three years later; Ferdinand junior became presidential assistant in 1979.

The support of the Filipino army was crucial. It was secured by allowing the military a political role for the first time in the Philippines, a legacy of the Marcos era that is reaching fulfilment today. Cavalier about elections, Marcos strengthened his grip on the country by means of referendums which extended his terms of office, gave him almost unlimited powers of decree, and subordinated the legislature to his will. Opposition to the dictatorship took on both non-violent and violent forms – the southern islands of Mindanao and Palawan passed into the hands of the Moro Liberation Movement, a Muslim guerrilla force unofficially backed by Libya and Malaysia, while elsewhere the New People's Army drew thousands of Roman Catholics to its banner. The Church itself gradually moved to voice its condemnation of the regime, especially after the assassination of Beningno Aquino in 1983 at Manila airport following a period of exile in the United States.

By 1986 it was obvious even to Ronald Reagan, the second-term American president, that Marcos had lost his grip on the Philippines. He could no longer deal with either the rebels or the rising demands for a fair presidential election. Running against the widow of Beningno Aquino, Corazon or Cory, the ageing dictator won, but the vote was so fraudulent that widespread protests unnerved the military and left Marcos without support. Television cameras revealed how a million Filipinos first formed a human barrier to protect Cory Aquino from police loyal to the discredited president, and then compelled him to seek refuge in the United States. A televised footnote to his non-violent deposition was provided in July 1990 at the acquittal of Imelda Marcos in a New York courtroom for any personal involvement in her late husband's gigantic theft of public funds. While Imelda Marcos was free to shop again, the new president Cory Aquino faced a growing rebel movement, a mutinous army, and crushing foreign debts.

During her troubled presidency (1986–92), Corazon Aquino came to depend on Fidel Ramos (born 1928), the defence minister and military chief. It was hardly surprising, therefore, that in 1992 he was the first soldier to be elected president. How Ramos will cope with the rivalries of the great Filipino land-owning families cannot be predicted: Corazon Aquino's own rich relations urged her to stand again as a candidate but, tired of politics, she endorsed Ramos instead. Cardinal Jaime Sin, the Catholic archbishop, also received a rebuff in the warning issued by the newly elected general, who is a Protestant. Ramos said that his election was a message that Filipinos had reaffirmed their adherence to the ideal of church and state 'separate but collaborating, co-existent but each supreme in its own domain'. With only 23 per cent of the popular vote cast in his favour though, he may have to look for allies wherever they exist in the troubled years ahead.

MALAYSIA, SINGAPORE AND BRUNEI

The British never re-invaded Malaya; amphibious forces for this operation were ready, but the Japanese surrender rendered these unnecessary. Instead of returning in anger to the scene of its most humiliating defeat, the British Army peacefully re-occupied Malaya in September 1945. The sudden end of the Pacific War also allowed the dispatch of troops to Hong Kong, so as to prevent the Guomindang from receiving the Japanese surrender there. Jiang Jieshi wished to confine the British to the island of Hong Kong, and confiscate the leased territories opposite on the mainland. He had the support of the US ambassador, instructed by Roosevelt to ensure that returning European powers should not bully China again.

Although Mountbatten had to delay the Japanese surrender ceremony in Singapore until after MacArthur had completed his own in Tokyo, the handing over of Japanese swords marked the end of American interference among the recovered British colonies. Yet not even the public receipt of these potent samurai symbols could erase the memory of the brief Japanese triumph. Force of arms had shattered, once and for all, the comfortable colonial world of British South-East Asia. The Brookes perfectly understood the changed situation: after ruling Sarawak as a family estate for more than a century, the last White Rajah ceded his kingdom to Britain as a first stage towards its eventual independence, and quietly retired to London. In Malaya the effects of the Japanese occupation were perhaps more far-reaching. The Malay sultans to varying degrees had co-operated with the Imperial Japanese Army, while some of the Indian population were enrolled in the pro-Japanese Indian National Army. The only steadfast opponents of the Japanese had been the Chinese, a group previously denied any political rights at all. That there was also in the Malayan jungle an armed Chinese guerrilla force under Communist leadership put any return to pre-war conditions out of the question. The force was disarmed, and its leaders rewarded with decorations, but it soon became a political party which condemned renewed British rule.

The chief political party, the United Malay National Organization (UMNO), was formed in 1948 as a protest against British moves to create a common citizenship for Malays, Indians and Chinese within a unitary state comprising the Malay sultanates and the Straits Settlements, with the exception of Singapore. The subsequent restriction of political rights to Malays triggered the Communist-led Malayan insurgency (1948–54), which kept the colony under a state of emergency until 1960. The largely Chinese insurgents received little outside support, possibly because Beijing had more urgent problems with Korea, but their activities delayed independence for a decade. Only the firm commitment of Britain to a programme of decolonisation averted a disaster akin to French experience in Vietnam, and in 1957 delivered the premiership of an independent Malaya to Abdul Rahman (1903–90). UMNO fears of a universal franchise were allayed by the formation of a new federation in 1963, which joined Malaya with newly independent Singapore, Sarawak and Sabah, former British North Borneo. Two years later, however, disputes between Abdul Rahman and Lee Kuan Yew, the premier of Chinese-dominated Singapore, led to the departure of this state from the Malaysian Federation.

Abdul Rahman accused Lee Kuan Yew (born 1923) of attempting to become prime minister of the federation, a not unreasonable aim for a rival politician, but in the eyes of his accuser it was nothing less than the subjugation of the Malays to Chinese control. The departure of Singapore left Malaysia's balance of population tilted heavily in favour of the Malays, but this in-built electoral advantage was not enough to ensure stability in West Malaysia. Discriminatory legislation in favour of the less economically advanced Malays caused resentment, and the unwise Malay reaction was the racial riots of 1969, which in Kuala Lumpur cost over 2000 Chinese lives. The spectre of renewed violence proved a useful excuse for the tough actions of Dr Mahathir bin Mohamed, who became president of UMNO and prime minister in 1980. Even though his Anglophobe stance took Britain by surprise, Dr Mahathir's eastward policy of disengagement from Commonwealth trade should be seen as a Malaysian desire to participate in the growing economy of the Pacific Rim. As he commented in 1988, at a time of political unrest:

> Our policy is not anti-British. But contracts should not go automatically to Britain, when the same goods and services are available more cheaply from Japan, South Korea and Taiwan. We have a lot to learn from these countries if we are to catch up.

Less anxious than Dr Mahathir about economic performance, Lee Kuan Yew's government in Singapore also placed emphasis on stimulating development. In the 1970s the gross national product, responding in part to American expenditure on the Vietnam War, clocked up an impressive 14 per cent growth rate. During the 1980s the figure fell back to around 5 per cent, but it was no longer sustained by entrepôt trade: on the contrary, Singapore's wealth derived from the very things that Dr Mahathir sought for Malaysia – thriving manufacturing and financial sectors.

The position of Brunei, a ministate like the island of Singapore, is different. This enclave within the Malaysian state of Sarawak is so endowed with oil and natural gas reserves that its sultan can be confidently termed the richest man in the world. Despite the ending of a British protectorate in 1984, a military presence survives in the form of a Gurkha battalion, which serves there on a renewable five-year contract. In 1967 Malaysia was confronted by Indonesia, which saw the new federation as a neo-colonial bulwark for European and American interests in South-East Asia. The strongest opposition to the setting up of the federation came from Brunei, where in 1962 there had been a local uprising in favour of an independent Borneo. Its crushing, and the containment of Indonesian infiltrators, was the last British military action in South-East Asia. Following the fall of Sukarno in 1965 peaceful relations have prevailed among the island powers.

THE REPUBLIC OF INDONESIA

Political protest in the Dutch East Indies had difficulty in finding expression, not least because police action circumscribed political activity through the extensive use of detention. Sukarno (1901–70), the son of a Javanese schoolteacher, was one of the earliest leaders to be sent to a penal camp. By 1934 he had been joined by Mohammad Hatta (1902–80) and Sutan Sjahrir (1909–66), two Sumatrans who had just returned from their university education in the Netherlands. So repressive did the colonial authorities become that in 1940 it was announced that the word 'Indonesia' could no longer be used. Relations between the Dutch and the Indonesians worsened as police surveillance was stepped up and the popular village sport of pigeon racing was outlawed in order 'to prevent bad news being spread abroad'. The fall of the Netherlands to Germany in May 1940 could not be kept secret, but the feebleness of the Dutch resistance to the Japanese in early 1942 still astonished the local population. Indonesians were quite unprepared for the sudden demise of three centuries of colonial rule.

But the Japanese made no concessions to nationalist demands for independence. Apparently they contemplated the indefinite exploitation of Indonesia's natural resources: oil, tin, rubber, iron, timber, quinine, as well as foodstuffs. But they clothed the policy in a propaganda campaign that promised modernisation as a reward for active co-operation within the Greater East Asia Co-Prosperity Sphere. Public opinion in Java was encouraged to strive for economic growth, and there were many who welcomed this aim until forced labour, rice requisitions, and the Japanese military police revealed the realities of yet another conquest. Still, anti-Western propaganda served to strengthen anti-Dutch sentiments throughout the Indonesian archipelago and contribute to the spread of the idea of independence.

The experience of Surabaya, a coastal city in north-eastern Java, can be seen as a barometer of the political change inaugurated by the Japanese occupation. The initial shock for Dutch and Indonesian residents alike was the destruction of the city's harbour, airfield and oil refineries at the orders of the Dutch colonial government. An upsurge of lawlessness was the second unexpected blow to the old order. Even the Japanese, who received the surrender of Surabaya in March 1942, were shocked by the robbery and violence. Their own ignorance of Javanese ways thwarted an eager wish to establish an anti-Western regime at once, because Dutch knowledge of local conditions was found to be essential for maintaining control. The Japanese interned the Dutch colonists so slowly they were lulled into a false sense of security. However, the Indonesians while they did not greet the Japanese with any warmth took undisguished delight in the downfall of the Dutch. As one officer wrote:

I quite understood that the Javanese didn't exactly worship the Dutch, but that they harboured such a hatred for us as then appeared came as a great surprise to me. I never thought it was that bad.

A visit by Sukarno three months after the city's capture led to a crackdown on local nationalists. While the rostrum provided for Sukarno was decked with Japanese flags, and his speech concentrated on blaming the Dutch for Indonesia's ills, the enormous crowds alarmed the Japanese enough for a prohibition to be placed on all meetings and organisations.

Fearful of entrusting senior posts to Surabayans in the local administration, the Japanese confirmed suspicions about the nature of their occupation. The growing military weakness of Japan in the face of the American counter-attack forced in 1943 a loosening of control, even an attempt to enlist active support for the war effort. But the Putera (Pusat Tanaga Rakyat, or 'Movement for the Total Mobilisation of the Javanese People') had to be shut down after six months, as the Japanese authorities saw it was being used to further nationalist interests.

That a tide was running towards independence, and especially among the young, Mohammad Hatta was equally convinced. A sense of aimlessness, he noted, had been replaced by 'a sense of responsibility for the nation and the people'. One vehicle for this new commitment was the Japanese-sponsored paramilitary organisation, the Peta (Pembela Tanah Air, 'Protectors of the Fatherland'), which in October 1943 began training against the eventual return of the Dutch. From Australia the colonial government-in-exile was becoming involved in the Allied advance, and during 1944 a number of its detachments took part in Australian landings on the islands of Timor and Borneo. In Surabaya though, young Indonesians were destined to fight Anglo-Indian soldiers following the Japanese surrender.

In March 1945 Tokyo virtually acknowledged the end of its authority by asking Sukarno and Mohammad Hatta to devise a formula for political co-operation, which was founded on the so-called five principles of nationalism, internationalism, representative government, social justice, and Islam. They were also allowed to draft a constitution for an independent republic, which was to incorporate under a strong presidency not only the territories of the Dutch East Indies but those belonging to Britain in Malaya and Borneo as well. Because the Indonesian leaders did not want independence as a gift from the Japanese, on 17 August 1945, two days after the surrender of Japan, Sukarno proclaimed the Indonesian republic. In Surabaya a local council of Indonesians had taken over the running of the city under the effective control of the Japanese. Since the Netherlands had no troops available, and British forces were already spread thin in South-East Asia, this unreal arrangement lasted several weeks. Released Dutch internees were just as bewildered on their return to Surabaya, especially when the first British officers to arrive by parachute gratefully accepted the protection of the surrendered Japanese. Collaboration between the Dutch and British lit the fuse in the city, whose explosive response had by November sent a shock wave round the world.

As in Saigon, the colonists started the violence by direct action. Their attempt to raise the Dutch flag over the British headquarters provoked a popular reaction that could not contained by the Japanese garrison, the sight of whose bayonets was too much for the Surabayans to stomach. First the Japanese were overwhelmed and executed; then the Dutch found themselves reinterned or slaughtered in their homes; and last of all, a newly arrived British unit was cornered and its commander killed. The subsequent ten-day Allied assault from sea, land and air all but destroyed the city; the sacrifice of Peta volunteers and residents in its hopeless defence staggered the British, who were unaware of the strength of Indonesian nationalism; but the Dutch refused to heed all advice about opening negotiations. Between 1947 and 1949 they tried to reimpose colonial rule by force, a task entirely beyond their means. Even the United States, worried as it had become about the defence of Western Europe against Communism, felt constrained to lean on them to make concessions. The Republic of the United States of Indonesia thus gained recognition as a sovereign state four years after Sukarno's declaration of independence.

The problems that beset the new republic were due in part to the suppression of politics under the Dutch, the other source of instability was the diverse traditions to be found in the archipelago; even the Muslim majority were far from homogeneous in culture. On Bali Hinduism resisted all encroachment from Islam. Large Christian populations, too, dwelt on Amboina, the southern Celebes, and Sumatra.

For fifteen years Sukarno endeavoured to unify Indonesia. An abortive rebellion in 1950 of demobilised colonial troops, led by a Dutchman, was followed by the abolition of federal arrangements, and the establishment of a unitary state. But centralisation alone could not solve the problems of political rivalries, which were compounded by economic stagnation and official corruption. Seizing the nettle, and ignoring the objections of Mohammad Hatta, Sukarno announced in 1957 'guided democracy' as the only means of attaining consensus in national affairs. In spite of serious rebellions Sukarno held on to power with the support of the Communists and the armed forces, an uneasy alliance compounded by his need to declare a state of siege and pass day-to-day authority to local army commanders. One of these officers was Suharto (born 1921), who had joined the Royal Netherlands Indies Army a year before the Japanese invasion.

It fell to Suharto in 1965 to deal with an alleged Communist coup. Over the next three years he gradually pushed the still-respected Sukarno from power, ended confrontation with Malaysia, and secured his own personal rule. The massive 1973 price increase for oil, initiated by OPEC, helped in the recycling of the debts accumulated under Sukarno, but economic recovery eluded Indonesia during most of the 1980s. While Thailand and Malaysia developed tourist industries and Singapore took full advantage of its position on the Pacific Rim, Indonesia still struggled to weld itself into one nation. Apart from Bali, where tourism has taken root, the archipelago continues along its own obscure course. Now self-sufficient in foodstuffs, the world's largest population of Muslims can look forward to a period of sustained economic development, providing the immediate future is not blighted by either renewed secession movements or increased corruption.

SELECTED BIBLIOGRAPHY

The following notes and references are intended to assist the reader in pursuing topics of special interest. They draw attention to publications that may provide greater detail themselves or suggest ways in which further investigation can take place. It has to be said, however, that East Asia presents considerable difficulties to anyone who wishes to range between its various traditions and countries. Quite apart from the diversity of the languages spoken there, the different European colonial powers have introduced another complication by writing in Portuguese, French, Dutch, Spanish and English. There are fewer problems with China, Korea and Japan than South-East Asia, a factor perhaps in the dropping of the latter from subsequent editions of *A History of East Asian Civilization* by E.O. Reischauer & J.K. Fairbank, Boston and London 1960–5. This pioneering study evolved at Harvard from a lecture course which started in 1939. That it was the first attempt to provide a general approach to East Asia is a testimony to the enterprise of American scholarship.

CHAPTER 1: CLASSICAL CHINA

For the Shang dynasty two books by K.C. Chang offer the best introduction: *Shang Civilization*, New Haven, 1980, and *Art, Myth and Ritual: The Path to Political Authority in Ancient China*, Cambridge, Massachusetts, and London, 1983. Documents relating to the Early Zhou dynasty are contained in the *Book of History*, J. Legge, new edition, London, 1972. The oldest narrative history, the *Tso Chuan*, covers the period from 722 to 468 BC: a selection is available in a translation by B. Watson, New York, 1989. Later political intrigues and wars appear in J.I. Crump's *Chan-kuo T'se*, Oxford, 1979, a large collection of historical anecdotes covering the period between 300 and 221 BC. For the Qin dynasty there is *China's First Unifier*, D. Bodde, Leiden, 1938, reprinted Hong Kong, 1967, as well as my own *The First Emperor of China*, London and New York, 1981.

Although the translation of Sun Zi's *Art of War* by S. G. Griffith, Oxford, 1963,

323

has an excellent introduction, the detailed commentary alongside the text and translation made earlier by L. Giles, London, 1910, deserves study for anyone who wishes to read properly what is the oldest military treatise known in the world. An overview of political thought in general, including the use of coercive power, is provided in *A Political History of Chinese Thought: From the Beginnings to the Sixth Century AD*, Hsiao Kung-chuan, translated by F. W. Mote, Princeton, 1979. Books on individual philosophers are *Confucius and the Chinese Way*, H. G. Creel, New York, 1960; (Lao Zi) *The Way and Its Power: A Study of the Tao Teh Ching and its Place in Chinese Thought*, A. Waley, London, 1934; (Shang Yang) *The Book of Lord Shang: A Classic of Chinese Law*, J.J.L. Duyvendak, London, 1928, reprinted 1963; and *Mencius*, D. C. Lau, Harmondsworth, 1970.

CHAPTER 2: THE EARLY CHINESE EMPIRE

Translations of the Han historian Sima Qian include B. Watson's two-volume *Record of the Grand Historian of China*, New York, 1961, and *Records of the Historian written by Szuma Chien*, Gladys and Hsienyi Yang, Hong Kong, 1974. While Sima Qian's narrative comes down only to about 100 BC, Pan Ku's *History of the Former Han* encompasses the entire dynasty as well as the usurpation of Wang Mang. H. H. Dubs' three-volume edition offers the text, a translation and notes: it was published in Baltimore, 1930–55. Other works of note on the Han dynasty are *The Han Civilization of China*, M. Pirazzoti-t'Serstevens, translated by J. Seligman, Oxford, 1982; *Han Social Structure*, Chu T'ung-tsu, translated by J.L. Dull, Seattle, 1972; *Trade and Expansion in Han China*, Yu Ying-shih, Berkeley, 1967; *Crisis and Conflict in Han China*, M. Loewe, London, 1974; and *The Bureaucracy of Han Times*, H. Bielenstein, Cambridge, 1980.

For the crisis of the early Chinese empire there are *Inner Asian Frontiers of China*, O. Lattimore, New York, 1951, and *A History of China*, W. Eberhard, revised and enlarged edition, London, 1971. The arrival of Buddhism and its metamorphosis, especially during the Tang dynasty, is chronicled in K. Chen's *Buddhism in China*, Princeton, 1964, and his *The Chinese Transformation of Buddhism*, Princeton, 1973, as well as E. Zurcher's *The Buddhist Conquest of China*, Leiden, 1959. An account of the persecution of 845 can be found in *Ennin's Diary: The Record of a Pilgrimage to China in Search of the Law*, translated by E. O. Reischauer, New York, 1955. Explanation of dynastic decline during both the Tang and the Song periods is given in *The Background of the Rebellion of An Lu-shan*, E. G. Pulleyblank, London, 1954, and *China among Equals: The Middle Kingdom and its Neighbours, 10th–14th Centuries*, edited by M. Rossabi, Berkeley and London, 1983.

A useful insight into the Song dynasty is available in *Daily Life in China on the Eve of the Mongol Invasion, 1250–1276*, J. Gernet, translated by H.M. Wright, London, 1962. For the Mongol invasion itself there are I. De Rachewiltz's *Papal Envoys to the Great Khans*, London, 1971; *The Secret History of the Mongols*, translated by A. Waley, London, 1963; *Mongol Imperialism. The Policies of the Grand Qan Möngke in China, Russia, and the Islamic Lands 1251-1259*, T. T. Allsen, Berkeley, 1987. China's other early rival appears in C.I. Beckwith's fascinating study of *The Tibetan Empire in Central Asia*, Princeton, 1987.

CHAPTER 3: EARLY KOREA

General surveys appear in *The History of Korea*, Han Woo-keun, translated by Lee Kyung-shik, Seoul, 1970, and *A New History of Korea*, Ki-baik Lee, translated by E. W. Wagner, Cambridge, Massachusetts, 1984. Commissioned by a Koryo monarch in 1215, *Lives of the Korean Monks: the Haedong Kosung Chon*, translated by P. H. Lee, Cambridge, Massachusetts, 1969, throws interesting light on the motives behind royal patronage of the Buddhist faith. J. H. Grayson's *Korea: A Religious History*, Oxford, 1989, records the rise and decline of Buddhism, as well as the newer faiths in evidence today. The impact of the Mongols on the Koryo kingdom is detailed in *Korea: The Mongol Invasions*, W. E. Henthorn, Leiden, 1963.

CHAPTER 4: EARLY JAPAN

The published volumes of the *Cambridge History of Japan* are strongly recommended as a general framework, along with J. M. Kitagawa's *Religion in Japanese History*, New York, 1966. Treatment of the Japanese state in its formative stage can be found in *Early Japanese History (c. 40 BC–AD 1167)*, R. K. Reischauer, Princeton, 1937, reissued Gloucester, Massachusetts, 1967, and *A History of Japan to 1334*, Sir George Sansom, London, 1958.

CHAPTER 5: EARLY SOUTH-EAST ASIA

The countries of mainland South-East Asia, prior to European colonisation, are admirably covered in *The Making of South East Asia*, G. Coedès, translated by H. M. Wright, Berkeley, 1966. Whereas *The Birth of Vietnam*, K. W. Taylor, Berkeley, 1983, charts the course of Vietnamese history up to the attainment of independence from China in the tenth century, D. P. Chandler's *A History of Cambodia*, Boulder, Colorado, 1983, almost reaches the present day. The Angkor period, however, is also dealt with by *The Ancient Khmer Empire*, L. P. Briggs, Philadelphia, 1952. For early Indonesia there are *The Making of Greater India*, H. G. Quaritch-Wales, London, 1951, and *The Indianized States of Southeast Asia*, G. Coedès, Honolulu, 1968.

CHAPTER 6: THE LATE CHINESE EMPIRE

The victory of Zhu Yuanzhang at Boyang lake is recounted in *Chinese Ways in Warfare*, F. A. Kierman and J. K. Fairbank, Cambridge, Massachusetts, 1974, along with the capture of the Ming emperor Ying Zong by Mongol tribesmen at Tumubao in 1449. The early Qing (Kangxi) period is well represented by *K'ang-Hsi and the Consolidation of Ch'ing Rule, 1661–1684*, L. D. Kessler, Chicago, 1976; the late eighteenth century by *Shantung Rebellion: The Wang Lun Uprising of 1774*, S. Naquin, New Haven, 1981, and *An Embassy to China: being the journal kept by Lord Macartney during his embassy to Emperor Ch'ien-lung, 1793–94* (Qianlong), edited by J. L. Cranmer-Byng, London, 1962; and, the period when China was under siege, by *The Opium War Through Chinese Eyes*, A. Waley, London, 1958, and *The Taiping Revolutionary Movement*, Jen Yu-wen, New Haven, 1973.

CHAPTER: 7 CONFUCIAN KOREA

Admiral Yi Sun-shin and his Turtleboat Armada, Yune-hee Park, Seoul, 1973, offers an account of Korean resistance to Toyotomi Hideyoshi, including the successful naval strategy of Yi Sunsin. The tragedy of 1762 is recounted in *Memoirs of a Korean Queen*, translated by Choe-Wall Yang-hi, London and New York, 1985.

CHAPTER 8: FEUDAL JAPAN

The second and third volumes of Sir George Sansom's history cover the period down to the Meiji restoration: *1334-1615*, London, 1961, and *1615-1867*, London, 1963. Medieval warfare is analysed in S. R. Turnbull's *The Samurai: A Military History*, London, 1966, and private passions are explored by *The Love of the Samurai: A Thousand Years of Japanese Homosexuality*, Tsuneo Watanabe and Jun'ichi Iwata, translated by D. R. Roberts, London, 1989. The biography of *Hideyoshi*, M. E. Berry, Cambridge, Massachusetts, 1989, illuminates warlord politics, just as the accompanying religious turmoil is graphically recounted by N. McMullin's *Buddhism and the State in Sixteenth-Century Japan*, Princeton, 1984. Also recommended are *Confucianism and Tokugawa Culture*, edited by P. Nosco, Princeton, 1984 and the sound but somewhat old-fashioned *The Christian Century in Japan, 1549-1650*, C. R. Boxer, Berkeley, 1951.

CHAPTER 9: SOUTH-EAST ASIA

Several of Zheng He's voyages are recounted in *Ma Yuan: Ying-Yai Sheng-lan: The Overall Survey of the Ocean's Shores (1433)*, translated by J. V. G. Mills, Cambridge, 1970. The coming of Islam is documented in *A History of Modern Indonesia, c. 1300 to the present*, M. C. Ricklefs, London, 1981. Burma can be approached via V. B. Lieberman's *Burmese Administrative Cycles: Anarchy and Conquest, c. 1580-1760*, Princeton, 1984, and *A History of Burma*, Maung Htin Aung, New York, 1967. And *Thailand: A Short History*, D. K. Wyatt, New Haven, 1982, gives excellent coverage from earliest times. For the battle of Nong Sarai as well as an explanation of military tactics there is *Ancient South-East Asian Warfare*, H. G. Quaritch-Wales, London, 1952. Almost Braudel-like in its scope is A. Reid's *Southeast Asia in the Age of Commerce*, Yale, 1988.

CHAPTER 10: THE EUROPEAN COLONIAL INTERLUDE

Early travellers who left accounts were Tomé Pires, *The Suma Oriental (1515)*, translated by A. Cortesão, London, 1944; Fernuão Mendes Pinto, *The Travels (1614)*, translated by R. D. Catz, Chicago, 1989; and Peter Munday, *The Travels in Europe and Asia (1609-67)*, edited by R. C. Temple, London, 1919. General studies include C. R. Boxer's *The Portuguese Seaborne Empire 1415-1825*, London, 1969, and *The Dutch Seaborne Empire 1600-1800*, London, 1965; J. I. Israel's *Dutch Primacy in World Trade, 1585-1740*, Oxford, 1989; B. H. M. Vlekke's *Nusantara: A History of the East Indian Archipelago*, Cambridge, Massachusetts, 1944; and H. W. Morgan's *America's Road to Empire: The War with Spain and Overseas Expansion*, New York, 1965. *Raffles of Singapore*, Sir

Reginald Copeland, London, 1946, is a thorough, if partisan account of this great imperialist's career with the English East India Company, while J. G. Butcher's *The British in Malaya 1880-1941*, Kuala Lumpur, 1979, unashamedly exposes the social consequences of his acquisitions.

CHAPTER 11: IMPERIAL JAPAN

Born in the year of the Meiji restoration, the novelist Junichiro Tanizaki records in his *Childhood Years: A Memoir*, translated by P. McCarthy, London, 1990, the amazing transformation of life in Tokyo, whose early years as the new imperial capital are also the subject of E. Seidensticker's *Low City, High City: Tokyo from Edo to the Earthquake, 1867-1923*, New York, 1983. An overview of the modernisation programme can be discovered in *Japan's Modern Myths: Ideology in the Late Meiji Period*, C. Gluck, Princeton, 1985. For international relations there are Akira Iriye's *Pacific Estrangement: Japanese and American Expansion, 1897-1911*, Cambridge, Massachusetts, 1972, and I. N. Nish's *The Anglo-Japanese Alliance: The Diplomacy of Two Island Empires, 1894-1907*, London, 1966. Quite different were the problems faced in 1905 by the doomed Russian commander, Vice-Admiral Rozhestvensky, in R. Hough's *The Fleet That Had to Die*, London, 1958, a compelling narrative of the disaster at Tsushima.

Japan's own progress towards catastrophe is charted in the translations so far made of *Taiheiyo senso e no michi: kaisen gaiko si (The Road to the Pacific War: A Diplomatic History of the Origins of the Pacific War)*. They are edited by J. W. Morley and published in New York as *Japan Erupts: The London Naval Conference and the Manchurian Incident, 1928-1932*, 1984; *The China Quagmire: Japan's Expansion on the Asian Continent, 1933-1941*, 1983; and *The Fateful Choice: Japan's Advance into Southeast Asia, 1939-1941*, 1980. An American perspective on this sad era appears as *Japan Prepares for Total War: The Search for Economic Security, 1919-1941*, M. A. Barnhart, Ithaca, 1987. The little-known brush with the Soviet Union is detailed in A. D. Coox's *Nomonhan: Japan Against Russia, 1939*, Stanford, 1985.

CHAPTER 12: THE REPUBLIC OF CHINA

Hsiao Kung-chuan's biography of the would-be reformer Kang Youwei, *A Modern China and A New World*, Seattle, 1975, explains less successful Chinese efforts to deal with the foreign pressures that had galvanised Japan. J. Ch'en's *Yuan Shik-k'ai* (Yuan Shikai), Stanford, 1971, covers the early republican period, and his *Mao and the Chinese Revolution*, Oxford, 1965, the events leading up to 1949. *The Last Manchu: The Autobiography of Henry Pu Yi, Last Emperor of China*, edited by P. Kramer, London, 1967, relates from an unusual vantage point the final collapse of the imperial system. Guomindang rule, on the other hand, is frankly described in J. H. Boyle's *China and Japan at War 1937- 45: The Politics of Collaboration*, Stanford, 1972. The Communist defeat of the Guomindang receives detailed military attention in *The Communist Conquest of China*, L. M. Chassin, translated by T. Osato and L. Gelas, London, 1965, while J. F. Melby's diary *The Mandate of Heaven*, Toronto, 1968, provides a graphic account of US involvement.

328 *East Asia*

CHAPTER 13: THE END OF EMPIRE

An outline of the military bid for hegemony in East Asia is provided in *Japan's New Order in Asia: Its Rise and Fall 1937- 45*, F. C. Jones, Oxford, 1954, while *Japan's Colonialism and Indonesia*, Muhammad Abdul Aziz, The Haigh, 1955, reveals the adverse effect of colonial policies in one part of the Japanese empire. Two books in particular offer an inside view of Japanese strategy in action: *The Japanese Navy in World War II: In the Words of Former Japanese Naval Officers*, edited by D. C. Evans, Annapolis, 1986, and *Singapore 1941-1942: The Japanese Version of the Malayan Campaign of World War II*, Masanobu Tsuji, translated by M. E. Lake, Sydney, 1960. Just as invaluable is A. J. Marder's two-volume study of one dimension of the war at sea, *Old Friends, New Enemies: The Royal Navy and the Imperial Japanese Navy*, Oxford, 1981-90. The decisive American naval engagements are well presented in R. Hough's *The Longest Battle: The War at Sea 1939-45*, London, 1986. Terence O'Brien's *Chasing After Danger: A Combat Pilot's War Over Europe and the Far East, 1939-42*, London, 1990, captures the confusion of the fall of Malaya in the same way his *Out Of the Blue: a Pilot with the Chindits*, London, 1984, and *The Moonlight War*, London, 1987, describes the painfully slow British recovery. Quite remarkable, too, for its appreciation of the difficulties of fighting in Burma, for both sides, is Field-Marshal Viscount Slim's *Defeat into Victory*, London, 1956.

CHAPTER 14: PEOPLE'S REBUBLIC OF CHINA

Recommended for post-1949 developments in China are *The Political Thought of Mao Tse-tung* (Mao Zedong), S. R. Schram, New York, 1963, as well as R. MacFarquhar's study of cultural revolution, two volumes of which have been published to date: *The Origins of the Cultural Revolution: Contradictions Among the People 1956-57* and *The Great Leap Forward, 1958-60*, Oxford, 1974 and 1983 respectively. However, *The Second Chinese Revolution*, K. S. Karol, translated by M. Jones, London, 1975, is still a readable, though uncritical, narrative of the Great Proletarian Cultural Revolution. For a Chinese viewpoint on the 1960s and the 1970s the relevant chapters of *Zhou Enlai: A Profile*, P. J. and L. G. J. Fang, Beijing, 1986, are illuminating. The tragic events of June 1989 can be followed in *Tianamen: the Rape of Peking*, M. Fathers and A. Higgins, London and New York, 1989.

CHAPTER 15: TWO AMERICAN SETBACKS

Of the numerous works on the US reverses suffered in Korea and Vietnam these are especially useful: *The Origins of the Korean War*, B. Cummings, Princeton, 1981; *The Edge of the Sword*, A. Farrar-Hockley, London, 1954; *The Role of the Chinese Army*, J. Gittings, Oxford, 1967; *Korea and the Fall of MacArthur*, T. Higgins, Oxford, 1960; *The First Vietnam War*, P. M. Dunn, London, 1985; *Vietnam*, H. Higgins, London, 1975; *General Giap: Politician and Strategist*, R. J. O'Neill, London, 1969; *55 Days: The Fall of South Vietnam*, A. Dawson, New York, 1977; and *Neither Peace nor Honour: The Politics of American Military Policy in Vietnam*, R. Galluci, Baltimore, 1975.

Selected Bibliography

CHAPTER 16: POST-WAR JAPAN

For the early years there are M. Schaller's *The American Occupation of Japan: The Origins of the Cold War in Asia*, New York, 1985; J.W. Dower's *Empire and Aftermath: Yoshida Shigeru and the Japanese Experience, 1878-1954*, Cambridge, Massachusetts, 1980; and *The Yoshida Memoirs: The Story of Japan in Crisis*, Yoshida Shigeru, translated by Yoshida Kenichi, New York, 1962. Later developments are included in *Protest in Tokyo: The Security Treaty Crisis of 1960*, G.R. Packard, Princeton, 1966; *The Fragile Superpower*, F. Gibney, New York, 1985; *The Japanese Way of Politics*, G.L. Curtis, New York, 1988; *Crisis and Compensation: Public Policy and Political Stability in Japan, 1949-1986*, K.E. Calder, Princeton, 1988; *The Japanese Company*, R. Clark, New Haven, 1979; and *Between MITI and the Market*, D.L. Okimoto, Stanford, 1989; *Japan: The Coming Collapse*, Brian Reading, London, 1992.

CHAPTER 17: SOUTH-EAST ASIAN INDEPENDENCE

Two works stand out as excellent introductions to the post-colonial era, H. Grimalls *Decolonization: the British, French, Dutch and Belgian Empires, 1919-1963*, translated by S. De Vos, London, 1978, and J. Cady's *The History of Post-war Southeast Asia*, Athens, Ohio, 1974. Studies on specific countries include *Thailand: Reform, Reaction and Revolution*, D. Morell and Chai-anan Samudvanij, Cambridge, Massachusetts, 1981; *Sideshow: Kissinger, Nixon and The Making of the Indonesian Revolution*, W.H. Frederick, Athens, Ohio, 1989; *Waltzing with a Dictator: The Marcoses and the Making of American Foreign Waltzing with a Dictator: The Marcoses and the Making of American Foreign Policy*, R. Bonner, New York, 1987; *Vietnam Under Communism*, Nguyen Van Canh, Stanford, 1983; *Singapore: Ideology, Society and Culture*, J. Clammer, Singapore, 1985; *The Richest Man in the World the Sultan of Brunei*, J. Bartholomew, London, 1980; and *The State in Burma*, R.H. Taylor, London, 1988.

CHRONOLOGY

CHINA	KOREA
Shang dynasty c. 1650–1027 BC Early Zhou dynasty 1027–771 BC Spring and Autumn period 770–481 BC Warring States period 481–221 BC	

Unification, 221 BC
Qin dynasty 221–206 BC
Former Han dynasty 206 BC–AD 9
Xin dynasty (Wang Mang)
    AD 9–23
Later Han dynasty 25–220
The Three Kingdoms 221–65
Western Jin dynasty 265–316
	First Korean State
	Choson 194–108 BC
	Chinese commanderies
	    108 BC–AD 317
	
	Koguryo founded AD 12

Tartar Partition, 317–589 Tuoba Wei dynasty 386–550 Eastern Jin dynasty 317–420 Liang dynasty 502–57	Three Kingdoms c. 350–688
Reunification, 589 Sui dynasty 589–618 Tang dynasty 618–906 Five dynasties period 907–60 Song dynasty 960–1279	Destruction of Koguryo 688 Silla 688–918 **Unification of Peninsula** Koryo 918–1392
Mongol Conquest, 1279 Yuan dynasty 1279–1368	
Chinese Recovery, 1368 Ming dynasty 1368–1644	Yi dynasty 1392–1910
Manchu Conquest, 1644 Qing dynasty 1644–1911 Republic 1912–49	Japanese Annexation 1910

PACIFIC WAR 1941–5

People's Republic 1949	North and South Korea

Vietnam annexed to China 111 BC

Adoption of Chinese Model
Taika reforms 646
Nara period 710–84
Heian period 794–1184

Shogunate Begins
Kamakura period 1185–1333
Ashikaga period 1338–1568

Warlord Era 1568–98
Oda Nobunaga (died 1582)
Toyatomi Hideyoshi (died 1598)

Late Shogunate
Tokugawa period 1603–1868

Imperial Period 1868–1945
Meiji restoration 1868

Srivijaya (Sumatra) c. 650–c. 1300
Khmer empire (Cambodia)
   802–1440
Pagan (Burma) 849–1287
Vietnamese independence 939
Majapahit (Java) c. 1350
Ayudhya (Thailand) 1351–1767
Malacca founded 1402
Later Le dynasty (Vietnam)
   1418–1789
Toungoo dynasty (Burma)
   1486–1752

Arrival of Europeans
Portuguese seize Malacca 1511
Chakri dynasty (Thailand)
   1782 onwards

Franco-Thai War 1940–1

PACIFIC WAR 1941–5

Post-war Japan   Independence movement

INDEX